YOUR LOVING SON

by Shirley Cadmus

A TRIBUTE TO OUR FATHER
R. Robert Cadmus

March 27, 1923 - February 25, 1998

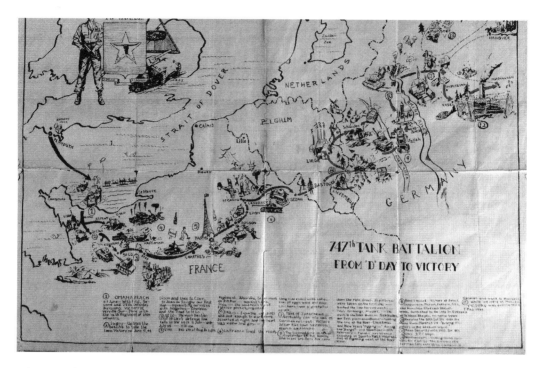

(ABOVE) 747 CAMPAIGN MAP

DEDICATION

Your Loving Son is dedicated to all World War II veterans, and to all who have served this country. Without your sacrifices, the world would not enjoy the freedoms we take for granted today. Thank you and God bless.

ACKNOWLEDGEMENTS

With special thanks to:

Our grandmother, Olive Milden Cadmus, for saving and keeping the letters safe and passing them on to our mom, Natalie Zirkle Cadmus.

Our mother, Natalie Zirkle Cadmus, for marrying our father! And for keeping the letters hidden and safe.

My youngest sister, Betty Cadmus, who kept the letters safe for many years, and especially for all the hundreds and hundreds of hours she worked on organizing and typing the 300 plus letters, some consisting of multiple pages of all shapes and sizes, some barely legible.

My sister, Nancy Cadmus Franklin, for her extensive work in organizing, editing, and support.

My brother-in-law, Charles Franklin, for his help deciphering, editing, and support.

My friends Jean Scott and Angela Daniel, for their support, hours of proofreading and encouragement in this endeavor.

Wayne H. Drumheller for his outstanding editing, trouble shooting, and publishing support.

The Army Heritage Center Foundation, Carlisle, Pa., for their time in locating and printing information pertaining to the 747 Tank Battalion, and for being a friendly and professional support team!

d. On 31 December 1944: Officers: 43
            Warrant Officers 2
            Enlisted Men: 660

4. Stations (permanent or temporary) of units or parts thereof.

Station	Component Part	Date of Arrival
Camp Shanks, New York	Entire Bn	1 Feb '44
Palmer Estate, Fairford, Eng.	Less B and D Cos	26 Feb '44
Stow-on-the-Wold, England	B and D Cos	26 Feb '44
Artillery Range, Okehampton, Eng.	Less D Company	5 Apr '44
Braunton, England	B Company	12 Apr '44
Artillery Range, Okehampton, Eng.	D Company	12 Apr '44
H.M.S. Raleigh, England	Less B Company	21 Apr '44
Antony Park, England	Less B Company	25 Apr '44
Antony Park, England	B Company	12 May '44
LCT 1049 Invasion Force	Entire Bn	2 Jun '44
St. Laurent Sur Mer, Fr. T676891	Entire Bn	7 Jun '44
Carretour, France T556776	Entire Bn	9 Jun '44
Chippelle, France T576766	Entire Bn	15 Jun '44
St. Jean de Savigny T568715	Entire Bn	17 Jun '44
Le Mesnil Herman, Fr. T452553	Entire Bn	31 Jul '44
Beau Coudray, France T470465	Entire Bn	2 Aug '44
St. Vigor de Monts, Fr. T491401	Entire Bn	4 Aug '44
Mesnil Clinchamps, Fr. T551332	Entire Bn	5 Aug '44
La Julliere, France T608280	Entire Bn	11 Aug '44
La Fresne Poret, Fr. T665185	Entire Bn	16 Aug '44
Sees, France Q445296	Entire Bn	20 Aug '44
Nonant Le Pin, Fr. Q478392	Entire Bn	21 Aug '44
Limours, France R861203	Entire Bn	25 Aug '44
Janvry, France R918201	Entire Bn	26 Aug '44
Sceaux, France R972328	Entire Bn	27 Aug '44
Dammartin, France S313630	Entire Bn	29 Aug '44
Peroy Les Combriar, Fr. S426742	Entire Bn	30 Aug '44
Largny, France S610870	Entire Bn	31 Aug '44
Crecy, France O 035282	Entire Bn	1 Sep '44
Landrecies, France O 098896	Entire Bn	2 Sep '44
Pommeruil, France O 043767	Entire Bn	3 Sep '44
La Fourchtmagne, Fr. O 630510	Entire Bn	6 Sep '44
Long Champs, Belgium P521626	Entire Bn	12 Sep '44
Weiswampach, Luxem. P812727	Entire Bn	16 Sep '44
Eichenbusch, Germany P926755	Entire Bn	18 Sep '44
Wilre, Holland K615532	Entire Bn	27 Sep '44
Hetrooth, Holland K625506	Entire Bn	29 Sep '44
Schinnen, Holland K704613	Entire Bn	1 Oct '44
Susterseel, Germany K743682	Entire Bn	4 Oct '44
Ribmurg, Germany K844585	Entire Bn	30 Oct '44
Zu-Ubach, Germany K878573	Entire Bn	20 Nov '44
Schleiden, Germany K948552	Entire Bn	21 Nov '44

Station	Component Part	Date of Departure
Camp Swift, Texas	Entire Bn	29 Jan '44
Camp Shanks, New York	Entire Bn	10 Feb '44
Palmer Estate, Fairford, England	Less B and D Cos	4 Apr '44
Stow-on-the-Wold, England	B Company	4 Apr '44
Artillery Range, Okehampton, England	B Company	12 Apr '44
Stow-on-the-Wold, England	D Company	12 Apr '44
Artillery Range, Okehampton, England	Less B Company	21 Apr '44

<u>S E C R E T</u>

H.M.S. Raleigh, England		Less B Company	25 Apr '44
Braunton, England		B Company	12 May '44
Antony Park, England		Entire Bn	1 and 2 Jun '44
LCT 1049 Invasion Force		Entire Bn	7 Jun '44
St. Laurent Sur Mer, France	T676891	Entire Bn	9 Jun '44
Carretour, France	T556776	Entire Bn	15 Jun '44
Chippelle, France	T576766	Entire Bn	17 Jun '44
St. Jean de Savigny, France	T568715	Entire Bn	31 Jul '44
Le Mesnil Herman, France	T452533	Entire Bn	2 Aug '44
Beau Coudray, France	T470465	Entire Bn	4 Aug '44
St. Vigor de Monts, France	T491401	Entire Bn	5 Aug '44
Mesnil Clinchamps, France	T551332	Entire Bn	11 Aug '44
La Julliere, France	T608280	Entire Bn	16 Aug '44
La Fresne Poret, France	T665185	Entire Bn	20 Aug '44
Sees, France	Q455296	Entire Bn	21 Aug '44
Nonant Le Pin, France	Q478392	Entire Bn	25 Aug '44
Limours, France	R861203	Entire Bn	26 Aug '44
Janvry, France	R918201	Entire Bn	27 Aug '44
Sceaux, France	R972328	Entire Bn	29 Aug '44
Dammartin, France	S313630	Entire Bn	30 Aug '44
Peroy Les Combriar, Fr.	S426742	Entire Bn	31 Aug '44
Largny, France	S610870	Entire Bn	1 Sep '44
Crecy, France	O-035282	Entire Bn	2 Sep '44
Landrecies, France	O-098896	Entire Bn	3 Sep '44
Pommeruil, France	O-043767	Entire Bn	6 Sep '44
La Fourchtmagne, France	O-630510	Entire Bn	12 Sep '44
Long Champs, Belgium	P521626	Entire Bn	16 Sep '44
Weiswampach, Luxembourg	P812727	Entire Bn	18 Sep '44
Eichenbusch, Germany	P926755	Entire Bn	27 Sep '44
Wilre, Holland	K615532	Entire Bn	29 Sep '44
Hetrooth, Holland	K625506	Entire Bn	1 Oct '44
Schinnen, Holland	K704613	Entire Bn	4 Oct '44
Susterseel, Germany	K743682	Entire Bn	30 Oct '44
Rimburg, Germany	K844584	Entire Bn	20 Nov '44
Zu-Ubach, Germany	K878573	Entire Bn	21 Nov '44
Schleiden, Germany	K948552	Entire Bn	

QUOTE BY HOMER D. WILKES
Probably given at an annual 747 reunion, July 4, 197?

July 4: Commendation
Formal Commanding Officer, 747 Tank Battalion:

"Sir, through you and to you veterans of the 747 Separate Tank Battalion are hereby commended for the following feats of arms and administration while supporting the 1st, 2nd, 4th 28th, 29th, 79th, and 90th infantry divisions plus two Ranger Battalions, one Belgium Brigade from June 6, 1944 to May 9, 1945. In addition, you served the military Government of several areas. Omaha Beach, simultaneously supporting 3 infantry divisions and one ranger battalion while also providing the 5th Corps 2 reserve; Holland: supported 1st Brigade taking direct fire; Battle of the Bulge; taking indirect fire as a division of the 9th army front; Rhine River Crossing: transporting and helping infantry divisions across the river; Military Government: served as such in numerous areas after the Rhine River Crossing when military government teams were not available.

Your deeds in the interest of great principles of the American Constitution were so extraordinary as to sometimes border on fantasia. For your companions who fell in action."

Homer D. Wilkes

INTRODUCTIONS

The Letters

Dad frequently wrote home throughout his tour in the army. From boot camp to D-Day to VJ Day, Dad's letter writing maintained the close bond he had with his parents. Our grandmother kept every letter and turned them over to our mother when she married Dad. Tucked away in an old wooden box held secret from us kids, Mom kept the letters safe until she and Dad retired and sold their home. At that point Mom turned the letters over to me but it wasn't until Dad passed away that my sisters and I got the letters out, organized them by date, and typed them.

We learned a lot about our father in this exercise. The letters made us feel closer to Dad, gave us a better understanding of him, made us laugh and made us cry. In addition to the letters, Mom told us what she remembered of the stories Dad had shared with her over the years.

Dad had been a puzzle to us when we were growing up, as he could be happily joking with us but switch to being angry or withdrawn in a matter of seconds. We never knew what would trigger his mood swings caused by what we now know was PTSD. Dad was engaging and fun, a hard worker, a great businessman, a loving father, and he fought the after-effects of war from the day he was discharged until the day he died.

I tried to talk to Dad about the letters several times in the past and he went into a rage each time. He didn't want them saved or read. He was angry with Mom for giving them to me, and angry with me for bringing them up. No doubt he would have been doubly upset if I'd told my sisters about them. The letters were such a source of pain and anger for him that I put them away. I never read beyond the first few days of boot camp, and did everything I could to forget they existed.

Betty Cadmus

Photo by Nancy Franklin

Regrets

I never knew these letters existed until years after my father had passed away. As I read them, I came to realize how the war affected him. I remember him as a fun loving prankster and storyteller - a strict authority figure with an inner sadness that came out periodically, when situations I can only assume, revived memories of the battles he fought and the carnage he saw. As he aged, those memories became demons that plagued him. The D-Day anniversaries were sad times for him.

I was embarrassed as a child that my dad only had an eighth grade education. As an adult, I was extremely proud of him and his accomplishments. He became a shrewd entrepreneur who made a good living and was able to sell the businesses and retire at age 50. In the letters, he tells how he "wheeled and dealed" his cigarettes, rations, and even his rain coat for cash to have a good time on his three day passes. He carried that throughout his life in real estate and in his businesses. He knew how to make a buck. He studied hard in basic training, was an avid reader, and excelled in his duties. He really was a very smart man.

I remember a story he once told me about why he skipped school so much. Dad walked to school, and this one intersection provided him two choices. If he turned left, he went fishing; if he turned right, he went to school. He said more often then not, he turned left. He loved to fish. However when he went to school, he was bullied about his first name Rynier, and he hated it. So off he went fishing.

I am grateful the letters weren't destroyed as he had wanted and we were able to read about how he spent his time in the Army and of the ravages of war. I regret that he did not want to share those letters or share with us the details of his service. He kept that pretty close to the vest.

Nancy Cadmus Franklin

Photo by Nancy Franklin

TO PRESERVE HIS LEGACY

It wasn't until about ten years after his death that I found out about the letters. I was very excited and couldn't wait to read them. This has been a healing experience, realizing why he had acted the way he had, realizing what a caring person he really was. Realizing what a hero he was.

We also found letters, old newspaper clippings and a cassette tape sent from several of Dad's friends. He never saw the coveted **Croix de Guerre with Palm Citation and Medal** awarded to his battalion. I've included letters, articles and memories from his lifelong battalion buddies. We never knew about or found the many photographs he mentioned in the letters.

Joe Skelly, his former gunner, attended a special ceremony and sent Dad's medal to my mother a year after his death.

My father, Sergeant "Bob" Cadmus, drove a Sherman tank onto the shore of Omaha Beach on D-Day. He was a member off the 747 Tank Battalion Company A, attached to the 29th Infantry. His gunner recalled, years later, "he (Bob) had become physically sick at the sight of the carnage and being forced to drive (his tank) over those who had fallen."

Dad drove the first allied tank to reach German soil. He was one of the liberators of the concentration camp in Nordhausn, Germany. Wounded several times and, like many others, he still had shrapnel in him when he died.

As I read and reread the final compilation of letters, I learned a lot about my Dad and chuckled at habits and food preferences we were familiar with all our lives. Sometimes I felt like I was right there in the tank with him or digging the

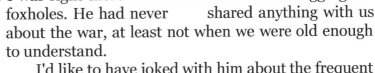

foxholes. He had never shared anything with us about the war, at least not when we were old enough to understand.

I'd like to have joked with him about the frequent references to ice cream, the shrimp cocktails he was able to concoct during this ordeal, the stolen ham, all the packages of food his mother had sent...

I hope that more support will be given to those returning from war. The soldier who returns with PTSD is not the only one who suffers.

Shirley Cadmus

ABOVE: SHIRLEY AND BOB CADMUS, EARLY 1950'S OCEAN BEACH, NEW JERSEY

CONTENTS

DEDICATION/ACKNOWLEDGEMENTS   3

747 PERMANENT/TEMP. STATIONS   4-5

QUOTE BY HOMER WILKES   6

INTRODUCTIONS   7-9

LETTERS FROM 1943   11-114

LETTERS FROM 1944   115-218

NATIONAL ARCHIVES PHOTO   183

LETTERS FROM 1945   218-314

DISCHARGE PAPERS   315-316

CROIX DE GUERRE   318-319

747 CAMPAIGN MAP   320-321

SIGNATURES ON BACK OF MAP   322-324

SAMPLE LETTERS   325

LETTER/ARTICLE FROM JOE SKELLY   326

DAD'S MEDALS   327

(PHOTO) DAD WITH TANK   319

ARTICLE/LETTER FROM KEN FORTNEY   328-329

MEMORIES BY RICHARD CAMPLONE   330-336

ARTICLE/INTERVIEW JOE SKELLY   337-340

EPILOGUE   341-342

ABOUT THE AUTHOR   343-344

LETTERS FROM 1943

1/6/1943
Dear Mom and Dad.

I hope you can read my writing as I am in a funny position trying to keep warm. I am standing on top of a stove in our tent. It is only 20 degrees in hear and you can't get warm no matter what you do.

I am in a tent with Ray Daly and Ralph Hollister and a fellow from Roselle and two from Brooklyn. I am having the time of my life despite the cold and hard work.

I guess you are wondering how I like the food, well it is fine and all you want of it. Today we had roast lamb, baked potatoes, Beets, Cabbage, rice pudding, Ice cream, pie, good Coffey and then bread – 5 pieces of Butter, peanut butter, apple butter, 2 kinds of jellies, and chocolate milk. I do not eat breakfast because it is not worth losing sleep for it.

I get up at 5:30 and stand for inspection, then go back to bed till 7:30 instead of going for Breakfast.

We got to Dix 2 o'clock Monday and almost froze to death after we got here. As soon as we got off the train we had to stand in line for lunch. There were 1800 men on the train and I was the 30th man from the end of the line. We stood in line for 2 ½ hrs with the temperature 10 above and the wind would blow you down. When I finely got to the mess hall I got a half pt of cold milk and two slices of bread with one slice of bologna.

Then we marched to get a physical, then got our clothes, needles, lecture, and by the time we got to our tent it was 2 in the morning. Then we had to march to get our blankets, then make our beds and build a fire clean up our tents. We just got under the blankets and the whistle blew to get up. Then we marched from 6:30 till 8 o'clock at nite. Boy did we sleep that nite. I woke up during the nite with the worst tooth ache I ever had and shivering so much I could not talk or get out of bed.

Things are getting better now we are getting warmer cloths and the weather is getting warmer we have all nite tonite off.

There is a movie picture house about a 1000 ft from our tent with all latest pictures. A service men's club about 300 ft away and the mess room is about 100 ft away.

We took our I.Q. test to day and I got 109 the average mark is 90 Ralph got 140 and will go to O.T.S. He had about the best score in the company. Ray got about 100. We have about 242 men in Company M all swell fellows not every body likes it here but of course we have a few cry babies.

Here is a list of things I want you to send me as soon as I send you a card with my new address.

Shaving lotion   pen   pencil

Tooth powder   watch case

Razor blades   send toilet kit that Fritzie gave me

  List of addresses   Cigarettes

Have these ready to send me when you get word. My watch is no good at all to me the way it is it stops all the time and I am getting in trouble for being late. The strap will have to be changed because it keeps coming off every time I change cloths. It does not keep correct time. When I send it to you don't send it back till you are sure it keeps perfect time and the strap won't come off. It fell off on the parade grounds today and nearly was trampled.

I got a hunch I will be shipped out tomorrow but you never can tell. I went to the corporal about my tooth and he said to go to the hospital and have them taken care of but the sergeant had other ideas, he said I did not have time this morning and to wait till tomorrow morning. So I expect to go in the morning.

We got two needles and we can hardly move our arms but they will be alright in the morning. Our tent was about the cleanest in the bunch so we did not get K.P. yet most every body in our Company had it already.

I got my uniform the first day including two pair of shoes that fit me perfect. We got 42 pieces of clothing and we have to carry them in two bags at all times because we are likely to be shipped out of here at any minute of the day or nite.

Am sorry you can not write me here but I will send you address as soon as I get in permanent Camp.

I will not get much time to write so I am making this a long one. I hope Dads cold is better and everything is ok home. I hope you will go on a vacation now that the store is closed and take plenty of rest.

Well I had better get to bed because we will have a hard day tomorrow.
Your loving Son,
 Bob

Camp Dix
Pvt RYNIER R. CADMUS
1229 R.C. Company M
Ft Dix NJ

Dear Mother Dad

Well I got to the hospital this morning and they drilled a hole in my put a drain in it. My whole face is swollen up from the puss. I have to hospital again sat. to have it pulled. They took x-rays of my whole head major and two Lieutenants worked on me for 2 hrs. When I got back fro hospital Ray had been shipped out and I found out that my name was cal   go to Arizona or California and I just missed the Train. I think Ray is going down south.

Well the weather is getting nice and warm and I am beginning to enjoy my-self. My work here is about done. I am hoping to be shipped to morrow but I mite be stuck hear now for a few weeks for missing the train.

Don't send anything but a letter till I tell you to!!

All of my friends left this morning and I am now waiting for my new tent mates to come in from the drill field.I did not eat breakfast this morning on ac-count of my tooth ache and I did not get back in time for lunch so I am pretty hungry now. I hope I get a big supper.

I found out that they want to send me to an ordnance unit but I hope to get in the artillery.

I mailed my cloths home a little wile ago I don't now when you will get them.

Mail me a letter special delivery as soon as you get this letter. I don't think I will be here to get it but it is worth the chance.

They called us out on the drill field earlier this morning just to see how long it would take us to get their.

I will write you soon.

Bob

Camp Dix Sat 9,
Dear Mom Dad,

Well the time has finally come for me to be shipped. I am going down now to get a final checkup I will leave camp this afternoon. I just got out of hospital. I have been in since yesterday morning; my whole face was swollen up so I could not see from the tooth. I went to hospital in ambulance but I am all better now. Boy they got swell doctors and nurses.

Well, hope I go south west where it is nice and warm. It is getting colder here every day. I saw a movie last nite 'China Girl'. It was pretty good.

Will write you as soon as possible. See if you can get a small mirror to shave with. Please have everything ready to send me as soon as you get new address. Ralph is still here. Well it looks as though they have finally split us up.

It is so cold here you don't have to shave but 2 times a week, and then it is so short it is not necessary. Well I have to go now so be good to your self and take it easy.

Your loving son, Bob

.S. Train is coming now. I can hear the Bell.

Camp Bowie Texas
Jan 13, 1943
Dear Mother & Dad,

I don't know whether they mailed my letter Saturday from Dix but as I said, I left Dix Saturday and rode till Tuesday. We had a swell trip. We went through Pennsylvania W Virginia, Indiana, Ohio, Illinois, Arkansas, and Texas. When we saw this camp we could hardly believe our eyes it was so big. All you can see for miles and miles is barracks and churches, tanks, trucks and thousands of trucks. This is a brand new camp and up to date in every sense of the word.

I guess you got my telegram yesterday. We all had to send them collect. It is sure costing mea lot of money to get started. I had to by small case to carry our kits on the train, haircut, coat hangers and many other things.

I hope you mailed my pen and pencil and every thing I asked you for, because it is hard to get along with out it.

Roy it is a pleasure to stay here every body is so nice. You don't get up till 6:45 in morning and we sleep in barracks. We just came back from mess and is it good. I eat till I can't move. We have corn bread and it tastes like cake. Pork chops with all the trimmings.

I just got another shot in the arm but it does not bother me. Some have the chills now and a fever.

I got instructions on the Thompson sub machine gun today and we go to firing line tomorrow for target practice. The gun shoots 700 shots per minute. The day after we learn to operate a tank and all units of the tank corps. You ought to hear the roar of those tanks it sounds like about 10 airplanes all together.

They keep us so busy you can't keep track of the days one seems to run in to each other. I had to stop in the middle of this letter to go to a movie on the sub machine gun. We are going until all hours of the nite.

Tell Mrs. Hollister my address so she can send it to Ralph. See if you can get in touch with Ray Daly send me his address. I am waiting patiently for mail which does not seem to come from you. I hope to get one by Friday if you sent it yesterday.

Well we just got orders for lights out at 9:30 and it is almost that now we will have to get up at 4:00 for special Duty. Will try to write more tomorrow.
Your Loving Son
Bob

Jan 17, 1943
Dear Dad,

I just received your letter, it was the first letter that I received since I left home. It was good to hear from home. I thought you forgot to mail the letter.

I have some bad news to tell you. It's bad as far as I am concerned anyhow. We just got notice that we will not get home till after the war. But there is one chance that I mite see you and Mom. Before I get shipped out, which will be any time after June, you can come to live in this camp for a few days. They have a place here for relatives of the men to live.

At the rate things are going we may leave sooner. Our basic training has been cut from 13 weeks to 4 weeks. We were supposed to go for maneuvers in June but there is talk of cutting that time too.

My tooth is still draining but the pain is gone. The major is trying to save my tooth. It has not cost me any time since I left Dix. I will go to the hospital in a few days and have a check up.

I went over the hill last nite and went swimming for a little wile. The water was fine but late at nite it gets very cold and when we came out of the water we had to run all the way home, about 3 miles. We can leave camp any time after we are dismissed for the day and don't have to be back until 6:45 in morning unless we get orders to the contrary. Some days we have to start 5:30 in morning till all hours of the nite. Most nites we go to instruction classes and they last until we learn the lesson no matter how long it takes.

We have to go to Fort Worth to the nearest town it is only 140 miles away. This town we have here has 35000 people but the town covers about 1.00 mile. We have 11 movies in camp and they have the same pictures as New York. We also have 11 churches all of which are new. We also have a service club a few miles over to the other side of camp, with every thing you could ask fore. We do a little boxing and play baseball when we get time. I haven't had time yet myself. We had Inspection of field equipment this morning and the C.O. said our hut was the best in Co A. Our Battalion Commander is only 27 years old and is 5 years out of West Point. He is a swell major, everybody likes him. He has his heart set to make our battalion the best in the world and he is well on the way to success. We are gong to do all we can do to help him. We are the best equipped armor division in the world. In case you did not know it this is the highest branch of the army it is on a par with the air corps. We cannot get a transfer because we can not get in a higher branch. Only the men with the highest marks in our I.Q. and adaptability test. The latter I got Excellent the best in our Co. I got 110 at Dix the average is between 90-80 with 110 you can apply for O.T.S. I really like it here and wouldn't change with anyone outside the army.

Don't know whether I told you or not but I fired the Thompson sub machine gun the other day. Boy that is some gun. It fires 700 rounds per minute I did pretty good for a beginner. We learn to shoot a 45 revolver next week.

How is your cold coming along? I hope you are all better by the time this letter reaches you. I hope Mom and Roy don't catch cold from you. Did you go to the doctor yet, if not why?

Mother said in her letter that she cleaned the cellar why didn't Roy do it? Mom worked enough already.

Well how does it feel to be rid of the store? Did you get rid of all the equipment?

Hope you will excuse the writing because all the boys are raising the roof. I got hit in the eye with a dirty sock about 9 times during the course of this letter. I will call you up on the phone as soon as I get to Fort Worth. I hope to hear from you and Roy in the near future. I know Mom will write but I know you and Roy.
Your Loving son
Bob

Jan 20, 1943
Dear Mother, Dad,

I received all your letters from Dix and two that were addressed to this camp. Helen sent me a letter saying you were over to Bayonne. I will not have time to answer her so please tell her I was very glad to here from her.

You did not state clearly how Dad's cold is if he is sick I want to know about it. So Dad wants to hear about Texas. Well I seen plenty of it yesterday we went on a 9 mile hike if you could call it a hike I would call it a cross country race. We left camp at 3 in the afternoon and were back at 5:35. We had a 5 minute rest in the middle and started back. You had to run to keep up in line. You would run a few steps and walk a few mostly run. I managed to make it but the boys were dropping out like flies. I did not see a house or farm since I got in camp. The country is very pretty but it all looks the same.

You asked me where abouts in Tex I am well the nearest town is (Brown wood) 1 store and 1 post office. The nearest city is Fort Worth is 140 mile away.

I am doing all kinds of work, from mopping the floor to driving the tanks, half tracks, trucks, jeeps, peeps, tractors. I am still learning all about the sub mach gun. I am getting to be a better shot. I got notice I go on guard duty for 24 hrs tomorrow so I will not have time to write you tomorrow.

I hope you all are feeling fine. I know I am all except for being a little tired. So I'll say goodbye for now.
Your Loving Son,
Bob

Jan 23, 1943
Dear Mom, Dad, Roy,

Have received letters from you nearly every day now and they sure cheer a guy up. I can't write to you so often because I don't have any time to my self. I have a letter here that I have been writing for 3 days, every spare minute would write a line and I only have 1 ½ pages finished.

    9 hrs later

I got off at 4 o'clock. We went to Brownwood. I had a picture taken there with my two buddies. I guess you will get them before you get this letter. I will have all day tomorrow off thank God! I am going to sleep till supper time.

Thanks for the dollar it comes in very handy. I spent it on a steak dinner in town to nite.

I will be driving 'Smutsy' the tank Monday and I will need plenty of rest. You ought to see me in a jeep. I only use one wheel at a time to save rubber.

We had to use our feet the other day but I think I told you about that. The sergent said if we kept knocking down all the trees he was going to make us cut them all up in to toothpicks.

We do very little walking and I mean very little. We don't walk we run, we run for gas, we run to eat, we run when our tank is put out of order, and we don't stop running after retreat till we are out of sight so we don't get extra duty. They blow a whistle at chow time and you got to be seated in the mess hall in 4 minutes or you don't eat. I was never late for that except when I did not expect to eat.

It is time for lights out now so I will finish this letter sometime tomorrow.
Sunday

Well I am going to finish this up today or know the reason why.

I just woke up it is about 10:30. I did not sleep as long as I thought I would. I am going to play a little ball today if I get the ambition. My arm is stiff as a board from a needle yesterday so I am going to punch the bag for a while to take the soreness out of it.

Don't buy any dress hat or belt because we are not allowed to wear them in the tank corps. I am sending you the patch we wear on our arm.

I am really sorry about this bad writing but did you ever try to write a letter in bed. I forgot to tell you but I got the package the other day.

Yesterday I received a letter from cousin Kittie I was glad to here from her.

Did I tell you how hot it is here? I got a swell tan but I had sunburn first and that was not so nice. This evening I think I will walk out to the river and sit in the shade and let my feet soak in the water. Do I love Sunday. I really appreciate a day off now.

I put in an application to go to gunnery school. I hope I make it. I think the school is at Knox. Did I tell you I walked guard the other day? I hope I don't have it for a long time again. You don't get any sleep for two days if you are lucky, and that Tommy gun gets darn heavy after a couple of hours. It is about 10 pounds but it feels like 50 lbs. Did not see anything but rabbits on my tour of guard. I saw as many as 5 rabbits at a time, and me with a machine gun. What a temptation.

I did not have K.P. since I got in the army, although I would have had it Sunday at Dix but I was saved by the train.

How is everybody in the family? Is Gramps alright and how is Dad's cold and speaking of Dad when is he going to get ambitious and send a letter and Roy also. James Lectner sent me a card. He was on the same train with me but they switched his car of at Harrisburg. Did you hear from Ray yet? Ralph wants to know my address to tell Mrs. Hollister. I don't know where he is either so get me his address.

A funny thing happened yesterday during the parade (tanker) our mascot dog started singing with the bugler. The bugler started to laugh and couldn't finish. So the C.O. dismissed him from the parade.

I can't think of anything else to say so good by for now.

Your son,

Bob

Camp Hood

Dear Mother and Dad,

I just got word that we go for our Commando training Wednesday. I am not sure it is true but I am getting ready for it anyway. It was supposed to start next Monday.

Sunday is sure a day of rest down here and do we need it. I was a table waiter yesterday and the Company Commander gave us a party last nite. They had 30 cases of beer and 20 cases of soda. The boys sure had a swell time. It was the first amusement we had since we went in quarantine. 50 of the fellows went over the hill last nite. God help them when they get back. They are getting disgusted because they can't go out that I don't blame them. They should have some kind of a show for us in our Rec hall.

Helen sent me a letter today and it only took 3 days to get here. Yours take 4 and 5 days. Some fellows get them in 2 days from N.Y.

You asked me what Adele sent me well it was sure a good box. It had cookeys and candy, cigarettes. The community house sent me a dollar bill.

If you can get me some 40 in shoe laces, brown, send them at once.

I sure am anxious to see whether we leave this camp or not. It isn't so bad but after Bowie and with us in quarantine we are getting pretty disgusted with it.

We had chicken for dinner today but I was too lazy to get out of bed. I got up about 2 this afternoon and took a shower and washed my socks and went back to bed. One day our tank broke down and we were 20 miles from camp so we went to a farm house to get a meal. They gave us a swell meal and wouldn't take any money for it. They said they never had visitors so begged us to come back in the near future. The next day I get off I am going back and get me some good home cooked food. The army feeds good but theirs is some difference.

I have to sew a hole up in my fatigue pants and there is only an hour left so I had better say good nite for now.

Your loving Son,

Bob

Jan 25, 1943

Dear Folks,

I am sorry I could not write to you but as I say they keep you very busy here all the time. I got your letter today with the clipping in it. I went to the dentist today and they pulled my tooth out |_||_||*| this is the one. They are making a bridge for it but it looks funny now. _||_||_| I missed a 10 mile hike by going to dentist but I was ordered to go. All the fellows are getting packages from home so we all eat. One seems to come every nite but I did not see any from Linden. There are 19 of us here. I guess I did not tell you but all the boys in my hut are between 18 and 20. I am almost the oldest one here. My sergeant sleeps here too. His name is Ben Fuller and he is the best sergeant in the camp. He is from West Virginia.

The boys in the picture with me are two swell boys and we have a great time every nite. The short fat one is Erne and the other is Semore. They are both from New York. That picture is terrible but it is the best we could get.
All that sunshine I told you about is gone as you can see by the clipping.

Last nite when we went to bed it was 82. That was 10:30 and at 1 o'clock it was down to 17 above. We all got up and put on our long johns and dragged out the blankets. We went to bed with no covers at all and had our canteens full of ice water trying to keep cool. Last week the same thing happened. We were playing baseball yesterday in our shorts and today we are doing double time in our overcoats to keep warm.

We had to go over the optsticle course this morn and only 4 out of 350 made it. I was not one who made it but I made it last week.

This morning it was so cold we had to do double time for 55 minutes and when we finished they said go over the course. I was so tired after I went over half of it I couldn't of gone over a 2 ft wall with a step ladder. I did better than average at that. Last week I went through the hole thing the first try but I had plenty of rest before I did it. I will try to draw a diagram of it for you on another page.

I signed up to go to school for gunnery. I think it is at fort Knox if I make it I will get home or know the reason why. The school will last a couple of months at least.

I am learning to be a scout, on foot, that is map reading and all kinds of Indian tricks. They are also teaching us to fight unarmed and I mean fight. I hope I never get in a fight where I have to use the tactics they are teaching us because one of us would get killed sure. In this outfit you have to be a better shot than a sniper and a better fighter than any man in the infantry besides being one of the best tankers in the world. We have to be able to scout better than any other outfit in the army. Our training is tougher than any other branch of service including the marines. When we go on a hike it is only 10 miles but it is double time 2/3 of the way. And you only get one 5 minute rest in the middle and we get no water. I am not only glad to be a tanker but I am also proud to be able wear the emblem of the tank corps. These men are tough and I mean really tough. Any tanker after a 12 hr tour of duty they can run a mile at top speed. I have given up smoking almost altogether because it was cutting my wind. I have only smoked 6 cigarettes in the past 7 days. I can trot for 2 miles now without stopping but at the end I drop in my tracks.

There is only one thing I don't like here and that is inspection. The top kid says, "Bob please pick your pants up of the floor and if you don't mind I would like you to shine your shoes." Or he says 'Bob its 9 o'clock you don't mind getting up just for me do you" (oh yeah?) But no kidding we have swell officers to work for, they do everything we do. They sleep with us and eat with us. The same food, same beds, same work. We don't mind doing all the things it takes to be a good tanker under those conditions and besides we all got our heart set on being the best in the world. We even practice drilling, fighting, and any other subject we think we are not good enough at on our time off. Col. Brown says that with our spirit the battle is half won. He said, 'just to show you boys that I know what you are going through I will go with you on the opsticle course and the hike, and he kept his word. He is a Lt Col and only 27 years old he is 6 or 7 years out of West Point and every man in his Battalion would follow him to the four corners of the earth. He also said when we get shipped across he will be along with us.

We get instructions in chemical warfare pretty soon. Really I did not think I had brains enough to learn all this stuff in so short a time. And everything we take up we have to become experts and they really mean it we get examinations every day to be sure we did not miss a thing they taught us if we miss one question an officer comes to give you special instruction, because his life depends on us as well as ours on theirs. They are also going with us where ever we go. That is why we are getting such a rugged and complete course on being a tanker.
Well I think I have said enough about my self. How are you and Dad lately? I sure miss you, but I guess that can't be helped at this time. I miss fighting with Roy too, but we can take care of that after the war. What I really miss is a letter from the two men of the family.

We have pie for super once in a while and it is good but when I think of your pies Mom I get disgusted with it.

They try to keep us so busy we don't have time to think of home I guess maybe it is all for the better because you can't think of two things at once. A mistake here means someone's life.

For the first time in my life I am learning what it means to be careful. You have to be reckless and yet careful here or you get in plenty of trouble.

I guess you are wondering how we spend our time on Sunday. We played soft ball in the morning and pitched horse shoes in afternoon and just to keep in trim we run around the track. We ended up at the movies at nite and went to bed early so we could be in condition for this week. Well its time for lights out, so good by.
Your Son,
Bob

Jan 26, 1943
Dear, Mother Dad.

Got a new idea, I take this book with all the time and when I get a rest I will write to you. I received the letter from you and Dad. And will try to answer all the questions you sent.

I don't know where I am any more than you do, in fact I know less because I have not seen a map. I did get your letters from Dix. I will go on K.P. tomorrow fore the first time since I have been in the army. I was out scouting today and if it was real I would have been shot. I stuck my head up at the wrong place at the wrong time. I guess I read my compass wrong. I ended up in the enemy camp. We go on an over nite hike Friday. They have a surprise gas attack when you are asleep. I hope my mask works.

I went to the moves tonite. Casablanca was playing.

I am glad Ralph got what he wanted. I can't understand what happened to Ray he must be going to China.

I still did not here from Roy has he got a broken arm. I here you can't get gas HA HA   I get all I want and no stamps needed.

We just heard about F.D.R. in Africa. I guess that is good news but we did not get the details.
Well I can't think of any thing to say so good by for now
Your Son
Bob.

Jan 28, 1943
Dear Mom

I just got off K.P. and I am plenty tired I had K.P. yesterday and table waiter today. We just served tables at meal time today and in between we went on duty. Between 12 noon and supper I went on a 12 mile hike and didn't we go. It took 3 hrs when I got back I was bowl legged. Than I gook a shower and went back to kitchen we served meals and scrubbed out mess hall. Tomorrow we go on an over nite hike God only knows how far we are going. We had a real gas attack to-day on the hike and I just got my mask on in time.

Next week we drive all the time, that's the work I like. We have done very lit-tle driving this week, because we are getting special training in scouting and gas warfare.

Grand Pa wrote me a letter today but I have not had time to read it yet.

We got notice to be ready to move at a minutes notice. We are going to an-other camp in the near future. We got our needle today and it was not due till Saturday so maybe we will be gone sat.

The weather is better know but its not warm enough to take a sun bath yet. It mite be hot tomorrow, I hope so anyway.

When is Dad and Roy going to send me a long letter. If I don't get one by Sunday I am going to stop sending letters home. I got enough apples, grapes, oranges in my locker to last me for two weeks. I got them in the kitchen.

I can't think of anything more to say know so goodbye for know.
Your loving Son,
Bob

Jan 29,
Dear Mother, Dad,

Your letter of the 24 took 4 days to reach me. It must have come by Pony Express. Fritzie shouldn't spend any more money on me, although the mirror will come in handy. Tell her to drop a line once in a wile. Red sent me a card today, it is the first I have heard from him since I left home. Its too bad about Bill Rielly, his Dad was a fine man.

It's a lot better to think of you home taking it easy than is was when you were in the store. I know you won't stop working, but at least when you get tired you can sit down and rest.

I sent Hazel and Ed a letter yesterday. I want to write to cousin Kitty a soon as I get time. Will you please explain how hard it is for me to write? Maybe she will understand. So Dad don't like the bosses, well its about time you found out what I was going through at work. Dad you're a fine guy. Afraid of a little crowd (*hard to decipher this word*).

By the way Dad and Roy when are you going to give up 5 minutes of your time and write me a full length letter?

The boys all get a great kick out of the cartoons you send down. We can buy papers here, but we don't get time to read them. I haven't seen any war news since I left home and I don't want to see any. Nobody talks war or politicks here. You asked me if I wanted cookies. No we get so many of them from the families of our boys that we are tired of them. The 19 of us like nuts, candy, cake, raisins and fig newtons. I say 19 but there are only 10 of us left. 9 are in the hospital from the hike yesterday.

Sergeant Fuller is in bed here sick as a dog but he wont go to hospital. We have to make him take his medicine.

I went through a gas chamber this morning to test my gas mask. (It works, thank God.) We also had a tear gas drill, I was a little slow and my eyes are a little sore yet. We are getting in new tanks which are twice as fast as these. They are M4.

So Ray Daly ended up in the artillery. What a racket he got. All but the cold weather. We have to be artillery men as well as tankers and infantry men. We shoot the 75mm and the 37mm the same as I got home. The 30 cal Rifle and 50 cal mach gun, Tommy gun, the 45 cal revolver and we even throw stones.

For the past hour no one has bothered me. It looks funny to me. Any minute I expect someone to throw a gas bomb in the window.

I went to the dentist to have a tooth made but he could not take care of me today. He was too busy. I hope to get a tooth before we move to another camp. Those pictures I sent you are terrible but the best I could get. We are not allowed to have cameras here any more.

Jan 31, 1943
Dear Mom Dad

The weather is good again today so I went to town with one of my pals. We had these pictures taken in the same place as the others. I went to the U.S.O. to make a recording of my voice but the machine was out of order. I bought a dinner and it cost me 80 cents and it wasn't as good as they had at camp. I am going to the movies to nite to see the (Avengers.) Yesterday I seen (The Crystal Ball).

I seen a map in town today and I just found out that we are 16 miles from the geographic center of Texas. I am going to San Antonio as soon as I get time and money to see Art Kiefer. I might make it next week. The song Deep in the Heart of Texas was written by a soldier in this camp.

I believe you asked me about the U.S.O. It is very nice we have three of them here. They have a dance floor, pool tables, ping pong tables, checkers, piano, radio, victrola, eats, and many other nice things.

The people down here play dominoes like you play Bridge. They have clubs, and all the members come and play every nite.

All the fellows that were sick and in the hospital are getting better, two of them came home today from hospital. Sergeant Fuller is all better and will go on duty tomorrow.

The other nite when I was writing you the lights went out and I did not have time to finish, so I put it in an envelope and used a match to address it. Then I felt my way to the mail box and mailed it. You may get other letters not finished so you will know the reason. I haven't received any of your letters in two days, I guess their will be one for me tomorrow.

I sent cards out to everybody yesterday. I guess you know we are not allowed to have cameras on the post, and are not allowed to wear dress caps, or belts, not even the gold buttons on our lapels. We don't get any medals for shooting or any thing else or I would have one. We have to wear our hats on the left side of our head instead of the right. Our hats have green trim on them. The tank corps is supposed to get new uniforms they are dark green with lite green tie. I don't know just when we get them but I hope its soon. I went to the movies in between lines and just got back. The picture was <u>terrible</u> it was an English picture that's why. Its almost time for lights out so I'll say goodbye and love to all.
Bob

Feb 1, 1943
Dear Mother and Dad,

I received your letter telling about Gramp Davis. It was very sad news but I guess we all expected it. There still might be a chance although it sounds very bad in your letter. Tell Bob, Dick and Elaine and Janet I am looking forward to receiving their letters. It might take me quite a long time to answer them but tell them I will answer as soon as possible.

I am very tired now as I have been driving cross country all day and it is a rough ride. Its swell and we have a lot of fun, but you still get tired. I have a picture of a tank enclosed that is exact in every detail to the one I drive. The picture was taken in Africa.

I got paid today for the first time. $27. It wasn't much but I invested it and got $40 now.

We have new tanks in camp; they are the newest model out. They are swell. I can't tell you anything about them, but they cant be touched by any other in the world. I hope to get one next week.

You ought to see me make a bed. I didn't know I could do it. I shine my shoes twice a day and like it. We all try to have the best shine and shave for inspection.

I did not receive the mirror from Fritzie yet, I guess it will come soon. Please thank her for it and tell her how much I appreciate her getting it for me.

Well Dad I think the army is doing me a lot of good. On Saturday I had the neatest bunk and the neatest uniform in the hutment. Saturday we have a full field inspection by Col. Brown and he is from West Point so you can imagine how strict he is.

I went to the show again tonite and seen 'Fall in' and 'One Dangerous Nite' they were both very good. We get new pictures every nite so we go as often as we like. I fall asleep in them quite often. The movie house is a block away from our hutment.

I wore two pair of shoes out already. They have to get new soles. Maybe you can imagine how much running we do. I am going to bed so its so long for now.
Your loving Son
Bob

Feb 4, 1943
Dear Mother, Dad,

How do you like the snow up their? All we got was an hrs rain. It was the first rain I have seen since I left home.

The new tanks came in today, and were we glad to see them. They are the M4A4 type or the 'General Sherman'. We drove tanks all morning by radio instructions. All my orders came over the radio. It was the first time I ever talked over a radio. It's great fun not to see where you are going and all of a sudden run into a trench and almost go on your head. Yesterday they put me in the turret with my head sticking out and it rained and the mud from the other tanks flew up in my face all day. You should have seen me. I wouldn't recognize myself. This afternoon we took a track of the 'Gen Grant tank' that's the old ones I got blisters all over my hands but the work was very interesting. I would rather change a flat tire though. I wish I could tell you about the new tanks but you know how it is.

The mess sergeant is still feeding us good. We had beans every day this week. We had roast, beans, spinach, potatoes with cheese melted on them, pudding, coffey, bread, and more beans for supper today.

We learned to drive the motor cycle this week, it was fun but I would not drive one steady.

I went to the stage show last nite and had more fun than I had in years. There was a man that is supposed to be an expert at the bull whip. I was in the front row so he picked on me and a few of the boys to demonstrate on, he snapped a cocoa cola bottle cap out from my teeth. My knees were shaking for an hour after. Then the originator of jitter bug gave us lessons on the stage. Our partners were all girls from the stage in Fort Worth. You should have seen me. I'll never live it down but I had so much fun it was worth it.

I received a letter from you today and also Fritzie's mirror, it comes in very handy around here. I believe you asked me where all the boys are from that live with me. Some are from Brooklyn some from Kentucky, Mississippi, and Oregon. Fort Worth is North East of here.

Enclosed find $20 save it for me I might need it later on. If I keep it here I will only spend it. I got 20 left to last me for the month. It might do. As I told you I was broke when I got paid, my pay was 27 dollars and got the rest playing pool. I got the game beat so I am going to quit now for good. I am very tired so I'll just say thanks for the letters and keep sending them.
Your loving son
Bob

Feb 6, 1943
Dear Mom, Dad.

I received your letter from Schenectady today. I am very sorry to hear about Gramp Davis, he was a swell old fellow. How long did you spend in Schenectady? Was it cold up their? I guess you think that is a long way but we go that for the nearest big city.

Thanks for the money Dad, it always comes in handy.

The new tanks we got in are swell. I took one out today for a wile and it's the best their is. You aught to see them go. They got 500 horse power and are stream lined. I would sure like to take you for a ride in them. You would have a lot of fun but not mutch room. I came cross country in a truck yesterday. I was the first in the convoy. I had to follow a jeep wherever he went, I was plenty scared and I am not fooling. Their were 3 men in the back of each truck and when we hit the big curve, which looks like a S standing up and down two of the men in my truck got so scared they jumped out. One of them got a sprained ankle, and the other broke his nose. I made it but the third truck to follow me turned over 3 times and no one was hurt. The men that jumped had to ride that hill all day and got K.P. for a week. The driver of the truck had to get in another truck and go over it 5 more times. We also went up a hill so steep the truck slid down backwards with the wheels still going forward.

You asked me if the U.S.O. gave anything away. I have never gotten anything for nothing in this army and never expect to. You pay for insurance, laundry, tooth past, all shaving equipment, patches for your arm, coat hangers, shoe polish, of which I use a can every two days.

We had a real dust storm yesterday you could not see the sun we had to wear our dust respirators and goggles even to go and eat. The whole sky was red all last nite but this morning it was all gone.

You asked me if I lost any weight, well I don't know but I lost 7 inches around the waist.

I got a letter from cousin Kitty yesterday and also one from you. You can never write   enough so keep them coming.

 As ever
Your loving Son
Bob

Feb 8, 1943
Dear Mother, Dad,

Your cards and letters got here alright, I got 2 letters from you today. You asked me about my watch. I can't mail it till I get to town on a work day when the post office is open.

We got orders to move to camp Hood next Monday. Your mail will follow us just the same.

The Co. Commander told us our basic training will be over this Wednesday. Its no wonder we been working so hard. He said we had everything the Infantry gets in, in this 13 weeks. I thought our obstacle course was bad but you ought to see the one they are building for us at Hood. I seen pictures of it today. You go all through barbed wire with live shells bursting all around you then you swing over a cliff on a rope after you do that if you do it you swim with full pack across river and on the other side is a 9 ft wall to clime over. Then all you have to do is jump 8 hurdles and run all the way back.

Today we had classes on gunnery, we started 3 o'clock this morning and studied guns 45 minutes and then 10 minutes break and repeated that all day until 11 o'clock at nite. It is now 2 o'clock in the morning and I can't sleep. I don't know what's the matter but we don't get up till 8 in the morning.

We start advanced training next week. I will let you know how I make out.

You must have misunderstood me about being captured in the games, I was never captured!!!! I was shot.

I am getting my new tooth Wednesday. I hope it fits.

They gave me a haircut the other day and it's not a quarter of an inch long at the longest point. It looks funny but a lot of us got them. My new nick name is baldy. Some of the girls from the U.S.O. made us go to church Sunday and then invited us to dinner. It was swell getting some home cooked meals. I don't want to leave here now. We have so much fun. We go to the service club every week and that's a riot. There is always a good show and plenty to do.

It's sure getting hot here it must be summer coming in. I never sweat so much in my life. It's about 80 in the shade and there is no shade. If I wasn't so tired I would go swimming at Lake Brownwood. I got lost the last time I went in the dark and had to get a taxi back.

I have pictures of the new tank we got. They are beautiful aren't they? We will go into battle against the Tank Destroyers at camp Hood. God help them. The first Battalion of Tank Destroyers that went across was chopped to peaces they can't stand up against a good tank.

The fellows here get packages from home at every mail call. We get everything we want to eat. Today we did not even go to mess. About five salamis, three cakes, and more cookies then we know what to do with.

Did you ever go to the Squacome Inn near the shore? Mrs. Keller owns it and her son is one of my best friends. He is 18 and the baby of the hut. His name is Sam but we all call him sonny. He hates it. He is sure a swell fellow. Some day I will send you his picture. There are only 2 or 3 fellows older than me and they are 20 or 21. Its nice to be with boys your own age. My Commanding officer is only 23 and most of the sergeants are not over 23 or 4 some are not even as old as I but they sure know their stuff. Our Battalion Commander is a Lieutenant Colonel and he is only 27 and 6 years out of West Point.

I just got your letter saying you mailed the package. I am glad as I am the only one who has not received one. Thanks allot.

Did you get the $20 yet? I hope. I will probably need it later but if I keep it here I will only spend it. I have to laugh about the gas up north, I burn a hundred gal a day and never think any thing of it. Don't you wish you could get it? We only get ½ mile on a gal if we are lucky. The tank holds 160 gals and 25 gal reserve.

I got extra detail for leaving my hat on the bed. Just stepped out for a minute and they had a surprise inspection. I had to clean up the orderly room it took about 2 hrs of my own time and that time is precious. I was glad to hear from you Dad please write more often.

I had all my cloths cleaned and pressed it cost me 3$ and we are going to have to put them in barracks bags to be shipped and they will have to be done all over again.

I received a letter from Fritzie and Dick. Tried to answer both but did not do a very good job. I just thought of something that Dad wanted to know. There are rattle snakes all over here we see them all the time. When we sleep out one man stays up all the time watching for them. Before we get to sleep we beat the brush just to make sure. A guard shot one the other day right in camp. He was new and only hit him once with the Tommy gun out of thirty shots. The shots sure scared me I thought we were being attacked. The major hit one with his revolver the first shot. I never got chance to shoot one yet but their will come a time. I ht the target towed by a jeep 5 times out of 40 shots which is excellent. They say you are good to hit a still target 5 times out of 40 at that range. All 40 shots are gone before you can take your finger off the trigger. They fire 70 shots per minute. 45 cal bullet.

your son, Bob

Feb 9, 1943

Dear Mother Dad,

Well its final that we leave here Monday. Its almost as if I was leaving home all over again. I love it here, but maybe I will like the next camp to. I can't leave camp any more till we move so I guess I seen the last of Brownswood.

We had school all morning, and this afternoon we had a race in the tanks. We had to blow up a bridge and get back to camp in a certain time. At the bridge there were guards made of wood and looking like real men. They were moved by tow ropes and we had to run over them. It gave you a sickish feeling when you run over them but it will come natural to us later, they tell us. We were fired upon by 50 cal machine guns all along the route just to give us the feeling of war. You ought to hear those bullets splash off our tank. Coming back we opened fire on a concrete pill box we blew it to peaces with our 75. The sound of the tank with the motor wide open knocking down everything in your path makes goose pimples run up and down your spine, especially when you got the 4 machine guns and the 75 all blazing away at once. I would not miss this life for a million dollars. It seems there is no limit to the power of these tanks. I don't think there is any thing in the world that could stop them. I got a chance to shoot each gun shoots 8 shots per second. Tonite we are having more school on the Browning machine gun. I could take it apart with my eyes shut but we can't name all of the 74 parts yet so we wont get out of school till we can, if it takes till Monday.

Yesterday we had the same thing on the Thompson sub machine gun and I got that down pat.

I received a letter from Mr. Keiffer today saying John is in Ireland and you told me the same time.

The fellow with me in the last pictures I sent home is Skelly he is one of my pals an I still don't know his first name. Everybody is called by their last name here (Thank God).

I am getting very good in jujitsu or what ever you call it we practice every morning before dawn. Its regular commando training. Its just in case our tank gets knocked out at the front.

How about you sending me a picture of yourself and Dad and Roy. Don't forget I will be waiting for you to send it. I can't think of anything so I guess its goodbye for now.

Your Loving Son, Bob

Feb 13

Dear Mom Dad.

Boy have I been busy lately getting ready to move. We work from dawn till dark on the tanks and then go to school till you can't see. We have to load the tanks on flat cars this afternoon. I am sorry I could not write you for the past few days but there are just not enough hours in the day. I haven't received any letters from you for 4 days either.

How are you and Dad feeling? Is it cold up home? It's a little chilly here in the morning but in the middle of the day it hits 75 or 80. Every day is what you call a beautiful day. You only get the kind of weather we have about 2 weeks a year. There is never a cloud in the sky we only had rain once since I left home and that only lasted 5 hrs.

I received your package, and it was the best one in the hut. All the boys thank you. Enclosed is a negative of Sgt Fuller. Save it for me when I get home.

I want to grab a little sleep so good bye for now.

Your Loving Son,

 Bob

Feb 15

Hello Folks

I am not allowed to say anything to you about anything right now. I am not receiving any of your letters but I will get them in a few days or weeks. I am in good health so don't worry about me.

As ever,

Bob

Camp Bowie Texas

Feb 18, 1943

Dear Mom, Dad.

I sure wish I could tell you what going on down here but that is impossible. I haven't had a letter in two weeks from anybody and we are not allowed to write except what they tell us. My address has been changed but I can't even tell you what it is. I will get all my mail Monday. I guess their will be quite a pile of it. I will write to you either Sunday or Monday but even than I wont be able to tell you what happened this week.

Did you receive the letter with the picture in it? I don't know whether they mailed it or not. Maybe they wont mail this either. I don't know.

How do you like the cold weather up their? I hear its kind of cold. We are having a heat wave here it is about 90 degrees in the shade. I never heard of such crazy weather as we are having. The temp will sometimes drop 60 degrees in 2 or 3 hrs at nite and than as soon as the sun comes up the temp goes up just as fast as it went down.

In any emergency where you need me at home in a hurry, get in touch with the local Red Cross and they will get in touch with our Red Cross and I will be on my within the hour. That is the only way we can get an emergency furlough. The Red Cross is doing fine work for the boys here. We get all the inside information about the war and the Red Cross is always on the job. If any of you get the chance to give blood to the Red Cross I wish you would because it is saving thousands of lives, especially on Guadal Canal. They give us books, writing paper and they will even lend us money at no interest.

I guess I will have to close now as the lights go out in 5 min.
Your Loving Son,
Bob

Feb 21.
Camp Hood Texas
Dear Mom Dad.

Well at last I can write to you and say what I want. I am at Camp Hood Texas. We had quite an experience in the last few weeks that I cant tell you about until after the war.

We have regular barracks here and most of the boys like them but I would rather sleep in the hutments that we had at Bowie. There are twice as many men in the barracks as what we had in the other and we have to floors. One good thing is that we have a lot of big towns about 100 miles away. We are near Temple, and Waco Texas. There is a town called Kileen about 3 miles from camp. It has 2 stores and a railroad station. The people in the town are worst of all. They live in shacks and the pigs go rite in the house. On a windy nite you can smell the town.

The water here smells, you have to hold your nose to drink it. All we do is rinse our mouth out with it. It has sulfur and a bunch of other stuff in it. I only drink coca Cola and coffey.

We have a big service club and movies near by. I went to the movies this morning and also to the club.

Today is Sunday and last nite I had the first sleep I had in four days. Its real tough here, about twice as hard as in Bowie. We are going to have battles with the tank Destroyers from now on. In two weeks we have to go over the Commando obstacle course. It takes a whole week to go over it. It is worse than I thought.

I just tried to call you up on the phone but it would take 6 hours and I haven't got time to hang around that long.

Cousin Kitty just wrote me and told me how cold it is up their. I had to laugh when I read it because I was sitting in the shade in my undershirt. It looks as if summer is really here. It is about 90 degrees here and getting hotter every day.

Monday I have to go out on the range and try to qualify for marksman on the rifle, browning mach gun and the 45 cal Colt automatic pistol. Please wish me luck. I made expert on the Thompson sub mach gun. Its about time you sent me another letter Dad. And how about you Roy. I got the paper this morning but I would also like a letter from you. How are you making out in school? The lights go out at 9 at nite here and we have to get up all hrs of the nite to go on a hike sometimes we go to the service club and when we come in to go to bed the hole company is gone on a hike that's when we get in a nice mess and I mean a mess. That's the mess hall doing dishes for 16 hrs. We don't have to be in bed at any special time but if they are called out any time and we are not there we get all the details of the following day. I never get to bed before 2 in the morning because we are all over to the service club till they throw us out. I came in one nite so tired I could not see and there they were in full pack ready to march. I got my pack and started after them. It took me 45 minutes of double time to catch them and then we marched 15 miles and pitched tents, dug rain ditches and were just going to sleep and they got us up and on the move. It takes the heart out of you after all that work. When we got back from the hike they gave us 35 minutes to wash shave and change our clothes and go to the parade grounds for inspection. After inspection they gave us an hour rest and than we went to school for 9 hrs. 60 out of 160 went to sleep in our seats and I was one of them. Every one that went to sleep had to go out and run for 10 minutes. We get used to that stuff we get so mutch of it.

I will let you know how I make out tomorrow on the range.
Your Son, Bob
P.S.
My address is the same all except for the name Hood instead of Bowie.

Camp Hood
Feb 24, 1943
Dear Mom Dad,

I just received 9 of your letters all at once. It was sure swell to hear from you after all this time. This letter will be the last one this week as we are gong to the firing range for 4 days. We will leave in the morning and it will take us 7 hrs to make it, and that will be quite a march. It is 32 miles out there and the same back. When I get back Friday I will be about dead so I will probably write Satur-day. We got up at 5 o'clock this morning and marched 7 miles to the hills for map reading and scouting and that scouting is really tough. I traveled about 3 miles on my belly over stickers and through dust that was so bad you could not breathe. The temperature was 90 degrees in the shade and after the 7 miles home I am pretty tired now.

I got Adele's package and also the one from Bayonne. Please don't send any more for a while or we will all be sick. Tell Adele I am grateful but I will not be able to write her for quite some time. The next time Grand Pop and Grand Mom come out tell them we all liked the candy very much and also the wrapper.

I am sure glad I am down here where it is hot rather than freezing up north somewhere. I tried to call you up again tonite but I could not get a wire through.

I guess I told you about the water here. I just found out it s the same kind of mineral water you get up at Saratoga Springs or wherever it is we got it. It is so bad I came back from the hike today with my tongue hanging out and a full canteen. My tongue is still swollen but had a quart of milk for supper and I feel better. I am not even going to take my canteen with me on the hike tomorrow because it is heavy and I wouldn't drink it anyway. Our full pack weighs 104 lbs. Our commanding Officer says it will make men out of us. They make us carry a pick and shovel and an 11 lb sledge hammer with us just to make it a little heavier. We will not take it tomorrow though.

Honest Mom I would like to write some more but I can't even sit here in bed and write I am so tired. I hope to get another nice bunch of letters next Friday.

Goodbye for now and Love to you all

Your son

Bob

P.S.

I sure do like to read those cartoons you send me. Keep them coming.

(Buy Bonds)

Camp Hood Tex

Dear Mother, Dad

I just got back from the firing range and I did a good job. I made marksman with the Tommy gun and will get a medal for it as soon as they come in. I will send it home so you can see it.

I told you about the hike I expected before I left. That was supposed to be a road hike but we went through the woods instead. We left Tuesday morning and we got one surprise after the other. We went by compass only. We started out alright for the first 3 miles and then we came to a river with a 40 ft cliff on the other side. We couldn't climb over it so we had to follow the river for about 3 miles before we could cross then we marched over all kinds of hills for about 5 miles when we came to a poison gas area. We had to detour around that, which took 2 more hours. Then we got a 10 minute rest. We were about dead from the heat and so tired I didn't think I could get up again. We started out again and walked for about another hr when we came to a dry river bed and on the other side was a hill almost straight up. I got about 50 ft up the hill and slipped and slid all the way down again. I had to lay there for 5 min before I could try again. When I did get up I took my first mouth full of water. As bad as that water smelled it tasted swell to me then. We then marched for a few miles and it got dark and we had to halt. We slept for 4 hrs and stood guard the other 3 hrs. We were supposed to be at the firing range that nite and that's where the chow truck was, so we did not eat. In the morning we finished the rest of the hike, which was as bad if not worse than the first half. We came to a small river and we all jumped in as soon as we saw it. We got balled out by a lieutenant but it was worth it. The temperature was in the 90's and with that full pack it felt like a hundred and ninety. I am so sunburned I can't touch my face. When we reached the range we pitched our tents and dug slit trenches before we could eat. After we ate we fired 100 rounds on the Tommy gun for practice and then we shot for the record at bobbing targets. We could have done better if we were not so tired but did good enough. After that we fired the 45 pistol. We did not shoot that for record though. We went to bed after that and it got cold. It went from 93 degrees to 25 degrees over nite. All we had was two blankets one over us and 1 under us. We were so thirsty that we could not sleep so we, that is Sgt Fuller, Joe Skelly and myself slipped past the guard and went about 3 miles for water. We found a small fast running river and filled our canteens and drank all we could hold. We came back to camp and sold the water for 25 cents every 2 ounces. I made $2.50 and gave it to the cook for 5 oranges. Today the measles broke out in camp so they brought 50 of us back in the trucks to stand guard. I just got off guard and I go back on in 3 hrs. I will have to keep this up until the rest of the company comes back tomorrow or Saturday. This guard duty is rotten you think the time will never pass. On top of that we are quarantined for at least 21 days to the company area. We will go on duty and all that but we can't go to town or to the movies or Post Exchange or anywhere on our company grounds.

I got a letter from Hazel and Ed today. I might get time to answer it soon but I don't know.

I hope to get some mail from you tomorrow as that will be our only pastime from now on.

I want to get some sleep so goodbye for now.

Your son

Bob

Camp Hood Tex

Dear Mother & Dad,

I don't know what to write about any more. I told you about everything I could think of. I am still on guard duty. I will walk 2 more hrs and will be finished. I just looked up my name on the K.P. list and I got that tomorrow. I seem to get everything at once. I will probably have table waiter Sun, then I will be threw for a month I hope. I haven't had my shoes or clothes off in 3 days. When you get relieved on guard you still have to sleep in your clothes. You are not allowed to take them off until you are all finished and off duty. It will sure feel good to take my shoes off and soak my feet after all this time. That Tommy gun sure gets heavy after you carry it a few hrs. I think I have a groove worn in my shoulder from the strap.

Three o'clock this morning a captain drove up on my post in his car and parked there by a fire hydrant. I did not know he was a captain it was so dark. After he parked he started off in the dark. I made him halt and I gave him a bawling out, and after I finished I seen those 2 silver bars. You should have seen my ears get red. I'll bet you could have seen them in the dark.

Two corporals came on the company grounds and I turned them in. The Commanding Officer put them both in quarantine for 21 days. They will have to live in tents for 3 weeks on the cold ground.

The laundry hasn't gone out in three weeks because of us moving and now it can't go until the quarantine is lifted. So I guess I will spend Sunday washing clothes.

I got the pictures you sent me.

(2 hrs later)

I just put in another tour of guard and put my feet in a bucket of water. I sure was glad to hear you got the money alright. I will mail some more home about the 10th of March. I won't get paid til then. I still got 8 dollars left out of my pay and I can't spend any now for the next 3 weeks at least. I will sure be glad when Monday gets here. We will spend all next week in the tanks. That will be a lot better than the field work we just had. The week after next or the week after that we go to the Commando obstacle course and that isn't going to be fun. It takes 7 days to go over it.

They have a tough opsticle course that we have to drive the tank over but I like that because the tank does all the work.

Did you ever see the jeeps go over a bump in the movies? We have to do that too. The first time I did it my hair turned grey but now it's fun. I didn't go over it yet with the motorcycle but I watched some of them and it gives you plenty of excitement. I can't wait til we go on maneuvers against the tank destroyers. We will murder the bums.

I don't know whether I told you about the gas attacks we had on the hike or not so I will tell you again anyway. We were practicing how to decontaminate a tank of mustard gas when all of a sudden they blew up a gas mine of Lewisite, a gas that will kill almost as fast as snake bite. We were sure surprised and we had one casualty; our pet mascot 'Tanker' a little mutt that we raised from a bottle. He was under the jeep sleeping and never woke up. Our top sergeant took him to the dispensary but it was too late. We gave him a military funeral. We brought him from Camp Bowie in a tank. He used to eat better than we did and we would give him water from our canteens when we were too thirsty to talk. He slept in the orderly room like a king. We sure will miss him.

We caught an armadillo in the woods and a southern boy cooked him for us. It was sure the best meat I had in years. The worst thing about sleeping in the woods is the wood ticks. We were covered with them every morning and we had to have them burned out with a red hot needle. I had 9 of them on me and am still sore all over from the burns.

I think I will like this camp a little better as soon as we get settled. We can go to Temple and Waco Belton and Caldwell.

The lights are out Bob

Camp Hood Tex

Dear Mother Dad,

This has been the day of all days. I got up at 11:30 and went to dinner and then back to bed til 2 o'clock when we had a dress parade for Major J Witfield who later made a wonderful speech telling all about his fighting in the last war. He has a Congressional medal for heroism. He rates the same as Sgt York. He got separated from his company in the Argon forest and killed 19 men single handed and wiped out 3 machine gun nests. He told just how he killed each man. We were so interested in his talk that 2 hrs slipped by before we knew it. We then went to eat supper and as soon as it was over I hopped in bed and that's where I am now.

Yesterday was real tough. I put in 17 hrs of K.P. I washed dishes all day and peeled potatoes at nite. My hands are so raw from the strong soap that it is painful just to write. I am glad I am through with that for this month.

This week we are going on blackout driving. I guess that means we will get no sleep all this week again. I don't think you know what black out lights are. They are round like any other bulb but the front looks like this (--------). The slit is where the light comes out and that is the actual size of the slit so you can imagine how close together we drive. All I hope is that my tank is not the first in line as I am likely to lead them into a lake or over a cliff.

They had a surprise check on our field equipment and I was short one tent peg so they will charge me for it. 6 cents. It's going to break my heart.

I can tell you something about the week I did not write. I was out of the country, but I can't say which one I was in. I'll bet you can't guess which one I was in.

You asked about a letter addressed to Hood. I got it.

That's all for to nite.

Your loving son

Bob

Camp Hood

March 1, 1943

Dear Mom Dad,

This sure was a tough day, but I enjoyed every minute of it. We went out in the tanks and we were told to try and wreck the tank if necessary but show the captain some real fancy driving. I got in and got the tank going about 30 miles an hour and went over a steep hill and the tank left the ground. Then he told me over the radio to drive into a tank trap and see if I could get out of it. I got in it alright but I never did get out. I had to be pulled out with 3 other tanks. After I got out the Lieutenant got in and did he give us a ride. I'll never forget it. I think I would get gray hair if I had to go through it again. It's a wonder to me that the tank held together. I was standing up in the turret and could see each bump and ditch coming. I got a sickish feeling in my stomach just before we hit but when we hit there was nothing to it, although I wouldn't want to do it without my safety helmet on. We go out again tomorrow and he promised it would be worse. I will have to go down a hill 100 ft long and it is almost straight up and down. At the bottom there is a bump and the tank takes off just like a plane. I guess it will be worse than the roller coaster. I don't mind it just so long as I am driving but every man in the tank does it too and that's when you get scared.

We will go over the opsticle course in a jeep in the middle of the nite with the blackout lights on. I am sure that will be fun. I only hope I land on all four wheels.

We are getting up at 5:30 in the morning and going to bed at 9:00. We were plenty mad about going to bed at 9 but we are in bed by 9 most of the time, we are so tired. We still can't go anywhere because of the measles so we play baseball in our spare time.

Believe it or not we are having a thunder and lightening storm now. It is the second shower we had since I left home. The ground is so dry we have dust storms every day.

Lights out
  Your son Bob

Camp Hood
March 3, 1943
Dear Mom Dad,
  Well we are off again. We leave 5:30 in the morning and we won't be back until Saturday. We are driving all nite and sleeping 2 hours during the day. We have to feel our way around in the dark. It sure feels funny to go crashing through the woods in the dark. I drove a truck last nite and hit a tree. If it wasn't for our safety belts I would have gone through the windshield. The tanks got stuck in a ditch about 14 feet deep dug for a rain ditch. We just got our winter all at once and we sure feel it. It went down to 15 above last nite. I only hope it gets warmer before tomorrow nite or we will freeze. Company B came back from a 4 day hike today and they said they did not sleep the whole 4 days because of the cold. They had to stay up all nite and jump around to keep warm. All we have is 2 blankets and we have to put one under us and one over us. It sure is cold. During the day when we were on the last hike it was 95 and we almost died from the heat and the same nite it went down to 20. We got together about 5 men and put 2 blankets on the ground and put 8 over us. I am beginning to wonder why we have barracks. We sleep out more than we sleep in.

Did you hear Bob Hope the other nite? He made a broadcast from Hood but we could not go because of the measles. Next week Hellzapoppin is on the stage at our Rec hall. That's out too.

I just got 2 letters today one from Bayonne and the other from the social civic society of Raritan Rd. Linden with a dollar in it. I sent Grand Pa a letter the other day but I did not have his letter yet because it was mailed Feb 11 so please explain it to them, and thank them for the nice card.

I have $6.25 a month taken out for bonds every month so you will get a bond in 3 months. I won't get paid this month until the 10th because I wasn't in camp when they signed the payroll. I just got another pair of shoes fixed and my others are ready to get new soles and heels. That makes 8 soles and heels I wore out. I am glad I am not paying for them.

I won't be able to write til Sat or Sun and the lights go out in a few minutes so I will have to say good nite.
love to all
your son
Bob

Camp Hood
Dear Mom Dad,

I just got back from the driving range and I am so tired I can hardly lift the pencil to write this letter.

The first day we drove through mustard gas to get practice in decontaminating our tanks. That nite at 7 we started out over a 25 mile cross country drive with blackout lights. I drove for 8 hrs without stopping, going over all kinds of hills and ditches. We got lost and drove all over Texas before we got back on our course. We started out with 22 tanks, 5 jeeps, 6 trucks. 7 tanks were disabled and two trucks have not been heard of yet, as they have no radio.

I went over a wooden bridge about 12 ft wide and about 20 ft deep. When I got half way over, down we went. Did I get a scare – I thought I went over a cliff. We threw a track and broke the radio and we all got a good bounce. We sent out scouts to get to a radio. It took 2 hrs to find a radio to call the maintenance crew. They fixed us up in an hour and we were on our way. We could not find the convoy so we went by compass til we came to a road and we radio'd for a jeep to guide us in. It was raining all the time and it was too dark to see the road so quite a few, I think it was 4 tanks hit rain ditches going sideways and turned over. Everyone is strapped in so they never get hurt.

<u>9 hrs later and still no sleep</u>
They called us out for repairs on our tanks. I had more damage than I thought. My track was very bad; there were two cracks in it. I don't know how it held together. My sprocket was out of line. I guess I hit a rock or something. We all worked as hard as we could for 9 hrs. I am so tired I can't go to sleep now. I haven't had a wink of sleep since Tuesday. 3 days and nites without sleep is no

joke. We have to scrub the floors and wash windows tonite for tomorrow's inspection.

Got a letter from you today. It was good to hear from you. We don't have anywhere to go in our time off so the letters are our only means of passing the time. Some of the boys read their letters over 10 times.

Four new cases of measles broke out yesterday so we will be in here for 21 more days at least. If we get 2 more cases we go into quarantine inside of our barracks til it's all over. I thought you would like to know how mutch gas we burned in our tank for the 4 days. It was 820 gallons. Wouldn't you like to have it?

I turned in my name to get war bonds out of my pay but they called us out a little while ago to sign up; there was a big line so I did not wait. I suppose I will have to explain to the top rank but they got some nerve calling us out tonite after all we went through.

We are about to go nuts if we don't get some kind of amusement. They even took the radio out of the day room.

I hate to think of getting up and washing my socks and underwear yet tonite.

I just got word I go on table waiter tomorrow. That's all I needed. There is a baseball game going on tonite but all the men in our company are too tired to play. Most of them are in bed now.

Joe Skelly, the fellow in the picture I sent home, is in the hospital. He has been there two weeks and he sent us a letter saying he won't be back for at least two months. The doc says he doesn't know what is the matter with him. Joe thinks he has meningitis. There was quite a bit of it back at Bowie.

Sgt Fuller got the measles this morning and they had to drag him to the hospital. He will sneak out tonite most likely if he can get his clothes.

Ernie, the short fat guy in the picture has measles too. He got them yesterday. All you can see here is empty beds. I just got information through a friend of mine who works in Battalion headquarters that we are moving in 2 weeks. I don't know how true it is but I just hope so.

Next week is commando training week. I get chills every time I think of it. Half the boys are going to get sick that week but I will try anything once. I hope I can go through it all the way because that is a very rare thing. Only about 5% go through it all the way. I guess I told you it takes a week to go over it.

I made a good score on the rifle yesterday. That means I get another chance for a medal. I can't wait to shoot for record with the 50 caliber machine guns. I sure like it. We just got a new type of sights for it and it improves your shooting 100%. One of the missing trucks came in and you should see it. It isn't worth 5 cents. They were carrying eight 5 gallon cans of gas in the back and a limb of a tree punched a hole in a can and it somehow caught on fire. The driver will lose his stripes and will lose 2/3 of his pay for a year because it was carelessness. At least that is what is supposed to happen to anyone who causes damage through neglect. He is not worth having in this outfit if he is that careless. In here it only takes one minute to kill the whole outfit.

I guess I have changed since I left home about being careless with that kind of thing, because we play for keeps here and our lives may depend on our equipment. You don't know what war is until you get in the army. It always seemed like a game to me before I came in. We get books written by men over on the other side and they sure go through hell. We got a book called The Fighting in Guadalcanal. It was written by the marines on the battle front. Each man from private to general put in just what he thought. The book is restricted or I would tell you what they said. It is unbelievable in parts how tricky the japs really are. I don't think it is going to be easy to beat them because it's going to be one tough job.

I was posted in the woods on the second nite of our driving and I had a lot of funny experiences. They put me on a steep river bank to guide the tanks by that dangerous spot. I went on post at 11 at nite and it was cloudy and dark as the inside of a boat. The tank convoy was due at 1:30 at that spot. I got cold as usual and I was not allowed to builda fire and only use my light in an emergency. It was 50 miles from nowhere and very quiet. All of a sudden I heard a man walking through the brush. Waited til he got very close and then I expected to scare him to death and yelled 'Halt!'. But the noise kept coming. Then I got scared. I yelled again and still the noise came nearer. I raised my Tommy gun and was ready to fire. I then flashed my light where I heard the noise and there staring me in the face was a great big opossum. Hit him in the head with the butt of my gun and gave him to the cook in the morning.

As I said the tanks were due at 1:30 so I was jumping up and down trying to keep warm and waiting. 1:30 came and went and so on til 5 in the morning when one lonely tank came by. The whole convoy was lost except him. The rest came to camp after daylight. You might think it's funny to lose a whole tank battalion but all you have to do is go over 1 hill and look around and there won't be a tank in sight. There are so many hills and trails you can't tell one from the other.

I had better bring this letter or book to a close before lights out or I won't get it mailed til morning.
 Goodbye and lots of love
Your son, Bob

March 10, 1943
Dear Mother, Dad,
I am sorry I did not have time to write any letters to you in the past few days but as you have probably guessed I have been busy all day and far into the night. I have not had time to breathe and from now on god only knows when I will be able to write letters.

Yesterday I got 10 letters and I haven't had time to open 3 of them yet. Tomorrow we have a review before the battalion commander. It is a very disagreeable task because he is so fussy. Our commando training has been postponed till next week, and we are firing the Browning machine gun Friday. It is going to be blind shooting by that I mean we can't see our targets. We take the range over the radio.

Put all the money in the bank that I send home until I have $100 and then buy bonds. I got paid today for the second time since I got in the army, and they took out $3.25 for insurance, $2.00 for laundry, 1.00 red cross, 25 cents for old soldiers' home, 6 cents for tent peg, 10 cents for shoe polish and when they got all that done they said I would have to wait till next month to get all of my pay. I got 25 bucks as part payment, because of being out of camp when they signed the payroll. I have a load of work to do tonite so I will have to close now.
Your Loving Son,
Bob

Dear Mother Dad,

Your pictures arrived today and they sure look good. I am glad to hear you are having a good time bowling because I am not. It's getting very bad around here with no way of having any fun. All the boys are getting mean and everybody is fighting and arguing. The first Sergeant is working us from 6 in the morning til ten or eleven at nite to keep our mind off getting in trouble. Company B got out today and they all left for Ft Worth to have a good time, which makes us feel worse. I hope our company is out next.

We had a very rough week, every bone in my body aches. I just got in from the tank after a 6 hr drive. It is lots of fun but twice as mutch work.

We had a rugged inspection on our equipment today. I scrubbed out the bore of my 75 gun on the tank til it shined, and Colonel Steel looked down it and asked me f I ever cleaned it. He said I didn't clean either that or the 50 caliber machine gun. I felt like shooting him. Just about 10 minutes later major Freeze came down and complimented me on the excellent care of my arms. This Army is just nuts I guess.

Honest Mom I am tired and hungry so I am going to close for today. I might be able to write tomorrow.
Yours as ever
Bob

March 13,
Dear Mother Dad,

Maybe you thought I forgot to write you but its not that. We just don't get time. I am afraid you won't get any more mail for quite some time, because we leave for the commando course tomorrow. It will be a day's march out there and it takes 6 and a half days to go over it so it will be quite a while before I get a chance to write again. Maybe the orders will change again, I don't know. You just can't figure out this army.

I made expert on the Browning machine gun after a lot of sweating. I had the second best score in the company. It will be another medal. I sure hope I can do as good on human targets.

Please tell all the Schneiders, Helen, Granpa pa and Grand Maw, Hazel, Ed, Mrs Mollender, Edd Milden, Cousin Kitty, Mrs Wilburg, and anybody else that you think of that I won't be able to answer their letters for at least 3 weeks and maybe more. I will receive mail but will not be able to send any.

I hear we will get out of quarantine when I get back. There is not mutch to tell you about so it's about time I close this letter.

Your loving son, Bob

P.S.

I just sent in my income tax report and in order to get out of paying it I told them I had no money in the bank. So you take all my money out of the bank and put it in your name. If they knew I had money I would have to pay now.

Bob

March 21, 1943

Dear Mother, Dad,

The commando course is over thank God! It was the most interesting experience I have ever had, but also the hardest to endure. There is not a man in the company who did not lose at least 15 lbs in the one week.

I know you will be surprised to hear that three quarters of the whole battalion are in the hospital. There are 33 men in my barracks on the bottom floor. Out of the 33 only 8 are left including myself. We lost 4 men in the first 3 minutes of the obstacle course. Farara, a fellow from Plainfield broke his leg on the first wall, Miller from Linden had his two fingers blown off while going under barbed wire, Bo Combo from New York was hit by a 30 caliber machine gun bullet which skinned his shoulder. McGuire fell off a bridge, which you have to climb on a rope. He landed on his back and we haven't heard what happened to him yet. I came out of the whole thing in one piece, but in sad shape.

I have a cut in back of my neck about 1/8 of an inch deep and 4 inches long, and my hands have very little skin on them. My whole body is scratched from the barbed wire, my clothes are in ribbons scattered all over Texas. Our clothes were practically all torn off of us the first two days so you can imagine how we made out under the barbed wire after that. We had to go over the infiltration course twice, once on Monday and again on Friday. It is a stretch of land about 500 ft long and 200 ft wide. It has barbed wire all over it and big holes with 4 or 5 sticks of dynamite in each, and at the end there are two 30 caliber machine guns. You line up at the front and start to run and after you run about 3 steps there is an explosion and you hit the ground and crawl, wiggle, and squirm under the barbed wire and every second there are mines going off within 4 ft of you in the in the holes. The noise is terrific, your ear drums ring for hours, and over your head is a steady stream of machine guns bullets they fire from 5 to 9 inches over your body and if you pull your nose out of the mud they usually take your head off. As I said one of our boys was hit in the shoulder. Once I got on the ground I was so busy getting through that it did not bother me mutch. I was scared before I started and so was everybody else. When you watch someone else do it and see those tracer bullets only 5 inches over their head, you get a little chill when you think that you are next. But as soon as you start it all leaves you and all you think about is getting out in one piece.

You will be surprised as I was when you hear about Sgt Fuller and Sgt Bowman and about 50 others. I was watching a bunch go through and I saw someone in the back caught on a barbed wire entanglement. He could not get through it and he was all torn up from pulling. It was Sgt Fuller and next to him was a mine which might blow up any minute. It would not hurt you as long as you were down and had your head away because it will blast up. I guess he just lost his head. After the men were all through we went out and carried him in. He was sweating and shivering all the same time. It was a very sad sight to see. Although I seen it every day, it seemed funny until it happened to him. This morning he went over and turned in his stripes. He is now a private same as me.

There were dozens of other cases the same way and even a 2nd Lieutenant was broken on the field by the Colonel. We went through 7 solid days of that and I mean it is the toughest thing there is. At nite you would just fall down and lay for 2 or 3 hrs before we could move. We would never get any meals because we were too tired to go get them.

At night after we rested up we would go down to the river and swim for a while and get clean. After that we would catch our meals on the run. We would use flash lights and catch an armadillo and cook him at our camp. Our camp was way out in the woods. Just five of us would get together and go out and build a camp. We were so well hidden that the C.O. did not find our camp all the time we were there. One nite we were hungry so we went out and dynamited the river and we got 11 big bass. All we could eat was 3 so we gave them to the cook and we had them the next day.

We were sitting around the fire one nite all of us were starved but too tired to go out after food. All of a sudden someone came plowing through the weeds and came up and handed me a big package from you. It was like a gift from heaven. I forgot I was tired and jumped up and ate til I was full. The boys sure enjoyed it too. But the next nite what do you think happened! In from the woods came another fellow with another package for me. It was those darn books. Of all times to get books. You can imagine me carrying those books on my back for 30 miles back to camp besides my full pack. I thought I would die. I dumped my water out to cut down the weight.

I had a new pair of shoes when I started out and all I have left is a pair of leather inner soles. When you get time will you go over to the shoemaker and see if he can make another pair of those arch supports? I will have to have them pretty soon. Did you get the $10 I sent you? I just got your mail and it was sure a surprise to hear from Dad and <u>Roy!!!</u> I was sure sorry to hear about 'Slim', the bus driver. He sure was a swell guy.

I have a lot of work to do so I will have to close for now.

Your Loving Son,

Bob

P.S. I think we are going out again this week to the firing range so don't expect any letters.

March 22

Dear Mother Dad,

Did you let all the people know that I did not have time to write them? Don't want them to think I don't want to write. Hazel wrote to me last week and wanted to know if I wanted her to make a sweater for me. I sure could have used it this month but I won't need it from now on.

I am glad Dad quit his job as foreman, as it is too much of a headache. I can't understand why the work is so slow in the yard. Is it because they can't get steel? I got a letter from cousin Kitty saying how much she enjoyed your visit. She also bought me a subscription to the Readers' Digest. I don't know when I will be able to answer her letters so I wish you would thank her in your next letter. I am going to try and write Grand Pop and the rest tonite. They are really putting us through some rough training. We have to get up at 5 o'clock every morning now and double time to the firing range which is 5 miles away. We make it in 48 minutes. This morning on the way, 2 men fell out and were taken to the hospital. It seems we are sending them to the hospital faster than they send them back to us. I shot down our anti aircraft target with only 700 shots from the 50 caliber machine gun. It is a model airplane and the average shot is 950. We will be shooting 10 hrs a day for the next 6 days. It sure is good practice. I have been recommended by the officer in charge of the commando course for special training in dirty fighting and knife fighting. He said I was the best dirty fighter in his class at the course. That is called judo or a combination of jujitsu and just plain dirty hand to hand fighting.

The marines are going to build a course just like the one we got here. They had men from the marines observing us while we went through it. They said if they had one before the war we might not have lost so many men because they could have weeded out the cowards that spoil all their well laid plans. We were taught to shoot in the dark at a bottle and hit it almost every time, just by sound. We also shot the Graund Rifle from the stomach and hit what we aimed at. It is realy unbelievable what you can do with a gun if you are taught how.

I had the stitches taken out of my legs and the back of my head today and I am healing up slowly but surely. My hands are still raw but in a few days I will be as good as new and just a little bit better a soldier.

I would have given my right arm to get out of the training while I was going through it but now that it is all over I am the happiest guy in the world, because only the tankers and the tank destroyers are given the opportunity to go through it. I know now just how I will feel in battle and I have confidence in myself and in my weapons.

I can't tell you all that happened to us last week in a month of writing so I will tell you about it as soon as I get home. If am going to write to the Mildens I will have to close for now.

As ever

Your loving son

Bob

P.S. the measles are still breaking out and no relief in sight, as far as getting out of camp. I just heard that the Tank Destroyers are still in quarantine after 7 months.

March 25

Dear Mother, Dad,

I just sent a money order home for 20 bucks. Don't buy bonds with it as I will need it if I ever get a furlough. Next week I will send you $30 more to add to it. I have very good news about my shooting. My score was 86 out of 100 and was only beaten by two men in our company. Sgt Pollie got 87 and Sgt Wolf, my tank commander, got 91.

On this target if you get 50 you make marksmen and 60 to 70 is sharpshooter and over 70 is expert. Only 11 men made expert. We are shooting a full 9 hours a day. As much as I like shooting, it gets pretty tiresome after a while. We are getting more practice on the machine gun than any other outfit in the army ever got. I don't see how they can make the bullets as fast as we fire them away. A colonel was out watching us today and gave me some very helpful hints on how to shoot. I am sure that is why I got such a good score. This colonel is about 75 years old and you ought to see him shoot. He made fools out of all of us. He told us that the training we are getting will make our battalion the best the country has ever turned out. He said that the commando training we had will increase our chances of getting out of this war in one piece by 50%. As you know the machine gun is our main weapon and at the end of next week anyone who does not make expert is going to be transferred to another outfit.

The papers and magazines that you mailed me came yesterday and I have been swamped with birthday cards. I wrote to cousin Kitty yesterday and also the Mildens. I am going to try and write to the Schneiders tonite.

If you think you have had weather up there you ought to see it here. It has been raining for 3 days and I mean really raining. It rained so hard yesterday that we couldn't see our targets, much less the markers on them. We lost another man out of our platoon today; he got pneumonia. Joe Skelly has it too and not what we thought he had. We got in two dozen new men to replace some of our non com battalion. Some of our measles boys are coming back, but we are sending others back to replace them in the hospital. We had another case break out Wednesday so we have another 21 days slapped on us.

I just got word that I go on KP tomorrow and Battalion guard on the 27th. So now you can imagine how I will spend my birthday. I am so used to getting stuck with those details that I don't mind it any more. The reason I am getting it so soon after the last time is because of all the men we are missing.

I heard that the week after we left Bowie the whole camp was quarantined to their hutments for spinal meningitis, so maybe we were lucky to get away with the measles.

I am glad you are enjoying yourself. You sure earned it. Remember me to Mrs. Welburg and thank her for the card she sent me. I will have to close now if I want to write to the Schneiders so good bye for now.

Your Loving Son, Bob

March 28,
Dear Mother, Dad,

I have a surprise for you about my birthday. Our company was voted best on the commando course so we got out of all details for Saturday and Sunday. I spent the day resting and I sure did appreciate the rest. It was the first time in three weeks that I had any time off to myself.

This morning I got out of bed at about eleven o'clock. It was just like old times. We just had dinner and it was the best one we ever had in the army. Our mess sergeant went to the hospital during the commando course and we have been eating like kings ever since. We all sent letters to the C.O. telling him how good everything is since he left. He said he would make the cook that has charge now, the new mess sergeant. The officers had a big party last nite so we all went out to the service club and some went to town. It is the first time I went out in 6 weeks and I sure feel like a new man today. I bowled 2 games last nite and got 133 and 105.

The new story is that we are going to California soon but you can't believe half of what you hear.

I tried to call you on the phone last nite but it would take 5 hours so I could not do it. Nothing ever happens here so it is hard to write a letter of any size. I will write again in a few days.

Yours as ever,
Bob

March 29
Dear Mom, Dad,

There isn't anything to say in this letter except that the weather is really getting like summer. The temp is 80 in the shade.

I have a clipping here about the training we had last week and the pictures were taken while I was on the course. I went over every single thing in the no. 3

course. These pictures will give you a very small idea of what we went through. They are not allowed to print the truth about the course as there would be 90 thousand families here trying to get their kids out of it. It says the bullets are 30 inches over you but you can see that is a lie because they admitted a boy was hit in the head. The truth is he was hit in the shoulder because I seen him get hit and he sleeps across from me. The paper doesn't tell 1/1000 of what went on.

I spent another lazy day because all the men that didn't make expert on the machine gun are still out there trying and the eleven of us that did make it just stay in bed while the company marches out to the range.

I saw a new picture today of the war which you will see after the war is over. I think I will go to sleep for a while now.

Your loving son Bob

P.S. I just got papers.

March 31, 1943

Dear Mom, Dad,

I had a bad day at the range today. But I guess everybody has their off days. My score was so low that I was scared to show my target to the score keeper. The 1st Sgt sent for me this afternoon and wanted to know what happened. I told him it was just one of those days. He doesn't take answers like that so I ended up back there with him this afternoon. He made me shoot until I made expert. He said he wouldn't put my first score in to the books because it would pull my average down. I have the best shooting average in the 3rd platoon and he said he was going to see to it that I keep it that way. He said if I wasn't so lazy I could go into competition with the 7th tank group. I don't like to go through so many dry runs though. We lay on our target for as high as 4 hours at a time. You get so you see targets that aren't there. I already shot more bullets away than 10 people could make in the rest of their lives. We will spend a total of 3 months on the firing range. I guess we ought to be good shots before they get done with us.

My platoon sergeant called me in to his room tonite and told me that I would get the job of tank commander on the new M4 tanks, that is, the General Sherman. I don't want it because it is too much responsibility for the money. I will get to be a corporal for a start and if I make out alright the job calls for a sergeant. I told him I did not want it but the C.O. recommended me so I will have to take it when the tanks come in. The ones we have now are all commanded by the old timers. I will be the first new man in the company to be a Tank Commander. It might be a month or two before they are ready to run.

I will say good nite now as the lights are about to go out.

Love to all,

Bob

April 4, 1943

Dear Mother, Dad.

We got some more good news this week. We are all going to get furloughs starting April 24. I will probably get mine in about 2 months, don't depend on it though. Joe Skelly got out of the hospital last nite and left for home on a 10 day leave. I gave him your phone number so he will probably call you up. We are about to shoot the 75mm gun, it sure will be good to see what they will do to a tank.

Was on guard last nite, it was sure one rotten job. I had to guard the homes of General Durham and Col. Biddle. It is right across the street from the officers' mess. I had to salute about 400 officers that live near there. my arm is so sore today I can hardly lift it. I can't think of anything else to write about today, it seems there is nothing of interest going on. Although there was a guy shot last nite over at the motor pool.

Our quarantine is just about up so it is about time someone else gets the measles.

I had oysters for lunch today. I had about 50 of them. We had oyster stew a few weeks ago and I ate them for 2 hours. I don't believe you could carry all the food I have eaten since our mess sergeant left for the hospital. It is about time for the afternoon roll call so I had better call it quits for today.

Your loving Son

Bob

P.S. no letters from you in 3 days.

April 5, 1943

Dear Mother, Dad,

I have already written to you once today but I just received your letter and I thought I would answer it. There is a little news that leaked out since this afternoon. You said that the colonel might break if he went over the course. He did go over the course. He made it better than we expected he would. All officers in the Battalion had to go over it with us by order of the Br General.

I went over to the hospital this afternoon to see the company and while I was there, they brought in a corporal from the T.D. (Tank Destroyers) who was going over the course. He had his arm blown off. They say he was caught on the same line of barbed wire that had me caught. The only difference between him and myself is that I kept my head and he lost his arm. He rolled over and did not look where he was going and put his arm on top of a mine. He has nobody to blame but himself.

I am getting to be just like an old man, every time I sit down I can't get up. My bones are so stiff that sometimes I can't get out of bed in the morning. Everybody is the same way. We have to double time for a mile or two to get loosened up every morning.

We get out of quarantine tomorrow at noon (IF).

We got a radio here now and I heard McGee and Molly the other nite also Bob Hope. It was good to hear some of the programs. I might go to town for the first time tomorrow. It is only 170 miles on the bus. People around here don't think anything of riding 170 miles to spend the afternoon seeing a movie and bumming around town.

I sure would like to be going to NY instead of Ft Worth, but that's the army.

It sure is getting hot. The temp was 100 in the shade today and those helmets are sure hot. The tanks were so hot you could not touch them. You ought to see me sweat and with the dust flying you look just like a mud ball. We squirt the hose on each other to keep cool.

Did you tell Mrs. Mallander how busy I am and thank her for the letter?

Doctor Dwire is here from Linden. He is a Captain. He patched me up on the Commando course. Sidney Creage from Cranford is in our Battalion. He is in the service company and drives a motorcycle. No he is not in the 'Guard House' yet. Bob Combs has been transferred because of his feet. Erne is out of the Hosp, and on K.P. Bob Ackerman just got a discharge because he has a bone disease that can't be cured. The fellow that broke his leg will be in the hosp for 6 weeks yet. Every day they come drifting back from here and there.

I am going to get a slip from the C.O. so you can get me a pair of dress shoes. Remember me to Adell and Lucille and Mrs. Welburg.

Is Keifer still at Mather Spring?

Yours as ever,

Bob

April 11, 1943

Dear Mom, Dad,

It seems this camp is just a jinx to me. I had my first chance to go to town in 2 months last nite and it turned out to be just another piece of bad luck. Worked all day Saturday and about six at nite I got off. I was going to take a nap and then go to town. I lay down and the first sergeant saw me and a little while later they needed a detail for cleaning guns so I was about the only man in camp. He put my name down for the detail. Before they got to me a friend of mine told me about it, so I grabbed my clothes and ran out the back door pulling on my clothes on the way to the bus station. I just got out in time. When I got to the bus station there was a line a block long waiting for busses. I finally got one and after four hours of riding I got to town. I then went to a restaurant and ordered a meal and before I got it a race riot broke out down the street. Three men were killed including a cop, an M.P. and one pvt. Orders came from the Brigadier general to get every man in town back to camp. So tired and hungry I got in line for the bus back. After 5 hrs of standing in line we got a bus. But that was just the start of our misery. The bus broke down about 75 miles from camp. So we got out and tried to hitch a ride. A truck stopped and picked us up. He took us to Killeen, a town the size of Gresser Ave. As we got out one of the boys hanging on the side fell off and the truck rolled over him. He was still alive when the ambulance took him away. We then had to walk 7 miles to camp. I just got in, in time for breakfast. I am going to try and go to the movies tonite but it will probably burn down before I get there.

There is more talk of moving out of this darn camp. <u>I Hope</u>. I am sure we are going to the desert either in Cal or Nevada. I can't wait to go.

It is about 100 in the shade and there is a gale blowing. The dust is so thick you can't see a man over 10 feet away from you. If you had this weather up home there would be 2 million fires at Coney Island. We sure were a bunch of fools to take Texas into the union. Our commanding officer said if he owned Texas and New York he would lease New York and sell Texas and live in Hell. When you make that trip around the country Dad, if you are smart skip Texas.

They shipped in bout 500 WAACs yesterday. You would die laughing if you could see them. They came in all dolled up in their new uniforms. They came over to the PX a little while ago and if you ever saw a funnier sight in your life I would like to see it. They had a mouth full of mud and mud dripping down their faces. Their uniforms were so dirty you could not see what color they were. It does not look so funny to see a man that dirty but when we saw them come in we rolled on the floor we laughed so hard. One of them started to cry when she saw herself in the mirror. They just joined up a few weeks ago. Every time we passed them in the PX. We would salute them just to get them excited. They did not know whether we were officers or whether they were supposed to salute us or not. There was one trying to drink a coke and every time she picked up the bottle one of us would go past and salute her. After about 10 minutes she was so befuddled she left for home. I never saw or heard of a more disgusted bunch of women. I'll bet they are so sorry they ever joined up.

We got newspapers and magazines here now so you don't have to go through all the trouble of cutting out the comics any more. The Red Cross has them sent to our day room. There is a fellow from Linden here and he gets the Elizabeth Journal so I am all set for now.

---------- Other half in other envelope   ------ second half of letter

I got a letter from you today that was mailed in March. You forgot to put the 747 on it that's why I did not get it on time.

I wasn't surprised to hear about Daly getting pneumonia. If you knew what we went through at Dix you could understand it. Next to the commando week that was the worst week I have had in my life. If it wasn't for my tooth I would have been with him now. I don't remember whether I told you about getting the new tooth for nothing. I can't even tell which one it is. You could look all day and you could not tell which tooth is false.

The doctors fixed my back at the hosp at Bowie, and I haven't had any trouble since.

I am going to take out another $5000 insurance policy as soon as I can get over to Btn Headquarters. Are you still keeping my other policy going? If you are

I will send home money to pay for it. I did not want to take out the whole 10,000 til I got straightened out on the pay problem. I will need about 75 dollars for my furlough and I don't know where I am gong to get it. I am going to send my watch home soon so you can get it fixed. When it is fixed I want you to check it. It has to run for 24 hours on one winding and it must keep perfect time. If it will not do that don't send it back because I can't use it.

--- second half of letter   see other envelope -----

If the watch is wrong even 1 minute it is liable to cause a bad accident. We get orders over the radio to go on so far in one direction and in so many seconds go some other way and if it is the wrong time we are liable to get in a sad fix.

I hope you got track of my money because I don't know where I stand. Give Keifer 3.00 and ask him to get me about 25 yards of fishing line and twelve hooks (6 hooks Eagle claw no.8, 6 cat fish hooks, long shank) (line about 16 lbs test) (one roll cat gut) heavy 16 lb test. Ask him to get the cheapest they got because I may never use it but I want it just in case I get the chance. When it comes put it in the smallest box you can get it into so I can carry it in my pocket. It might go in a tobacco can.

The rattlesnakes are out in all their glory. I killed my first one on the range. There is no need to be afraid of them because they only make you sick when bitten by one. It is the shock and fear of most people that makes them die. They will make you so sick that you wish you were dead. They tell us that there are more snakes in this part of the country than any other state. There are also black widow spiders here and they are even less dangerous. It is only the fear that kills you.

I have been taking extra lessons on dirty fighting and the lieutenant says I am doing very good. I can kill a man with one hand (empty) so fast he couldn't even have time to open his mouth. We have to be able to do this because we are liable to have our tank disabled behind the enemy lines and have to fight our way back to our lines. We are also supposed to be able to fight better than anyone with a knife.

My instructor was in the Philippine Islands fighting japs and he sure knows his stuff. He had me stabbing at a slide for 4 hours one day. It sure is good practice.

There is a slide like this

They drop a board on the other side of it and as it goes by the opening you stab it. I got so good after hours of practice that I could hit it 5 times out of 10. The whole thing is being fast and hitting what you stab at. They also make us go through a field a mile wide with guns about 2 ft high. There is a machine gun in the middle and he tries to get you in his sites. You start to wiggle for about 15 ft and then you get up and run. Zigzag for a few ft and drop and crawl and run again till you cover the mile. If he gets you in his sites you are considered dead. At first they got us in the sites every time but now they can never get us unless he can guess just where we are going to get up and run.

April the 15ᵗʰ we change into our summer uniforms. It will be a relief to get out of these hot woolen clothes. I changed my mind about going to the movies because of the heat. I am dripping wet now and I only have a cotton pair of coveralls on. I couldn't stand a woolen shirt and blouse. I see the law was changed about soldiers getting dress shoes. I guess I will have to wear these clodhoppers. I am about the only one here that hasn't a pair of dress shoes. In fact I haven't even got a good pair of shoes. I have one pair coming for the ones I ruined on the course. As soon as they come I am going to turn these in for another new pair. These shoes have been resoled so often that the quarter master knows my name. It takes about a week and a half to wear out a pair of soles and heals. I got one pair out of the supply room and turn one in every week and a half or two weeks. I am glad I don't pay for them.

I don't think I ever told you about the night firing we had or not. They blind-fold us so we can't see a thing. Then they take a bottle with a stone in it and tie a string on it. Then they wiggle the bottle and you jump around to the sound and fire at it with a pistol. You shoot from a squatting position with the gun waist high and in the center of your body. We have to practice this for hours at a time after 30 or 40 hrs of this you get pretty good. You never know where the bottle is going to be. I got so I can hit it 2 or 3 times out of every 10 shots. We also did this with the rifle. The rifle is very hard on the stomach though because sometimes you don't have it in the right spot and it knocks the wind out of you. We also use the Tommy gun in the same manner.
They took us in an underground tunnel as dark as, well anyway you couldn't see your hand in front of you, and made you walk along with the gun and every once in a while a target would light up for a split second and you have to shoot it.

Have to drive the Company Commander's tank tomorrow in a cross country race. He said if I don't win I had better not show my face around this camp till he cools off, and if I do win I will get a 3 day pass in a week or two. Each company has 2 tanks in the race that makes 8 tanks. I know darn well I will win because the other companies only have NY men and they can't beat a Jersey Cowboy. My only problem is that I can't get a crew, they rode with me before and are not going to take any more chances. The C.O. tells us to go like we would if we had the whole German army after you. These boys are afraid to open it up and I am never satisfied til I have the gas peddle in the floor. There is nothing to worry about because we all have safety belts on and rubber padding all around. If the tank does turn over you wouldn't feel it. The trouble is most of them never drove anything before in their life. I will let you know how I make out in a few days.

I am going to mail our cap paper to you. Let me know how you like it. I guess this letter makes up for the week I did not write. I want to get 3 letters in return for this one Roy, Dad (Mom) I know you will write Mom

Your loving son
Bob

Dear   Mother, Dad,

Three days have gone by since I mailed you a letter; it seems like yesterday. The days go by so fast that it seems like Sunday comes up twice a week, but the months drag by like years. It seems like 3 years since I waved to you from the train.

Please stop giving my address to everybody as I just haven't got time to write back to everyone. I am about twenty five letters behind. I got about 20 birthday cards. I did like to get them but if everybody thinks that they are going to get a letter in return they are nuts. I am only going to write to cousin Kitty, Grand Pop and you. I don't have the time nor the news to write to everyone.

It looks as if my luck is changing for the better. I made that race I was telling you about but was sure a lot tougher than I had expected. In the first place the company commander acted as tank CO, was supposed to stay in the camp. It seems all the Company Commanders had a bet on and they wanted to see how and why they were going to lose or win their bet. He made me a little nervous because I did not want to show him up too much. The race went as follows. We started at 4:30 yesterday morning out to the starting point a few miles out. The race started at 5 o'clock. It was still dark. I got off to a bad start and for the first 4 miles I was in sixth place. We came over a long winding hill and I saw my chance. I put it in fifth gear and let her go. I was plenty scared but not half as scared as the men in the crew. The Commander in the turret was sweating blood. He is the one that really gets the bouncing around. The tank will only go 40 miles per hr but down that hill I hit fifty five. When we hit the bottom we took off as if we had wings and, when we landed it was quite a jar. I called the Commander on the radio to see if he was still there. When no answer came I though he flew out, but he was just trying to get his breath. He said if I lost that race after what he went through I would get KP for a month. I made the next hill in third because of the speed I had. The others had to go into second so I gained about half a mile on them. I thought I had the race in the bag but after we had gone 16 miles I ran out of gas. I was ready to shoot myself because I had trusted my 75 gunner to take care of the gas. The other tanks were almost up to me when we discovered only one of the gas tanks had the valve open. We started out again and after a long hard race I did manage to come out 9 minutes ahead of the rest. I am sure to get that new job I was telling you about and I won't have the Commander to worry about because I know he will never get in a tank with me again.

This all happened yesterday. Today we went to the firing range again. I am getting so tired of shooting I hope I don't ever have to shoot again till we are shooting at live targets. Lights are going out so good nite.
Your loving Son Bob

PS. I got a 3 day pass for next week.

4/17/43

Dear Mother, Dad,

I started to write to you the other day but just as I got started news came to me of the arrival of my tank at the railroad station. I had to go and get it and I have been busy on it ever since. The paint is still wet on parts of it. It is called the M4-A4. It has five Chrysler engines in it, and has 400 horsepower. It cost $75,000 and it is all mine. The name you would know it by is the General Sherman. It has three 30 caliber machine guns and one 50 caliber, and one 75 mm gun. I took the job of commander because it is a big step forward on the way up. It calls for a sergeant's rating but I may only get corporal stripes to start. I told the First Sergeant I wouldn't keep the job unless I got Sergeant's rating in 2 months. It is too much of a job for $66 a month. I have already worked myself half to death getting it in shape.

Our ratings should come through by the 24th of this month. I hear we are moving out to the woods to live some time this month. I knew it was coming but did not expect it so soon. The 744th tank battalion just came back in after 3 months in the woods, and we follow them where ever they go.

So you took off from work again and went out. I haven't been out of camp except for that one nite that I got out and got chased back, since I got to this darn camp. I got free one nite and went to the movies and after waiting in line for two hrs I sat down and started to enjoy myself when there was a call for every man in the 747th to return to the barracks for a surprise inspection. I will have even less time to myself now that I got this tank to worry about. Half the camp went to town over the weekend but I spent it down in the motor park working on the 75 gun in the tank. I got it about finished now. It is Sunday nite and I am in the barracks waiting for supper. I will go back tonite and check up on everything so I can go out in it tomorrow. I expect to finish about eleven or twelve. Did I tell you that our day starts at 4:30 instead of 5:30? By the time it gets light we have a half day's work finished. We have no more drilling and not many hikes any more. All we are doing is shooting and driving. I had so much shooting that I hate the sight of a gun. I never thought that was possible. When we go out to the range we get no water from 4:30 in the morning til we get back at nite about 5 or 6 o'clock. I got out of the habit of drinking water like I used to. The heat is getting unbearable. The tanks get so hot you can't touch them. It still gets cool at nite and we can get a good nite's sleep if we get time.

Why don't those two brainstorms in Albany join the army? We could use some of their brains. Have a good time for me on your vacation when you get it. Maybe I will get one too. It looks bad for me though. All the jews got a week's pass for all this week, starting tomorrow. They call it a holiday. They got all the soft jobs and all the office work. They work 7 hrs a day and get every weekend off.

I am going to town next weekend if it means the guard house. Our Battalion is giving a big party for the W.A.A.C.s, which I won't be able to attend because of a problem with the Tank Destroyers on Tuesday nite, which will last all nite, and I understand we are going to have an ordinance inspection Wednesday. That is about 48 hours that will go by without even seeing a bed. I have a plan for that nite and if it works I will tell you about it in my next letter. I get a kick out of making fools out of those Tank Destroyers.

The chow is ready so I guess I'll eat. I will write soon.

Your Loving Son,

Bob

April 18, 1943

Dear Mother, Dad,

It has been a long time since I sent you a letter. I have been very busy and I did not have much to write about anyway. I can't think of anything of interest to tell you yet.

Last week I had a very interesting experience doing something that I have often dreamed about but never expected to do. We went out to the dumps in Kileen, which is a dump, and put a show on for the newspapers and civvies. They had about five or six hundred cars that they wanted smashed for scrap metal. They had them lined up in a column of twos. I put one track on each line and went down over them in a General Grant tank. They took all kinds of pictures of us for the papers. I suppose you will see the pictures sooner or later so you will know that I am driving the first tank.

I went out on that problem against the Tank Destroyers and my plan worked to a certain extent and saved us a lot of time and work. They gave us a 30 minute start and then started to chase us. I know all the woods and all the rivers around here for 30 miles so I had my trail all picked out. I went to Coppers Cove, which is a deep gulley and only one possible way through at the bottom over the other side of the river. I put a line of empty tin cans that I stole from the mess hall. When the Tank Destroyers outfit came they were afraid to go over them because it might have been land mines. If it were, the judges would have declared them out of action. Their only other way was go all around the mountain. They figured I would be 5 miles away by the time they got around, but I fooled them again. I pulled up in the thick woods about half a mile from the woods. We spent about two hours camouflaging our tank and then went to sleep. I woke up about 4 hrs later and there was no Tank Destroyer around. We started out for home in fifth gear. When I hit the river there were three Tank Destroyers shouting at the cans trying to see if they really were traps. Before they got their guns in action my gunner got a bead on two of them and we got credit for knocking out two of them and won the problem by a very wide margin. The third TD might have hit me but a tank has more chances of beating a TD than the other way around so I took the decision. That nite our boys were kidding the 716th TD about the beating they took and it ended up in a good fight, which we lost. I am glad that I had to work that nite on the tank or I would have been in it.

I was on table waiter today (Sunday) so as usual I did not get to town.

Try to get me a pair of dress shoes if you can. I tried it tonite and you need a ration stamp no. 17 to get them. Everybody else got them before they got in the army. I wear size 13EE.

I heard another rumor today saying that we are going into a heavy tank outfit and the only one we got is in Kentucky. I don't believe it but I hope we don't because those heavy tanks are too slow.

It sure was good to hear your voices on the phone. It was worth a hundred letters. Joe Skelly got in Saturday nite all tired out and got a weekend pass and left for Temple. He sure gets around.

Remember me to all the folks and I am thinking of them even if I don't write. Write to cousin Kitty for me and Hazel and Grand Ma and Grand Pop & Helen.

I don't know when I will be able to write again so until then good luck to all.
Your loving son
Bob
P.S. Your package arrived, arches, books, letters, cards, and papers.

Sat 24
Dear Mother, Dad,

I got guard over the weekend. It is tough but I will live through it. There is not much doing here. I still haven't had any time off, I am working 18 hours a day, seven days a week.

I got your Easter package and it was swell. The fishing line came too, just what I wanted. It is getting hot here. It's too hot to sleep.

I got to go on guard so I will have to close now.
Your Loving Son
Bob

May 5,
Dear Mother, Dad,

The letters that you have been sending me in the past week have made me feel pretty disappointed in all of you. You should know by this time that if I can possibly find time to write home I would surely do it. I haven't written to anybody in so long I can't blame them if they are mad. I will do my best to make this one long, although I can't think of a thing to write about that you would be interested in.

I was plenty worried about you being so sick, and it was a relief to hear that you are getting better. I never heard of a tumor being cured without an operation. I want to know first how serious it is. If I am not satisfied with your answer I will be home in a few weeks regardless of what the army will do to me.

I got a card from some W.A.A.C. that is in camp and is from Linden. I don't know who she is or how she got my address, unless you gave it to her. Her name is signed Dotty Cranson if you know who she is will you please tell me. I will go and see her as soon as I get time. At present our whole company is under restriction to our barracks on off duty hours. We went on strike for shorter hours. We worked til we could not keep our eyes open without any time off at all so the whole company went to town for three days last weekend. When they blew revelry Friday morning there wasn't a man in camp and we did not come back til Monday morning. All ratings were cancelled until the General has time to figure it all out. He said he never heard of such a thing in his 40 years in service. We don't care if they shoot us all, we had a good time over the weekend for the first time in 3 months.

I have been up for as much as three days without even sitting down except for driving.

Over the weekend I went to the following cities and towns: Lampasas, Pelten, Temple, Killeen, Copperas Cove, Nuttner. I left here with only $2.00 which wasn't even enough to last an hour. We hitch hiked and slept in the railroad stations and ate at the USO. We had a swell time.

We are all ready for maneuvers. We just sent all our tanks to Pine camp and got all new ones. The new ones came this week. I wore the other one out before I got a name for it. It is no longer a first line tank. It will be fixed up and used for training in NY. The new ones that we just got are a much better tank. Instead of having five engines it has an airplane engine (Wright Cyclone). It has 450 horse power. It will go about 65 miles per hour on a flat road. It sure is costing the Gov a pile of money to train us. Can you imagine wearing out a $76,000 tank in a month? Those tanks will be good for another three or four months of training but no good for any real driving.

I am glad to hear that Roy's team won the game in Elizabeth. We used to play ball back in the good old days back at Bowie. We do so many things here that it seems like we have been in the army for about 3 years. It seems almost impossible that we have only been in 4 months. We have learned more in that 4 months than I did in my whole life all put together.

We finished all our firing and I am sure glad that is over. I made 479 out of a possible 500. That is about as good as you can get. We fired about 8000 shots altogether for record. I made a score of 150 out of 150 on the 75mm gun, which is perfect. My score was only beaten by the Company Commander who got 483. Our scores are added up on all the different games and then averaged.

It is about 3 in the morning and I can't keep my eyes open so I will have to close for today. I have to get up in two hours and I still have to wash my coveralls.

Love to all,
Bob

May 7, 1943
Dear Mother,

I received your letter today together with Dad's. I can never forgive Dad for not telling me what was going on. I knew you were seriously ill when you went to the doctor, because you would not go unless it was something serious. I went to the first sergeant the other day and told him I thought you were sick and that I wanted a
furlough. He said I would be able to go home on the 19th of May. Unless something turns up I will see you about the 22nd of this month. Why didn't you go to Muhlenberg Hospital? I never seen or heard of a decent room in any Elizabeth hospital. I can't wait to get home to see you. Please don't hold any news back from me as it is enough to drive me nuts. It is a lot easier for me when I know what's going on than it is to guess all sorts of things. Mom we are going to have a big inspection by General Duram tomorrow morning and in 3 hours I have to get up so forgive me for writing such a short letter. I just know you will get well soon. Each day will seem like a year until I am permitted to see you.
Your Loving Son
Bob

May 9,
Dear Mother

Dad says you are getting along fine. It sure is a relief to hear that. I know you don't like the hospital because you can't get up and around but it is the only place for you. If you were home you would get up too soon and you would get worse. Now that I know that you are getting the proper care and rest I feel better. Dad sure must miss you around the house. He says it is so quiet that he doesn't know what to do.

There is no change in schedule for my furlough as yet. Unless something turns up I will leave here on the 19th. We are leaving here in about a week for the woods. The first week out we are scheduled to go on the commando course. I will probably get two days of the course before I leave for home. If you see me come limping home all scratched up and looking like a piece of cube steak don't be scared or get excited and think that I was in a train wreck, as it is just another week in the life of a tanker.

I got the money last nite that Dad sent me. I bought some clothes and I will go to Temple next week and buy my ticket. I am going by way of Chicago. I think I can make better time that way. It takes about 46-8 hours. The train fare alone costs $44 and it will cost a lot more for eats and everything that goes with it.

I tried to buy shoes in town but they did not have my size. I got a pair of pants and a shirt. Size 38 pants and 16 ½ shirt. I weigh 235. I put on a lot of weight in the past month as we have had no hikes or drilling or exercise of any kind. We have been shooting and driving and working on tanks. We have had inspections every day this week and more are coming. I will tell you all about them when I get home.

The boys are so disgusted with everything as it is that they are going A.W.O.L. at the rate of 25 per day from this Battalion. These inspections are enough to drive you crazy. We never get done til midnite. The reason for them giving so many inspections is because they want all our equipment ready for maneuvers, which was postponed until August. I was disappointed to hear that it was postponed.

Mom it's getting late and there is another big day in front of me so I'll say so long.

Your Loving Son

Bob

May 11,

Dear Mother an Dad,

We finished all our inspections yesterday. It was a riot. Everybody in the company had the best laugh in months. Major Freeze had his shirt torn off his back by the inspecting general. He had a tear in his shirt sewn up and he thought it was not noticeable, but these Generals don't miss a trick. You should have seen his face. He then inspected the mess hall. He looked in the garbage can and there were rodents in there. He made the mess sergeant pick them out and wash them and serve them for supper. I will tell you all about it when I see you next week.

Your letters came today saying the summer reached you at last. I wish you could see what we got. I think it is a little too hot to call it just summer, even when you take a nap you dream that you are roasting in hell.

Maybe by the time I get home you will be out of that hospital. I will leave here next Wednesday nite. I will be home sometime Saturday (May 21) morning I hope.

I can't think of anything to write about tonite. I will have a lot of time home to tell you everything you want to know.

Lots of luck

Your loving Son Bob

May 15, 1943

Dear Mother, Dad,

I am in Belton Texas at the USO. I came in last nite to buy my ticket home. The train leaves Temple at 2:30 in the afternoon next Tuesday. If I miss that one I will have to wait until 2 o'clock in the morning. It will take me about fifty hours to get home so you can figure it out.

I am so glad that you are out of the hospital. Please take good care of yourself and don't get a relapse. My furlough papers are all signed and waiting so I don't think there will be any slipup. I got a three day pass again. It started Fri to Monday, that's how I got to Belton. The first sergeant said I had some nerve asking for a pass when in only 4 days I have a 15 day leave coming.

There isn't much doing in this town but at least it is away from camp. I got a pair of shoes in Temple this morning. They are not the kind I wanted but I can't be fussy.

I just can't think of a thing to say so I will close for now. When you get this letter I will be on my way.

Your loving Son

Bob

June 5,

Dear Mother, Dad.

I got into camp 2 o'clock Thursday afternoon just two hours late. The trip wasn't bad at all. We got the streamliner in Chicago and the seats were swell, I got a good nite's sleep. It took me all afternoon to get my equipment straightened out. Yesterday we had a physical endurance test. It almost killed me after that long vacation. I got blisters on my feet from these shoes. My G.I. shoes did not get here yet. We finished the test about 4 in the afternoon after which we had supper and at 5:30 we went out in the tanks on a problem with the TDs. The problem lasted until today at 5 in the afternoon. I did not get more than an hour's sleep last nite. The meals have improved 100% since I left for home. That is the way here, one week you starve and the next you get more than you can eat.

What show did you see in New York when I left? I'll bet you went to the Roxie. We are going out of the camp Monday to live in tents for 4 months. I believe the address will be the same.

Please mail me a camera and a few rolls of film as we can have them out in the woods. I can send you some very interesting and funny pictures. I think I left a few things home by mistake if you come across them send them on along with my shirt. I have a slight headache from over work and loss of sleep so I am going to turn in now, as I have a big day ahead of me tomorrow packing up all the equipment.

So long until next time.

Your loving Son, Bob

Newspaper clipping

3 of 7 Fleeing Nazis Nabbed in Texas

By the United Press

CAMP HOOD, Texas, June 9.----

The third of seven

Nazi prisoners who escaped from the internment area here was recaptured shortly after noon, public relations officers announced today.

He was 21-year-old Hans Massoeur, captured by military police eight miles southeast of the Camp Hood Reservation near the small community of Flat. Officers said he offered no resistance.

Tips from residents in the vicinity sent searchers into the area. Headquarters believed that the other four were at large near by.

Two of the seven who crawled under a fence at the cantonment sometime between midnight and dawn were recaptured before they got off Camp Hood.

June 13, 1943
Dear Mother, Dad,

This is the first time that I have had time to write and tell you about the new camp. In the first place we are out in the woods so far that we have to put out guards for Indians. We live in tents which I like better than barracks. We have no drinking water so it all has to be hauled in from town. We eat out of mess kits and there is no mess hall.

The only place we have to wash is in the river about a mile from camp. We go in swimming every nite after we are finished with the day's work.

We have no light except 4 candles per week per tent. There are a lot of fish in the river and I expect to go fishing the first time I get a chance.

The temperature is terrific. It gets so hot you have to gasp for breath.

Three days later

Dear Mom, Dad,

I had to go on special guard and man hunt for those 7 German prisoners. We caught three of them so far and I hear there are 2 more in Dallas. They are both dead. I did not get in on any of the excitement but I thought I had one captured in the mess hall of another company. I was on patrol around the battalion area about 3 o'clock in the morning when I heard someone in a mess hall. I got another guard and we went in. We caught two men from B company stealing food. I did not turn them in because I like to eat, myself.

We are going out in the woods tomorrow for a 3 day problem. I mean further out in the woods than we are now, if that's possible. You ought to see the snakes out here, we kill them

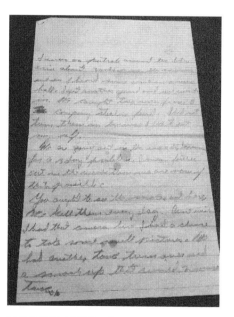

LETTER WITH CANDLE DRIPPINGS
PHOTO BY NANCY FRANKLIN

every day. I sure wish I had that camera here I had a chance to take some swell pictures. We had another tank turn over and a smash up that ruined 2 more tanks. We don't have many mosquitoes <u>but</u> we have <u>chiggers</u>!!!!! They are very small but they give you a lump like a bug. We are bumps from head to foot. You can't help scratching and especially at nite when you are asleep. We wake up covered with blood. As you probably have guessed I am writing by candle light and my candle has burned almost out so I will have to say so long pretty soon.

Don't think that I forgot your birthday but I just couldn't get even a card to send you, so I will make it up to you next year or the year after. The same goes for you Dad. I will be thinking of you on Fathers' Day and hope to be with you next year.

Happy Birthday Mother
Your loving son, Bob

June 18
Dear Mother, Dad.
Before I forget it my new address is

PFC Rynier R Cadmus
747 Tank Btn. Co A-M
32603063
Cotton Wood Camp #3
Camp Hood Texas

We just came back from the three day bivouac. I am a sorry sight with all kinds of bites and bumps from all the chiggers and mosquitoes, spiders in the whole state. We worked from 4 in the morning until 9 at nite. There was no water of any kind where we were so we did not wash or shave all the while we were out there. I was never so dirty in my life. I went down to the river and washed and shaved today and it sure felt good.

We killed 7 snakes in the 3 days. The temperature was 109 in the shade and about 120 in the tanks. I went to the hospital to see about those dizzy spells I have been having. The Dr. said it was from over amount of driving and nervous strain. He grounded me for 2 weeks, and after that I will have to report to him before he will give me my license again. He issued an order saying that no driver will drive a tank for more than 10 hours per day without a break of at least 8 hours. It sure will help us. Some of the men are nervous wrecks.

I can't tell you how much I enjoyed my time at home. It sure was swell to be able to eat what you wanted and when you wanted it. I lost all the weight that I gained while I was home in 4 days. We had a physical endurance test a day or two after I got back from home. I did 45 pushups, did the side straddle hop for 10 minutes, touched my toes 100 times, did a 200 yard dash in 47 seconds and then we made a forced hike with full pack. We hiked 4 miles in 43 minutes. It was mostly double time. When I got back I dropped on the ground exhausted. I lay there for an hour before I could get up and take a shower.

(Next day)

Fri

Hello again

I am out under a tree near my tent cleaning guns. It is real hot in the sun but it is nice her in the shade. It is only 8 o'clock in the morning now that is why it is still cool.

We are getting ready to go out again tonite on another problem. We will be back in tomorrow nite.

I am sorry I got this paper so dirty but under the conditions it can't be helped.

(3 in afternoon)

I hope I get time to finish this letter this try.

I received the package with the shirt and shrimp, cookies and we enjoyed them <u>very</u> much. The shirt will come in handy as I cannot get my uniforms cleaned out here. I bought another pair of pants in Gatesville for $2.50. I still have a shirt in the cleaners back in Killeen. Maybe I will get time to get it one of these days. Sunday Joe Skelly and I ducked out of camp for about 12 hours. We went to Center City, Goldthwaite. It was a change from looking at the same camp all the time. Center City is over a hundred miles away and the population is 34. We had a swell time there as it is a Ghost town. It used to be a busy city.

All the prisoners were captured. I hear that it was a put up job. They just let them escape to see where they would go to get help. The story that I heard about 2 of them getting shot was untrue. I thought it might just be a rumor at the time.

Buy the July 6 issue of 'Pick'. It has an article about the 747th. I am going to close now so I can get this in the mail before it is gone.

Lots of Love from your Son

Bob

June 19

Dear Mom, Dad,

I am in the darnedest town of them all. Joe and I got today off so we thought we would see some of the country. We hitched a ride to Waco last nite and this morning we went to Temple from Waco. From Temple we went to Rogers, and then to Buckholts and we ended up here at Cameron at about noon. We met a couple of girls here that invited us home to dinner. We had roast beef. It sure was good. It reminded me of your cooking. The girls' mother is a swell person. She wants us to stay for supper but we haven't got time. We are going swimming in a little while and then go back to camp. We have a long ride ahead of us. It is about 150 miles back to camp. We should be able to make in 2 ½ to 3 hours, if we get a fast driver.

We are going on a problem tomorrow morning which will last 2 weeks. I don't know whether I will be able to write until I get back or not so don't expect any mail although I might get to send one in on the chow truck.

We just came back from a problem yesterday. It only lasted 3 days but it was the 3 hardest days I have had in a long time. I did not drive out or back but just during the attacks.

We did not get any sleep in the past four days and that is why we got today off. Joe is dead on his feet but I don't feel so bad. We had 2 hours sleep on a park bench in Waco last nite, that was enough for me. We will get in camp about midnite tonite and be up at 4 in the morning.

How did you enjoy your birthday? I hope you had a good time. Do you feel as good as when I was home? I hope you are feeling good enough to enjoy your vacation.

How is the heat in the shipyard Dad? You ought to be here. It is 102 in the shade right now and I am not even sweating.

We are going swimming now so take it easy Mom. I know Dad will.
Love to all
Bob

June 23,
Dear Mother, Dad,

Words fail me every time I sit down to write a letter. Maybe as I go along I can think of something to write about. We haven't had rain in about 6 weeks, everything is so dirty and dry I don't see how anything lives. The river that we wash and swim in is getting so low that sections of the river are dry. It is so bad that if it doesn't rain in the next week we will not be able to use the river because it is becoming stagnant.

June 24.
Hello again. I will try to finish this letter tonite so I can mail it in the morning.

It is still getting hotter all the time. Today it went up to 102 in the shade. I did mind it as all I did was sit under a tree and study and sleep. This afternoon I went for a swim and got a bad sunburn. It is good to get out of the tank for a rest. I hope I don't have to drive for a month. We went out to the range to fire the 30 caliber carbine. It sure is a swell gun. I did a lot better than I expected, too. I hit a target 10 inches in diameter at 400 yds 3 times out of 8 for record. We had to fire all day, from 6 in the morning until it was too dark to see. It is a new gun in our outfit. The Company all did very good. We have a very good average in marksmanship. We fired from a sitting position at 100 yds, squatting at 200 yds, and standing at 300 yds and prone at 400 yds. All with our gas masks on.

If you don't hear from me for 10 or 15 days at a time you will know that I am out in the field somewhere where it is impossible to write. There is a rumor that we are going to Ft Knox Kentucky. We all are praying that it is true. We are supposed to be demonstration battalion. We are the second best medium tank battalion in the country. I think we have Col Brown to thank for that.

The funniest thing you ever heard of is going on right now in our tent. John McGlocklin, who lives in Paterson NJ is tearing his hair out. His wife had a baby two weeks ago, and he couldn't get a furlough. So his wife just wrote him a letter telling him the baby's name. He can't read the first two letters in the name. It looks like Cileen but that is impossible he hopes! He has everybody in here trying to figure it out. He is now getting dressed to go down to the telegraph office and wire home to see what it is.

I am very tired so I think I will get some sleep. It is too bad you can't get a day off Dad, but you sure made up for it while I was home. Wish Roy luck at his new job for me. I hope he likes it.
 Love to all,
Bob

June 30
Dear Mother, Dad,

Your card arrived today. It is the first letter in 6 days. What is the matter at home? Is someone sick again?

How does Roy like his new job? Is he starting to find out what work is?

I have been out on the commando course for the last 5 days. I didn't tell you before because you might have worried. I am still in one piece although I wish I was dead. All my bones and joints ache so bad I can't sleep. It was worse than the last time. They made a lot of new torture equipment since we were there before. We only lost 104 out of 700 this time.

This morning it was cloudy for the first time in 3 ½ months. We all thought it would rain but it cleared up this afternoon. So we still have no place to swim. I sure miss my afternoon swim. We have to wash in a pail now.

I have to go on prison guard tomorrow. It sure is a rotten job. I have to do more work just guarding, than the prisoners do. I am going to sleep now as I have to get up at 3:45 in the morning.
Love to all
Bob

July 7, 1943
Hello Folks,

I am in Austin with Sgt Wolf. We left camp last nite at 6:30 and went to Bartlett and Llano. We stayed at Bartlett until this morning about 6 when we started out for Round Rock. We went to see some girls that we met at the USO but they were not home. We then went to Buchanan Dam and had something to eat (steak). After which we ended up in Georgetown about an hour ago. We didn't like the looks of the town so we left and came 50 miles more to Austin.

We have gone about 350 miles since last nite. I am in the USO writing this letter while Wolf is at church. They gave us cake and coffee a little while ago.

We haven't been paid yet as the finance office is so busy that they can't get all of us at once. We have 100,000 men at this camp now and they all get paid through one office.

I left camp last nite with 86 cents and I just spent 50 cents of it on supper last nite. I have to get a free meal some place today as I am getting hungry. We know a family near Dallas that is always glad to see us and always has a swell meal for us. He should have some musk melons ripe today. I just decided to go down there as soon as Wolf gets back. It is another 150 miles out there but we can't starve and besides we have until 5 o'clock tomorrow morning.

Your package arrived from Asbury (Park). It was very good and did not melt. Skelly was too sick and tired to come with me today. It was his first time over the commando course. It is the first time I went out without Joe in a long time. He wants to go more than anything but he is a very sad sight. He is all skinned up, his head is cut open and his ears are still ringing from the infiltration course. My ears stopped ringing yesterday. My nose is better today and the doctor said it was not broken.

I am getting a pair of dress shoes through the army. It will cost me $4.50 but they are worth it.

Will you cash in one of my $25.00 bonds and send me the $18.00 as I don't know when I will get paid.

Love to all,

Bob

July 9

Dear Mom, Dad.

I am hiding inside a tank as I am writing this letter. It is far too hot to work to-day,. The temp is 113 and I am dripping with sweat. I hope we get some rain soon as the river is stone dry. I haven't been able to take a bath since Sunday, when I took a shower in the USO. The dirt is so thick on us that we scrape it off with a knife. I am going to sneak into camp tonite and get a good hot shower. The meals are fine since we came back from furlough. We have had corn on the cob once a day. The goat meat comes in only once a week and no more horse. We have to eat out of mess kits all the time out here. Yesterday I had string beans, peas, carrots, potatoes and a pork chop and then a whole cup full of butterscotch pudding poured over the whole thing. It didn't taste bad. Of course it did not have salt or catsup on, so I know that you would not eat it Dad, but we get so we like it anyway.

I got weighed the other day and I lost all the weight that I had gained plus 4 extra lbs. I weigh 230. I just got two new pair of shoes and I am getting one more. I can't get my shoes repaired fast enough so the C.O. got me another pair.

A s soon as I get paid I am going to get that pair of dress shoes from the Quarter Master.

I bought a new mess kit and cup. I now have two sets. I use one to eat with and the other for inspections. I have seven sets of sun tans now. There is no way to get them cleaned so every time I go to town I buy another set. Some day I will be able to have them all cleaned. It will be swell not to have to worry about having clean uniforms.

Your package came last nite. It sure was a good one! We all enjoyed it very much.

Monday 13

I forgot what date I started this letter but things have changed since. We have had showers for two days now. It is the first rain in a long time. All of the crops were burning up. You should have seen it rain. We went to the river this morning, and it is deep enough to dive into from a tree. The whole company was off this morning as we haven't been to bed in three days. General Ward, our new post commander, made his first inspection and was very much dissatisfied. He gave Col. Brown 3 days to get the Battalion in proper condition. We worked 3 days and 3 nites to get it done. The camp was in so bad a condition when we got here that it was unfit to live in. Col Brown did a wonderful job of fixing it up. But the General did not see it when we came here and he was mad. He said if this camp did not pass inspection in 3 days that Col Brown would be tried by a Court Marshall for neglect of duty. He did not say a word to us about it; our C.O. told us and we volunteered to work from then until the time of the inspection without stopping. We even had the cooks working. We would not let them cook meals. At chow time they would run in and make sandwiches and coffee and come out and work til supper. The general came at 9 this morning. He could not believe his eyes, the camp is spotless. Col Brown called us together and said "I guess you boys earned a day off. Thanks Men". He took off and we were more than repaid just to see him get a square deal. Every man respects him more than the general himself. We know that if we ever go into battle he will be in front of us instead of in back.

I am half asleep as I write so don't mind if I leave words out.

Your money order came today. I don't want to go into debt any more, I would rather sweat it out until we get paid, so I am sending it back in this letter. Thanks just the same.

I am keeping 3 pictures and am sending the rest to you as I can't carry any more around.

Love,

Bob

July, 1943

Hello Mom,

I just got a picture at the USO and might just as well send it home so you can laugh too. I sure wish you would send me a camera and some film. I will <u>pay</u> for it. We can't buy any down here because there is no more left in the stores.

I mailed a package today too. You will probably get it the same time as you get this. Joe and I volunteered to fight a forest fire last nite so we got today off. We are too broke to go out so we are hanging around Killeen just to be out of camp. We went to sleep in a truck last nite when we were supposed to be fighting fire, so we are not tired today.

I had a lot of trouble with those German prisoners. They tried to make me believe they couldn't understand what I wanted them to do. I had them building a shower bath out in the woods. I got the interpreter and told them they would get the rock pile if they didn't do what I wanted. You should have seen them work then! They are a tough bunch. They all went through about 5 campaigns and they are hard as nails. The only thing they are afraid of is the rock pile or solitary confinement. I am going out with Joe to a show so take care of yourself and tell Roy and Dad not to work too hard.

Your son

Bob

July, 1943

Dear Mom, Dad,

Your letter came just as I was about to go out for the weekend. I haven't been in bed for 3 days as we just got back from a problem. I started to read your letters and I heard that we are being restricted for two weeks for not winning the problem. The reason we did not win is because most of our boys got so tired that they could not work so they camouflaged their tank and went to sleep. I don't blame them but I still don't want to stay in camp Saturday nite and Sunday, so I am out in the woods waiting for it to get dark so I can sneak out. I still have to shave. The company thinks that I already left before the order came out so if I don't get caught shaving tonite I will still get out of camp Sunday. I am glad you are mailing the camera, as I want to get some pictures of the things we do so that I can look at them after the war.

I did not receive any letters from Grand Pop although I did get the Hoboken news. I am going to try to write to Kitty and the Mildens tonite or tomorrow. I haven't written to anybody since my furlough. I just wrote to John Kemp in answer to his card.

The picture that I sent home was Skelly's idea of a funny picture. He thinks of the craziest things to do. I am not going out with him for a month as I need a rest, and I sure won't get it with him.

Sunday Nite Midnite

I fell asleep in the woods while writing this letter last nite. I woke up at 4 this morning, when I woke up I didn't know where I was but after stumbling around for a few minutes I found camp and shaved by candle light. I then went out to the road and got a ride on a milk truck into Camp Hood, then I got a bus to Temple where I took a shower in the USO, followed by a swim in the pool. It was then 9 o'clock and the USO gave me breakfast. I then got a ride with a rancher in a new car out to Dallas. He bought me a big dinner and gave me his address so I can come see him and his big ranch as soon as I get time. I did not stay in Dallas long as I wanted to go to Bartlett on the Farm and get me some melons. I arrived in Bartlett at seven tonite and did I get a feed. The farmer's son got in a big water melon from the well. It was ice cold but I ate so much French toast made with home made bread and milk that all I could eat was ¼ of the melon. They were glad to see me and were very much disappointed to hear that I will probably never get back to see them. I swill sure miss those meals but it will be worth it to get out of this camp. We don't know when we are going but it will be very soon. It might be only back to Bowie or it might be across. We are on the alert to leave with 6 hrs notice. We might be here for a year yet you can never tell.

I got your letter tonite Dad. So you think it is hot up home. You ought to be ashamed of yourself. It is so hot down here that the medics make us take 9 salt tablets per day. The paint gets so hot on the tanks that it peels off. It sure was swell to hear from you Dad. Please keep it up. I have some cards I am going to mail to you so I will close now.

Lots of love from your son

P.S. How is Roy and his job coming along?

July 24, 1943

Dear Mother Dad,

The mail did not come in yet today as we had a big inspection and the mail clerk couldn't leave until after insp.

July 25

I didn't get very far yesterday with the letter so I will try again. When the mail did come yesterday I got two letters. One from you and one from cousin Kitty. I am now guarding prisoners. I have 2 hours off to rest and then 4 hours on. I am making those prisoners wish they were never born. They are earning their 80 cents a day. I got them working like they never worked before. Yesterday one of them escaped again. The guard that was on then is being court marshaled. I can't find out how he got away but you can be sure there will be no get away from me. Col Brown was relieved of his command yesterday. In spite of all we did to help him they still caught him for something. We just found out why they didn't want him here. It was because this is a Tank Destroyer camp and we can, under Col Brown's leadership beat any 3 battalions of tank destroyers on problems. That makes it look bad for the big shots in the T.D. So we get a new Col. that won't be such a smart man. I for one won't do an ounce of work from now on. If they want a lousy outfit they sure will get one and they will have some tall explaining to do just why the 747 turned from the best in the country to the worst in the world. Every body feels the same as I do about it.

My time is almost up so I will have to close in a hurry when they come for us. Every time I get this guard I hate those men more and more. I would rather do KP for a week rather than guard for 30 hours. The time goes by so slow and it is so hot standing in the sun making those men work. And this tommy gun gets heavier by the minute it weighs 11 lbs. when you start and 50 when you get done. The camera did not come yet. I can't wait to get it. I want to get some pictures of the camp before we move, and I know I can get some good ones on maneuvers.

I will have to go now Mom so have a good time on your vacation.
Love to all
Bob
PS I don't know when I will get time to mail this letter.

July 1943
Dear Mother Dad

My insurance finally came through. I put in for it before I went home on furlough. I am sending you all my extra equipment and clothing as they are going to take it all away from us. It means we are going away very soon. Probably on maneuvers. There is an order out for us to be out of camp Hood by aug. 1st. I will send the clothes home this week and when I can get to town. We are not even allowed to have an extra pair of sox. Our tanks are all in ordnance getting new engines and gears. We are doing a lot of drilling and calisthenics. It looks good to us. We still have hope that we might move back to where there are roads and lights and people. I am beginning to feel like Dan Boone. When we go into town and don't know how to eat like civilized people. We sit down and order steak with nothing else and when we finish we order another. The people did look at us and wonder where we were brought up.

It doesn't matter where they send us it won't be as bad as this place. I can't find my new arch supports since I was home. will you look in all my old black shoes and see if they are in there?

I feel a lot better since I quit smoking. I haven't coughed since I left home. The reason I quit was a shortage of money but I don't miss them.

I didn't cash the money order yet as I don't have to have it until the end of the week. I will use it to mail the clothes home. I want you to cash my bond because I wanted to get out of debt. I had all my debts paid up and was flat broke. I wanted the 18 to get me by for the end of the month, and I could start next month with a clean slate. Now I have to pay you 10 and that will leave me with 20 to live a month on and I will be borrowing again next month.

I got Dads letter and also one from Grand Pa. I expect one from John Fisher.

Nobody has mentioned Roy lately. What happened. Did he lose his job or does he still get away with it. I am sending home a plan for the commando course that they have up at Ft. Knox. It is not half as bad as ours. Put it away so I an look at it when the war is over. I am getting a little more limber every day although I am still stiff and sore in every muscle when I get up in the middle of the night. Revelry is at 3 in the morning and we work till dark most days, that is why we get so any Sundays off lately. The food is fine and we all feel better since we heard we are moving. The 744 tank Btn left this camp before we came and they went on maneuvers. They all got captured in the first 2 days so they called off the maneuvers and sent them up to Indiana to start their basic training all over again and their officers were all sent back to O.C.S. They are all southern and western boys in that outfit and they haven't had the education of our battalion. Most of our men have a college education. You might wonder how I got in. I don't know! Your I.Q. test has to be over 110 to get in here and I got 114. They were supposed to go overseas a year ago but they just can't learn. We are on call to go at any time now with only 7 months training. We were congratulated by Gen Biddle for learning so fast and for working so hard. He said we did our 2 years work in the seven months we are in the army. He said up until now that kind of training was thought impossible.

I have to go to bed pretty soon because the candle is burning low. I will let you know when we are going as soon as I find out. It might be up north I hope.
Love to all
Bob

August 4, 1943
Dear Mother, Dad.

It has been a long time since I sent you a letter, but it isn't because I didn't have anything to talk about. It is because I have been working 20 hours a day since last time I wrote to you. We got Sunday off to rest up but tired as we were Joe and I went to Dallas as you already know from the post card I sent to you. It is 200 miles to Dallas and we made it in 3 ½ hours. We didn't have much time to spend there as we had to fall out 3 in the morning Monday. We did see it though and it is a very modern city. It had beautiful hotels and theaters just like New York. It has almost as many lights as Times Square used to have. We got a ride from camp right to Dallas and the driver was sleepy so he asked me to drive. It was a '41 Buick and I drove over 70 all the way.

I might as well tell you now as later what Joe and I are up to because you will find out anyway. We are taking up flying. Don't get excited, it is safe as driving a car. It will cost us $70 to finish the course. It cost $4 per hour and the course is 12 ½ hours. After that we will get our license to fly alone. We have had 2 lessons and we both love it. We pay as we go along. Now that I got that off my mind I feel better. It is a lot of work studying aviation and tanks at the same time but it is a chance in a lifetime and I always did want to fly.

Now to start on today's news. Hold your hat and sit down before you read this. I smashed my tank up again. Only one guy was hurt, he got a fractured knee. I was coming home this afternoon from a problem when it happened. I was in 5th gear coming down a long hill at the bottom of which was a bridge about 8 ft over the water. Just as I came down to the hill a jeep with 3 men were coming the other way. I could not stand to see them run over by the tank so I went over the side into the creek. What a jar! It was the first time in my life that I was really scared. Every man in the tank said a prayer to himself between the time we left the bridge and the time we hit bottom. We all sat in the tank for 10 minutes without saying a word. I was out cold for a few minutes from the jolt. But do you think we were scared, you should have seen the men in the jeep. They were white as a sheet. I only have about $1500 damage to my tank. It will be ready to run in a few days. I took a picture of it and will send it home as soon as they are developed.

I got your package and was surprised at what was in it but it sure tasted good. I hope the camera works. I guess you have my package of clothes by now. We had to get rid of all extra clothes and equipment. I will send for them some day when we get settled again. You keep the towel, and the wool cap will keep Dad's ears warm this winter. We wear them under our helmets.

I forget what I put in but you use all except the sun tans. They are all that I will need back. Let me know what size pants Roy uses as I have an extra pair for salvage that I will send him. I have extra socks that I am going to mail home for Dad. They are good army socks. Tell Dad to wear them all the time and as soon as they wear out to send them back to me (clean) and I will get new for them.

I am sending a clipping to you to show what we are in for next Friday nite. Wish me luck. It sounds pretty good. I can't see any more so will close before it is too dark to finish.

As ever,
Your loving son
Bob
P.S. Thanks for the $10.

The White Plaza Hotels
San Antonio, Texas
Aug 9,
Dear Mother, Dad,

The card that I mailed this morning has probably reached you by now. I hope you enjoyed the pictures as much as I enjoyed the real thing. It sure was a thrill to go into the Alamo and see all the old rooms where Bowie and Crockett died. We were in the room where Crockett drew the line on the floor. Out in back of

the Alamo is a museum which you can see in the picture. Inside of the museum are pictures of all the men who died in the Alamo, and Bowie's long rifle and the knife that is the original of the now famous Bowie Knife. The building is the same now as it was in 1823. You can see the bullet holes in the walls and you can picture in your mind the whole battle just as it happened. We stayed in the Gunter Hotel yesterday and we decided to change to this one today. It is a very modern hotel with all the trimmings. We can't sleep good on these soft beds but otherwise it is alright. We will have to start back tomorrow as we will have to sign in at 5 o'clock Wednesday morning. In case you don't know where San Antonio is I am going to mail you a map showing all the towns that I have visited. I guess my suit case has arrived by now. Just put the uniforms away until I send for them.
Your loving son
Bob

Aug 11/43
Cottonwood
Dear Mother, Dad,

I sure got a big surprise when I got back from my pass this morning. The 747th is going to the dogs. We don't have to work any more for a while. The medical department examined all the men and said that they were all unfit for duty. They ordered a two week rest for the whole battalion. All we did all day was swim and eat. We are getting double rations of food. The rest of the company are going to a movie tomorrow paid for by the government. and a USO dance tomorrow nite. I am not going as I got stuck for guard. I came on at 7 o'clock tonite and will be on til tomorrow nite at 7.

Next week we are going out to Buchanan Dam for 3 days just swimming and fishing. Joe and I know a couple of girls out there near the dam so we will sneak out at nite and go to Llano and see them. It is only 60 miles from the dam.

We had a swell time on our furlough. We went canoeing in San Antonio at nite on the river. The river is beautiful at nite. It runs all over town and is all lit up with colored lights. After that we went to Kelly field and then Randolph Field. We got a ride from San Antonio to Temple over 200 miles in 3 ½ hours, and we stopped for lunch in San Marcos.

I am glad you got your vacation and are enjoying it. It must be hot at home but the weather is getting worse all the time here. It is so hot you can't get your breath. When we were out at the Alamo it was 118 in the shade, and 105 at eleven o'clock at nite. That was the hottest day I ever seen. The average day is 106 to 110. You ought to get in a tank on one of those days. It is about 140 inside. It is so hot inside that you almost freeze when you get out.
I can't see any more so I will have to close now.
Lots of love
Bob

Aug 14/43

Dear Mother Dad,

I received your <u>short</u> letter today if you could call it a letter. If it was me that sent it to you it probably would be labeled a note.

I hope you can read this as I am trying to write while laying on my back on the floor of the tent and trying to share the candle with my two partners. It is too hot to sleep so we are all trying to write a letter. I think I wrote to you last when I was on guard. I am not sure whether I ever mailed it or not. That often happens as it usually takes 2 or 3 days to finish a letter of any size and most times you misplace it or throw it out before you finish.

The men that were hurt in my tank are all out of the hospital and almost as good as new. I went in for a final check and I am alright except for a few bruises. My tank is what I am really worried about. It is not even ready to roll yet. It seems that my tank is in for repairs all the time. It won't be out for 3 weeks as no one will work on it. This is still our week of rest. We can't get used to lying in bed until 5 o'clock every morning. I am up at 3 – 3:30 every morning and lay there waiting for the whistle to blow. All we do now is have inspections one after the other. This morning we had a big inspection in the ranks. Almost everybody was gigged. I was alright, all but one thing, I did not have my stripes sewed on my arm. He started hollering and crying about how careless we were about not putting them on. No one wants them or will put them on because as soon as you do you can't get time off. You work on books at nite after everybody else is done. We are very short of N.C.O. and no one will take it as a gift.

My candle is very low and it is the last one until Tuesday nite so I will close soon as the others finish.

Mrs. Mallander's letter arrived after a long journey from camp Bowie. It took 12 days to reach me. How did Jack get out of the army? Tell her that I can't write or that I got a broken arm or something as I don't feel up to writing her.

Our hair cuts have to be shorter than they were if possible and our uniforms must be kept cleaner (Says Him) and a few other little things have to be changed, otherwise every thing is still the same.

Two days later

I never had time to finish this letter the other day as we were busy all day and I just never got to it. Skelly finally made corporal too. He is a gunner in the tank. I never told you about it because I was afraid that I would be broken but I was made cpl while I was home on furlough. Now that I told you about getting my rating I will probably lose it right away.

I am going to try and get the job driving the self propelled 37mm gun. It is just like driving a pleasure car. I will let you know if I make it.

I just got that card from you Dad, let's have a letter for a change. How is the shipyard coming, is it still as hot as it was?? From your card I take it you did not have such a good time on your vacation. Talking about swimming I am going in for a swim tonite after I finish this letter. That is if I can get the jeep out of the motor park. We turned in our gas masks today and we got all new trucks in the Battalion. The latest rumor is that we are going to Indiana. I hope it is true as I will be able to get home on a 3 day pass from there.

I am going to close now so this letter can be like a rabbit.
Love to all
Bob

Aug 19
Dear Mother & Dad,

So your vacation is over, I am so glad you enjoyed it. My vacation is over too. We went back on regular duty Wednesday. You went to Asbury swimming and it was cold, I went in the creek and it was hotter than bath water. You can't win. No matter where you are it is either too hot or too cold. How are the flies up there this year? They drive you crazy here. They fly in your face and in your ears and up and down your back, and tickle your toes so you can't sleep.

I am sorry I did not answer your questions sooner but it slipped my mind. Yes, I did receive, cash, and spend check from Mather Springs. I have so much on my mind that I can't think of everything when I write.

You seen the G.I. roller skating at Asbury but you should have seen me and McGuire skating with 2 queens from Killeen. I fell down 4 times before I got around the ring once. Finally I got going fast and could not stop and went through the rail in the end of the rink. The M.P. tried to make us build it up again but to his surprise we had other ideas. We tripped him, took his club and took off for Waco. We still have the club here in the tent.

You shouldn't do so much canning again all at once. I don't hear you say anything about the cleaning woman. Do you still have her. I know Roy doesn't help and if Dad does there sure has been some changes made.

I still haven't heard from you Dad. I am sure you have more time than I do to write. What ails Roy? He went to school long enough to learn to write.

I guess Roy is having a good time up at Addie's. He always did enjoy himself up there, but he would be happy anywhere just as long as there was a radio and a baseball game on. I guess he is getting to be quite a golf fan. I could never see golf. You hit the ball and chase it all around the countryside.

How are Grand Pa and Ma, and Helen these days. I haven't received a letter from them in a long time. Thank Grand Pa for the Ho Bo News (*Hoboken News?*). It came today.

You asked me about flying. We had 1 lesson at Dallas and a lot of reading and studying here at camp. I flew for 1 hour on my first lesson. It cost $8. I have seven more lessons before I can solo. That will be quite some time as it sure costs lots of money. I only get a gross pay of $66 per month and after all the deductions come out I only get my 50 left. It's learning the hard way but it is the best way at that. At that price you can't afford to forget any of the lesson.

My latest whim is to drive a light tank. They go faster. We have two lights in our Battalion and I am going to try to qualify for a license to drive one.

I am going to get out of the mil unless we go across. The war might end soon and I don't want to waste all that I have learned in Texas. If we don't go across in 2 months I am going to transfer to the paratroopers. I will have to lose 13 more lbs but that won't be hard. They send you over in 2 months, and besides there is more action.

My candle just burned out so I am going to use my flash light until that goes.

We keep getting the run around about moving but we never seem to move. I am getting disgusted with this outfit. We never go any place except Texas. We all want to be shipped across and we sure let them know it. We got rid of General Ward. He is the one that took the first armored division to Africa. He should have died with the men he murdered. When he was in Africa he was fighting Rommel and one nite he made his men take all their guns apart for a full field inspection. When he had the guns out of the tanks Rommel made an attack and all his men were killed. Now they send him here to try and get us. We soon got rid of him. The whole camp made a protest and he has been recalled from his command. He is the one that got rid of Colonel Brown back from Ft. Knox. They put him in charge of an induction center. That is a disgrace to any officer.

We have a new wave of men going A.W.O.L. The last roll call we had tonite we were short a total of 15 men for today. Don't worry about me going over the hill. They could never break me no matter how bad it gets. The men that leave are not worth having anyway. If they can't take it over here they can't take it over there.

I think I can get out of my tank if I keep trying. I saw the top Sgt tonite again trying to get on the 37mm gun carrier. It is a swell job.

We fired the 75mm and the 37mm again for record. Joe Skelly got the highest score in the battalion on the 37mm and I got 140 out of 150 on the 75mm. I was beaten by 3 men in the battalion. Expert score is only 105. We got a letter from Colonel Steel saying we were the best battalion ever trained in the med tanks. He said it is a miracle how we ever did it. The only one who can take the honors is Colonel Brown and he isn't here to get them. Since he left we have lost 3 problems against the T.D. Battalion. When he was here we never lost out of 79 problems.

The heat rash that I have is getting worse. It is all over my body and itchy something fierce. Everybody is getting it. It seems there is nothing you can do for it.

Those films that I sent home are probably not much good because I stood too far away from the camera. I will know better next time.

I hope you got the socks as I did not insure them. I had a lot of extra equipment and we had to get rid of it all. Ed Brady, one of my pals, hid his civilian shoes inside of mine so they would not take them. But it so happened that there was a shoe inspection and they found them. The captain called him in his office and gave him extra K.P. He laughed and said it was worth a K.P. just so he could tell his kids that he had a pal that had shoes big enough to put his inside. The Capt. did not like him laughing and gave him 2 extra K.P. instead of one. Then he called me in. He said if he ever caught me hiding something like that again he would take my stripes. Then I got mad and told him he could have them. I said you give me a $16 raise and want me to do another $50 worth of work. He did not like that, he said "I will not break you this time but the next time it will be different." He gave me an extra 'Charge of Quarters' and let it go at that. I was happy as a private anyway. Some day I will hand in those two headaches and get my $50 per.

I have two extra pairs of shoes I will have to send one of them home before I get caught with them. As soon as we move I can send home for the uniforms again but now it must all go.

The light is almost burned out so I will close for this time.

Your loving son,

Bob

P.S.

When Addie comes down tell her to make a big lemon pie. Then you eat it and think of me.

  Did you get map?

Did " " socks?

  "   "   " films?

  Please answer

Aug 21, 1943

Dear Roy,

I just received your letter this morning. I was glad to hear from you after all this time. So you got a vacation too. It seems like everyone is getting one of those things. It is too bad I didn't know that you were looking for a job this summer. I could have gotten you a job here at camp working in the 'Post Exchange'. You would only work 3 hours a day and get your room and board free with a pay of $175 per mo. It would have been a swell chance to see the country and also see what the army is. After the war you can get all kinds of college courses free and take up any kind of trade. So don't think that the army is so bad. We also have more fun in one month here than you could have in a year at home. When we get a Sunday off we appreciate it more than you would appreciate a month off. You might think you would miss going to the movies and going to see the Yankees play ball but you are so interested in doing your work and having such a good time just being with your friends that you don't even think of those cheap civilian ways of passing time.

I have more friends here in the army already than I could even begin to get in a lifetime in civilian life. Joe Skelly is a swell guy as I have already told you. He and I go all over the state without spending a dime. You would laugh if you could see Joe and I on a Sunday morning with only 35 or 40 cents between us starting out for Austin or San Antonio over 200 miles away. We always get to where we are going, get plenty to eat, see a show or go boating or fishing and have a swell time and get in camp about 2 minutes before revelry the next morning. There are so many fellows here that you can always find one that likes to do the same as you. Joe and I are like twins. We both like to do the same things. We never had an argument about where we should go because we can have fun no matter where we go. Mack is another one that likes to just go out and have a good time. He is taking flying lessons with me too. Mack's right name is McGuire. He comes from Matawan New Jersey. We are going to Buchanan Dam fishing one of these days soon. That is a beautiful big lake. It is the main source of power and light in Texas. The dam itself is 2 miles long and very high. Buchanan Dam is the 3rd largest dam in the world. Mack is a very religious fellow. Outside of that we get along fine. He is always trying to drag me into church.

Say, you ought to see some of our baseball teams here at Hood. I'll be they could play the Yankees and not get beaten too badly. We have many famous players from the minor leagues and some from the majors. There are some famous hockey players from New York down here too. One of my best friends is a former trumpet player for Johnnie Ling's Band. His name is Dick Papari. He used to be my assistant driver. He is only 18 years old but you should hear him play that horn. We think he is as good as Harry James. I recommended him for a driver in one of the new tanks. He can drive as good as anyone in the battalion. So you see that in a way we are better off in here than we were outside. Of course a guy likes to go home and see his folks once in a while but for a real good experience and lots of fun it's the army.

Joe and I are figuring out some new ways of making some money. I walked guard the other day for a $5 bill, and did K.P. for 8 bucks. That gives me enough for one more flying lesson. It is a hard way to make money but it is the best way that we found yet. If you have any suggestions let us hear them.

I got a pair of dress shoes that should fit you or Dad. We are not allowed to have them here so the fellows are getting rid of them. Keep a good shine on them and they will last you a long time. They are in the mail now. Talking of shoe shines you ought to see mine. I have 3 pair of G.I. shoes. I spent 2 hours on each shoe. 6 hours altogether. You can shave with them. When you walk in the tent you need sun glasses to cut down the glare from the shoes. The first thing I did was wash them in hot soap and water. I then scraped them with a knife, then let them dry. After that I rubbed saddle soap on them and let that dry. Then I dyed them and then polish and then wax then Johnson's floor wax. The inspector said they were the best he ever seen. I have 3 pair of shoes and 1 more coming in salvage. We are only allowed to have two pair so I will send two pair home some day. They are very expensive shoes and will come in handy after the war.

Did the socks come yet? I don't know if they will fit you or not but if they don't I can always use them after the war.

There is not much more that I can think of to say except that – enjoy getting mail from so keep up the good work. Your brother, Bob

Aug 23

Dear Mother, Dad.

The news of Mr. Keifer's death was quite a surprise to me. I had no idea that he was even sick. It must have been quite a shock to John and Art. I lost a very good friend, one that I will never forget.

The cards you sent me were very amusing, I mean the one about the customers telling you that I wasn't in school. It isn't so funny now as I could sure use some of those lessons. It isn't too late yet. I am taking up a General Science course. The Army Institute is an organization run by and paid for by the Army. They give you the lessons on your own time. I might be biting off more than I can chew but I am sure going to try to take these courses that they give you. I am going to start with a general science course to get started. I always liked that subject and it comes in handy every day. After I finish that I am going to take a course in math.

I go out tomorrow to take my exam in the light tank. I am not so sure I can pass but I will try my best. Those light tanks are tricky and you can't tell how they will take a bump. It takes months of practice to be able to judge a certain kind of ditch or bump so you don't hit it too hard. I have to go with a major in the light tank obstacle course. If I get through in the proper time I will get my license. That will be another one of my ambitions fulfilled. I have a lot of things I still want to do but at the rate I am doing things now it won't be long before I am satisfied. I won't be able to take another flying lesson until pay day as I am flat broke until the 10th of the month. That 3 day pass is what ruined me this month. The next one I am going to take one flying lesson and spend the rest of my time studying. Joe Skelly and Ed Brady are in main camp tonite signing up for a course like mine. The company commander approved mine this morning. I had a long talk with my C.O. I told him that going to classes every day and most nites was enough work without driving the tank. He said he would speak to my platoon commander and try and get me the job that I want on the 37mm gun carrier. If I get it I will be driver and gunner. I will have an assistant gunner and an assistant driver under me instead of a whole tank crew. It is a very soft job. No headaches and very little responsibility. I will then have lots of time to take care of all my lessons. I finish up the judo and knife fighting next Wednesday. The map reading will be over in a week and a half. Then things will be swell.

I bought a coat from a guy who needed money real bad. I paid 3 bucks for it. I am sending it home today. Put it away for me where it won't be eaten up by moths. If it fits Roy he can use it next winter if he promises to take care of it. It is a good coat and I don't want it ruined.

Next Day.

I just got back from the driving course. I got my license. I went over the course in 44 minutes. It had to be done in less than 50 min to get your license. I got the rest of the day off to rest from it. It was about the roughest 45 minutes that I ever had. The major did not shoot me as I thought he would when I jumped a ditch instead of going down and up the other side. We had 3 more men go over the hill this morning. One of them was on guard and deserted his post. When he gets caught he will probably be sent to federal prison for the rest of his life. The mail goes out in half an hour so I will close this letter and get it in there before it is too late.

Your Son

Bob.

If these socks don't fit Roy or Dad, save them for me.

As ever

Bob

P.S.

If you need Brillo soap pads let me know. I can buy them for you. I can also get you chewing gum.

Aug 26

Dear Mother, Dad,

I have some bad news to tell you. It looks like we are not going to leave camp Hood for the duration. They made school troops out of us. We are going to train Tank Destroyers. Unless there are some unforeseen developments in the war they won't need us. The men are very disappointed as we were supposed to sail this week. The order came today to paint "School Troops" on our tanks. We are now allowed to have our civilian shoes back and all our other equipment. I didn't tell you the whole story about what has been going on. We had our gas masks all checked. We got all new guns for our old ones, we have 58 new tanks at the railroad station. I expected to be on the ship by now. Well I almost made it. Maybe I can get a transfer to some combat unit in another outfit. I sure am going to try.

I didn't get any letters from you in the last two days. I hope there is one tomorrow. I got a letter from Helen Milden and also a package of cartoons. I am not going to answer Mrs. Mallander's letter because I don't want to start anything and besides I don't know what to write to her. Did you get the shoes, socks, coat, and film yet? I want all the pictures sent to me until I see them and then I will mail them back to you. Send the enlargements as soon as you get them. I mean the ones from Chicago.

Do the shoes fit Roy or Dad? How about the socks? The coat fits me, does it fit Roy alright? Tell me how much the pictures cost you and I will send money on the 15ᵗʰ of next mo. As that is when we get paid. I will be glad when we get paid on time again for a change.

A lot of our letters are not reaching home. One of the fellows' wives sent a letter to the company commander wanting to know why she never heard from her husband. He said he wrote to her every day so if you don't hear from me you will know that the letter is held up or lost.

I guess I will have plenty of time to finish my flying lessons now. I lost all interest in the tank corps as soon as I heard the news today. It don't seem possible that we are stuck here for the duration. I am going to refuse to drive a tank here. It isn't worth it. You work like a horse and take all kinds of crazy chances for what? Just to train T.D. Btn and they aren't any good after we teach them the problems. I am going in tonite and tell the top sergeant to take me out of the tanks. It might mean getting broken but if he gives me the job I want I will keep the pay.

Next Day
Hello again,

I went to see about getting out of the tanks last nite and I did alright. They are giving me the 37mm gun carrier. That means I keep my stripes. I have a picture of myself in the carrier. It is in those that you are having printed. I will take it over tomorrow. Now I can study all I like as I have the best job in the company. I have an assistant gunner to keep the gun clean and an assistant driver to keep the carrier clean.

I had better close this letter as you are probably tired of reading by now. Take it easy and remember me when you go in swimming down the ocean.
Your loving Son
Bob
P.S. I am bucking for another furlough. Maybe they will give it to me in another two or three months.

Sept 1
Dear Mother, Dad.

I guess this letter will make you laugh if you remember the last one. The orders have changed again. Last nite the major called a meeting of all non commissioned officers and told us that we are no longer going to be school troops. He said that the orders from the 7ᵗʰ tank group said to be ready to go on maneuvers on or before the 28ᵗʰ of this month. We are going to Louisiana until Nov 15. We never will know where we will go from there. I am sending home all my extra clothes and camera. There will be a rain coat, 1 pair of pants, 1 pair of goggles, some underwear, and some other small items. I have so many clothes I don't know what to do with them. Does the coat fit Roy? How about the shoes? The coat is a good G.I. Coat. I can salvage it when it wears out and the same with the socks so don't throw them away. I have 6 pair of socks in salvage now so I will mail them home later. When are you going to send the pictures back?

I feel a lot better now than I did the other day. That was an awful thing to happen to a tank Btn (School Teachers). I never want to get a scare like that again. It looks like my flying lessons are shot for a while. Last Sunday I went on guard at 1 o'clock in the afternoon. We had a good guard until 4 o'clock Monday afternoon when a truck driver that I sent to camp with a load of trash to dump, came walking into the guard house. He told us that the prisoners beat up the guards and took their guns. They then put the gun in the driver's back and made him get out and walk. The truck and the two prisoners have not been found yet. I am going to the hospital and see the guard tomorrow. They say he might die. The prisoners were not japs or german. They were our own prisoners. If the guard dies they will be shot when caught. The guard was a private from C Company. I am getting most of the blame because there is no one else to blame. It will all blow over in a few days. That is what is bad about being cpl of the guard. You get blamed for everything.

I haven't much time to myself now as we are getting ready to go. So don't expect any letters for weeks at a time. If I get time I will write but you will understand if they don't come often.

As ever, your loving son
Bob

Sep 5
Dear Mom, Dad.

We are very busy again. That is why I haven't written letters. I have to go before Major Fries Monday to be questioned on the escape of the prisoners. The guard is still out of his mind so he can't answer any questions yet. He will ask me what instructions I gave the guards before they went on guard. It so happens that I read the rules to them in the morning, so I am covered completely. We found the army truck on the outskirts of camp but still no sign of the two prisoners. We called in the FBI to work on the case. The two prisoners will get 44 years in prison and if the guard dies they will get death. I'll be glad when the whole works are over.

I got your letter Dad. I am glad you liked the socks. All I wear is the wool socks. We just keep the cotton for inspections. I will try to get you some more. Do they fit alright? I can get any size you want. When they get a hole in them just send them to me and you will get a new pair for them. Send me all your old socks that are brown or even look a little like those I sent you and I can salvage them for new.

I have to wash my clothes today so I won't have much time to write. The two bucks came and it made me the richest guy in camp. It could not have come at a better time. Thanks a lot. We get paid the 10th I hope then I am going on a 3 day pass. I got it coming for making the best score in the company on the pistol.

Since I stopped smoking my average came up from 88% to 93% on the pistol. I will send home my score card. When are the pictures coming! I can't wait to see them. Didn't the enlargements come from Chicago yet? Please send them as soon as they come. I am going to chow so it's good bye for today.
Your Son
Bob

Sept 7,
Dear Mother, Dad.

This letter is probably going to be short as I am writing just to let you know how I made out today about the guard. They asked me all kinds of questions and after a long time I finally made them see that it wasn't my fault. I am cleared of all matters connected with it. The guard was a lot better when I went to see him today. His brother was here to see him. I took his brother out to see a show this afternoon. He feels a lot better than he did before he seen his brother.

Well Dad I guess you can see now why I don't want any rating. The higher up you go the worse it is. The lower you go the less work and trouble you get.

In about 3 or 4 months when I get caught up on my money I am going to ask to be reduced to a buck private. The army really is a pleasure when you are a private.

Well the tanks are being loaded on the flat cars today. I guess we are really moving this time. We are not supposed to go until the 20th at the earliest but you can never tell. All I hope is that they move us the heck out of Texas. I would rather be in China than in this God forgotten place.

What is the matter with the pictures? The guys are hounding me for them every day.

The rainy season is here with a bang. We have had rain every day for the past 5 days. You ought to see it rain here. It comes down so hard you can't see 100 ft ahead of you. We had more rain last nite then we had since I have been in Texas all put together. Up until this week we have only had 4 days in 8 months that the sun hasn't shined all day. It is also the hottest and driest summer that they had in 44 years. It is hotter than I have ever seen it right now. You can't get your breath at all and you can't stay in the sun more than 5 minutes at a time. All the corn was ruined this year. It is all burnt up. The cotton did not grow over 12 inches high this year and they can't get a n- to pick it. Labor is so scarce that they can't get 12 year old kids to work 6 hours a day at the P.X. for $50 per week and their room and board. They hire 14 year olds in the shipyards in Houston for $10 per day.

Better start saving your money Dad as it looks like the end of the war is near. Maybe more than you think.

I will write tomorrow if I get time. How about you all doing some of it.
As ever,
Bob

Sept 9

Dear Mother, Dad.

While I am waiting to be paid I might just as well write you a letter. I got a pass from today at noon when we get paid until Monday morning. I was supposed to go Friday til Tuesday morning but we just got notice that we have to go over the commando course starting Monday morning, so I get one day cut off. I got the pass because of my score on the pistol. I don't know why we have to go over it again, we went over it twice already. I don't know if I can make it again like I did before.

I don't know where I am going this weekend but I will end up somewhere about 400 miles from camp. I might go into Mexico or New Mexico. This will be my last time out of camp in Texas for a long long time. Major General Aundry (*Illegible*) was here yesterday and said that "thanks to Col Brown up in Ft Knox we are going to be a combat unit." Col Brown is trying to get back with us. He is pulling strings for us in Ft Knox. He is the one that got us into maneuvers and will get us across. We are in 1A. That means we are the next tank battalion to go. We should be in Louisiana in two weeks.

I am sorry to hear about Tim Albens. He is lucky they didn't shoot him for disobeying an order. I hope when my time comes I won't disgrace the US Army by turning yellow. If he obeyed his orders the other planes might have had a chance. I wouldn't want that on my conscience all my life.

I got the cookies from Bob and Marge and sent them a letter.

The Hobo news came from the Mildens but I just didn't have time to write them. I might drop them a card this weekend from some town that I visit. I still can't think of a place to go to. I want to see something I haven't seen before.

How did Roy make out on his trip? He sent me a card from Asbury. I sure would like him to go with me for one weekend. I travel hundreds of miles in a day here. I have gone to Austin 100 miles away at nite after work and seen a movie and come back the same nite.

I just got pass

As ever Bob

Sept 11

Dear Mom, Dad.

We just got back from Lake Austin where we hired a motor boat and went fishing and swimming. The fishing wasn't so good but the swimming was swell. They have a swell beach and diving boards and everything you want at the lake. June is an expert diver. She made me dive off the 20 ft board. I almost broke my neck but you ought to see her do it. The only thing is she don't realize that everyone can't dive like that. She says there is nothing to it but I am never going to try it again no matter what she says.

We are going bowling as soon as she gets back from her room. She is putting on a clean uniform. I have a funny feeling she is a good bowler too. If she beats me in that I will never live it down. Tomorrow I am going to Waco and get one more flying lesson in before we leave here. It will be my last one for a long time.

I still didn't get the pictures, what happened to them? We are getting hotter days and colder nites. Every nite before I go to bed I put on my "long Johns" and role up in my 1 blanket, but before midnite I am up after my overcoat. The rainy season has started for good. Every nite it rains now, and I mean it really rains. So after I get all nice and warm in my long johns and 1 blanket and overcoat it starts to rain, then I get up and get my rain coat and then try to get under it but it never does any good. It rains so hard that the tent starts to float away and we end up not getting anything but cold feet and wet blankets and no sleep. It happens every nite without fail. Ah yes the army is lots and lots of fun. But you haven't heard anything yet. Wait til we hit Louisiana. The only thing there is to bother you there mosquitoes, alligators, snakes, swamps, rain, cold, ticks, chiggers, and getting separated from the mess truck. I am sure I will have a swell time, don't you?

My new job is a racket. In the morning I go to revelry at 3 o'clock and breakfast at 3:30 and report at the motor park at 4:00. I check my crew and then hunt for a place to sleep til dawn. At dawn I get up and see that the guns are cleaned and see that they check the carriage and stand inspection for complete unit. At 8 o'clock I drill the platoon for 15 minutes and then another Cpl drills platoon including me for 15 more minutes. Then the whole Btn has exercise for 1 hour. Then we go to work. We check our guns and vehicles and go out on a problem which may last until midnite or maybe 5 or 6 hours. We eat in the field. No matter what time we come in we clean all guns and gas up all tanks and trucks and other things. We then check them to see that they are ready to roll. After that we go up to the tent and scrub it out, shine shoes, and then stand on inspection in ranks for shoes, shines, class uniform, teeth clean, haircuts. After that we are off, usually about 10 at best. I then stagger into the guard house and study. I go to the guard house because that is the only place they have light to read by. I go to bed at eleven thirty and try to talk myself out of writing letters but I usually end up with a candle, a pen, and ink anyhow. I am always afraid you will not write as often as you do if I don't keep my end up. We have to take a physical exam every week now as the men are run down again. If you are very bad they give you a 15 day furlough. I will never get one I guess because I seem to thrive on these hours. The most I get is a 2 or 3 day pass to catch up on sleep.

I am up in the Balcony of the USO and can see June coming down the street so I had better finish up now.
Your loving Son
Bob

P.S. We had two steak dinners today. The steak was about 1 inch thick and big across as a dinner plate. It was the most tender steak I ever had in my life. Price 80 cents each.

Sept 13

Dear Mom, Dad,

I just got back from my pass. It is midnite and I got the mail clerk up out of bed to get me your mail. To my surprise there was two letters and one of them was very big. I enjoy those long letters but very seldom get them.

I sure could use a good <u>knife</u> on maneuvers but it would have to be a good one and I don't know what make is good. I need a knife "knife spelled without the K as you had it" about 6" long. It must fold as I have a fighting knife on my belt now, but it can not be used for cutting anything except human meat. The only other thing I need is a sweater without sleeves. I don't know what size but it must fit good so it don't bulge out from under the other clothes. It must be "olive drab", the color of the winter uniform. It is very cold in the morning and at nite. Don't let anybody send me anything else for Christmas and I'll need the sweater before that. It still goes over 100 in the shade in the daytime but goes down to 40 at nite. If they don't issue us blankets we will freeze soon. We turned our comforters in because you can't have them on maneuvers.

Don't worry about me getting hurt. I never get hurt. Only a scratch once in a while. If you are careful you don't get hurt so easy. I always wear my safety belt and my crew doesn't have to be told too. I give them crew drill at least twice a week. There is no reason why we should get hurt and I am going to see to it that my crew doesn't get hurt if I can help it. They all have wives and kids and I feel responsible for them to a certain extent. I don't want any serious accidents on my conscience.

I need a good razor and brush. Someone stole mine and I had to buy a 7 cent razor and a 10 cent brush. My Gillette blades are almost gone, see if you can get me some more. I can't use my other kind of blade with cold water.

We left Austin today about noon. I had a swell time. I forgot I was in the army for a day anyhow. June is a good bowler but I kept up to her in 2 games and she beat me one. I took her home tonite. She lives back in camp about 3 blocks from where I used to live. She took me up to the W.A.A.C day room. I felt about a foot high. There was 200 WAACs and only one man besides myself. I played ping pong with darn near all of them and never did win a game. I stayed until Taps and then came home to the woods. I will never see her again if we move this week but I will never forget the fun we had together.

There is not a candle or flashlight in camp. When I came in I could not find the company. I fell over trees and stumps for a half hour before I got home. I used matches to read your letter. I used up 3 boxes of matches and burnt my hand 3 times. I then tried to sleep but could not so I ended up down here in the guard house writing letters. It is the only light in the 747 tonite. We can't get candles and our flashlights are in ordinance for a check before maneuvers.

We are all praying for Col Brown to come back for maneuvers, as our chances of going over all depends on this. It is next thing to real battle. If he were here I know we would win. We could win any battle with him as our commanding officer. We had a check made on our Btn by a general from Ft Knox and he said it is a miracle how we got our training so quick and said we had the best tanks in the country. He said that he never saw tanks in such good condition as ours. There is an investigation going on to see why Col Brown was taken out. I'll bet some one will have a lot of explaining to do. "Gen Ward".

I am sending you a booklet called Fighting on Guadalcanal. Read it as soon as you get it and then burn it. (And then forget it.) Don't let anyone see it but you and Dad. (That means no one!!)

I am going to bed now so I can do my best on the commando course.
Love to all
Your son
Bob

Sept 13
Dear Mom, Dad,

The orders are changed again about the commando course. We were all sent to the dental clinic this morning. The whole btn. I had one cavity filled and had my teeth cleaned. The commando course will come tomorrow instead. We are going to pack our bags this afternoon. In one we put all our clothes that we don't need on maneuvers all except 1 uniform. We are only allowed to take 3 pairs of socks, 2 sets of underwear and two pair of coveralls, plus our toilet articles. It looks like the real thing at last.

I left one letter here to be mailed before I went on pass but they forgot to mail it so I put it in the box this morning plus another one I wrote last nite.

I am at the service club in camp. I will stay here until retreat. It is better than working.

I am going to buy my dinner there. It smells like corned beef and cabbage.
Love to all
Bob

Dear Mom, Dad.

We just got our new address. But don't use it until I tell you !! We are still at Camp Hood. When I write and tell you that I have moved then you can use it.

Cpl Rynier Cadmus
747 Tank Btn M Co A
A.P.O.# 403A
c/o post master

Shreveport Louisiana

Major generals Ward and   (*he left a blank space – maybe meant to go back and fill it in*) were out to our camp today. They sent for Gen Ward all the way from Ft Knox to come out and see our camp. We don't know what he had to come here for but we sure can make a good guess. We were never supposed to come here in the first place. They also probably want to know why we beat the T.D. so badly and why our Col was relieved of his command. I would hate to have to explain all that if I were Gen Ward.

Roy's candy came today at noon. It is now 3 o'clock and it is all gone. It sure was good though. I didn't get any letter from you today. That makes 3 days and tomorrow will be 4.

I just want to say hello today and let you know we are still here.
Love, Bob
P.S. I am going to mail another package tomorrow as we have to get rid of everything.
P.S. Commando course was cancelled for good. We haven't time for it now.

Sept 19
Dear Mom, Dad.

I haven't had time to write in the past week as we are head over heels in work. We will tear our tents down the first thing in the morning. Four German prisoners escaped from the prison camp last Wednesday. They caught 2 of them in Pottsville the next day. Friday I was on guard and a jeep came into our camp and they said they saw the other two about two miles from our camp. We went out after them. Pairs of us. We found their footprints in the mud and trailed them for an hour, then we lost their trail. By that time we had the MP out helping us. They then brought the bloodhounds out and we surrounded the whole area. The 106th cavalry came out to help us; we had a man every 5 feet for 3 miles. At 7 o'clock at nite they came out of the woods just about 2000 yards from my tent in the woods. A Texas Ranger shot one (a paratrooper) and captured the other. The reason so many escape is that they give us so many prisoners to guard. We just got in another 5000 Italians. We only have room for 1000 altogether. It doesn't matter much because they can't get away. All the farmers have guns and know how to use them. They always get caught in a few days. There are always a few at large. I have never been on guard yet in the army when there wasn't any excitement.

Well we will have to live in pup tents for the rest of the week until we move. I might not have time to write until after we move so don't worry if you don't hear from me. Keep using this address until I tell you to change. I got your 2 letters today.

I sent the rest of my extra clothes home. You will get them soon. I have so many clothes I don't know what to do with them all. I won't want to buy anything any more when I get out. I got another pair of G.I shoes. They are worth $12 at home but we get them for $3. In civilian life they would last a lifetime. When I get in another camp after maneuvers I will get about 5 pair of new shoes and send them home. I could never get 5 pair of shoes in a store for $15.

Today is Sunday and I did not go out. I was one of about 30 that didn't go out. We had chicken for dinner. There was enough chicken for 144 men and 30 of us ate it all up. I had at least 5 whole chickens today. I ate til I almost burst and then ate some more. We had 300 sticks of ice cream. I had 9 of them. Every time I get so I can hold some more I go in the icebox and get another half of chicken. I got a leg here in bed with me. I will eat it when I get done writing. I also had 3 quarts of milk.

You think it is cold up north well we had ice on the puddles the other nite. It was so cold in the tents we went outside and built a fire and sat around it all nite. I will send my watch home as soon as I get a chance. Give it to Roy as I can never get it to work. It hasn't run for 5 days altogether since I got it. I don't want to lose it in maneuvers.

Good nite for now.

Your loving Son, Bob

Sept 22

Dear Mom, Dad.

Well we are finally going to move. You can start to use the new address now. I will be in Camp Polk by the time your mail gets to me. We tore down all the tents and we are now in pup tents. The tanks go on the trains Friday Morning. We will arrive in Polk Sunday. We will only be in Polk for a few days. We go on maneuvers from there. We start maneuvers on the 28th. They will last about 6 weeks. After that your guess is as good as mine.

The new address is

Cpl R Cadmus
747 Tank Btn. Co A – M
32603063
A.P.O. 403A c/o Postmaster
Shreveport Louisiana

I mailed my watch and another package home yesterday. We are very busy now so I will close until I get to Louisiana.

Your loving son   Bob

Sept 22, 1943

Dear Mom, Dad,

I am leaving in the morning. I ducked out tonite to see June for the last time. We are going to a show and then report back to camp. I am glad to be leaving

Texas but I had a great time here. We are liable to be up in Jersey in about 7 weeks. Let's hope so.

The next time I write I will be in Camp Polk. It will be at least 7 days before I write again so don't expect any mail before that.

Your loving Son, Bob

Sept 28

Dear Mom, Dad.

I am writing this letter on a troop train, so don't mind the writing as it is jerking all the way. We left camp 5 o'clock this afternoon. We got a big send off from the T.D. They had their 60 piece band out and played all afternoon as our trains moved out. June was at the loading platform to see me off. We had 3 trains for the Btn. They were all at least ¾ mile long. It took 2 engines on each train. We sent the first train out at 1 o'clock and the second at 3. I am in the last. Joe Skelly and Ed Brady are on guard on the others. I didn't get stuck this time thank God as it is raining and has been all day. I am in a coach where it is warm and comfortable. I would hate to be out on the flat cars all nite in this weather.

We should hit Camp Polk in the early afternoon tomorrow. I got your letter and the Readers Digest just as the train left. I read them both all the way through. Tell Kitty that I will not be able to write until after we leave for P.O.E. as we won't get any time to ourselves here.

I don't know when I can mail this letter but I might get a chance to drop it out the window for someone to mail. So don't be surprised if it is mailed from some hick town here in Texas.

The train has stopped again. It seems to stop every mile or so. But I am used to this all these trains are the same.

We are getting coffee and donuts at midnite, don't you wish you could have them served to you while you lay on the nice soft floor. I will close now as I might get a chance to mail this soon.

Your Loving Son,

Bob

P.S. Did the watch and the other package come yet?

SELF PROPELLED GUN

Sept 29, 1943

Dear Mom, Dad,

I'll bet you couldn't imagine where I am at this time. I am in Louisiana at Camp Polk. It is 7 miles from Leesville in a bivouac area in the woods next to a swamp. Camp Polk is back about 2 miles from where we are. But here is the real surprise. I am in a black out area so could not use the flashlight to write so I put the tarp over the front of my "S.P." self propelled gun and turned on the headlights. I am now under the front bumper writing to you.

We got in camp at 3 o'clock this afternoon and went out to our home in the woods a soon as we got here. The ground is sandy and soft. The tanks sink in the dry ground about 14 inches. Wait till it rains! They will go in to the turret. It is very beautiful country here but it is the funniest place you ever heard of. All you have to do to get wash water is dig a hole in the ground and wait a few minutes and it is full of clear water.

We will camp here in the woods for 1 week and then we leave for maneuver Self propelled gun s all over the state and then some. We can always use eats if you can get them without points. We may have to go days with only a few canned rations.

I thought we had all the prisoners of ours at Camp Hood but you ought to see them here. We are only 1 mile from the largest prison camp I ever saw.

I can't tell you much today because I just got here but I will write in a day or two and let you know all about it. I gave a (letter) to the brake man on the train to mail to you. Did you get it? Where did he mail it?

Well I m going to try to get some sleep now so good nite for now,.

Good nite and Love to all

Bob

P.S. I don't know when I will get a chance to mail this letter.

Dear Mom, Dad,

I am in the same spot that I was last nite, under the S.P. It is still raining and hard. I am as dry and warm as if I was in a hotel room. I found out a little more about this place today. It is worse ground than I thought. We went on a scouting mission today to see how the ground would be for our tanks. It is all rivers and swamp. On high ground you sink in up to your knees in mud. In one spot we counted 7 bridges in 15000 yds. They were 16 ton capacity. We can not use them but we still have to cross the rivers. The engineers are going to have some job. We had 3 jeeps go in mud up over the engines already and we haven't even started maneuvers. Can you imagine how deep those 32 ton tanks will sink?

We were surprised this morning when we got up by 7 pigs running around camp. One big one and 6 small ones. One of the little ones crawled in bed with a buddy of mine and scared him half to death. They belong to some farmer about 6 miles away. He lets them run wild. We played with them all afternoon.

In the first letter I wrote you, which I did not have time to mail yet, I told you about the German prisoners they have here. They bake all the bread we have here. It is very good bread – looks like Jewish rye? We saw hundreds of them working in camp today. They are swell looking fellows and all well built. I got to Leesville today. What a hole!! I won't go there again.

Ed Brady got his Cpl rating today.

Joe Skelly is camped half mile through the swamp from me. I seen him early tonite. He got a different train from the one I was on and he got stuck in Houston for 4 hours (lucky bum) and seen the town.

I will put in with this one the letter I wrote you last nite and pray that I can mail them tomorrow as you will probably get another one in the same envelope. I have 2 rolls of film here so will send you some pictures as soon as we have some good wrecks as sunken tanks.

I will close for now and get some sleep.

Your loving Son,

Bob

P.S. We did not get any mail yet at our new address. It will start tomorrow.

Sept 28, 1943

Dear Mom, Dad.

It has stopped raining for a few hours at last. It has not cleared up though. I am up at Joe's tent. We are sitting around a fire and listening to Judy Canova on the radio. Cary Grant is now talking. We sure enjoy this portable out here in the woods. It is warm tonite for the first time since we been here. You didn't think that I would need the sweater but I can't wait til it gets here. We need a sweater every nite and morning here. I have been wearing my long Johns for the past week.

They took us into camp today on trucks to take a shower. It is the first one since we left Hood.

George Burns and Gracie Allen just came on.

Myself and a few of the boys were practicing Judo just before it got dark. Our company commander came over and told us he was pleased to see us so interested in our work. He had me teaching him some of the tricks I learned in school. I threw him a few times and he didn't mind it at all. He couldn't do much with me because I could tell what he was going to do. I have to give instructions Friday over in B Co.

I haven't received any letters yet at my new address.

I just got the first two letters I wrote you mailed tonite. God only knows when I will get this on its merry way.

The pigs raided our kitchen last nite and ate 100 lbs of potatoes and a bushel of apples. The light from the fire is not so good so I will close this letter pretty soon. The boys are starting to sing a few songs so I had better stop now.

I hope I get some mail tomorrow as I was about the only one not to get any today.

Your Loving Son,

Bob.

Sept 30

Dear Mom, Dad,

I haven't mailed the letter I wrote last nite yet but I am writing as often as I can because when I leave here for maneuvers on the 3rd I won't be able to write very often.

The latest is we found 5 coral snakes this morning between our blankets. They are more deadly than a rattler. They are very pretty snakes. All colors of the rainbow. We are going to set out guards for them tonite. I just heard from the orderly room that they have stopped all work until the cold weather on a big dam they are building here on account of snakes. They have been blasting the rock around it to kill the snakes. They got 65 snakes in one day.

The Jews got a 3 day pass for their New Years. It looks like a real riot will be taking place soon. If you remember they got one last Easter and when our Easter came they got off again and we did KP and guard.

I will have to close as it is getting dark and we have a blackout tonite again. As ever, Bob.

Sept 30, 1943
Dear Mom

Just a note to explain what I need done to these things if you don't mind.
1 films have printed and all good ones enlarged.
2 Mail me some more film
3 Their will be some more pictures mailed to you because I might have a new address by the time they are enlarged. send them to me.
4 Take soles to Crisanti and have them relined or fixed as best he can.
5 Find $2.00 as part payment until payday.
6 I will mail you letter tomorrow

Oct 2, 1943
Dear Mom, Dad,

We left the woods around Camp Polk last nite at 7 o'clock and drove a distance of 20 miles to the north. It was all cross country driving and through swamps. It took us until 3 o'clock this morning to reach here, in the middle of a big swamp. It was 20 miles on the map but I drove 41 miles. It was all in 1-2-3-4 gears. I only got into 5th gear once the whole trip. I got stuck up to the engine twice and had to use the winch to get out. We left one tank in the swamp in up to the turret. We will send the engineers back to get it.

We will leave here tonite and go into position for the first attack on the 3rd or 4th. It will be another 35 miles on the map. That means about 75 miles of rough driving tonite and from then on it will be steady driving day and nite. We are allowed 3 ½ hr sleep a nite now but once we start you can only sleep if you halt for a few minutes. We are attached to the 3rd army now. We are the only tank Btn on the blue side. The reds have the 749th and 742nd tank Btns plus the 1st tank group 2 tanks. The 749th started down in Bowie the same week we did. They are classed 4A and we are 2A. When we get in 1A we will be in the post of implementation.

We had a very serious accident last nite when the company commander of B company shot his first lieutenant through the lung with a 45 pistol. We can't find out whether it was an accident or a murder. If it's a murder it is the 3rd in our Btn. We had one in Cottonwood when someone killed a guy that worked in the PX. We never found out who did that yet. It is someone of us but no one will ever know, I guess, who it was. We had another in Hood in the PX when Skelly got in trouble for not shooting a TD who was trying to kill a First Sergeant. The First Sergeant was killed. I just got word that the officer that was shot still has a 50/50 chance to live. The captain is in the guard house. He was relieved of his command. Our best officer, the best in the Btn was just transferred to B Company to be company commander. That is one reason I never carry live rounds for my 45.

I am glad we got away from Polk because we would spend all our time chasing the German prisoners. I just heard that the guard that was taking those prisoners back to the stockade when I was on guard has had a relapse. He is not expected to live. I sent him a carton of cigarettes last week. I thought he was all better. That will make 4 murders. There are only 509 men in this Btn now. There are a good percentage of murders, don't you think?

We had 800 men to start. We lost 300 men either discharged or transferred for different reasons. I have to gas up now so will have to close.
Your Loving Son,
Bob

Oct 2
Dear Mom, Dad,

Well maneuvers are on, and we are off to a good start. They officially started 1 hour ago. Two umpires just came around to inspect our camp. They came to my S.P. and when they came the Captain was on the running board shaving. They couldn't even see him. They said it was hidden very good. They said you could hardly tell it was a dispatch car. You should have heard the captain laugh. They did not even see the 37mm gun. We worked on it 7 hours so it should have been good. They almost fell in our fox hole before they seen it. We make our first attack tomorrow sometime. We are about to leave here any minute. We will be driving steady from now on. We have all nite to get here. It is very pretty country. Lots of big trees and about 10 miles up a dirt road from town. There is a farm house between here and town. I got about 50 lbs of hickory nuts in my S.P. We found horse chestnuts too. I haven't seen them since we used to get them in Kriegers yard. We killed a rattle snake last nite as we left our camp. He was under the S.P. This morning we killed a coral snake and a black snake 4 ½ ft long. We are near a lake full of alligators but I haven't met any of them yet. We were bombed yesterday with flour sacks.

We will start toward southern Louisiana tonite in blackout. We are the blue army. The red army will start north until we contact them. Then we fight it out til someone gets to their destination.

I haven't received any mail for 4 days as it can't catch up with us. We may get it once in two weeks if we are lucky. I guess I will get a pile of mail when it does get here. The chow whistle just blew so I will go get my last hot meal for some time.

Your loving son

Bob

P.S. The mosquitoes are thick and as big as your fist.

Oct 9

Dear Mother, Dad.

It is nite now and we are in a rest camp. And I might add a well deserved rest. The last time I wrote to you, I told you that maneuvers had started. I had no idea how hard or how nerve racking it really is. Just after I finished writing to you last time, we left our camp. We were blacked out. We drove over the worst stretch of country I have ever seen. How we ever got across it is beyond me. It took us 11 hours to go 21 miles. The road or cow path as you would call it was hardly wide enough to get a jeep through. And the trees were too big to knock down with a tank. So we went as best we could. The whole 21 miles are lined with fenders, bumpers and bows and tarps from the trucks. I was the luckiest guy in the whole 3rd army that nite. I never even scratched the paint. I did hit two stumps which stopped me in my tracks, but otherwise we didn't even so much as knock the (*illegible*) of the sides. It was so dark that the top Sergeant who rides with me had to get out and walk in front of me for two miles at a time. He would carry a dim out flashlight so I could see him. I went over 40 or 50 bridges made of two by fours that I never even seen that were only about 8 feet wide and no side rails. Lots of times I would hear the back wheels bump off the last board on the bridge. It was the coldest nite I ever seen. I put on the tops of my long johns and two pair of coveralls and a field jacket. We were still frozen. We finally came to a deep mud hole. There were 3 tanks stuck in the mud and there was no sense us trying to get the wheel vehicle through. We called up a company of engineers to get us through. We took 3 tanks to knock down trees and 3 bulldozers and 400 men and we built a new road around this creek bed. In ½ hour we were rolling. We finally came to a farmyard and they told us we had reached our destination. I pulled out a blanket and went to sleep in the front yard. One hour later I was awakened by the tap kid. It was starting to get light. We hid our vehicles and waited to be called to the front lines to support the 84th infantry division and the 99 infantry division.

We had no water and no place to get it that we knew of. It is my job to get it or find out where we can get it. This is where my training came in. We had special training to find where water is most likely to be. I went out and scouted the countryside. I found a good looking spot but there was a farm yard up the creek about 200 yards and it was red territory beyond the farm house. I went back to the 84th infantry and got 3 platoons of foot troops and a platoon of engineers.

There were two lieutenants in command. We went back to the road and the infantry made their attack. I fired blanks to counter their attack. My 37 sure sounded good as it was the only major small gun in the attack. We were beaten back and had to send for a mortar platoon which put the odds in our favor and we took the water and the engineers put up a filtering tank in 1 hour. We sent for the water trucks and on their way to the water, the red planes bombed them and then their ground troops brought up the whole 742nd medium tank Btn and we were all killed. That's just one example of what we are doing.

We have had about 75 trucks and tanks turn over in 3 days. No one was hurt very bad. The tanks left us the first day of this problem and I have been scouting around the front lines finding their location and getting parts and once in a while I sneak them some extra iron rations. I get fired on every once in a while and get a chance to fire on them.

We pulled in to this rest camp early this morning and built fires and went to sleep. This morning my assistant gunner found the soles of his shoes left where the whole shoe was. The only thing left of his leggings was the buckle and his blanket had a hole in it about 3 ft in diameter. He is from Wall St Cranford. He knows the Albans and worked with Calis Detzel on the coal trucks. His name is Joe Hogen.

I got your package today and it was just what I wanted the sweater is swell. The knife is the best you can buy and just what I wanted. It might save my life some day, if I get bit by a snake. I will need the blades next week as mine are just about gone. I got two darn post cards from New York after waiting a week. I don't know if it is lost or if you didn't write.

Don't put HQ platoon on my address any more as they mistake it for HO company and it takes me an extra few days to get it. I am glad Roy likes the shirt. I didn't think it would fit him. I would like to taste some of your chili sauce as it was always good when you made it. We get all the good food we want but it still isn't your cooking. I have to get some sleep so good nite all.
Your Son,
Bob

Oct 11
Dear Mom, Dad.

The mail just came in for the first time in a week and a half. I got so many letters I didn't know where to start. I got 3 and a card from you and 1 from Dad and 1 from Nisters and 2 from Jane.

You asked me about the medals. I didn't know that you wanted them. As soon as I finish this letter I will see if I can find some of them and put them in the letter. I am keeping 2 of them to wear on my blouse when we change uniform. We had to turn in the cheap ones like I brought home and we got silver ones.

I think I told you about the sweater getting here. I wear it every nite and morning, as it is just as cold here at nite as it is at home.

We are going to reorganize the Btn after maneuvers. We are getting in a company of light tanks with us, also a mortar platoon. The company commander called me to his tank late last nite told me that I would be tank commander in one of the new light tanks because I was one of the few who had a license to drive one. I told him if he made me a tank commander I would go over the hill so he would have to bust me. I told him I would not be a sergeant under any conditions. I just want to be one of the boys and not have to give too many orders. Joe Skelly wants to be a pvt again too. We had so much fun when we had no stripes and no worries. We get blamed for everything that happens that is wrong and if we do something good we don't get the credit because the officers get it all.

I had to take a smart alec [redacted by author] out in the woods and pound some sense in his head yesterday. He couldn't see why he had to stand crew drill with the rest of us. I don't care if he does burn to death when we turn over but he isn't going to be on my gun unless he can get out and not block the way for us. I get so mad at these guys I can hardly stop from killing them. That's all I would need is someone getting burned up on my gun and I would be tried for neglect of duty in not having enough crew drill.

The officer that was shot is out of danger now. I guess the captain that shot him feels better.

Skelly's tank broke down on the road yesterday and he didn't get in camp til 6 this morning. He is lucky we didn't pull out early this morning and leave him. We are waiting for a call from the infantry to come and help them.

We are getting ready to move out so good bye for now.

Your loving son,

Bob

We are supposed to go to camp Swift after the maneuvers. Guess what state that's in. I will tell you in the next letter.

10/12/43

Dear Mother, Dad,

The two letters that you mailed Sunday arrived yesterday. I am sorry to hear that Helen is sick again. It seems she has a bad spell every year about this time. I am glad you think it is not muddy around here. It is not sand and it is not hot. It rains every day and we march up to our ankles in mud.

We had a bunch of nurses from the GI Hospital here to see our tanks yesterday. Ours are the first tanks ever in this camp and they never seen a tank before. We took them for a ride in the afternoon. I had a nurse as tank commander and asst drivers. I gave them a ride they will never forget. I hit trees and went through big ditches and all kinds of maneuvers. They couldn't get enough of it. We had them out all afternoon and they still wanted to ride some more. Everyone stops work and watches us ride by in the camp. They can't get over how fast we can drive through the woods. All kinds of high ranking officers come to see us drive.

It looks as if we aren't going to be in this camp long. We will probably leave within a month or two. All I hope is that I get out of there on my way home before they move. It is only 9 more days til I leave. Once I leave here I don't care if they move to California the next day.

There is an article in the camp paper about us, I will bring it home to you. It is about how the boys acted when we got back in a building with heat and water and lights.

We got a big inspection tomorrow but I am not going to get ready for it as I have had about all the inspections I intend to stand for a while. Every day some big shot gets an idea he wants to inspect and we are supposed to stand on our heads to get ready for him. If they don't like the way my equipment is now it's just too bad because I'm not working any more today. All they can do is give me extra duty and I will get out of that.

My feet are still sore from the 25 mile hike. We made it in 7 hours. That is 1 hour less time than the infantry does it.

I need a new pair of shoes now as there is no soles left on my shoes. I hope to get them before I am home. You shouldn't have bought those things for the Lakes. They wouldn't want you to do it, but they will appreciate it.
There is nothing else new so I will close and go to supper.
Your loving son
Bob

Oct 15
Dear Mother, Dad,
    I am sorry that I can't hold my end up on the letter writing but I know you understand the reason why I can't.
It really is tough but I wouldn't miss it for anything. We have fun no matter what they put us through. Last nite the second problem ended and we were allowed to have fires. We were feeling pretty low and tired out, but as usual Joe Skelly came to the rescue. He and half the third platoon came over to my camp and dragged my crew and I out of our blankets and back to the third platton area. They had coffee and bread and jam and a few mickeys in the fire. Joe started to sing some of his funny songs as only he can sing them, such as "The Old Red drawers that Maggy used to wear" and "Who put the Overalls in Mrs. Murphy's Chowder". He knows a hundred verses to all those songs. And you should hear his voice. He has a real Irish tenor voice. He would sing the verse and we all came in on the chorus. After an hour or so of that we got out the old portable radio and heard Joan Davis and Bing Crosby and a few others. I was thinking of you when Bing was singing because I am almost sure you were listening.

    Your package or I should say packages came last week just after I wrote you last. I am sorry I couldn't write you as soon as they arrived. The mail is coming in pretty good now. It makes us all feel better to know that everything is alright at home. That's the only worry we have in the world. It is a big worry when we don't hear from home.

I can hardly see the lines on the paper now as the fire is going down.

I had to hide in the woods and eat my shrimp. I would share my blankets or my last drop of water with anyone that needed them but not my one and only can of shrimp. Our food is scarce now out here in the field. We get enough to eat but it is cooked terrible because the kitchen is moved so often that they don't have time to cook anything right.

You asked me about my Christmas package. I don't need anything that I can think of so don't spend a lot of money on anything because I probably won't be able to use it. All I want for Christmas is to be home with all of you. If I can manage that it will be my happiest Christmas. I am trying to figure out what I can get for you. There isn't anything in the south that is worthwhile buying. People down here can't afford any good things so they just don't have anything. I will figure something out by that time though.

We came to a swell spot in the woods for a rest camp this time. There are beautiful pine trees and a creek only a few hundred feet away. I took a bath in it this afternoon. It was the first time I had my shoes off in 8 days. And 8 days ago I only had them off for 10 minutes while I washed my feet in a bucket. I have had my shoes and leggings and pistol belt on all the time except for about 30 minutes since I left Camp Hood 18 days ago. Yes I burned my socks after I got them off. We move sometimes 3 or 4 times a day and we are not allowed to get undressed at any time. If you are caught sleeping with your shoes off you are court marshaled.

We are rationed to 1 gal of water per day. We have to wash our face and hands and brush our teeth and shave every day and we can drink any water that's left of the gallon. That must sound pretty bad to you but after a while you get used to it. One of our officers that was in the battle in Africa said all but the killing this training is 3 times as bad as battle. He said when we get over we will have a picnic compared to this. He said that our men would get caught taking a bath or sleeping undressed and be all killed before they could get their clothes on. He said they wanted the ones that are not strong enough to stand this filth to get sick now and not on the other side. For every man that gets sick over there it takes 4 men to take care of him.

I am sleeping with my shoes off tonite and it feels so good I never want to put them on again.

Did you ever get those arches fixed that I sent home to you? I can use them now as these don't get time to dry out.

It will be some time before I can send you any socks again as I am burning mine every time I get time to change them and I will have to make up the shortage.

Tell Roy to wear my coat that I sent home because I don't want it wasted this winter. The rain coat will come in handy some day too. Don't be afraid to wear it. I wear mine every nite. It helps to keep out the cold. I have had my sweater on for a week now and no intention of taking it off til it is warm out or summer gets here again. I have my woolen undershirt and my fatigues and field jacket and the sweater and rain coat and still freeze every nite while driving. The other nite we made a fast drive over 45 minutes of rough ground. It was the coldest nite I ever remember. We froze til we were numb and I couldn't even feel the steering wheel. We don't have any top or any windshield. I would have given a month's pay for a hot coffee.

I am glad Roy is on the team this year. I always wanted to get on it but I am glad he made it anyway. All the boys are glad to get the scores. We have some boys from Roselle Park and Cranford and Carteret and all the towns around. I am always bragging about Roy being on the Linden team. We have some big arguments about who has the best teams.

I can't see any more as my eyes are strained from the blackout driving so I will have to close now.
Your Loving Son,
Bob
P.S. I received a letter from Kitty and a paper from Grand Pa.

Oct 20
Dear Mom, Dad,
We have been on a problem ever since the last time I wrote to you. We are in the middle of an attack now. I am in reserve and won't be called up til late in the morning. It is just after sunrise now, and as cold as I have ever seen it. We have been driving all nite to reach our attack position. We traveled over 40 miles in rough country since 4 o'clock yesterday afternoon. That is 13 hours of driving and 20 minutes break. Our kitchen truck has been captured and we ran out of food 3 days ago. I don't know what it feels like to have my belly full any more. The rations have been cut in half and we don't get any water unless we come across it by accident. We don't stay in one place long enough to locate water fit to drink. I am pretty near thirsty enough to drink this bottle of ink that sets before me, as we haven't had a drink since yesterday morning when we had a cup of coffee that we begged from the anti aircraft batteries.

We have had two airplane crackups in the last 3 days. One was a P39 that hit a tree and the other a cub that had to make a forced landing. He hit a stump and went over on his nose. Yesterday a P38 one of those two tail jobs come down so low he clipped the radio antenna on the tank that Dick Papori drives. We have hundreds of planes dive at us every day.

The nite before last we laid down a barrage of artillery and machine gun fire at a big hill that was supposedly being held by enemy infantry. It was the first time in this maneuver that we fired live ammunition. We used tracer bullets. I fired 150 rounds of 37 mm shells. 50 tanks fired their 75mm and 3 machine guns on each other at the same time. Each tank fired 25 rounds of 75mm and each machine gun fired 700 rounds. That was 150 machine guns and 50 – 75 mm guns and 20 - 37mm guns. All firing was done in 14 minutes. It sounded like thunder, and lit up the area for miles around. Every time I fired my gun the whole carriage would leave the ground and it was so noisy I could hardly hear my own guns go off. After I fired 60 rounds the barrel of the gun was red hot, but we kept on firing. We looked the area over in the day time and not a mouse could have lived on that hill. It was just a mass of shell holes. General Gillem the head of the whole armored force was in a jeep not 1000 feet away from me. He sent our Btn commander a letter to be read to all the men. He said we are one of the best Btn's ever turned out in this country.

I got your letter telling about Radio City just before we left last nite. I am glad to see you are having a good time at home, and only wish that I could be going with you to NY once in a while.

Well Dad I hope it rains so you can get a day off. How long did it take you to finish your boat this time? It seems to me you are always getting a new one. They must be really working to get them out so fast.

The new Ford tanks that are coming out are all welded and are they fast. You can go 50 miles per hour on a road with them, and they have all the new inventions that will help us to shoot better and a lot of safety devices. Some of the welding looks like those women welders get at them but on the whole they are not bad. I have to clean my pistol now so must close soon.

How did Roy make out in the game with Perth Amboy? What position on the team does he play?

I hope Dad and Roy get some time to write once in a while. I am sure they have more time than I do to themselves. Don't worry about me going over before I see you. I will be home sometime around Christmas. I was going to try to get home sooner but I am trying to get one of the holidays at home. I got to start on my guns so good bye for now.
Your Loving Son,
Bob

Oct 24,
Dear Mother, Dad,

We have just finished a 3 day break. It has been the best week we have had. Joe Skelly and I made the best of it too. We pulled into the rest camp 4 o'clock Thurs morning. Joe was stuck back at a river crossing up to the turret. He came dragging in about midnite. We got in to a state forest of pines and hickory trees. It is very pretty with the leaves all turning color. The first day we just worked on our tanks and at nite we bought real southern fried chicken from the farmer. We watched them kill the chickens and fry them. We each got one and went back to camp and ate them around the camp fire. It was delicious. In the morning I got a gallon of milk from the farmer and he wouldn't let me pay for it. I only got about

1 small cup of milk out of the gallon because we hadn't had milk since we left Cottonwood camp. I was mobbed.

Here is where the surprise comes in. Early Saturday morning Joe and I start to sneak out of camp. Everyone was asleep we thought, so we dressed in our woolen uniforms and started out through the woods right past the 'old man' Cap Stuart. He didn't even open his eyes when we went past but when we got about 25 feet past him he said 'Cadmus!!!!! Take a jeep and go to Shreveport and get me a paper, and when you get back in the morning don't wake me up.' I almost died when he hollered my name but we ran and jumped in the jeep and took off before he could change his mind. Joe and I decided to go to Mansfield and then to Keithville and on to Shreveport 200 miles away. We got to Shreveport about noon. The first thing we did was go as usual to the USO and get a hot shower. We were surprised to see the best USO club we ever saw. It looked like a millionaire's mansion. We met a girl that worked at the fountain there and found out she was married to Sarg. Bland in C company. We left the jeep in the USO and walked to the Strand the best show in town and seen Sahara with Humphrey Bogart. It was all about tanks but it was not real enough. The tank they drove was an M3, the kind we learned on (the Gen Grant). We then drove around town for a while and went to the state fair on the outside of town. It was pretty good. We started back early and got to Mansfield about 9 at nite. We got something to eat and got going again. We hit Pleasant Hill at midnite and got to camp about 4 in the morning. Joe was driving up to our area when all of a sudden he jammed on the brakes and sat there looking at me. Finally he came out with 'We forgot the old man's paper.' I took the wheel and we drove 22 miles to Many to get a paper. We had to wait til 6 in the morning for it and got back to camp at 7:30 in the morning. The problem started at 12:00 noon today but we haven't been ordered out yet.

I am getting mail every day now and am glad to hear from you so often. For a while I didn't get any but you are making up for it now.

The Linden High paper came but got all wet and fell apart before I got it. I'm glad you got 3 days off Dad. I got 3 off too but I had to work 2 days after the 3 to get 1 off altogether.

I have some more work to do on my tommy gun as it got wet last nite. I spent all morning cleaning my pistol. That's all I can think of so goodbye to all.
Your loving Son,
Bob
You are right about Camp Swift.

Oct 27
Dear Mother, Dad.

Your Christmas package came yesterday and it was swell. The watch is working fine. I got a bottle of fluid for the lighter and it is swell. I always wanted a good lighter but never wanted to spend so much for it. I ate the candy in the box. It was the best I have had since I got in the army.

Both your letters got here this morning. I hope your back is better Dad. You seem to have trouble every year about this time. It is getting colder every day here. I have my wool gloves on now while I am writing. I have been shivering for the past 3 days as we are not allowed to build fires during a problem. I have a 2 day beard on now and am hoping I don't get caught. It is too cold to shave now.

I have a woolen undershirt on and your sweater and coveralls and a field jacket. I am still trying to find something else to put on. I wear my rain coat too while driving to keep out the wind. If you come across some of my old cotton t-shirts please send them down.

Guess what: Joe Skelly got busted. He didn't put grease in his back wheels. The captain heard about it and busted him yesterday. He is so happy as he has no responsibility any more. McGuire, and Capala and Daname, Seaton, Dick Papari and Lapapri all corporals were busted today as they are all over the hill. They all went out on our last break and did not come back on time and we moved out of the rest camp so they will never find us until we get to another rest camp next week. I am the only one left of our old crowd that haven't been busted this week. In the past month we have had 2 staff sergeants, 3 buck sergeants and 13 corporals broken. We have 28 men under arrest of quarters until we get to a new camp to be court marshaled. There are 9 men in the guard house of Camp Polk and 7 in Camp Hood. All from A Company. We only have 127 men to a company and now we are so short handed that in some tanks there are only 2 or 3 men instead of 5. We got 8 replacements from Ft. Knox. With them and the men in the guard house we will have enough to bring us up to full strength again. It will be 6 months before we get all our men back from the guard house, but then we will have another 30 in by that time. These men don't care if they do go to the guard house because they get worse treatment here than they can give you at the guard house. In the guard house you work for 8 hours and drill for 3 hours and 1 hour on the rock pile and you are done for the day. And you have a nice warm bed to sleep in and good food. Here you work 24 hours a day and try to steal a nap on the cold ground once in a while. Ed Reinhart thinks he has it tough. He ought to be here. It would kill him. If he has a sore arm now tell him to wait til he gets his yellow fever shot. It makes you sick for a week. I have walked 24 hour guard with my arm so sore I dropped my gun on the ground.

We are camped in a woods near Zoolie waiting for it to get dark so we can move into an attack position on the reds. We will probably make an attack in the morning. It is going to be a miserable nite as we can't get warm and we will drive probably til 3 or 4 o'clock and make an attack at 5 which will last until nite when we will move again to a new attack point.

Maneuvers will be all over in 2 weeks and then we will know for sure where we are going. It still looks like Camp Swift Texas. I won't mind going back to Texas now, just to get warm and dry. We are worried though because all big towns such as Ft Worth and Dallas – Austin are off limits to all men in uniform because of the fuel shortage. We will be about 15 miles from Austin and won't be able to go there. Furloughs are out now because of all the men in the guard house. We can't spare the men we have got now so I guess I won't be home til after Christmas. I was all set to get a furlough the 19 of December but it looks bad now. That is one reason I have been keeping out of trouble. The other is I might want to stay in after the war and don't want any bad reports on my service record.

I just heard the Yanks won the series and Notre Dame is going strong. I get the daily news after it is 2 weeks old but it is better than nothing.

We are getting a new major. His name is Nelson. He is now a captain and used to be Col Brown's right hand man. He is a very good soldier even though he did ball me out this morning for having a rust spot on my pistol. I still can't understand how it got there. It must have been the gremlins. It is the first gig I have ever gotten on any of my guns.

We are also getting a Lt Col. I hope he is better than the one we got now. We heard that Col Brown has made good up at Knox and is up for Brig General. I will let you know when he gets it. That is 1 star. You wait and see if this war lasts another year you will be reading about him in the paper along with McArthur and such.

The tanks are warming up now so we will be leaving in about an hour. I still have a little time so will try to finish this page.

In 2 more months I will be allowed to change my insurance into a 20 year life. I want your advice on the matter. It will cost about double. So I thought 5000 would be all I could afford in outside life at that price. I will keep the other 5000 until the war is over and just change the one policy. Should I pay the extra money to them and get this year counted on the 20 years or just start when I change over and have 20 years to pay. If you don't understand what I mean ask me what you don't understand in your next letter.

I am freezing now and it is getting colder so I will close and warm up my engine.

Your Son

Bob

Oct 28

Dear Mother, Dad,

I received another letter from you today. They are coming in every day now.

We just finished another problem. I have been driving ever since I finished writing you the last letter. 36 hours steady driving and only 2 hour break altogether during the trip. The country was so bad that we only averaged 3 miles per hour. Last nite was one of the worst nites I ever put in, in all my life. I was so tired I could not hold my eyes open. I had a bad headache from not eating, and we almost froze to death. I was so cold I was numb all over. My hands were so stiff from cold I couldn't feel the steering wheel and besides that we were driving as usual without lights. It was one of the darkest nites I ever seen. My eyes were almost popping out trying to keep in the clear. I hit a stump when we were going 10 miles per hour. It stopped me so short my head left my ears.

I was following Joe Skelly over a rough stretch of ground. He was about 200 ft in front of me. All I could see was two lights that look like cigarettes on his tail. All of a sudden I saw those lights go end over end. Joe's driver missed a bridge. I was shocked more than he was. I never expected to see him alive again. Joe was standing in the turret and when I got to the tank it was upside down standing on the turret. I ran down and looked at the turret and the doors were snapped off and it was buried in 2 ft of dirt. I then went to the driver's hatch; it too was buried. The timber from the bridge had the escape hatch blocked and the only other way out was the asst driver's hatch. It was 9 inches from the ground. It popped open and Mike from Plainfield came out uninjured, then the driver came out. He said he couldn't see Joe coming so I went in and expected to see a mass of bones and flesh but instead I seen Joe's boney head come squirming out of the basket singing 'Mrs Murphy's Chowder'.

I will finish in the morning.

As soon as I was sure everyone was alright we started out again. Joe and his crew stayed there. I went back last nite and gave them some C and K rations. The tank is still there. The driver was just starting to get shakey 12 hours after it was all over. He saved their lives by using his head. He pulled the battery switch as soon as he felt the tank going over. If he didn't they would all have been burned to death. We found the MP who was supposed to guide the tanks around the bridge asleep by a tree. He will be tried by a Generals court marshal. The least he will get is 5 years of hard labor. He is lucky nothing happened to Joe or he wouldn't live to get tried. I gave Joe my camera last nite so he could take some pictures of the tank today. I will send you the films as soon as I finish the roll. I have a picture of a tank I turned over. You can see the one I turned over by the gun. It is still showing. Joe's gun is buried in the mud. There isn't much danger as long as you use your head and pull the battery switch and use your safety belts. Joe's case was no exception.

We are going to reorganize our outfit as soon as maneuvers are over. I am leaving my S.P. They say they are obsolete. Instead I get a 105mm mortar on a medium tank chassis. It looks the same as the rest of the tanks except for a much larger gun. It has 8 men in the crew and 640 HP engine. It weighs 87 tons. Top speed 38 mph. The gun shoots 9 miles with accuracy. I am going to try and get Joe as gunner. If I do he will get his stripes back.

We also get a company of light tanks. They tried to get me in them but I wouldn't go. We will have 54 med tanks 80 trucks 80 half tracks 17 light tanks 6 motorcycles 16 jeeps 4 seeps 3, 105mm mortar tanks. The new tanks cost $80,000 apiece. The light tanks about $35,000 – Half tracks $9,000 trucks $2,000. That is pretty expensive equipment for 650 men. That will be the 4th time we got new equipment and wore it out. I would like to know how much money is invested in each man here, wouldn't you?

Each tank uses 150 gal of gas in 8 hours so you can see why there is a gas shortage. I have driven 3000 miles so far on maneuvers and only get about 50 miles on paved roads. I got 850 miles of blackout driving. I got a drivers medal for not having an accident in 1500 miles.

I have to close now as we are having a physical exam at 10 o'clock. I will write soon as possible. Maneuvers are over next week.

Your son
Bob

Nov 13,
Dear Mother, Dad,

I haven't had the chance to send you a wire saying that I arrived all right, so I will tell you all about it now.

We got to Mt Joy about 9:30 Tuesday morning. The prisoners were not ready so we came back for them in the afternoon at three. We went to the Roxey in the meantime. We saw Rosey O'Grady and Danny Kaye on the stage. He was swell. The whole show was fine.

I put the prisoners in the city jail and Joe and I went out and had a swell time. We met 5 girls that worked in the Red Cross (service men's canteen). They got off duty at 7 o'clock. We got 3 other soldiers and all went out together. We had supper at the best restaurant in town. I used the (G.I.) meal tickets so it didn't cost us anything. Then we went to a show and saw 'Swing Shift Maisie', a swell picture. We then went to Hazel's house (that was my girl) and had coffee and coke. We left there 3 in the morning. We were heading back to the railroad station when the MP's picked us up for being out. We got back to Joy at 3 and picked up the boys. We went to Grand Central Station. We had to wait until 7:30 for the train. I let them call up their families. Farra's family came over, to see them off. We got a swell train to St. Louis. We arrived there the next nite at 7:30. Just 24 hours. We were late and missed the other train. We had to wait in St. Louis until midnite for the next train. We went to the Fox Theatre and seen Roy Rogers on the stage. The picture was rotten. We got in Texarkana Thursday afternoon and missed the early train to Leesville. We were stuck there 23 hours. After curfew they took us to the MP station and we had to prove we were on special orders. They let Joe and I go but held the other 8. I don't know or care whether they got out today or not. After all they should know better than to go out after 11 o'clock.

We got a train at 11 o'clock this afternoon and got to Shreveport at 1:30. We had another layover there for 3 hours. We got into this camp about 9 o'clock tonite. We are in tents. We will be here until our company comes for us. I have to stay up and watch the prisoners so I am catching up on my mail while on guard. I am going to write to June and Hazel yet tonite so I will close now.

Your loving Son, Bob

Nov 13
Dear GrandPa Ma; Helen,

I am just dropping a line to let you know that I arrived here at Camp Polk all right. We had no trouble at all with the prisoners. I put them in jail in Texarkana for 23 hours. That gave me some time to have some fun and get a little sleep. The trip took us over 3 days but it wasn't because of the breaks in between. We also stopped in St. Louis and seen a show.

I want to thank you again for everything and it was swell seeing you all again. I have to go and eat now so goodbye until next time.

As ever, Bob

Nov 16

Dear Mom, Dad,

We finally caught up to the company. They were over in Texas, just across the Sabine River. We were 15 days away from the company. It was a swell break to get home and not have to pay for it. We had more fun in that 15 days than any other pass I have ever had.

I still have my prisoners to watch as they will not be put in jail until we get to Camp Swift Texas.

I got 13 letters and a package when I got back. I didn't open the package last nite because I thought it was only clothes. I opened it this morning and found the shrimp. It was good on bread and a bottle of catsup.

As soon as I came in last nite Joe Skelly came over to me and said they were going to transfer him to the light tank co. We went over to see the top Sgt and had his name taken off the list. That was a close one, as I would hate to get separated from Joe.

I hear we are supposed to get in Camp Swift Texas on or about the 25th of Nov. We will reorganize the Btn in Polk I think.

My shoes came back from salvage. Now I can turn in these old ones. I can't think of any more new so will sign off.

Your Loving Son

Bob

Nov 19,

Dear Mother, Dad.

Maneuvers are all over but we are still living in the woods. We will leave here next Monday or Tuesday for Camp Swift Texas. Last nite was the coldest I have ever seen in the woods. I could not sleep so I got up and set by the fire along with the rest of the boys.

This morning we are having inspections on the tanks and our personal equipment. There is nothing new yet except that some of the boys are going to get furloughs around Christmas. Two more men went A.W.O.L. this morning. They are from Jersey too. Maybe I will be able to go after them sometime.

The sun is coming up and it looks like it will be a hot day. Joe Skelly is going to get his stripes back soon. He is going to be gunner on the 105 mm howitzer with me.

I got rid of the prisoners yesterday. It is good to have that worry off your mind.

I didn't get any mail today, but I got a letter from you and one from June and another from Hazel in Texarkana. When are you going to get the pictures for me? I thought they would be in today's mail.

I have been telling the boys all about the meals you gave me while I was home and are they jealous. We are still getting ham. Three times a day for over five weeks. I like it as I got a break while I was home.

I am going to sleep in the woods today for a while to make up for last nite. It will be time for chow by the time I address this letter.

Start using this new address.

Cpl R Cadmus
747 Tank Btn Co A – M
32603063
Camp Swift Texas

Your loving Son
Bob

Read this letter first

Thanksgiving Eve
Dear Mom, Dad.

Yes I am still at Camp Polk but won't be when you get this letter. We have been held up here because of poor railroad facilities. The tanks are going out now on their way to the train. We will leave here 6 in the morning. Thanksgiving dinner will be served here in the woods tonite about 9 o'clock. I will let you know how it is in my next letter.

I hope you were able to get a turkey dinner this year as they are so hard to get. I am getting my turkey twice in a month, but the meal they will give us here doesn't compare with the one you gave to me at home.

I hope Roy can stay out of the army until after he gets out of school. It would be tough to have to quit after all this time.

Roy I am sorry I couldn't buy you a birthday present or at least send a card but maybe next year it will be a little different. We can't get anything down here that would even resemble a birthday card. Let me know when you expect to go in the army and Joe and I will figure out a way for me to get home before you leave. I can make it a lot easier for you if I can explain what to look out for and what not to do. The army is only tough if you make it that way for yourself.

Joe and I went into camp last nite and seen a movie as there was nothing else to do in that camp. We seen Henry Aldridge in 'Haunted House' and 'The Great Gildersleeve'. They were both full of laughs but only second rate pictures. We walked 3 miles into the show and 3 miles back. We got back about midnite. It was too cold to sleep so we sat up around the fire all nite. I will get some sleep this afternoon in the warm sun. The temp was down to 35 last nite but it felt like zero because of the dampness.

I am going to Camp Swift in a truck. I chose the truck because we will layover in Beaumont Texas for a half day and we can have some fun looking the place over.

There is nothing new here yet so I will close wishing you all a Happy Thanksgiving and happy birthday to Roy.

Your Son,

Bob

Dear Mom, Dad

I got a letter from Mr. Lake's stepdaughter. She is only 12 years old. I thought you would enjoy reading it so am sending it along. I think from the letter you can see what kind of people they are.

Bob

Mr. Mrs. H.M. Lake
2206 Freeman St
Houston Texas

Read this last

Nov 26

Dear Mother, Dad,

We finally got out of the woods and into a swell barracks.. I just got here a few minutes ago so I don't know much about it. We have hot showers and beds with a mattress. There is a movie about 200 yds from here and a PX next to it. There are busses in to Austin. There are German prisoners all over camp. They have them working in front making sidewalks. I wrote you a letter the other day but lost it before I had time to mail it.

We had turkey dinner in the woods Thanksgiving Eve. It was delicious. We drove through Houston Tex on our way here and camped 1 nite on the outskirts of town. Joe and I got in to town 7:30 at nite on the 25th. We went to the USO and took a shower and shave and a swim in the pool. We went upstairs and a family took us to dinner at their house. They were the nicest people I have ever come across. Joe and I and three sailors went there and they had 9 chickens, mashed potatoes, candied sweet potatoes, pickles, dressing, biscuits, apple pie, lemon pie, and devils food cake, coffee, cigars, candy. The food was cooked perfect. I couldn't get enough of her sweet potatoes and I never ate them before. Their name is Young. They have 3 children all of them swell kids. A boy 5 years old and 2 girls about 12 or 13. I will put in the address so you can write to them. Joe has the address so I will put it in before I mail this letter.

It is raining and has been all day. It is cold and the trip was rotten except for the stop in Houston. There were 24 men in each truck and each had a barracks bag. You couldn't even breathe we were so jammed.

I just heard that we are going to get another complete turkey dinner. We were supposed to get here 2 days ago so they delivered the turkeys here also. That will be 3 dinners for me this year.

I can't think of anything else now so I will close now. If I find the other letter I will send it along too.

Your loving Son

Bob

WESTERN UNION
NT185 8/7 COLLECT=BASTROP TEX 28 1243P
MRS OLIVE CADMUS
10 GRESSER AVE LINDEN NJ

SEND $50 FURLOUGH EXPECTED IN DECEMBER
 CPL ROBERT CADMUS

Nov 28,

Dear Mom, Dad.

I guess you were surprised to get the telegram, but I had to do it so I am broke and need to have all my clothes cleaned and pressed and get railroad ticket. I wouldn't need it but we didn't get paid because of change of station. I can't understand why you didn't get mail. I wrote a few letters anyway.

I am supposed to get a 15 day furlough starting the 14th of Dec. I had to pull some strings to get it but it was worthwhile.

Our camp is called Wake Island. It is about 8 miles from the main camp. There are only 2 Btns of tanks here. 749 and 747th. The 749 was with us down in Camp Bowie. They started the same time as we did but they never left Bowie until maneuvers when they fought against us. We have a swell movie here. I seen Dorothy Lamore in 'Riding High' last nite. We get all the best pictures.

We are 8 miles from the main camp and we have 2 busses a day out of camp. Otherwise you have to work. That's the reason it is called Wake Island. You can't get in or out of the place. As soon as the money comes I will try to get a pass into Austin and get my clothes fixed up. I am so broke I had to borrow a nickel to call Western Union.

I will close now as it is time for chow.

Your Son

Bob

Nov 28

Dear Grand Pa, Ma, Helen

Yes I am back in good old Texas. I am getting to like the place. After all this time I am not only in Texas but in barracks again after 6 mo in the woods. We have a movie near camp and everything you could ask for. We will be here for a short time as we are ready to go overseas any time they need us. This is a combat camp. We have only combat tanks here. It is a camp for men to build them selves up and get ready for battle. We get all the food we want, plenty of sleep and we can go out to the firing range any time we want and fire any gun we think we need practice in. We have a 10 mile hike every other day and a 25 mile hike every Saturday. Two hours of exercise every day and 2 hours of drilling.

I will be home for Christmas. Mom wrote and told me you were having a big party so I thought I would drop in about the 16th til the 30th for a little visit.

I got your letter Helen but couldn't answer it because of the change in station. It has been so long I have forgotten what was in it so I hope you will excuse me for now answering your questions.

We have a big prisoner of war camp here. We get all the dangerous ones here because this camp is so well guarded with all these combat troops here. I seen in the paper where 8 more Germans escaped from camp Hood. I don't know whether they have captured them yet or not. We have them working in our barracks and building roads in our camp. They seem to be happy. They are always laughing and fooling around. They wouldn't get very far in this camp as we are all armed all the time, even in the mess hall. There are more prisoners here than in all the rest of the camps I have been in combined.

I had a swell Thanksgiving dinner at a home in Houston Thursday. I had more chicken than I could hold.

Well I guess I'll close now as there is no more news that I know of.

See you Christmas

As ever, Bob

Dec 1,

Dear Mom, Dad.

I just got some bad news about furlough. The trains are too crowded so we can not all leave on the 15th. Instead we are going 1 each day starting the 15th. I might be able to get home before Christmas and I might not. It will probably be by the end of the month anyway.

I sure was happy about getting home for Christmas but I should have known it was too good to be true. At least it will be near Christmas.

I went out last nite and got all my clothes cleaned and pressed and fitted. Your money-a-gram arrived yesterday and I spent most of it last nite getting all the things I need for the trip. I will get paid on Saturday and will get my train ticket then. We didn't expect to get paid until the 25th, but it came through early.

I wrote Christmas cards to most of the family tonite and will mail them the end of the week.

I went to the show last nite and seen Betty Davis in 'Old Acquaintance'. It wasn't so hot but passed the time away.

We went on a 12 mile hike today and it wore me down. It was double time most of the way we made it in 2 hrs and 40 minutes. I have my feet soaking in a bucket now. It was just a warm-up for Saturday's 25 mile hike. I dread those hikes. They sure are hard on the feet but do you lots of good. (I guess).

The 105mm hz did not come in yet and we don't know when it will be in so I was assigned to another tank today. The name is Agitator. It sure is an agitator all right as it is always breaking down. Joe is going to be the gunner on the 105 when it comes in.

The pictures came yesterday and the large ones were swell. What did you think of them?

The camp is swell for sleeping. Nice soft beds and showers but we are too far from any town. As usual we are way out of the main camp because of the tanks tearing up the roads. It is still heaven to us. We are going to do all kinds of shooting here on the 75mm guns. We have special guns in now, they are the latest thing out. You can't miss your target with them. I sure hope we get a chance to use them on live targets soon. Our chances look very good. They are teaching us how to destroy them if we think we are going to be captured. I don't know why because before I would be captured they would have to destroy the tank first to get me out of it.

I wrote to the Readers' Digest and had my address changed so they can get the book to me sooner.

That's about all the news from here so I guess I'll sign off.

Your loving son, Bob

Dec 3,

Dear Mother, Dad.

As usual my furlough has been changed. Maybe for the better or maybe for the worst. It is supposed to go on the 20th of Dec. but don't get excited. There is a rumor that we will leave here for California on the 25th. That will put an end to all furloughs. There is a 50/50 chance of getting home. We are supposed to go on a final maneuver in the desert at Indio Cal.

I got a letter from Dot Newsom in Texarkana today. I met her in the Red Cross canteen. She is a swell girl. I will send her letter along so you can know more about her. You always ask so many questions about the people I meet. This will save me a lot of time telling you about them.

We will make our 25 mile hike tomorrow. A little sleep tonite will help a lot tomorrow so I will cut it short now.

Your Loving Son,

Bob P.S. The papers arrived today but no letters from you.

November 30th.

Hello Bob:

 Was so very glad to get your letter & it was quite a surprise for I had begun to think you weren't going to write. But I'm glad you did !!!!!

 From what you said in your letter the scenery sounded beautiful. My scenery is just about as good, for my dog is practically sitting in my lap here on the couch. So if this letter looks and sounds crazy – excuse it please !!!!!!!!

 I think it's swell that you're getting a furlough. You'll be home for xmas too. That's wonderful!

 The man power shortage is really short here, and I'm not kidding – Amen !! I got an awfully nice letter from Jonny but he hasn't as yet answered my letter. If you see him tell him hello, and to answer my letter.

 I haven't been doing much. Went to Shreveport last week and shopping. That's all I've done just about besides working at the canteen.

 When you come through here again let me know when you're coming. Write me a letter or something, and let me know when you're coming just in case I should have something planned. The 15th came on Thurs. So maybe I'll be down at the canteen I'd love to go to dinner and a show with you. Thanks for saying so many nice things about me. I'll soon get conceited !!!

Must close now & go to bed. Please do write me soon.

Don't forget me!

Dot

Dec 5, 1943

Dear Mother, Dad,

 I just got your letter telling about the telegram. I am sorry you had so much trouble. If I thought it would cause so much trouble I never would have sent it. The reason I sent it is that I had no clothes that were fit to wear. Just coming out of the woods after so long you can imagine what they looked like. It usually takes two or three weeks to get them cleaned and pressed so I didn't have any time to lose, as I expected to leave on the 15th. Joe was broke too so I couldn't get money so easy. We had no idea when we would get paid as we move so much our money doesn't ever seem to catch up with us. As it was however we got payed yesterday unexpectedly. I don't ever want you to worry about me again. I told you that so many times and still you worry needlessly. If I had to have the money and you couldn't get it to me I could always dig up a couple of hundred one way or another. I thought the easiest way was to call on you, but the Red Cross will always lend you a hundred and between all the boys there is always another couple of hundred. So don't ever worry about money again.

 It is final now that we are going to California. But! When? That's the question. They wanted to leave here on the 25th of Dec. but we have too much work to complete here that we won't be able to leave for some time. It is still a fifty fifty chance of coming home. I am praying for one more chance to get home before we leave because once we leave it is likely to be a couple of years before I get home again, as we will have to police up Europe after the war. That will probably be Roy's job too.

It's too bad about your teeth Dad, as you don't have a heck of a lot of them left. I might have to have another one of mine pulled as I get a toothache every once in a while. I think I have another abscess but am not sure yet. I had another dental checkup the other day and had my tooth put back in. The army sure takes care of your teeth. We go to the dentist every 3 mo. And have a checkup.

I got another letter from Hazel in Texarkana and also one from Dot Newman and 2 from you and 1 from June this morning so I have plenty of writing to do this afternoon. Dot is sending me her picture, if it gets here by the time I go home on furlough I will bring it along. She is very pretty. I only met her in the canteen and never had time to take her out yet. I met her after I had taken Hazel home that nite in Texarkana.

I will close soon as there is a lot of work and letter writing I have to do today (Sun) because there is no time during the week.

Glad to hear Roy's team won the game. We had a few games among our companies. In the first game there was a broken nose, arm, wrist, finger, and black and blue marks all over the rest of us. I got a shiner and a kick in the face but came out alright. The boys play just a little rough as they forgot all about rules and regulations as we don't have any rules in our big game (over there).

Then we started boxing here in the club room. That too was a mistake. We broke all the chairs, tables and have to pay for them. I got a sock in the nose and thought it was broken but it doesn't hurt any more so I guess it's alright. I hit my partner in the chest and broke two of his ribs. Just then the Btn Comm. put out an order to stop all rough games until the men got well enough to work again. He said there was more broken bones in the football games in one day than we had in the whole maneuvers. He doesn't mind us killing each other but not to put too many out of duty at one time. So we started to play ping pong when what do you think happened. A pal of mine Ted Healy slipped making a fancy shot and broke his arm.

Joe Conti, the fellow I had with me when I was after the prisoners is going home on the 15th as his father just had a bad accident while working. He and his 5 men were on a scaffold putting bricks up when the whole thing fell. None were killed but all were hurt. He isn't sure about how bad his father is. He said they fell 50 ft.

I went to a show last nite and seen a swell picture. It was 'While Thousands Cheer'. Be sure you see it if you haven't already seen it.

Don't go to the Roxy or Radio City Music Hall, because I want to go with you when I get home. I saw the Roxy while waiting to pick up the prisoners. It was the best all around show I have ever seen. It had Danny Kaye in person, also a swell picture "Sweet Rosy O'Grady". They always have a good show there. Grace

Moore is singing in Austin this afternoon but I can't get away to see her as there is too much work to do. I also want to save money for furlough.

My two prisoners are getting their trial tomorrow. I will let you know how they make out. Major Nelson congratulated me in the way I brought them back. He said I used very good judgment in stopping in different cities for sleep. He don't know it but I didn't sleep, I was out site-seeing.

Now that the prisoners are safely in jail I can tell you something that I couldn't before for fear you would be worried. We could not get hand cuffs for the prisoners. We had to both stay awake all the time. I never said anything but I was sure sweating up a storm a storm when we took them through Grand Central Station and on the subway. I stayed so close to them I looked like I was glued to them. In Texarkana we had a little trouble, one of them got hysterical and we locked them up for a day to let them quiet down. We beat them and everything else trying to make them snap out of it, but it took a doctor to do the trick. We had to take them to another doctor at Camp Polk. That took another day. As much as I hate them I still can't help feeling sorry for them.

That furlough is a bonus for our work. Joe Conti and I are the first in Btn to go if we go. We earned every bit of it. If I ever have to do that again I hope it is to the same place as that 4 days at home made it all worthwhile.

Hoping to see you all soon,

Your loving Son,

Bob

P.S. If everything goes right I will get home about the day before Christmas and leave 3 days after New Years.

LETTERS FROM 1944

Jan 6, 1944
Dear Mom, Dad,

Well they are keeping us busy here as you can well imagine. I have no clothes left except one pair of coveralls. Everything else I own is in for new. We even turned in our shoes. I have 3 pair so when I've got orders to turn in shoes I had an extra pair.

I had to go on the nite infiltration course last nite. The bullets were very high and the barbed wire thin. The noise of the TNT going off was enough to burst your eardrums though. It was a pretty sight to see all the tracer bullets come right at you and then go over your head about 18 inches. The explosions lit up the sky. I only tore the sleeve off my field jacket and did not scratch myself very much.

I have to get 2 more needles and a vaccination this afternoon.

All furloughs are cancelled from now on. The boys that are home now will be back on the 19th. Any time after that we are likely to leave. It is always possible to have the orders changed so don't be surprised to hear we are not going over again. When we get there you can be sure. I just heard this minute that we are to turn in all tanks tomorrow by noon. I guess that settles it. We will not see any tanks now until we get across. We will probably leave here by the end of the month. Gosh Mom, it feels good to know that you are finally going to get your chance. I am so excited. It's just like the week before I got in the Army. We are going on the firing range day and nite from now on til we leave. I have to go to the medic now for shots.
Love to all, Bob

(this one was typed)
Jan. 8.1944
Dear Mother Dad,

I am on guard today as there isn't any one else here to do it. Every one is either home on furlough or in school. I am cpl of guard and have nothing to do except sit around here and play with this mach.

Joe Skelly got back from school tonite and got a nice surprise when he heard we were going over seas. I was on charge of quarters yesterday and didn't get to write any letters to anyone. You should see the jam I am in with June. Joe wrote

and told her that I was in the hospital with the grippe, she got a three day pass when I was home and went to the hospital to see me. Boy is she mad. The top sergeant said she would have shot me if she could have laid her hands on me. I am not worrying as I will probably never see her again anyway. I will try to write to you every day as there is no telling when I will have to leave here for P.O.E. Once we start we will not be able to write for some time. We have no clothes left and we have a blew norther a blowing. According to the papers it is the worst blizzard in 52 years. The temperature is near zero. The wind is blowing so hard it is hard to keep a car on the road and we have to change the guard every hour to keep them freezing. They are walking with blankets around to keep warm.We discharged all men unfit for combat yesterday and got replacements late last nite. They look like some good men, they came from another tank outfit. We won't leave until after the 20th, as that is when the men are due back from furlough. We were out firing the 75mm gun the day before yesterday. I got a scroe 192 out of 200, it was easy as it was direct fire. Everyone had swell scores as they really want to learn now. Before they didn't realize how important it was but they are waking up fast, and I mean really fast. Did you receive my package yet? I am sorry about sending it collect but I was near broke and didn't want to lose all those clothes. I still have more but they are not worth saving.
There isn't any more news so I'll sign off for today.
Your loving Son
Bob

Jan 11, 1944
Dear Mother Dad,
    Well another day has gone by and no more news since my last letter. No one seems to know what is going on. Our new clothes are in the supply room but they won't give them to us. I am walking around in slippers because my shoes are worn out, yet they won't give me one of the 2 new pair they have for me in the supply room.
    The last of the boys had to leave on furlough last nite and be back by the 20th. It only gives them 9 days. Boy was I lucky getting 18 days. I got payed the other day by surprise but it didn't last long. Some of the boys were broke and as this will be their last time at home I loaned it all out. Now I am broke. I am glad to see them go home though and don't regret lending it to them.
    There isn't anything new around so I'll close now until tomorrow.
Your Loving Son,
Bob

Jan 12, 1944
Dear Mother, Dad,

I hope you are not mad at me for not writing to you every day but there just isn't enough time to do it. We are kept busy from 5 in the morning until far into the nite. There is so much to do here that I don't see how we can ever finish. There are only 20 men left here in the company. The rest are home or in the hospital. We have to turn in the rest of our tanks tomorrow. There are 17 left and they have to be spotless. It is hard to clean them as every time you go in one you track in mud. It has been raining almost all the time for the past 2 months here and when you walk the mud comes up to your knees. Joe got 15 teeth filled yesterday and two pulled, you should hear him curse the dentist.

I still have no shoes, no clothes, no nothing. It don't look like I'll get a pass here in Texas again. So I'll just forget all of my friends here and save a lot of time writing letters. June sent me a letter today forgiving me. I am not even going to answer her as I won't see her again anyway.

I had a fight with the mess sergeant tonite at supper. He got me so mad I dragged him over the table and out in the mud and beat him until they dragged me off him. I never did like him and I just lost my temper tonite. I don't know how bad he is hurt but will find out tomorrow when he gets back from the hospital. The officers didn't say a word as they have been expecting someone to do it sooner or later.

I am going to bed now so good bye for now.
Your Son
Bob

- next day ---

I didn't get time to mail this letter last nite so I will add to it today. It rained all nite and all morning, it just started to snow this afternoon.

Our P.O.E. is supposed to be in NY or Boston so there is still a small chance of me getting home again. They give 24 hr passes in P.O.E. That will give me a few hours home if I am lucky.

My shoes are in but I can't have them. The C.O. says I will wear them out before we sail, so he won't let me have them.

I got your air mail letter this afternoon. Don't ever worry about me. You should know by now that I can take good care of myself. I will never go hungry and I think I am trained well enough to keep out of the way of enemy bullets. Remember good soldiers always come back. It's only the poor ones that don't.

I have a sore throat today from this weather. I haven't been warm since I left home. I will go on sick call tomorrow and get it painted.

You all can help me by just taking good care of yourselves and not worrying about me. So long for now.
Bob

Jan 15

Dear Mom Dad,

Another phase of our training has just ended. It was the closest thing to combat we will ever see other than combat itself. Remember in my last letter I told you we were having hail and rain? Well it turned into a snow storm. Yesterday morning in the worst part of the storm, we took tanks from the 749th and went on a 36 hr problem. The temp was around 17 or 18. We had only a pair of coveralls and a wool shirt to keep us warm. We drove to a camp area about 25 miles away. There we gassed up and started on to an attack position. We reached our position about 9 o'clock at nite and the snow had stopped but was 7 in. deep. We were allowed no light and no fires. We stayed there until 6 this morning. We were frozen stiff! At 6 we left for the attack. We made the attack at 8. We fired 25 rounds of 75mm and 500 mach gun. 100 Tommy gun. They had wood tanks for targets, we blew up everything in sight. When we hit those targets they just disappeared. It was one of the worst days I ever put in, in my life. I didn't think it was possible to get that cold.

About noon the sun came out and all the snow melted. The mud was so deep that 9 companies of tanks were stuck and they are not in yet. That is 140 tanks laying out there in the mud. The 612 Tank Destroyer Btn lost all their M10 Tank Destroyers. Some are up to the turret in mud. When you get out of your tank on to the ground you go over your knees in ice cold mud. It's really unbelievable. I never dreamed it could get so bad. It will be weeks before they get all those tanks out of the mud.

Here is the best part. I have had a cold and a sore throat ever since I've been home. Finally there is no sign of cold or sore throat. I seem to agree with the cold and wet.

I got your letter today Dad. I am always glad to get one from you. Thanks a lot. The address book came today too.

It looks like we will leave here for Boston or NY about the 30th or before. Let's hope it is NY. If it is I'll see to it that I get home again.

I'll have to close now as I am so tired I can't keep my eyes open. So until tomorrow good bye.

Your Loving Son,

Bob

Jan 19, 1944

Dear Mom Dad.

Joe and I are in Austin today. Joe has a 3 day pass and I have a hell of a lot of nerve. I couldn't ask for a pass just after furlough and Joe got one. I couldn't see Joe go out on his last pass alone, so I fixed it up at the office with the top kick. He won't hunt for me until Friday morning if I help him pack his furniture on a truck Friday nite and Sat morning. That gives me 2 full days off.

Now if the Company Commander don't want to see me for anything in these two days no one will be the wiser. If you see Pvt on my letters you will know what happened. It doesn't make any difference as you can't spend money overseas anyway.

I just thought I would write to let you know that we will probably be going within the next 10 days. Of course it might be 10 weeks too so don't stop writing to this address until you have a new one.

Your Son

Bob

Jan 22, 1944

Dear Mom Dad,

Today was the last day that anyone was allowed to be away from camp. We have 15 men missing. I got back last nite with Joe from Austin. No one said a word. My friend covered up for me and no one in camp knew I was gone.

We had a swell time on our time off but it didn't last long enough. I borrowed $10 from Joe and we had just as good a time of $10 as we would on $50.

I don't think we will leave here for at least a week if not more. Some of the boys are getting a pass tonite until Monday. 90 percent of all the boys in the whole Btn have been picked up by the MP's in the past week. They will be barred from towns if they get any worse. They get in fights with everyone. The boys coming back on the train slugged the MP and locked him in the closet.

Well they can't get any more work out of us now. The boys won't work or do anything like getting up for revelry or retreat. We lay in bed until 9 in the morning and keep the lights on all nite. When the guard comes in to turn lights out we run him out. They can't do anything to us because we don't care if they hurt us or not. If they put you on extra duty you just sit down on the job, so they just leave us alone. The officers are nice as pie to us now. I guess they are afraid of getting in the way of a stray bullet.

Ed Brady was due back from furlough yesterday but there is no sign of him yet. He will be court marshaled and get a week's hard labor when he does come back. They will have to give him back his stripes before we get overseas though so he don't care.

Well we just made out cards with our names and half of our address on them. When we leave here today they will fill out the full address and mail them to you.

It's time to eat now so I'll say good bye til next time.

Your Son

Bob

Jan 23

Dear Grand Pa Ma,

I received your letters a few days ago but haven't had much time to answer them. You are wrong about me leaving home early for the train. The only reason was, I wanted to be sure of a seat and I just got there 35 minutes before the train left.

Boy we had some cold weather here. We had a overnite problem in a 7 inch snow storm. The temperature was down to 7 above. It sure was cold sleeping on that snow covered ground. The past week has been different. The sun has been shining and the temperature has been up to 90. We will have no more work to do except hikes from now on, as all our tanks and guns are turned in. We won't get new ones until we get overseas. The government will mail you a card with my new address when I leave here.

I am no longer allowed to tell you anything about what we are doing so please don't ask any questions that are anything about what we are doing. You would be surprised to see some of questions I am asked in letters. If I answered them I would be arrested.

I just had an allotment for a bond a month to come out of my pay. It won't hurt much as I will get a 20% raise soon and that will help.

I took a 3 day pass on my own the other day. Joe had a pass and I couldn't see him go alone so I went with him. The boys covered up for me and they never knew I was gone.

Thanks for the cartoons Helen. They came a few days ago. Keep writing! I am always glad to hear from you.

How do the two Eddy's like the service? I know little Ed will like it but I imagine big Ed will find it hard for a while. All married men seem to have a tough time. They get homesick too easy. Tell little Ed he is lucky getting in the Jew navy as he couldn't wear pajamas in the Army. I am sure he will get used to doing without them when he gets overseas.

Well there isn't any news left so I'll close wishing you all the best of health and lots of good luck.

As ever,

Bob

Jan 23,

Dear Mom Dad,

I wrote to you the day before yesterday, but I just found that it never got in the mail until this morning.

There is nothing new here. We just hang around and do odd jobs. This is Sunday and I got up about 10 o'clock and am waiting for dinner now. I will go to the show at 1:30. We are eating like kings now. We had all the chicken and ice cream we wanted yesterday. There is always plenty of food now. They want to treat us good now before we leave.

We are having beautiful summer weather now. It makes you feel good with all the grass starting to turn green again. I suppose we will have another cold spell again but lets hope not until I get out of here.

Ed Brady came back yesterday. They never said anything to him.

I have new shoes now that I can wear until we leave here and then I have to bury them as we are only allowed to have 2 pair but I have always had 3 or 4.

Well I guess I'll close now as there is nothing doing and that leaves me with nothing to write about. Oh. I forgot! I took out bonds through the pay roll. You will receive a $25 bond every month from February on.

Well so long until next time.

Your Son, Bob

Jan 24

Dear Mom Dad.

There is no more news yet. I am just dropping you a line to let you know we are still here. Please excuse the paper as it is all we can get here.

The good weather has ended again. It just started to rain. The temp is up around 75 though. We have two hikes on for this week. One is 10 miles Tues and 18 miles on Fri or Sat. That's all we will do for the week. We are going crazy here doing nothing. We just sit in the barracks all day and read and write. I wrote a letter to the Mildens yesterday.

Harry Bock came in this morning 4 days late. He has to see the C.O. this afternoon to hear his sentence.

There are only a few left over the hill now.

I think we have at least another week or so yet here. We haven't got all our clothes yet. After next Monday we will be able to leave here at a minute's notice.

I went to the show yesterday and seen two rotten pictures. They were 'Rookies in Burma' and 'Career Girl'. It was a waste of time. I seen a few good pictures lately but most of them are bad.

I am going to try and send you some of my pay this payday. Keep $50 in the bank for me so I can send for it on my next furlough. After the war the rest will all go into bonds. 18.75 per mo.

There is the news as it stands today.

Your Loving Son

Bob

Jan 25

Dear Mom, Dad,

There is still no news about leaving. We have no work to do and the weather is bad. That just about clears that up.

We got a bunch of the new $8.50 sub machine guns in. We are learning them and will use them overseas. They are made of tin cans and look like Buck Rogers' rocket gun. I am enclosing a paper about the bonds. Keep it as a receipt.

The boys are getting worse every day. They act like wild men. They are all glad they are going over, and just can't wait.

Well that's all I can think of now so until tomorrow.

Your Son, Bob

Jan 26, 1944
Dear Mom Dad,

There is no new news today except that we will probably be on our way for POE by Monday. I will write you as soon as we get there. We will probably be at least 3 weeks before we sail after we get to the POE. It is still supposed to be NY or Boston. Let's hope so.

I am writing you very short letters now because there is nothing I am allowed to tell you.

So until you hear from me again good nite.
Your Loving Son
Bob

Jan 27
Dear Mother Dad,

Well we are still here as I am writing this letter but probably before it reaches you we will be on our way for P.O.E. Keep writing to this address until you get the card with my new address. I will call you up on the phone at my first chance after I reach P.O.E.

I would like to tell you just what we are doing and other things but we are on our honor not to tell anything.

Our mail will be censored when we leave here. I won't be able to tell you where I am or anything else like that. Your letters will be censored on occasion and if they find anything in it that they don't like they destroy your letters and we will never know what happened to it. Don't!! put anything in your letters about the war! Nothing about how many ships are built in Dad's place. If you just think before you write all of your letters will reach me wherever I am.

I took out another $12.50 per mo in bonds today. You will get the slip on them in a few days. That makes $31.25 per mo. (almost as much as you Dad)

Mom, papers are being forwarded to you making you my power of attorney. That gives you the power to sign my name on anything you want to. It's just in case anything comes up where you need me and I can't be had at the time. You will receive a $25 bond every mo and a $50 bond every 3 months. You can do with them as you please. If you ever need money don't be afraid to take it..

Boy its hard to write a letter when you can't say anything about what's going on but we will just have to get used to it.
Well so long til tomorrow.
Your Son
Bob

Jan 31, 1944
Dear Mother Dad,

We have been moved out of that hole Texas, but are still in the US. It's swell to be in the east again. I was going to stop in and see Fritzie and Bernie before I left Texas but we left very suddenly and were restricted the last day in camp. I saw Virginia before I left, and she was sick and on a Orange juice diet.

How is Roy making out with the draft board? I hope he can stay out of the army until the cold weather is over.

I guess you have my new address by now, but if you haven't copy it's just as it is on this letter.

Our mail is being censored now so I can't tell you anything about the trip or where we are. I probably won't be able to get home again, but just in case I do you had better tell Mrs. Riley or Mrs. Nisher where I can get a hold of you in a hurry!!

Tell Dad to keep a full tank of gas on hand in the car.

I guess that is all the news that can be told at this time, so until you hear from me again, good nite

Your Loving Son,
Bob

Feb 4 1944
Dear Mother Dad,

After a pretty good trip I arrived in camp last nite to find everything upside down. There were different troops in my barracks and everyone was running around with barracks bags over their shoulders. I finally found my company in another Btn area. They were in with the 749 tank Btn. I hunted for Joe Skelly and found he left for camp Clayborn for special training in anti aircraft gunnery. All the gunners are there for 14 days. Joe is a cpl again. The tank commanders are in another camp for other training.

They are taking all our summer clothes away from us and we had to turn in all our equipment for new. They took all my clothes, blouse and overcoat and even 2 pair of my shoes. All are going to be replaced with new. I had one more day so I took all my extra clothes and left for Austin again last nite. I sent them home by railway express this morning. Half the btn is going home on a 10 day furlough tonite and when they get back the other half will go.

We are getting our shots for yellow fever and a few others over again. We were put on full alert a week after I left. That means we can leave in 3 days notice.

Our mail will be censored from now on so don't expect any more news about us going over until you get a telegram saying I am over there already.

I got to Chicago in 17 hrs and was in Ft Worth 24 hrs later. It took 7 hrs to hitchhike to camp.

Thanks for the swell time when I was home everybody. I got a swell rest and plenty to eat.

I'll give you all the news I can when I find out more so until then so long everybody.

As ever Your loving Son

Bob

Feb 7, 1944

Dear Mom Dad,

You probably have guessed what has happened by this time. Our passes have been stopped and I won't get home any more. I got back in plenty of time the other day. I even got some sleep before breakfast. My cold is much better now since I got some sleep.

Don't send me a pen as I already have one. I got it in NY the other day. There is nothing new as yet so I'll close until tomorrow.

Your Loving Son

Bob

Feb 28, 1944

Dear Mother Dad,

This is the first chance we have had to write letters since we left the ship. Our barracks are a whole lot better then we expected. They look like half a tar barrel with a door in either end. There are lights in them and a small coal stove. We sleep on cots with straw mattresses. It's cold inside but we have 4 blankets so sleeping is comfortable.   I will send you pictures of the place as soon as we get a clear day so we can use the camera.

We had a long train ride from the ship to our camp. The trains were better than we expected too. Each compartment is made to hold 6 men. There is a door in each compartment to get off the train. I think it is a lot better than we had at home. The freight cars or boxcars are about $1/5^{th}$ the size of ours and are called 'goods wagons'.

We are rationed in most anything you want to buy and have ration books. We are not allowed to tell you how much of each thing we are allowed to buy but you can imagine. When you write to me write 1 Vmail and 2 regular mail. Keep them in order so I can tell if any are lost. Send me a package when you get time. Put in some razor blades and candy (Babe Ruths) and a picture of you and Dad and Roy. All three in one picture if possible.

Joe got a letter from his Dad and it said you wrote to him thanking him for the picture.

Well that's about all the news for now. As soon as I can get a pass I will go to London and then will tell you all about it.

Your Loving Son,

Bob

Mar 1, 1944
Dear Mom Dad,

I arrived last nite from the place that we docked. I sent a regular letter this morning giving you the full details. It will probably arrive soon after or before this one. Thank Kitty for the carton of cigarettes and tell her I will write to her soon. Joe and I are having a swell time and are both in good health. Write and tell the Lakes that I will also answer her letter as soon as possible.

I hope you started writing when you didn't hear from me, as the mail is already coming in. How are you coming along with the draft board Roy? I wish you a lot of luck.

Love to all

Bob

Mar 3, 1944
Dear Mother Dad,

After a swell trip we arrived somewhere overseas. I didn't get sick but a few of the others didn't feel so good after we left. It was very calm all the way. No excitement except bucking the chow line.

I guess you were wondering what had happened when I didn't get home again. We just up and left all of a sudden and that was that. Don't send me any money as I have more than I can use. You forgot to give me Rip Binisanos *(illegible)* address with the rest. Please send it to me so I can write to him.

Don't worry about me and take care of your selves .

Until next time I remain your loving son

Bob

Cpl R Cadmus

747th Tk Btn Co A

APO 308 c/o PM

NYC NY

Feb 3, 1944 *((he wrote Feb but must have meant March, as he didn't arrive in Europe until late Feb))*

Dear Mom Dad,

I received your letter of the 19th today. It takes about 10 days. You asked me if I wanted fruit cake. You should know me better than that. Yes send me fruit cake and candy if you don't need it yourself.

I am sorry to hear about Bernie. Be sure and let me know if there is any change. We get paid within a few days so I will have more money than I will know what to do with. I still get $54 per mo. even without the bond money. I am going to make out an allotment for about $20. per mo. You can put it in the bank for me when it comes. Your letters are too short. Please keep your lines closer together and you can get a lot more on the sheet. We went to town and found it almost impossible to spend more than 2 shillings in a nite. Joe will find a way to spend more I suppose. He is going to buy a bike. They cost 4 lbs. I am glad you like the picture as I never seen it. I met a girl that lives in London and am going to see her as soon as I get a pass. She is staying here while there is still danger from bombs in London.

Your Loving Son
Bob

March 3
Dear Mother Dad,

There is nothing new here yet. The weather is still cold and damp and the sun only shines a few hours a day. We went on a short hike today and it felt good to get the exercise. I didn't get any mail today as there was only a few letters for the co. Kitty's letter came yesterday and I answered that last nite. Is Ed still in Hawaii? Or had he been moved again. How about little Eddy Milden has he left the states yet? Is there any news about Roy and the draft board?

Put in some flints for my lighter in the next package. There is no more news that is not restricted so I'll have to quit now before I get in trouble. Before I forget it I met an old customer by the name of Highe from Cranford. You can call up his folks if you want.

Your Loving Son
Bob

3/8/44
Dear Mom Dad.

We went on a short hike this morning and had a class on gunnery this afternoon. That's about all we do over here. That and clean up the joint. I'm beginning to think that's why they sent us over here just to clean up all the Army camps just as we did in the states. I go to town every nite but its about as lively as a graveyard. The food is swell. We have chicken at least twice a week. We have canned peaches or some other fruit every meal. We get all our cigarettes at 5 cents a pack so don't ever send me any. You can send me fruit cake and candy and blades. That's all I need. Joe and I are going to London and see what it's like as soon as we can get a pass. Write soon Dad if you can find time.

Your Son
Bob

3/8/44
Dear Mom Dad,

I was surprised today with two letters from you. I didn't quite understand all of it as I didn't get any letter telling what happened to Fred Meyers.

What happened to him did he get in an accident? You just said he has bad spells. Does Roy still like his job as much as he used to? Or is he really working.

Eddy is lucky to be so near to Hollywood. Tell him to enjoy himself while he is still in the states as there isn't much to do in other countries.

We had another hike this morning. I guess that's all they have for us to do. It is still damp and cold here but it should warm up soon. I can't understand why my mail isn't reaching you.

Love to all   Bob

3/9/44
Dear Mom Dad,

Still no news. We do nothing here but go on hikes and rake leaves. Anything else that goes on we are not allowed to write. I didn't know that George Story was in the army. Even if he is over here I probably never will see him.

How is Artie Kieffer? Is he still in Texas? I don't have to ask about Ray Daly. He will never change.

How is the war coming along? Is the US still mad at Japan?
You keep asking if I want candy. Yes. Send me candy, nuts, and a big steak!
Have a good time and take care of yourself. Until next time I get time to write so long.

Your Son
Bob

March 9
Dear Mom Dad,

There isn't anything to write about yet so I'll just write a few lines so you will know I am alright. I got three of your letters yesterday and am anxious to hear how Bernie is. Can't he come up north and get a good doctor? How is Kitty is she married yet? I guess you were surprised to see her. It is still cold and damp here. It seems you can never get warm. It gets nice for a few hours in the morning and then cold and damp in the afternoon.

You can write regular mail and put an air mail stamp on it and it gets here sooner than Vmail. As soon as I get paid I will buy some stamps and write you some long letters. Glad to hear you're working a little Dad. Keep it up.

Your Son
Bob

March 13, 44
Dear Mother Dad,

I have a day off so I will try to write a longer letter than usual.
I went on guard last nite out in the tank park

_____ (*actual cut out in the letter,*

censored) from our camp. The guard house is in the middle of town and the tanks are a short walk from there. I had cpl of the first relief and was all done at 10 o'clock. After that I took in the town. I went to a hotel and bought a meal. It wasn't bad either. I had roast beef, buttered beets, soup, cheese fries, and some *rotten* coffee. The bill came to 5' 6 shillings about $1.10 in American money. I then went out and had a glass of cider. You wouldn't like it because it is sour. By that time the moon had gone and it was blacker than the inside of a boot. I had to feel my way back to the guard house. When these people say blackout they mean just that. There is no light whatever showing. The guard house is a house with two rooms and a fire place. No beds and no lights. We just lay our blankets out and go to sleep next to the fire place. I got off at 8 this morning and came back to camp. I had breakfast and went to bed for an hour. I got up and the sun was out so I went for a long walk around the river and then to see a farmer I know _____ (*other side of the page where the cutout was*) day off. We got paid the day before yesterday. I got 12 lbs or $48. Next mo I'll get $54. They took out my first bond so I guess you will have it by the time this letter reaches you.

I'll tell you a little about the place we are staying. It used to be a big estate owned by some rich family. There is a castle here with over a hundred rooms in it. They use if for all the officers and P.X. – barbershop, btn supply and all the officers sleep in it. It is hundreds of years old and built out of stone. The grounds are enormous. They used to have over a hundred gardeners working here. They used to have horses here for hunting and hundreds of cattle. We live in huts in the grounds of the estate. The church we go to was built in 1490 and is still going strong.

The town is very small and has only a few stores. Every house in town is at least 200 years old and some a lot older. The people are very nice and most of them are Irish. The cars are very odd looking. They have the steering wheel on the right and you drive on the left. Some cars only have 1 wheel in the back and are run on a motorcycle engine. The busses are double decker.

Joe went to Oxford last week when I was on detail. He didn't like it at all. He didn't have much fun either, I guess that's because I wasn't there to think up some trouble to get into. I got Jack Reid's address but lost it so send it to me again if you don't mind.

I just got another letter from Dot again and a big picture. I'll have to quit writing to her as she is getting too serious. That's 3 letters in two days. Your mail didn't come today so I'll expect 2 or 3 tomorrow. I am going to send you about $30 this payday and then have 25 per mo sent home through the Army.

I have no desire to see anymore of England so I'll stay near camp and save my money for after the war. My vacation check will arrive soon, so you just sign my name to it and put it in the bank. Don't ever send money over here as it is worthless. We use it for poker chips. We get news papers here almost every day and they give us all the news from the states.

If you ever see a good pen send it to me as the one I have is shot. Boy it sure is windy out. It rained for a few minutes a little while ago but the sun is out again and the wind is blowing up cold.

Well remember me to all my friends and relatives. I am feeling fine so don't worry about me. Hoping you all are in the best of health I remain,
Your loving Son
Bob

3/20/44
Dear Mother & Dad,

Just a few lines to let you know that I am alright and still having a good time. There is never any excitement of any kind. There is nothing of interest to tell you about. The food and weather is still the same.

Well I close now hoping you are all in good health.
Your Loving Son, Bob

Houston Texas
March 22, 1944
Dear Friend –

At long last I am going to write you a few lines. It is now 10:30 pm everybody is in bed and all is quiet. We were so glad to hear that you had heard from Bob overseas. Maxine had received two letters from him and we have gotten one from him and are we glad to hear from him. I just finished a letter to Bob and I teased him, telling him that when Maxine got a letter from him Hal and I got the finger-itch in other words, we can't wait until Maxine gets home to hear what he has to say. But today came a letter from him, so it was my turn to tease her that I I didn't have to wait. You have every right to be so proud of Bob. He is so considerate. Maxine has written him several times but so far he says he hasn't heard from here since he left the states.

I hope Bob won't be bashful in writing and letting us know what he wants most, for we would like to send him whatever he wants. You help encourage him to do so, will you?

I am rather ashamed to send this letter on to you as my writing is rather bad tonite. What with a leaky fountain pen, tired arm and just a wee bit sleepy with it, I just can't seem to get my characters straight.

Doing my office work and running the house leaves me pretty tired when bedtime comes.
Canning season starts pretty soon. We have quite a few things put up from last year but there is quite a few more to be put up this year. We have 121 chickens put up. I have to can mostly pork & beans, snap beans, carrots, pickles and corn and a few more bell peppers this time.

Here I go talking too much about my household and not asking you anything. Do you can? Do you have a garden? Chickens? I hope you don't mind me asking questions like that. I love to talk on and on about the home with others, in so doing it often gives me some valuable ideas.

We are all doing fine and hope it is so with you. Give my love to your sister that made those pretty little do-dads.

Well I think I will close for this time and save some for next letter. I'll promise not to wait so long in writing.
Your Friend,
Anna Marie Lake

March 23, 44
Dear Mother Dad, Roy,

I should be ashamed of myself for not writing in so long but I get so tired of writing the same thing every day. We are not allowed to tell you very much anyway. This has been a very odd week. A little of everything has happened to me. I had guard and a few other details to begin with. I met a swell girl from the W.A.F. and have been going with her every nite, in fact I just took her back to her barracks a little while ago. Joe goes with her girlfriend. We meet them every nite at the canteen at 7 o'clock.

There is nothing to do except walk and once in a while go into the canteen for a cup of tea. The good points are you can take her out for a week and it costs you about 7 or 8 cents for all expenses over the whole week. The bad point is they live over 3 miles from our camp and we have to walk them home every nite. They have to be in camp and in bed at 11:30. I tell you that 6 miles every nite is killing me. I don't mind the 3 out there but that walk back is sure a long one. I got my first argument with her tonite when I was late meeting her. My asst driver just got some bad news from home as I was about to leave camp tonite. His wife gave birth to a baby girl and a few hours the baby died. She is in very bad condition yet and its a matter of time before they will know whether she will live or not. I stayed in with him for an hour and that is what made me late.

I have a pass starting tomorrow morning. I am going to Bristol. Marge didn't like the idea. She said I ought to stay here. I made a date with her for Sunday and will take her to the city. I think that will be our last date as my feet tell me it isn't worth it.

How is everything these days? Are you all in good health? I want you to tell me if anything goes wrong. I would rather have it that way.

My tooth was knocked out again in a little fight among the boys. The whole company looks like they went through a meat grinder. Black eyes, broken nose, cut lips. We have a swell time when we go to town and find the 4F medics looking for a fight.
<u>next morning</u>

I'll say so long til next week as my pass starts in 15 minutes. Don't worry as I am having the time of my life.
Your loving Son and Br
Bob

March 26
Dear Mom Dad,

This is not intended to be a letter but just a line to let you know I didn't get hurt in the crossing. I hope Roy was as lucky.

I haven't been to bed for over forty hours so I know you will understand me writing such a short letter.

I'll tell you all about it in a few days.

God bless you til we meet again

Your Loving Son
Bob

March 26
Dear Mother Dad Roy,

I just finished writing you a Vmail to let you know that I am alright. I suppose this letter will take mo. to reach you.

We went to Bristol on a pass the other day on my first pass since I got over here. I enjoyed the visit very much. We seen all the bombed buildings and all points of interest. I met a few girls from different branches of the service. One of them gave me the surprise of my life. I had met her in the morning and we spent the day together. We had dinner in a nice place and wasn't a bad meal at that. We later took a walk in the park and just passed a quiet afternoon. At nite we went to a movie and seen 'This Is The Army'. After the picture was over a news reel came on and it showed a picture of a bombing raid. She looked up and said 'That's the kind of a gun I shoot!'. Well I could have died! I figured she worked in a office or something. She has 2 enemy aircraft to her credit.

The next day we went to Bath. It is only about 12 miles from Bristol. I liked Bath a lot better. It is more like an American city. There is a large business section and a few buildings almost new (at least they aren't more than 2 or 3 hundred years old). Maybe you never heard of this town. Do you remember studying about the Knites of Bath? Well that's the place.

The meals are not bad in town <u>if</u> you have a very good imagination! And if you like food, and <u>if</u> you don't like to eat much, and <u>if</u> you can find it!! The coffee tastes like water, the tea tastes the same and the <u>milk</u>!! Well you just dream about that.

Well Joe just came in so I guess I had better get ready to go pick up Marge and Audrey.

Well keep the mail coming and take care of yourselves.

Your Loving Son & Brother
Bob

Mar 26, 1944
Dear Mother Dad & Roy,

Well I guess it's about time I got busy and try to answer a few of your letters. I get your mail almost every day and it is one of the big events of the day when we have mail call. As soon as I finish this V letter I will write you a longer one and send it by air. I got back from Bristol this morning. We had a swell time. We seen the whole town. We were very careful not to miss anything as I never expect to go back. We spent a day in Bath too. It is also a big town, and was also visited by the German bombers. There has been a big change in the weather. It is a beautiful spring day and I am sitting next to a tree getting some much hoped for sun.

I am going to spend my birthday morning with Margret.
Your loving son
Bob

March 28, 1944
Dear Mother, Dad, Roy,

Well it looks as if Spring is really here! We have had beautiful weather for 3 days in a row. I had a swell time on my birthday, I just layed around all morning and then went out with Margret all afternoon and nite. Of course it couldn't be like it used to at home but it was the next best. If I don't have to work next Sunday I am going to see England from the air. Margret's brother (a pilot in the RAF) said he could get permission to take me up in a four engine bomber any day that I could get off.

Your mail is coming in good so just keep up the good work. I'm feeling fine so don't worry about me just keep yourselves in good shape.
Your Son & Br
Bob

March 29
Dear Dad,

Thanks for the swell letter. I was beginning to give up all hopes of ever hearing from you. The letter only took 6 days to reach here. It beat Mom's Vmail by a day. I'm glad to hear you're able to work steady again, but don't make yourself sick going it. I wish you would use my bonds to pay off the house as I won't need them for some years yet. It would sure save you a lot in interest too.

What makes you think the boys didn't get sick on the way over here. Only about 95% were sick and what a mess. It wasn't only the enlisted men either.

Don't believe all you read about these English girls in the paper. There are all kinds here as well as home. If everything goes alright I'll be in London next week. It's the only town to go to on pass if you want a good time. You see before you can get a pass to London you have to have a room to go to. I have a friend that lives there so I will stay with him.

We get paid this Sat. so I'll get a pass Tues or Wednesday. I wish I could go with you to Virginia on your vacation but the odds are just a little against me.

I wrote you the other day and made a slight mistake of 100 lbs. I weigh 229 not 129 as I said.

I got 4 more pair of shoes this week. That makes 7 brand new pair I have now. I guess they are afraid of running out of those very large cows it takes to make me shoes. Thank God I'm not paying for them!!

Well I guess that's all the news from here. Tell Roy to write once in a while.
Your loving Son
Bob
April 5, 1944
Dear Mother, Dad, Roy.

I guess you are wondering what has happened to me. I got a pass the other day to London and we can't write letters away from camp. I had a swell time there with Joe. We went to the Tower of London, Buckingham Palace, Westminster Abbey, 10 Downing St., and all other places of interest. At nite we just raised hell in general, and managed to have a good time from start to finish. We were there 4 days and that was about the best pass I ever had. I sent you $100. last Sat and kept $50 for myself. The 50 lasted 3 days and on the 4th day we had to take it easy. I will sweat out the rest of the mo. until pay day and try to do it all over again if possible.
Love to all,
Bob

April 5, 1944
Dear Mom Dad Roy,

I'll finish telling you about London on this page or bust.

We stayed in American R Cross for $1.60 the four days. Real beds too. We had some pictures taken which I have already mailed to you, GrandPa, Kathy. I have one large picture here and I can't find any way to mail it. I'll find a way some how though.
That's all the news from here or at least all I can tell you, so please don't ask or expect any more information. If I answered the questions you asked in the last letter I would be in hot water for the rest of my days. I'll tell you everything in the near future I hope when the war is over.
With all my love,
From your son
Bob

April 13, 1944
Dear Mother & Dad,

I was surprised today with 5 more letters. I had 5 yesterday too. I got 5 all from you yesterday and 2 from you today. Also 1 from Dot Newman, 1 from

Hazel in Tex. Your regular mail takes 1 mo to get here. If you send it by air mail it takes 8-10 days. Vmail takes 10 days. Send a lot of air mail as I would rather have long letters than the short ones. We drove our new tank today for the first time. They are swell ones to drive.

It is still cold and damp. Kitty R. sent another subscription to the Readers' Digest. I'm going to write to her today.

It's too bad about Fred Meyers. I sure hope he pulls through alright. We had steak today for dinner and it was really good. Well that's all the news for today so until tomorrow so long.
Your Loving Son,
Bob

Dear Mother Dad Roy,

There is no news today, so I am just sending a Vmail to let you know that I am alright. The weather is beautiful now, at least it has been for the past two days. It is almost as good as we had in Texas. It is almost time for supper so I suppose I will have to finish when I get back.

I went to the tent movie last nite and saw 'The Man From Down Under'. It has been nice to catch up on all the movies I missed. The picture was very good but it was very hot in the tent. I came out dripping wet. I wrote to Helen, Kitty, and the Lakes yesterday. That should hold them for a while. The mail came in today and it was all burned around the edges. I did not get any so I guess mine was burned up altogether. That's 4 days with no mail from you. It will probably come in all together. Don't forget to take my advice and go on a trip Roy!! If you don't you will be sorry. I was. Why don't you go down to Fritzie's for a few days?
Your Son & Brother
Bob

Dear Roy,

I started to make a suggestion in the other letter but didn't have enough room. You will see what I mean when you get in the service. Why don't you hitch hike to Washington D.C., stopping along the way in each town seeing all the sights and having a little fun. You can stop in Baltimore and see May & Bill and I hear Baltimore is a great town to have some fun in. After you leave there, hitch into W.D.C. You will find plenty to do and see there. Spend at least 3 days there and then take a train to Fritzie and Bernie's. It's only 2 hours on the train from there. You can't get lost as all you have to do is ask. If you need money Mom will give you all you need out of my money. Don't worry about paying it back. That is the trip I am going to make as soon as I get home.
Brother Bob

April 13, 1944
Dear Mother, Dad Roy,

We just got in from the field this afternoon where we had a little maneuver and also got used to sleeping out in this rotten climate. Even Louisiana had better weather than this. The sun shines about 12 minutes a week and the rest of the time it either rains or is foggy.

My class E allotment starts this month. You will get $15 per month or $180 year. I would rather spend it in the states than throw it away over here.

Well that's about all the news here except that I'm feeling fine and the food is really swell. Your mail comes in every day.

Your Loving Son,
Bob

4/14/44
Dear Mother Dad & Roy,

Today has been a red letter day as far as the mail is concerned. I got 3 letters from you in the morning and 3 more in the afternoon, also 4 letters from Texas. The sun was out 3 times today, I guess summer is really coming.

Your first package came today. We enjoyed it to the last piece. Everything was in good condition. I'll be glad when the pen comes as the one I am using does not belong to me. I hope the Razor Blades are on the way as the ones we have won't cut butter, and they are made in Newark too!

Well I just got some bad news just now. I'm on cpl of the guard tomorrow nite. I sure hope it stays warm til I get off.

That's all the news for today. Hoping everything's ok at home.

Love,
Bob

April 19, 1944
Dear Mother Dad & Roy,

It has been a long time since my last letter, and I'm really sorry, but it just can't be helped. We have been kept busy for the past few weeks and there is no sign of a letup. I wrote a letter the other day and it was all blacked out and sent back to me. I don't know of anything I can tell you, except that I am alright and everything is fine where I am.

The weather is still rotten and the food isn't bad.

I got a few letters from you about 4 days ago telling about being down at Fritzie's. They took 7 days to get here by air mail. Tell Addie I don't want to go to those addresses and tell Mr. Dunbar the same! I can't tell you what cities I am near or anything like that.

Well I have some work to do now so I'll close for today.

I'll send a Vmail tonite or tomorrow.

April 22, 1944
Dear Mom Dad & Roy,

Your second package arrived last nite. The Coke was swell. I enjoyed it more than anything that I have eaten since I left the state! Everything was in good shape.

We had our first summer day today, it was really beautiful. It is the only day we had   that we didn't need our coats. We are working every day now and it makes the time go faster.

If I write any more they will only black it out so I'll close for now.
Your loving Son
Bob

April 24, 1944
Hello Folks,

I just got 2 letters from Grand Pa and 2 from Helen all the same day. I can't tell you anything except that I'm in good health, unless I lie about what I think. Thanks for the cartoons Helen, we don't see very many things to laugh about here.
I hope you all are in good health, and are not working to hard.
APO. 230
As ever,
Bob

April 28, 1944
Dear Mother Dad,

I just received your letters of the 8th-12th. You wanted to know how I spent Easter. Well for once we had a clear, warm, sun shines day. We had a day off and were supposed to have church services out in the field. Everything was fine up to this. I got dressed and walked to the spot where the protestant service was supposed to be held. I was the only one in the Btn to show up except the chaplain.

I came back and went to sleep next to my tent in the sun. A little wile latter I got up and got ready for chow. But was rushed out on a work detail. I missed chow with the company but when I got back the cook had saved me half a roast chicken, and that made everything ok. I don't believe you missed me as much as I missed being home that day. Yes you are right about being satisfied right where you are. I'll be glad when I am back their too.

You asked if we have ice cream over here. Ice cream is only a distant memory. I don't mind doing with out a lot of things just so you have it waiting for me when I get back.

I can't tell you all I would like to about the food or the country as we are only allowed to tell the good things. I don't know weather Joe would like your idea or not but it is ok by me. You see a lot of things I tell you might not worry you but is likely to worry his folks.

Tell Roy to go out and do everything he ever wanted to do before he gets in the army. Eat all you can hold of everything you like best. In other words live like a king for a short time any way. Once you get in it will be a long time before you can do it again.

I am going to quit now as it is too dark to write.

Your Loving Son,

Bob

May 3, 1944

Dear Mother Dad,

Your air mail letters are coming in very regular now, and it only takes 6 to 10 days. You asked me to request a package and I will be very glad to do same. Didn't want to ask for to much as you would probably think I was starving. Send some more fruit cake like the last one. Also a box of chocolate candy. You are allowed to send a package weighing 5 lbs. and an 8 ounce pkg with out a request.

I have already received two packages and they were in good condition. I'm glad to here you and Helen and Hazel are having such a good time. I sure would like to go bowling with you. Please don't write to me about Reg and Roy any more as I get tired of hearing how hard they work in the cold and wet class room with the hard seats.

Don't bother to send me a ballot so I can vote as you have to go through so much red tape. If you want to do me a favor just vote for the guy with the mustache, as I don't want to see Eleanor elected again.

No I didn't put the money in an envelope. I sent it through the finance dept of the army. You will get a check from Washington. It takes a long time so don't worry about it. You will get 4 separate checks one for $100, and 3 for $20 each plus 1 check each month for $15 each plus 1 twenty five dollar bond each mo. I should be able to buy some kind of a fliver when I get home.

Well wish Roy a lot of luck for me with the draft board. By luck I don't know weather it would be bad or good if he does get drafted.

Tell Hazel I appreciate her wanting to send me a package but there is nothing to write about in a letter and I wouldn't feel right asking her for a package.

It's getting dark folks so I'll close for tonite.

Your loving son

Bob

May 4, 1944

Dear Mother Dad,

I can't understand why you haven't been receiving my mail. I try to write as often as I can but some times a week will slip by before I can get around to writing you. I wish you wouldn't worry so much about me as there is really nothing to worry about. Please stop using your imagination as to how we feel. We are not having the best time in our lives but it is far from being the worst. We do a lot of walking and plenty of eating and enough sleep to get by on.

We don't have passes like we did for a wile but if you have cloths you can still go to town nights. I haven't a coat so I can't go out any more at all. I have been after them to get me a new coat for a long time but they don't bother. I can wait til after I get home to have my fun anyway.

Joe is doing fine and looks good as ever.

I went to the doctor today to see about arch supports as mine are getting thin. I will go to the clinic Mon to have my feet measured for them.

Don't worry about me getting in any more fights. I'll try to keep the rest of my teeth til I get home anyway. You can stop looking for the large picture I sent because I just found out that it was never mailed. The guy that was supposed to mail it lost it.

I got Dad's letter today. It took 17 days to get here. I guess it got lost. Keep sending air mail letters as they get here quicker than V mail. Besides I don't like v mail letters.

Don't worry about your income tax Dad, just remember it takes me a whole year to earn that much money. I still owe $275 on my income tax but they will have to hang me to get any satisfaction.

Yes Dad I still get letters from June, Dot, Hazel. They will get tired of writing pretty soon though as I never answer them. I am too darn far away from them now and I never expect to go to Texas again anyway unless the army drags me their by the heels.

Here is another request for a package, now that you asked for it. 1 bottle of catsup. 1 egg in any shape or form except dried. Razor blades. Chocolate candy! If you can't send the egg send a picture or a reasonable facsimile. I guess I'll have to wait until I get home to get some of your chili sauce but remember !! save that last quart.

Well Roy it won't be long now. Just go out and raise hell until they send two M.P.'s up to the door and drag you to your new home. Don't take it too hard as the first year is the hardest. Just stay the hell out of the kitchen and don't be a cook! Stay in the crowd with the men. I'm glad you are going so well in base ball this year. You ought to be in good shape for the army.

I don't know weather I told you that I got a letter from J Keiffer or not but he says he's working hard and hopes to be going home soon. I wish him luck.

I'm glad to here Helen and you are having such a good time. It is just what she needs. I got letters from Grand Pa in Virginia and also from Kitty.

I'll close for now, as it is too dark to keep writing and besides the censor will blow a fuse if I write much more.

Love to all

Bob

May 7, 1944
Dear Mother Dad,

I received a package from you last nite. It was the one with the chocolate cake in it. It stayed in good condition and was not too stale as the raisins kept some moisture in it. We sure enjoyed it, as the cake you buy over here has very little sugar in it. I have to use pencil as this paper is to poor to take ink.

This is Sunday and they gave us a day off. The sun is shining for a change and it is fairly warm. I am washing my cloths and reading the Readers Digest in between time.

I slept until 9:30 this morning and missed breakfast, but it was worth it as we have to get up 6:30 every other morning.

Got a package from a girl in Brooklyn the other day. She sent a can of fruit, home made fudge, nuts, and a fruit cake.

Wish I could help you out with the garden this year. What are you planting? I guess it's the same as last year.

Well my clothes should be boiled out enough by now so I'll go and rinse them and hang them in a tree to dry.

I'll try to write more often from now on as we have a little more time to ourselves than we did before.
Your Loving Son
Bob

May 12, 1944
Dear Mother, Dad,

I just got your letters of the 1st 2nd 3rd and 4th all at once tonite. I am sorry about the mail Mom, but the weeks slip by so fast and with nothing that I can tell you about happening it's hard to write much more.

I just got this week's copy of the Cranford Chronicle. I'll give you the news just in case you haven't been there lately. The four Connelly brothers are in the paper this week. John is in the S Pacific with the marines, Mark in the Navy, Edward is here in England, Joe is in India.

Bogen's daughter got married to a cpl in the army. Jerry Vogel from Bayonne got married last week to one of the local boys.

I was sorry to hear about Billy Albens, although it is the best thing that could have happened to him. Maybe he found out he is not as tough or smart as he thought he was.

I don't think you believe me about the food being good Mom, from your last letter. It's the truth though. We are eating better here than at any time in the states. Of course we don't get everything we want but that is to be expected. I do miss the fresh milk and eggs but the rest of the food is delicious. We have some new cooks here from the north, and they cook the food as we like it. I haven't heard any of the Rebels kicking about it either.

I'd give anything to see your garden after all that work you put in it. I could hardly believe the beans were up already. None of the farms over here have anything up yet. In fact they are just planting now.

The last 3 letters from you were Vmail. I wish you wouldn't use it as they always come in bunches and don't get here as fast as air mail. Some times I get your air mail in 6 days. Vmail takes at least 12 days.

William Donald the guy that went to school with me in Linden and later moved to Cran. just got his commission as flight officer in Ark. He was a very smart kid and a swell guy.

I glad to hear Fritzie is coming up to the Yankee land for a visit. There is some beautiful land in Vir but it can't compare with Jersey for my money. How is Bernie coming along? And how about Fred Meyers?

It's getting dark and the mosquitoes are getting thick so I'll only write a little longer. This is the only place in the dam world where the flies and mosquitoes are worse than Jersey. They gang up on you here and you have to beat them off with a club.

That's all the news excepting that Joe raised a family of mice in his barracks bag and didn't know it til it was too late.
Until tomorrow
I remain your Loving Son
 Bob

Mothers Day
May 1944
Dear Mother, Dad,

Today is Mothers' Day, so at 11 o'clock we stopped all work and put our guns away and went to a church service. It wasn't really a modern church as you have in the city, but just a small tent hidden in the woods. The army chaplain said a beautiful prayer in honor of our mothers. It made me a little homesick and made me realize how far I am from home. I couldn't help feeling sorry for all the boys over here who have no mothers to write to them and keep reminding them that there is some good in this world of ours.

After church we had a chicken dinner which was as good as could be expected in the Army, but it made me think of how much better it would have been if you cooked it, and of how much better I would have enjoyed it if it were you that I were eating it with.

At 1 o'clock we went back to work and preparing for anything that might be asked of us.

There is nothing new here except a few summer days once in a while, so I'll close now and get some rest so I can get some work done tomorrow.
Your Loving Son,
Bob
PS Your package with the candy came last nite. Bob

May 19
Sat
Dear Mother Dad,

It has been almost a week since my last letter and I am really ashamed of myself as I have no one to blame but myself. We have not been very busy, but the time did fly by. I guess you wonder why I use these blue envelopes every once in a while. You see our censor is my platoon leader Lt. Jasper Bailey a weasel eyed, bald headed goon who does not forget a thing you write in a letter. When you use the blue envelope he does not get the chance to stick his crooked nose in our business, as it goes to the base censor.

The fellow I told you about some time ago, Ralph my asst driver had his finger cut off last week and was transferred to a hospital unit. He is the one who's baby died at birth. Jasper made the lowest remark I have ever heard any man make about him. He said Ralph did it just to get out of our outfit. I got so mad I told him everything I thought of him and expected to be court marshaled for it but I guess Jasper didn't have nerve enough to do it. I have a new asst now and he is a good driver but very lazy. I have to keep after him all the time. He will snap out of it one way or another this week or I'll know the reason why. My gunner is the best in the outfit. He is from Canada. The tank commander is from Roselle Park. We all get along swell together and are satisfied with each other's work.

I go on guard tonite and will be on all day Sunday but will try to get off long enough to go to church. I got a letter from John Keiffer today. He is doing fine according to his letter.

I haven't written to anyone excepting you in a month I guess. If they don't like it it's just too bad, because I have no intention of writing to anybody else for a long time or at least until they lift the censorship.

It's 10 o'clock at nite now. I didn't have time to finish this morning. Can you imagine 10 o'clock and the sun just going down! It doesn't get really dark til 11 or 11:30. It is always light when we get up in the morning at 6. They tell me in June you have only 5 hours of darkness.

I went to the movies in a tent the other nite and seen 'Government Girl' with Olivia De Havilland. It was a swell picture. I really got a lot of laughs out of it. Last nite I seen Tarzan and the nite before that a USO show of the stage. It was a very good act. We have a loudspeaker in camp that plays all the popular songs and a lot of old and funny ones. They keep us very well entertained over here. We have a ball team and they play every afternoon.
Your letters are coming in fine – keep it up.

You can send me a box of fruit cake and candy when you get time mail it and it will be very much appreciated. The packages come in regular now we eat most every nite at midnite. Boy you thought I ate a lot when I was home! I eat 3 times as much now. I even get up for breakfast once in a while now. I hit the chow line

3 times for supper. We had roast beef, gravy, potatoes, peas, bread and jam, coffee and canned pineapple. I had 3 full course dinners. At noon we had hot dogs and catsup. Cocoa, beans, pudding, 1 chocolate bar and a pack of cigarettes or a good 5 cent cigar.

They took us on busses to a G.I. shower today. It was a fire hose and a tent in the woods. It was a hell of a shower but we did get clean. I guess the censor is tearing his hair out by now so I'll close for today.

Love to all
Bob

May 25
Thursday
Dear Mother Dad,

Your package and 3 letters came yesterday. We all enjoyed the candy very much. The pen looks good but I haven't had a chance to use it yet. It is hard to get good ink or paper that you can use ink on. I have enough razor blades so don't send any more for a while.

It is still cold and rainy here but the sun comes out once in a while, they tell me. We just had a swell supper tonite, meat loaf, creamed carrots, peas, gravy. It's getting dark now so I will have to close until tomorrow.

Your Loving Son
Bob

May 27
Dear Mother Dad,

I just received your letter of the 18th. Gee you must have a swell garden. We never had one that big before. I can almost see those ears of corn on the plate now.

Sunday

I didn't have time to finish last nite so I'll finish while waiting for church services to begin. The US Army Band gave a concert here last nite. It was rotten. The band was only half here and they tried to copy Harry James and other swing bands. It was the worst military band I ever heard bar none.

We had chicken for supper last nite again. It was pretty tough but we all enjoyed it anyway.

I didn't get up for breakfast this morning for the first time in a week and they had a swell breakfast. I seem to pick the wrong time to miss a meal every time.

I hear they are going to have a movie this afternoon in tent. I don't know what picture is playing but it usually is good.

I guess you are looking forward to your vacation next mo. I am glad you are lucky enough to get one and hope you have a good time. It will be hard for you to go any place far from home as the trains are packed at least they were a few months ago.

Try to get Roy to go on a trip for a week or two before they grab him. He can use some of my money if he hasn't enough. Give him all he needs and tell him not to worry about paying it back. It's time for church now so I'll finish later. I just got back from church and have a few minutes before dinner so I'll finish this up quick.

The sun is out today and it is getting warmer all the time. By 3 it ought to be warm enough to take off our jackets. I think I will go take a shower this afternoon if I can get up enough courage. You see the shower is an open air affair and though the water is hot the wind is plenty cold.

I guess I might as well tell you as you will hear about it anyway. I got all my hair cut off! Down to the bone. It is the only way to get rid of dandruff and besides it's clean. Almost all the boys did the same. It looks funny but feels great. We took turns cutting each others hair off with the clippers. It was lots of fun.

Joe just walked in my tent and what do you think he did. He got a big V for victory shaved in his hair. It looks like he_ _. I guess he will have it all off soon.

I can't seem to keep at this letter, it is now 7:30. I went to the movies this afternoon and seen 'Dangerous Blonds'. It wasn't bad but I seen it before. When I got back I took a nap until supper.

Well the boys are settled down to a nice quiet game of cards in one tent and the others are sitting around writing letters and reading the latest edition of the NY Daily News (Apr 10) that came in the afternoon mail. I got a letter from Helen M. this afternoon but none from you, I guess I'll get two tomorrow.

The company commander is outside our tent now with a big pair of scissors and scalping every man that goes by with any excess hair he just got a hold of Ed Brady. It's funny to see all the bald heads running around.

Well this is the last sheet of paper I have so I'll just have to close this time. Remember me to all the folks and neighbors, and thank Mrs. Fisher for the catsup. If you get time drop a line to the Lakes and tell them that I will write first chance I get.

Try to explain to Kitty and the Mildens that I can't write to every one and am trying to give you all the news so you can tell them what's going on.
Take good care of yourselves and don't worry about me as I'm in perfect health and doing fine.
God bless you all
Your loving Son
Bob

June 1, 1944
Dear Folks,

This is my third letter to you today. You must think I'm nuts but every time I finish one I think of other things I want to say. Tell Roy he can sell my 22 rifle for anything he thinks is a fair price. He can use the money for anything he wants to spend it on and you see to it that he has a good time doing it. Tell him it's for his birthday present (last and next).

Joe is in my platoon again so I see more of him now. You want to hear about all the trouble we get into but you must remember the censor is our platoon leader and he would love to know even more than you who is responsible for some of the jokes that are going on. (Only kidding Lt. B)

Don't worry about me Mom it's impossible for anything to happen to me and Joe; we were born with a horse shoe around our neck.
Bob

June 14
France
Dear Mom Dad,

There is nothing new here today except that we didn't go up to the front. The sun was shining all morning but those dark clouds are overhead again. It will start in raining any minute.

I just wrote a short letter to Bayonne and will write to Kitty as soon as I finish this letter. Roy's letter came today along with a card from Fritzie. None of your mail came in three days now.

We got paid today. What a laugh. I got paid 190 francs ($2.80) for 2 months. There is 3500 francs on the way home.

I didn't have time to finish before as we went to dinner. It was a swell meal. We had pie, corn, salmon, white bread, butter, carrots, coffee, and a hand full of hard candy.

We just had another mail call and I got one letter from you dated June 29. You said you received my first letter from France. You should be getting a lot of them soon. I also got a Vmail from Kitty just now. Joe spent part of the afternoon with me and when he seen me get my mail he left for his tank to see if he got any.

I have to close right now Mom, sorry I haven't time to finish. I will write in a few days.
Your Loving Son,
Bob

June 16, 1944
Dear Mother Dad Roy,

This is the first chance that I have had to write since we landed in France. Yes I'm still here in France as we haven't had time to reach Berlin with all these Germans getting in our way. In case you had any idea of seeing Europe after the war you had better change your plans as there won't be much left of it when we get done.

We have seen plenty of action as you can see by the papers. I haven't had a scratch nor do I expect to. Joe is fine and is now a tank commander. I see him every day or so as he is attached to my platoon. You can call his folks and let them know he is alright in case this letter reaches you before his gets home. Please don't worry about me as I can take care of myself. I was a little afraid at first but don't mind it at all now.

I haven't had a letter from you since the 2nd of June but I am sure they will all catch up to me soon. Just keep writing to me and I will be as happy as can be. You will have to get the news from the paper as I am too busy to find out what's going on.

We are getting all the wine we want and then some. We mix it with our water to keep it fresh.

I will write as often as I can, but don't worry if you don't hear from me as we are very busy and can't always mail the letters that we do write.

I will close now as the censor has plenty of work to do besides read a lot of minor details.

God bless you all

Your Son, Bob

June 16

Dear Mother Dad Roy,

I have only 15 minutes to write so please excuse the shortness. I'm still in good shape and fine health. We get plenty to eat but not much sleep. The French wine is pretty good but I haven't had time to find out about the women yet!

I wrote a long letter yesterday but it may not reach you for some time. Joe is fine and also Ed Brady. I hope you are all doing fine. Don't worry about me as I'm not worried about myself. We are sure making it hot for the Germans though. I can tell you all about it in 14 days.

Keep writing and some day I'll get the mail.

Your Loving Son

Bob

June 20, 1944

Dear Mother Dad Roy,

Last nite I received your letters of the 1st and 7th with the pictures enclosed. I was glad to get the pictures as the others I had were destroyed. Please send one of Dad and Roy again. We are in a rest camp for a few days rest. It is really swell to sleep all nite and half the day. I just got up at 1 o'clock and went to church. Thanks for the letter Dad it is swell to hear from you once in a while.

I will write a longer letter as soon as I can so don't mind the shortness of this one.

I slept with Joe in a haystack last nite. It was the only dry spot in all France as it has been raining the past couple of days

Love to all

Bob

June 21, 1944

Dear Mother Dad, Roy.

I have a little time on my hands so I thought I would write you a few lines. This is a German pen on French ink, G.I. paper and a hell of a writer so please don't mind what the letter looks like.

We are still in a rest camp and the weather is getting better all the time. The sun is out now so we may find a dry place to sleep tonite. I would liked to have seen Audrey in that homemade bathing suit. She must have looked like Daisy May!

I'm so glad to hear that Roy got out of school. You didn't say how he made out in Newark, but I can guess. I'm starting to like K Rations now and am getting fat on them. I am eating so much cheese I'm beginning to look like a cow. There is plenty of fresh milk here but we don't drink much of it as the cows are usually sick. We drink mostly cider that we get from the French farmers. It is sour but at least it is something to drink. We got some bread made by the French and it is hard and flat, but after three weeks of hard tack it is delicious.

We got some eggs from a barnyard and when we went to fry them out come some feathers (not the freshest I guess).

Joe Conti just came over to see me from D Company. You remember the little guy I had over the house from Roselle. He is OK and looks good. Sid Craig is sleeping about 100 yds up the field from me. He's doing alright too. He got busted to a private again. I guess he is happier that way. If we are still here tomorrow I will write to Kitty, but I will always write to you first when we get a break. I spoke to Joe and he said it is alright if you invite his folks out any time you want to now.

I was going to write you for a knife but I made a swell one out of a German bayonet. Your mail will come to me every nite as long as we are near the HQ where they can find us. No packages are coming in yet but will probably all come together.

I have only seen one nice French girl since we have been here and then under very unusual circumstances. We had to drive through her house to get to where we wanted to go and she didn't look very pleased so I didn't bother going back for an introduction. There are only old men and women and very small children left over here. I don't know where the rest of the people are.

Well good luck Roy in your new career and try to get in the F. Artillery or home guard, or if possible the Jew Navy (Sea Bees) where you will be safe and have plenty to learn at the same time.

Don't work too hard Dad, take all the time off you need to rest and have a good time while doing it. Don't you work too hard in that garden either Mom. Enjoy yourself but don't overdo it.

Til next time

Your Loving Son

Bob

June 22, 1944

Dear Mother and Dad,

The mail didn't come in yet this afternoon but I am hoping for a few letters anyway. I just got a brand new tank so there is plenty of work around this rest camp now. Joe came over to help me for a wile today.

I have to wash yet and I want to drop a few lines to Kitty so I know you won't mind me making this so short.

I am feeling fine and eating regular so don't worry. I might have some good news in a few days.

Your Loving Son, Bob.

June 23, 1944

Dear Mother Dad,

By this time I guess Roy is in Camp Dix or perhaps some other camp. I'm glad he had a good time at the graduation party. Let me know all about him as soon as he writes. You asked about when I left Shanks. It was on Lincoln's birthday and I arrived on Washington's birthday. I have been in Scotland, Whales, England and now France. I guess that will clear you up on all you wanted to know.

I'm working hard on my new tank and have a great time doing it. We have not selected a name for it yet but I will pass it on when we decide upon one. I am going to write you a full letter starting tonite, God only knows when it will get mailed.

Take care of yourselves and God bless you both.

Your Son Bob

June 24

Dear Mom & Dad,

There is really nothing to write about tonite as the mail did not come in yet. I'm having a hell of a time trying to write with Joe here fooling around. He won't leave either as I am using his pen. My pen is no more. I had to leave a place in a hurry one nite and I didn't have time to pick it up. The heck of it is my cigarette lighter was right beside it.

I cooked supper tonite for the boys, it wasn't bad either. We had a can of peas, lima beans, corned beef, cold biscuits, coffee, butter, a can of cheese and some black bread. It wasn't bad either. We eat 4 days' rations in one day in our tank, it's the only way to catch up on the meals we lost while we were at the front. Skelly's here practicing up on his French. You ought to hear him. I'm feeling fine now so you know the eats are good and the weather is grand (at last).

J'ecruai deamain, pour maintenant, bon nuit.

Votre fils Bob

June 24

Dear Mother Dad,

All your letters arrived today, some new some old, but I enjoyed every one. They answered a few questions I had on my mind too. I couldn't figure whose baby was running around the house. I didn't think about Audrey being up to see you. I don't know why my letters have been held up so long. I could not write for about two weeks but I did write every day up til the day we hit the boat.

We just got a whole steel helmet full of pancake batter and another helmet full of syrup. You ought to have seen us trying to fry pancakes in a mess kit over a blow torch. We burned a few and then the Lt got the thing in hand and turned out a bunch of beauties. We fried them in bacon fat that we had saved from morning. By the way I'm getting to be an expert at boiling water and frying bacon.

I was just thinking we would be in sad shape in case of an air raid with all our helmets full of food and engine oil.

The French kids are having a swell time around our camp. We give them most of our candy and a few other odds and ends. They love it. I have it nice now as my tank commander can speak French (4 yrs) and the gunner (2 yrs). Between the two we get along swell. The kids here wear wooden shoes, just like the pictures you see of the Dutch. Their clothes are not much more than rags. They do look fairly well fed as most of them live on farms.

We should have plenty of meat as we kill plenty of cows and pigs by accident but don't have time until a few days later to go after it, and by that time it is spoiled.

Well you probably want to know when I hit the beach so I might as well tell you. It was D Day. The landing was a terrible thing where we were. I never want to see anything like it again. If every one of you civilians had seen it there would never be another war. Yes the ocean was full of boats and the sky full of planes but that is only one side of the story. The rest was too rotten to describe. We had to fight our way all the way inland. My tank was the second tank in _____ ((*censor cut out at least one word*)) we took the town after a hot fight and I mean hot the whole town was on fire. I can't tell you of any other battles until 4 days after they take place. Ernie Pile gave a perfect description of the whole thing. Get that paper and you will have the whole thing. Many other things have happened that I can't tell you about. I told you all this because I promised I would give you all the news I could. You know I will tell you if anything happens to me so you can quit worrying. Joe and I are doing fine. There is plenty of work to do yet but I feel sure I will be home for (well maybe not Christmas) but soon after. I almost forgot to tell you I seen four German planes shot down before I hit the beach. I was one of many who shot at them from the turret of the tank. Who knows maybe it was me who made the hit.

Dad I can now see that you knew what you were talking about when you said I would be glad to see some of those Destroyers you build floating around me. You should have seen those little devils shell the beach. The best yet was those 16 in naval guns from the battle wagons, they really make all hell break loose. I wish you would answer me one question Dad. Why the hell don't you weld some wheels on them so they can come along with us?

Take care of yourselves now and go out once in a while and enjoy that swell country you're in.

Your Loving Son

Bob

June 25

Dear Mom Dad,

I guess you are surprised to see so many letters come in from me lately. I'm writing   every day while we are here in the rest camp as it will be very seldom that I write once we get to the front again. I had the nearest thing to a bed last nite as I had since the draft board caught up to me. I put a big arm full of straw in my fox hole and three blankets over me. It was the best nite's sleep since we left Plymouth. Not even an air raid to bother us. I stood my guard in bed and rather than climb out and wake up my relief I stayed on guard for another relief and daylight.

The nites are getting longer now, it's dark from midnite til 5 in the morning. We hate the dark when up at the front as that's the only time the Germans have nerve enough to send their planes up.

I will be sending a roll of money home one of these days if we ever get paid. They just gave us 200 francs in French money before we left England. That's 4 bucks. I lost all mine in a poker game on the boat, but it doesn't make any difference as you can't spend a thing here.

Are my bonds still coming in? How about the other $15 per mo.?

I wrote to Kitty the other day also a few lines to the Bayonne mob.

Don't mind me if I just ramble on, as there is nothing new to write about.

Did you know that D Day was a day late? We were halfway over here when we turned back to wait for better weather. It was supposed to come off on the full moon so we could fight nite and day. The moon is just starting to come out again. It reminds me of how we waited for the last full moon.

The weather is beautiful here now. It's just like back home in the summer. The trees are very thick with leaves and the bushes are so thick you can't see more than a hundred yds in any direction. That's why it is so hard to fight over here. It's the same as Indian fighting used to be.

The snipers get in the brush and you just can't see them. We found one way to get them though. We spray all the brush and hedge rows with our mach guns. We fire til our barrels are red hot and the empty cartridges are up to our knees. We went back through the woods one day after an attack and found Germans dead 4 and 5 deep in the bushes and ditches. We have captured loads of prisoners and equipment. I have a German mess kit, bayonet. I had a swell rifle but it was destroyed in action. I also had a beautiful hand made knife which was really a work of art. I was going to send it home but it was also destroyed.

John Nunzo from Kenelworth is here beside me reading the latest issue of the Stars and Stripes , our newspaper.

I have a new tank and crew now. The tank commander and censor is Lt Bulvin from Pennsylvania. He is also my French, English, and Spelling teacher. The gunner is Fitler from Brooklyn, our gunner Joe Patula from Patterson NJ., asst driver pvt Fortney from Wisconsin, in the army 17 weeks. All I have to do now is teach him to drive.

I guess you are wondering why the heck I took the sergeant's rating. Well it wasn't my fault I was tricked into it. They had it all cut and dried before I knew it. Well it means a little more money for after the war anyway. That will bring my pay up to $93.60 per mo.

The packages you sent didn't catch up yet but will probably all come in at once. I better request another now as maybe by 1945 I'll get it. What I really want is more of that fruit cake you sent once before. It was swell. Also a box of Schrafts chocolate would hit the spot.

I can't wait until the other packages arrive. They always make it seem like Easter morning. Remember those days? We get plenty of hard candy and G.I. chocolate but it is strictly Army. I don't know how the people over here can live and be happy without a soda fountain and an ice cream store around the corner. People over here don't know what that stuff is.

I think after the war I'll open up a string of hotdog stands from England to China. These people don't know what they are missing. By the way do they still have Coca Cola back in the States?

I have a lot of work to do tomorrow so I won't have time to write until maybe two or three days so don't worry. I'll try to drop a Vmail if nothing else as often as is possible.

If you are still home Roy I want to wish you all the luck in the world in your new job. You will probably hate it at first but it might do you some good. Don't be a fool and save your money in the States but go out every chance you have, and have a good time. Try and get a mail clerk's job as it is the best in the army. If you can't get that get the company clerk job by hook or crook. Don't let any of those corporals give you any lip, just sock a Jew and they will leave you alone. Then when you get out of the guard house you will be a good soldier.

Well folks it's time I do a little work around here such as eating supper, so I'll close for today hoping you're all in the best of health.
Your Loving Son
Bob

6/27/44
Dear Mom Dad,

There has been nothing new going on here since my last letter. The only thing that has changed is the weather. It is raining almost all the time now. It makes it hard to work and almost impossible to sleep. The sun comes out about every half hour for a few minutes and then it rains again. My foxhole is fairly dry as I have it covered with heavy timber and lined with straw and leaves. I get all full of mud when I have to climb in or out of it though. This has been five straight days with no mail from you. I got 2 letters from Mapl.. Donn (*illegible*) this morning. Your mail will probably be in tonite's mail, so I'll just wait. I'm feeling fine and dandy and the rest is doing us all a lot of good.
Best wishes to all,
Bob

June 29 1944
Dear Mom Dad,

Three of your letters came in today. June 10, 11, 11,. I'm sorry to hear that Audrey is such a poor mother. I thought she was doing alright. I was surprised to hear that you haven't been getting my mail. By now you should be getting my mail from France. You asked about the flowers that are over here. The fields have the same kind of flowers as ours in the states, only a few extra kinds scattered around. Poppies grow around the woods wild. The birds are all in the states I guess for I haven't seen very many. I seen a red squirrel running around the area today for the first time. There are millions of rabbits over here, both tame and wild. Every farmer has a bunch of them. I seen as many as 6 wild rabbits in one field of carrots at one time. Every farmer has a few cows, horses, chickens, ducks, and once in a wile a couple of donkeys. The trees are about the same as at home except for thousands of apple trees all over this part of the country. The houses are all stone as in England. Most of them are at least a hundred years old. At the camp where I was stationed in England the houses were built in 1000 AD.

I just got back from church a few minutes ago. That's about the third time this week. There is no set day for church any more. We just have it any time and any place when the Chaplain can catch us. Most every one goes to church now, as it's not like it used to be. Men are going now that have never been in a church before.

GrandPa sent a letter today for the first time in weeks. It was even shorter than Dad's if possible. Let's have a few letters once in a while, Dad. You have more to write and more time than I do. I gave up all hope of getting one from Roy.

I'll put in the menu we had today so you can see what kind of stuff the army is putting out to keep us going. Well there isn't another thing that I can write and not have the censor jumping down my neck.

Say hello to John and the rest of the Fishers for me. Tell them we can't write very often but I'll try to drop them a few lines some day. Remember me to Mr. Claflen too the next time you see him. Enclosed find picture of Ann Puzzo. If you ever see her you can tell her I read all about her here in France. Tell her we need lots of pretty nurses here. Who knows maybe some day I'll be lucky enough to get wounded and see some of them. I just thought of something funny that happened a short time ago. Remember the German Lt. who had Skelly busted in Louisiana for putting grease on the Buggie wheels (mit der fingers)? He was bending over a slit trench and a sniper hit him in the can with a wooden bullet. It might not seem funny to you but it would if you only knew him.

Well I'll close for tonite wishing you both the best of health and lots of good luck.

Your loving Son, Bob

July 1, 1944

Dear Mom Dad,

We are still in the rest camp much to our surprise. It is swell to be back of the line for a change but there is nothing for us to do. All we do is sit around all day and wait for mail call. They brought some back around to us yesterday but they are either dry or about the war. I know too much about the war to be reading about it in my spare time.

I am waiting for the Readers Digest to come in. It is long over due. It will be good reading for a few hours anyway. I'm beginning to hope we go up to the front soon again as the time flies up there. About 5 days at a time is enough though. The last time was 13 days and it was far too much. You see we don't get any sleep all the time we are up there. When you do sleep it is right in the driver's seat.

Two of your letters came today, one from the 15th the other was an old one of the 29th of May.

We got three eggs the other day and have been saving them until we could get 2 more, one for each man. I put my foot on one last nite and today a little puppy got hold of another one and bit a hole in it before we could stop him. That leaves us 4 to go.

We got some veal chops from a farmer yesterday and they cost us 200 franks $4.00 to you. We just had enough for one meal for the crew. I sent home 3,500 francs yesterday. You will get it in a few months if you're lucky. That's $70. You should have received three checks for $15.00 by now. You haven't mentioned getting them yet. There is one due each month also one bond.

Has Fritzie arrived yet? Every time you write you say she is coming on a different date. I can hardly wait till she gets here. Don't mind me I was just dreaming I was home. You seem to think the war will be over soon, I hope you are right. The only trouble is the Germans don't know about it.

Tell Roy he's crazy to be working just before he goes in the army. He will be very sorry he didn't have a little fun first. He won't be as lucky as I was with all the passes and furloughs, although he might fool me and get stationed in an office some place in Jersey. I hope he does.

It is still raining off and on every little while. Now I believe the vets of the last war about the weather over here. You can tell Pam Albains I said so too. I read about Bill Albains in the paper yesterday. That's all the news from here so I'll close now.

Your Loving Son,

Bob

July 3, 1944

Dear Mom Dad,

We are still in the rest camp and it is still raining. Joe made sergeant today too. That is all the news in a nut shell. I am feeling as good as ever considering the weather and the country I'm in.

Two of your letters came yesterday but none today. No packages yet for me. I guess they will be in one of these days.

I hope you all enjoy the 4th at some beach or up in the mountains some place. I wish I could be going with you but I never enjoyed the beach anyway.

Until tomorrow so long.

Your Son

Bob

July 5

Dear Mom Dad,

I just found out about your birthday being last month Mom. I'm sorry I never thought of it til now, but things like that always did slip my mind and I guess they always will. It's a little late but Happy Birthday anyway. Dad I got to admit that I forgot about Fathers' Day too, but honest I was so darn busy around that time one day was the same as the next.

Helen guessed wrong this time, but I'm glad I was at the place where they needed me most.

When you don't get any mail from me Mom, that is the time you can stop worrying as by the time the mail stops coming in to you I am back in another rest camp. Sometimes it may be a long time in between letters but I promise I will write every chance I have. John Nunze from Kenelworth is now the gunner in my tank. He is one of the best. I'll have him over to the house some day when we get back. When I started this letter I thought I had plenty to write but now I'm stopped.

That's about all the news for today so I'll close and get a little sleep.

Your Loving Son,

Bob

July 6 1944
Dear Mom Dad,

    Summer is here at last. It was so hot today we couldn't stay in bed after 11 o'clock. It's the first day that it didn't rain, but the day isn't over yet. Joe and I went to a band concert this afternoon. The band was pretty good too! It's the first music we had in a long time. No mail came in yet today and no packages. The other fellows are lucky with the packages, mine must have ended up on the bottom of the channel. We have it all planned to make shrimp cocktails for the platoon when it does come. One shrimp and one shot of catsup per man.

    I'm really feeling fine now after all this rest, our nerves were pretty well shot when we first came to this camp.

    I hope you're all in the best of health and having a swell time on your vacation
Your Loving Son
Bob

July 9, 1944
France
Dear Mother Dad,

    I missed writing for the few days just past as we have been out on a little maneuvers and we also had a drill schedule. Forty five minutes of exercises every morning. I guess the Lt is trying to make a football team out of us or something. I'm not used to working any more, and my legs and back are stiff as a board. I'll be almost glad to get up to the front again. Well it's over a month already since we hit the beach of this God forsaken country. The time goes by so fast it's hard to believe. France is not as bad as England but it's plenty bad. It rains at least twice per day if not more.

    The only time we are allowed into a town is when the Germans are in it. As soon as we chase them out, the town is put off limits to all soldiers. I'm in favor of leaving the damn krauts stay here in France as they must like it here or they wouldn't fight so hard to stay, and I'm damn sure I don't want any part of the joint.

    The cherries are ripe now and I'm going out this afternoon and fill up on them. It's too bad you can't be here and mix up a few cherry pies for the boys. That's all we talk about now, food, food, and more food. We build imaginary cakes, home cooked dinners, ice cream sodas, hot dogs, steaks with onions. That goes on far into the nite sometimes and we end up eating some canned cheese, hard biscuits and coffee. Our emergency rations are almost gone. I'll have to go up and order some more before we leave here.

    We were supposed to have church this morning but the chaplain never turned up. I guess he got caught in traffic up at the front. I go to church twice a week so missing this one won't hurt me.

Joe and I have a post war plan that can't be beat. We are going up to his father's country home and do nothing but eat, sleep and fish for the first two months. We are going to spend all our mustering out pay $300 on food, mostly steaks. When that's done we will work about 30 hours a week until the next war. Then we will cut off our legs and tell the draft board to go to hell!

Roy's picture came yesterday in the late mail. What the heck is that outfit he is wearing, the latest zoot suit? Wait til he sees the suit Uncle Sam is going to give him.

The next time you write to John Kieffer, tell him I lost his address on D Day and that's the reason I haven't answered his last letter. Remember me to all the neighbors and Mrs. Bonnel. Tell John Kemp I said he shouldn't work so hard and stop trying to win the battle of production by himself. Tell George Claften not to be too darn anxious to go overseas.

I almost got you a beautiful German wrist watch Dad, but every time I tried to get out of the tank and grab it some damn sniper chased me back with a burp gun. The guy that had it couldn't tell time any more so I figured you could use it. Hoping you are all in as good health as I am, I remain your Loving Son
Bob

July 13, 1944
France
Dear Mother Dad,

I suppose you are wondering why you didn't receive any more mail in the past few days. We have been up at the front doing some good work. At least it looked good to me and we altered the map of Europe a little more.

Joe Skelly did some wonderful work with his big gun. He fired over our heads in support of our advance. We could see his shells landing on the enemy. I call him a 4F because he is so far behind the lines when he does his job. He burns up for a while but he can't stay mad long. He tried his best to stay in the fighting first platoon with me, but he was too good a gunner to waste on a little 75mm gun.

I couldn't tell you before but I had a tank shot out from under me in the first days of the invasion. No one in the crew was hurt. I was trapped behind the enemy lines for over half a day. When it got dark our boys made an attack and got me back to the tank. I drove for five more days as a replacement in different tanks and then we came back to a rest camp, where I got another tank of my own. I just found out yesterday from some of the boys that after I was knocked out Joe was refused permission to start a 1 tank attack on the enemy guns that hit my tank. He thought I was dead. I thought he had more sense than to think a damn German could kill me.

The weather has been very good all day today for a change. It's sure nice to be back here at camp again for a few days. For the first time in a month there isn't a shot to be heard.

They brought our mail up to us at the front lines yesterday and it made everyone feel a hundred percent better. I got one letter from you Dad and another of yours Mom. Roy's didn't get here yet.

The eggs finally came!! The package was squashed as thin as a dime. The smell was terrible. I just dug a very deep hole and got rid of them.

It's dark now so I will have to close for today.

Love to All

Your Son Bob

July 14

France

Dear Mom Dad,

We didn't go up to the front at all yesterday or today. All we did was work on the tank, eat, sleep. We are getting class B rations now and do we enjoy them. This morning we had some of the best biscuits I ever tasted, for breakfast. We are also getting in some real powdered eggs. It took us a long time to learn to like some of that powdered food we got in England and Scotland. I only received one letter today and it was from Helen. She didn't have much to say but I am always glad to get a letter from someone back home. I didn't see Joe all day today, I guess he was sleeping and getting some well earned rest.

I'll be glad to meet that fellow that you are working with Dad. He must be a right guy. I'll do my best to prove all those things you told him about me. I don't do any walking over here but I'll bet I can out sit him. I have gone 48 hours without getting out of the driver's seat. I have also gone over two weeks in the seat with only ten and fifteen minute breaks when the shooting let up a little. We haven't had our shoes off except for a quick wash and change of socks since June 1st.

If he likes fishing, tell him to hang around until after the war because that is something I am going to do plenty of. Roy's letter didn't come yet, maybe it will be in tomorrow's mail.

It's starting to rain now so don't mind if the paper is a little wrinkled. We did pretty good today, it hasn't rained in 6 or 7 hours.

I almost forgot to tell you that we had fresh oranges for breakfast. That's the big news for today. Yesterday we had canned chicken. It was a treat for all of us.

Please send me another picture of Dad as I haven't got but one of you and Roy. If possible send 1 picture of all three of you. I didn't have time to even get my gun out of the tank. I lost everything I had, including 1 pair of shoes that were tied on the back of the tank. All of my crew were made sergeants after the excitement. That's why I have a different crew.

I'll write tomorrow if possible, until then God bless you all.

Your Loving Son

Bob

July 18, 1944
France
Dear Mom Dad,

We are back in a rest camp today. On top of that we have the sun shining and are running around with our shirts off. What more could you want? They made us get up for breakfast at 8 but that's all the orders we had so far today. I went to church services yesterday afternoon. We have a new chaplain coming here from the Div. He is a swell guy. You can often see him up at the front helping the wounded. He is giving another service this afternoon at four o'clock. I think I'll go up again if there is no work to do.

I had company here last nite from HQ platoon. Joe Skelly by name. He is getting fat over here. I heard last nite he is supposed to get a Bronze Star for getting out of his tank under heavy artillery fire and giving first aid to a blind shell shocked soldier.

The mail didn't come in yet, but I am hoping for a few letters today. There is no news so I will just try to remember some of the things that happened before we hit the beach.

We came over here on an English L.C.T. with an all limey crew. The captain was about 35 and had a red beard and thought he was hot stuff. While we were at anchor in the waters off England, the captain fell in the water and almost drowned as he couldn't swim. The crew didn't like him so just stood and laughed. It was just about what you could expect from an English officer. Later on in the day we decided to go for a swim as the air was very warm and we were very dirty. I dove over the side and out about 15 ft. The water was so cold I couldn't breathe. I just about made it back to the boat and got hold of a rope. I stayed in for a few minutes hoping I would get used to the cold but I kept getting colder so I came out and lay in the sun all afternoon getting warm. I expected to see icebergs floating around that channel for the rest of the trip. We spent 8 days on that damn boat altogether. There was no excitement until the last day. We had an air raid to start with and at the time I thought it was plenty of excitement. It was after dark when they attacked. Three battleships and hundreds of other ships opened up on them all at once including me with a fifty cal mach gun in the turret of my tank. You can't imagine what it looked like. There were millions of tracer bullets flying in all directions. It lit up the sky for miles around. We shot down 3 planes within 10 minutes. They all crashed within 200 yds of our boat. They all came down in flames. It was some sight. The next morning you could see the wreckage all over the water. From then on came more excitement than I ever thought could happen before one man's eyes. You probably read about it in the papers but I don't think you can realize just how bad it was. If you read Ernie Pyle's column in the paper it will give you an idea of what it was. He hit the beach in the same spot as we did only a long time after.

I would like to tell you about a lot of things that happened to us in England and on that English boat and on other English boats that our boys were on but we are not allowed to tell any of the low tricks and mean things that our beloved allies do to make life rotten for any American on British soil. Who knows maybe we wouldn't be fighting the Germans alone (double meaning).

It's almost time for supper and I forgot about church, so I had better wash up and get ready for chow. I'll write a Vmail tomorrow.
Your Loving Son
Bob

July 19, 1944
France
Dear Mom Dad,

The mail man was very good to me today. He brought 5 letters all from you. I was sure glad to hear from you. I'm so glad to hear you are having such a good time this summer. After all that's just what I'm over here fighting for. There is no one in this world that deserves to have fun more than you. Keep going out to all the shows and beaches every time you get chance. When I get home I am going to see that you have more fun than you ever had in your life.

I'm sorry to hear that Bill Meyers and Ray McLean were wounded but maybe they were lucky. It is sometimes better to get wounded and spend the rest of the war in bed. It saves you going through hell for a long time.

It is too bad Fritzie couldn't stay longer and keep you company but her family must miss her too. I'm glad to hear Bernie can see things 1 at a time again.

From your letters I can see that you are letting your imagination run wild again. I told you before that if anything happens to me I will tell you as soon as I am permitted to do so. I have been through a lot and I found out that I can take good care of myself.

I'll talk to Joe about writing more often, I thought he wrote every day. Joe can take care of himself too, so there is no reason for his folks to worry. We are not taking any unnecessary chances as we have a lot of plans for after the war.

Thank Ester for writing to me along with the gang. I didn't have any idea who the hell she was but was afraid to ask for fear it was someone I should know.

Tell John Zulick he isn't a man until he swims the English Channel. It's worse than the North Pole.

Your two packages arrived today in perfect condition. Everything was swell. Joe came down and helped us finish it. I didn't open the shrimp yet, as it will be used for a special occasion. Thank Mrs. Fisher for the catsup. I had it on my supper tonite and saved enough for the shrimp. The boys get a kick out me putting catsup on pancakes and dried eggs. They started to nickname me 'Catsup' back in England. When I told them how you use it Dad, they wouldn't believe it.

Today was hot and clear, but it looks like rain for tonite.

No the boys in my crew weren't hurt. They are all sergeants and you can't have 5 sergeants in one tank. That is why my crew has been changed. No the gunner I had wasn't the same one that Bernie had working for him. This guy never worked a day in his life. That's why he isn't my gunner any more.

Mom I am going to have to ask you for another package. I need writing paper bad. I have to borrow every piece I use until it gets here. All they give us is Vmail. I don't want to start using that as you might do same and I hate a Vmail letter. You just start reading and its all over.

By the time this letter reaches you, your vacation will be in full swing. Have a good time and if you don't have enough time take another 2 weeks extra. Next year I'll be on vacation from Mather Springs about this time. I'll bet you can't guess where I'll go either. It will be in that big chair next to the radio. I might even hook up the ice box on the other side of the chair.

Throw in a pen or pencil along with that package too will you Mom? The boys want to thank you for the swell candy and cookies too Mom.

There isn't much more to write about, but I'll try to fill up this page somehow.

It just started to rain so I'll have to close til tomorrow.

Love to you all

Bob

~later~

P.S. Here is a list of stuff for the package: more shrimp. You will read what the special occasion was in the paper tomorrow. The boys thought they were home when we had shrimp cocktails.

See if you can get some pepperoni in some Italian butcher shop. The boys get it in every package and do I love it.

Bob

July 21

Dear Mom, Dad,

Well I missed writing yesterday but I'll try to make up for it today. Last nite after supper I was about to write you a letter when I got orders to go back near the beach. I went by truck and we passed through all the towns that a few weeks ago were still in German hands. We passed through one town that I remember very well, as my old tank was the first of the bunch in there. We captured a German ammunition truck as it was trying to supply the big guns that were shelling us. We later had to blow the truck up as a German was hiding in the back of it and we couldn't take any chances. The explosion could be heard for miles around.

Joe just came down to visit me in my pup tent. He is lying beside me now to keep out of the rain.

Well to get on with the story we saw sights yesterday that were almost unbelievable. The army has really moved in to stay. There are road gangs all along the roads building 3 and 4 lane highways out of these little cow paths that we came through. It looks like the old W.P.A. They have steam rollers, dump trucks, cement mixers, air hammers, etc. The people are all moved back in their homes, or what is left of their homes and life goes on as usual.

One railroad that we captured had a big Am. *(American)* locomotive and box cars running in full swing. I remember the day we captured the railroad station. I was in the asst driver's seat taking it easy for a while and manning the 30 cal mach gun. We came around a bend in the road and were fired upon by enemy guns in the rail yard. We opened up with everything we had. We blew up the station with the 75mm and sprayed mach gun bullets all over the place. I was up to my knees in empty shells. We took the town soon after with little opposition, except for dozens of snipers.

When we got back here last nite it was dark and I was unable to write, or even read the mail I had waiting for me.

The food is getting better all the time. I went out and bought a steak yesterday and it was delicious. Then we had a grand surprise for dinner, fresh pork chops. It is the first fresh meat since we left England. I guess it will be coming in regular now.

That's about all the news from here, so I guess I'll close and go listen to the news on the radio. I hope you are having a good time on your vacation. Be sure and tell me all about it.

Love to all,

Your son Bob

Dear Mom Dad,

This is a poor excuse for a letter but it has been raining so much I just couldn't write without getting the paper all wet. It has been raining steady for the past day and a half. Today looks promising, the sky is cloudy but it is streaked with blue. We haven't been doing anything except getting a good rest. Yes we did go to a band concert last nite. It was pretty good too.

Well it's starting to rain again so I'll have to close.

I hope you are enjoying better weather on your vacation than we are getting here. But after all I'm not on a vacation so I shouldn't mind.

Love to all

Your Son Bob

July 23

France

Dear Mother Dad,

Today is Sunday and a good one at that. At least it has been so far. This afternoon we went to a stage show put on by French actors. It was strictly <u>corn</u>!! But at least it took your mind off the war for a few hours anyway. There were 9 girls and 4 or 5 men. The girls were homely as the devil and the men were just a bunch of jerks. They had one good act, at least it was good compared with the rest. It was a little midget doing a dance by himself. If it wasn't for him the show would have been a flop altogether. This evening after supper we went to a movie in a barn. The picture cost about $65 to film. What do you think it was about? War naturally. The name of it was Private Hargrove. To top that as we left the barn after the show, we loaded up and what do you think we saw? That's right, German planes. Our anti aircraft drove them off in a few minutes but it all helped to make us forget the war anyway. It is 9:30 o'clock now and still fairly light but I will probably have to finish this up in the morning.

We have a radio set playing over in another camp near us but we weren't satisfied with going over there to listen to it so we ran wires over to our camp and into each pup tent. We took our crash helmets with the ear phones up to the wire and have gangs of music and news day and nite. It's the best idea we have had yet. Charlie McCarthy is on now. I missed today's letters so I'll finish this and listen to Charlie next Monday. Joe is here listening in too.

The day before yesterday I was taking a nap when all of a sudden I heard guns going off all around me. I thought the 'Bosh' had made a counter attack. I jumped up just in time to see our guns rip a German plane to pieces. He went down in flames. No matter how many planes I see shot down, I always get a thrill out of it. It is the only thing in the whole mess that seems exciting any more. Why after this war is over I wouldn't pay five cents to see a battleship float down Gresser Ave. There just isn't anything that seems exciting any more.

We seen a beautiful day fight a few weeks ago. It was between three Spitfires, and 3 ME 109 fighters. It was just over our heads on a clear day. Five of the Germans were shot down in smoke and the other by some trick of fate managed to get away. A little while ago it looked like it was going to clear up for a little while but the sky is dark again and it would surprise me if we had a little rain before very long. This country will never be short of water. It rains at least 363 days a year.

We are getting fresh meat every day now. Believe it or not we had a G.I. steak for dinner today. Pork chops and Italian spaghetti yesterday. There has been no mail from you in 4 or 5 days but I got 1 from Helen today. I suppose about 5 or 6 of yours will come all at once tomorrow.

I hope you are still getting my mail as good as before. It's not just me but no one is getting mail including Joe. It's getting dark fast now and also a little cold. I think I'll have time to finish up before it gets too dark though.

I was out with another fellow yesterday taking a walk when I met two French girls. I had out my French book and we were having a hell of a good one way conversation. She was talking and I was trying to find out what she was saying in the book. I was just about to try and ask her to go to the show with me when all of a sudden down the highway came not one, not two, not three, but four real American girls!! They were from the Red Cross and in a jeep heading back to the beach. I took one good look at them and then took another look at the two French girls and walked away in disgust.

Well I hope you are all in the best of health and enjoying your vacation.

I'll say good nite and God bless you, til tomorrow. Good nite.

Your Loving Son

Bob

July 25, 1944

Dear Mother Dad,

I haven't enough news to fill a regular letter so I'll just rattle off a few lines to let you know I'm alright.

I went to a swell show this afternoon. It was named 'Two Girls and a Sailor'. We really enjoyed every bit of it. After supper we went to another show called 'Cover Girl'. It wasn't as good as the first but it was still a good picture.

We had a quiet day and the sun came out this afternoon. That was the thing we enjoyed the most. Tomorrow we will have exercises in the morning and other odd jobs all day. It will help to pass the time of day.

I think Joe is out to the late show tonite as he hasn't been down to see me yet.

Remember me to all the neighbors and family.

Your Loving Son

Bob

July 25

Hello Folks,

Your letter came in yesterday Helen, thanks for the cartoons, we all enjoyed them very much. Thanks for the Hobo News Grand Pop, it is being read all over the Normandy area. There isn't much news around here that I am allowed to tell you about.   Mom will give you the news of any importance as soon as she sees you. I want to be sure she gets the news first, as if she heard it in Bayonne first there would be hell to pay!

Don't worry about me getting drunk over here Helen, it doesn't pay, especially if you want to go back home after the war (and I do!)

I am listening to Fred Waring on the radio now. Fanny Brice was on the last program. We have wires to all the pup tents and hooked up to our tank helmets. The other end goes to the radio about a half mile from here.

Remember me to the gang.

As ever,

Bob

July 26,

France

Dear Mother Dad, Roy,

It is just noon time as I start writing this letter, and so far it has been one of the most exciting days of my life. This morning about 9 o'clock great clouds of heavy bombers flew over our heads to the front lines. We counted 2000 bombers alone without the fighters. We could see them drop their bombs. The whole earth shook under the heavy assault. There were hundreds of fighters of all descriptions. Before the last plane had dropped its load our heavy artillery let go with all they had. It was the 9th wonder of the world. You can't imagine just what it was like. At eleven o'clock another large force of bombers came over and they are still coming. Hundreds of them at a time.

At 12 o'clock our company fell out in full dress for an announcement from the colonel. What in the hell do you think he did. He called Joe Skelly and me out of ranks to the center of the parade ground. Then he presented us both with the Bronze Star medal. He read off a gang of stuff that we did that we had already forgotten about. Mine was for an argument I had with some Germans after my tank was shot to pieces on June 12. The planes were making so much noise I couldn't hear the whole thing so I'll find out what Joe got his for later and pass it on to you. The boys are all up at a band concert now so I'll have to finish up before they get back. The medal will be sent to you but it will take months to reach you. I keep the ribbon here to wear on my shirt. The ribbon is red with a blue stripe running from the bottom like this.

I have another little thing to bring home after the war. It is a brand new 45 cal colt pistol. It was given to me by the infantry that we work with. I can't tell you what we have been doing but the enclosed clipping should give you some idea.

I'm trying hard to get ahead of Joe in just one thing over there but every time I get something he gets the same on the same day.

I hope when this afternoon's mail comes in I will get at least one letter from you. Yesterday all that came in for the company was a Cranford paper and one NY news. No letters for anyone. I'm feeling fine and dandy Mom so don't worry about me. The war can't last for very much longer. Then I'll be home and tell you all about it. I just now got orders to get busy so I'll have to close til tomorrow.
Your Loving Son
Bob

July 28
Dear Mother Dad,
    This is the first chance I have had to write in the past few days. We have been busy doing odd jobs.
    Your two letters from Albany arrived yesterday and there was one today. I'm glad you had such a good time up at Addie's. Do they still have the ice cream war on up there?
    We had a USO show here today and it was rotten. I could have enjoyed myself more if I stayed in camp and read a book.
    The war news looks good for a change, if they aren't feeding us a line. You can't believe anything you hear over here. There is nothing new around here, everything is the same as usual.

I'm feeling fine and the food is good. There isn't another damn thing to write so I'll close until tomorrow.
Your Loving Son
Bob

July 30
Dear Mother Dad,

As I am writing this letter I am sitting on top of my tank, looking at the greatest show on earth. Hundreds of planes are dive bombing the retreating Germans. It is a mass slaughter. This has been going on for two days. The sky is black with flack from the German AA guns. This really is a wonderful sight. I only seen 3 of our planes shot down today out of all that mess. The crews all jumped out in time. How do you like our new advance? I'll write you a real long letter tomorrow. Things are getting hot around here so I'll dive in my foxhole until tomorrow. Don't worry my fox hole is so far under ground it takes an hour to find my way out.
Your Loving Son
Bob

Aug 1, 1944
France
Dear Mom Dad,

We have been very busy in the past few days. You can see what I mean in the papers. It will be two weeks before I can tell you all about it. Yesterday we came into this new area about 6 in the morning. I started to dig my fox hole about 8 o'clock and didn't finish until 8 last nite. I wanted to write yesterday but the fox hole has to come first. It is a two man job this time. My asst driver is using it too. We dug down about 4 feet and then tunneled under. We have steel boxes filled with dirt on top to keep out overhead bursts from mortars. It would take a direct hit to get us. After all that work not a single shell or bomb came near us all nite.

I slept until 1 o'clock this afternoon as it is the first real sleep I had in 4 or 5 days. We came to some beautiful tank country in the past week. We can really fight the way we like to fight now. We can see all around us and have plenty of room. Before it was just like jungle fighting.

There are plenty of farms around here. They have potatoes, onions, beans, peas, carrots. We have a gasoline stove in the tank and have been cooking French fried potatoes for every meal. I cooked up some fresh peas the other day too. It really hit the spot. It is the first fresh food we have had since we left the states 6 mo. ago. It seems like 6 years ago.

The mail comes in regular up here at the front as well as behind the lines. Joe is about two fields from here now. I am going up to see him this afternoon. That's about all the news from here so I'll close now and go wash up and do a little work on the tank.

I hope you are all having a good time on your vacation and also hope you have weather as good as we are having now.

Your Loving Son, Bob

Aug 6, 44
France
Dear Mother Dad,

I guess you are wondering why I haven't been writing in the past few days. Well we have been trying like hell to catch up with the Germans. They have been running so fast it is impossible to get in gun range of them. We captured thousands of shells for their big guns. Yesterday we captured a barn full of parachutes. Everyone in camp has gangs of silk handkerchiefs and scarves. I'll put a piece in this letter for a souvenir.

The weather is beautiful over here now. If the good weather keeps up we will be in Berlin very soon.

I got a patch from a dead German soldier. He was from the Africa Corps. You can paste it in your scrap book if you want to.

I haven't been getting any mail this week as it can't catch up to me. This is all the paper I have and I won't be able to get any until you send some so don't be surprised to get Vmail from now on.

Our Btn has 4 stars to our credit. That is 4 major battles. I have been in all four from beginning to end. We are not allowed to tell which ones yet but we are getting a presidential citation for the last one. That is just A.C.O. We made the breakthrough all by ourselves. That will give me 5 ribbons and 4 stars to put on my dress uniform when we get back.

I don't know when I will be able to write again but don't worry. I'll write every time I get the chance.

I hope you enjoyed your vacation in good health, and hope it won't be long til you have another.

There is nothing more to write so I'll say good nite for today.

Your Loving Son,
Bob

Aug 7, 1944
Dear Mother Dad,

We did not move today as I thought we would. We just spent a lazy day sitting in the shade. I took a bath in a spring near here and was it cold. It sure feels good to be clean though.

The big guns from our field artillery are moved up to the same area we are in, and are they going wild. We won't get much sleep tonite. Our nite fighters are up now and doing a fine job. We haven't been bombed in over a week now.

It sure looks like the war will be over soon now. We have only a few miles to go before Paris. I don't see why the Germans keep fighting. We are cutting them to pieces. Their tanks and trucks are scattered all over the roads, burning and smashed. They must know they can't win.

Those guns just went off again and almost jarred me off my seat. They make more noise on the other end though and I know what I am talking about as they shelled the German lines the time I was trapped behind them. Every time the Germans shoot a rifle over this way we shoot 1000 shells in return. It is driving their men mad.

There is still no mail. I understand the post office is moving up nearer the front. I suppose I'll get a dozen all at once when they do come in.

I hope your knees are coming along alright Dad. It has been coming on for a long time. You needed the rest anyway. I hope it doesn't spoil your vacation though.

There is a farm house just a little ways from us Mom that I would like you to see. The woman that lives there has gone behind the lines, but she left a beautiful flower garden. I don't know the names of the flowers, but some are like yours and some different. They are all in full bloom and there are no weeds. It is a beautiful sight. The people must be well off, as they have electric lights and nice furniture. You would like to see the country around here (in peace time). It is all green. You can see for miles across the valleys. Every little village has a church and for a change they are all in one piece. We had to blow most of them up when we first came over as the Germans used to leave snipers and observers in the towers. They are retreating so fast now that they don't have time to send a man up in them now though.

There are a few fields of wheat around and that's where the poppies grow. There are millions of poppies in every wheat field. You see a few grow along the roads but not too many.

I just heard some more good news but can not tell you what it is for two weeks. We just took another Nazi strong point and our guns will be quiet for a while now as they are out of range. These guns shoot 10 miles and every time they get dug in word comes in that they are out of range again. So now they will move up again. Our planes are flying overhead like flies. I guess they are trying to smash hell out of the Germans as they retreat from this big city. I guess it's ok to tell you we are getting a Presidential citation for making the main breakthrough at St. Lo. It was just A Company and it is only A Company that is getting the citation. We fought there for a long time and fought like hell. I was beginning to think we would never take it. That was the beginning of this whole offensive and the biggest battle of France.

I have had enough battle to last me a long time. There is no one in the world can call me a 4F now. All I want now is to get the hell out of here and back to the good old USA.

I have $120 on the way home but it will take months to reach you. I guess I have enough to buy a jeep after the war haven't I? You can expect $50 every mo. now besides the other 15 and bond. We don't have to buy anything over here. We get cigarettes, candy, razor blades, etc., free. I just keep a few bucks to play poker with.

How is John Kemp doing these days? Still working 7 days a week? Say hello to Mrs. Fisher, Catherine, Cloflins, Mr. Bonnel, and all the rest for me will you?

What is Roy doing these days, surely not working? I just hope he is having a little fun before he goes. Ah yes give my regards to the Zulicks and family too next time you see them.

I just got a hold of some more paper so I thought I would make up for lost time. We have 3 little puppies here with us for the duration I guess. We named them 'Beach Head', 'St Lo', and 'Isiciny'. The mother got scared during a bombing last week and took off for parts unknown. They are just old enough to eat soft food and get in little fights among themselves. They are no trouble now but I expect they will be a nuisance once they get big enough to get in the way.

I just found out that the letter I wrote yesterday didn't go out yet so I guess you will get two at once.

I can't think of any more news for now so I'll close til tomorrow.

Your Loving Son
Bob

Aug 7, 1944
France
Dear Mother Dad,

A few minutes ago I finished my 4th fox hole of the week. If I keep on digging holes and ditches much longer I'll be learning to swear in Italian.

We keep pushing up all the time these days. In fact I think by the time you get this letter we will be in Paris. It can't last much longer now.

The mail is very bad lately. I have had only two letters in a week. One from you Dad and the other from Kitty. I guess the mail truck can't keep up with us.

I'm getting lazier by the hour. This weather is too good to last. I slept until 10 this morning and then put more spark plugs in the tank. That is all I did today except for the fox hole. I just hope we stay here long enough to sleep in it.

I can't think of anything to write about any more. Everything that happens is just what you read in the papers. There is no use of me telling you about it again.

Joe is sitting here trying to think of something to write his folks but is giving up in disgust. I'm feeling fine and the food is good.

I'll close for today and try to write soon.

Love to all
Bob

Sgt R. Cadmus
747th Tk Bn Co A
APO 230 C/O PM
NYC.NY

Mrs O Cadmus
10 Gresser Ave
Linden
New Jersey
Aug 9, 1944
Dear Mom Dad,

All your mail came in yesterday. It was from Albany. I sure was surprised to hear you were up there again. There is nothing much I can tell you now except that I seen one German plane shot down in flames last nite. It was shot down by our nite fighters.

A few enemy shells came over during the nite and we sent about 10,000 back. Altogether it made it impossible to get any sleep.

I took a bath in a cold spring this morning. It sure was cold too.

We had fresh ham and corn for dinner today. It wasn't bad either.

Joe and I cooked French fried potatoes all yesterday evening. They turned out swell. I am going to catch a chicken in a little while and fry it up for supper.

I hope you are all feeling fine and having a swell time.
Your Loving Son
Bob

Aug 15, 1944
France
Dear Mom Dad,

I hope you haven't been worrying too much about me in the past week. It has been impossible to write as we have been fighting. Before I left home you made me promise to let you know if either Joe or I got hurt. Well Joe did get hurt on Aug 10 in an enemy trap. We were all together when it happened. Joe's tank got hit just after I passed him. He got shrapnel in his leg and body. After he was hit he walked to another tank and got in. My tank covered them with smoke while they made their getaway. I didn't get back until that afternoon so I didn't see Joe before he went to the hosp. The boys told me the last thing he said as he was leaving was 'You can't kill a good Irishman' so he must be alright. I haven't heard from him yet and probably won't for quite some time. But as soon as I do I will let you know how he is and will also send you his address so you can write to him. Don't tell his family. He will write and tell them. Don't say anything until Mr. Skelly writes to you about it. The whole thing was very

_____

_____

_____

((*The bottom inch and a half or so of the page was cut off – censored...*))

I'm doing fine Mom. We are in reserve now so that means a good rest.

I have had no mail for a few days, but last nite as we pulled in here, they gave me a swell package. It was the fruit cake and candy. My crew and I sure made a fast job on it to. It was just as fresh as the day you made it too.

I wish you could see the sky here now. It is a beautiful day and not a cloud in sight. The air is thick with the roar of heavy bombers. It looks like another 2 or 3,000 plane raid. The sun is shining on the planes and makes them look all silvery and clean. These formations of 36 planes each are going overhead now.

Maybe it would make you feel better to know that the German Tank that hit Joe is nothing but a mass of burned up steel and ashes. Not a man of the German crew left that tank alive. It makes me feel better about it, how about you? We are in a beautiful camp area here. I have my tank parked under a good sized apple tree. It is so well covered we don't need the camouflage net. On our right is a wide valley with hilly land in the background. It is

———————————————————————————

———————————————————————————

———————————

((other side of the missing bottom of page))

On the left are a few farm houses, some whole and some blown up or burned. All around is green pasture land with a few cows, chickens, and rabbits running all over the place. You can still smell the dead in the air. A few fields down from here is a bulldozer digging big holes to bury the dead cows and horses. There seems to be about 50% of the livestock dead all the way across France. Each field has one or two dead cows or horses in it. After a few days they smell terrible. They swell up to twice their normal size and break open. The Dept of Graves came around last nite and carried all of the German dead away. They were all fresh bodies though and didn't smell too bad. By tonite they should have everything buried and the air will be fit to breathe again.

Last nite the German air force was out in full strength. I was on guard from 10:30 to 12:00 and watched the whole thing. They didn't bomb us for a change, but they gave some other outfit hell. It was about two miles away. First they dropped flares to light the countryside up like day. Then they came over to bomb but were surprised by hundreds of anti aircraft guns. There were so many tracer bullets going up it looked like sparks from a huge emery wheel. I couldn't see any planes shot down but they surely couldn't have done any effective bombing. After a while our men shot up rockets to show our nite fighters just where the enemy planes were. That was the last of the raid. Our artillery started in then. First the small stuff 105mm started pounding away and then from all around us the 155mm Hoz let go. They sound like a clap of thunder when they first go off and then the shell going through the sky sounds like a busy freight yard with hundreds of box cars switching tracks. When they had sent out a few tons of steel and tnt, their daddy the 155 long Tom from way back cut loose with everything but the kitchen sink. They kept firing until early this morning.

I couldn't sleep very well last nite as my legs would go to sleep and I would have to raise up my hatch and stand for a while to get the blood moving again. When the big guns stopped firing about 4:30 I climbed out of the tank and curled up on the engine compartment and tried again. I could hear the chatter of a few mach guns and German burp guns far off in the nite but finally went to sleep. At 7:30 I was called for breakfast of hotcakes and bacon. After breakfast I decided to write this letter and have been at it ever since.

That is the kind of nite we enjoy. It is the kind you dream about when you are up at the front. I have to gas up the tank and do a few other odd jobs on it now so I will have to close until tomorrow.

Remember me to everyone and take good care of yourselves.
Your Loving Son   Bob

Aug 17
Dear Mom Dad,

We are in a new area today. It isn't as nice as the last but at least we know we are going to be here for a while. We are in reserve and won't be used for at least a week. (I hope)

We came in last nite and was it dark. I didn't see the road the whole trip. It was just luck that I didn't end up in the ditch. The dust was worse than Texas. After we got here it started to rain. It dripped down into the tank and down my neck. That didn't help the sleep any either. This morning when I woke up it was foggy. It didn't clear until noon. The sun shined all afternoon I guess. I slept.

We are on a farm I think. There are potatoes, carrots, turnips, growing all around us. I can see why we have French fried potatoes while we are here. I'll have to get some fat at the kitchen tomorrow and fry potatoes and maybe a few chickens all day tomorrow.

I got a new pair of pants and shirt this morning. I'll bet you couldn't guess what size pants I wear now. Well it's size 34 waist. I guess those K rations don't help the waist line grow like your cooking. I haven't had a hair cut since I got the baldie in England. My hair is just right on top but it is the same length on my neck, so I'll have to get it cut this week.

There is still no news on Joe. It usually takes 20 days to get the new address so I guess we will just have to wait.

Next morning

I didn't have time to finish last nite as we had to gas up the tank and check up on everything. We had a quiet nite for a change. There were no planes as the rain made poor flying. We are so far behind the lines now we never heard a shot in 24 hours. It don't make me mad.

I will have to close now if I want this letter to go out in this morning's mail. I hope you are all in good health and not finding it too hard to go back to work.

Your Loving Son

Bob

Aug 18

France

Dear Mom Dad

All your mail and some others that I have been waiting for, have finally come in. Your letters were of Aug 2, 3, 4, 6, 7. I'm sure sorry to hear about you having so much trouble with your knees Dad. I told you, you should lose 60 or 70 lbs. Look at me I did. Ha Ha. It took a little will power but I did it. (with the help of the darn kitchen not being around).

Thanks for the letters Dad I really enjoy hearing from you. You sure have your troubles with that darn car. If I had as much trouble with the tank I would want to sprout wings. In fact I probably would, or at least a pair of horns.

Heck yes the candy keeps Mom. It gets here in as good a shape as when you send it. Don't send any more life savers, we get them free by the bushels.

I'm sorry to hear Joe Eldrige got the Purple Heart and don't let it worry you I'm not going to get one. Joe Skelly has one now and it is going to be good enough for both of us.

I hope Hazel isn't mad at me for not writing but I am not allowed to keep an address book for fear of the enemy getting hold of it, and I can't remember all the addresses.

I will have to close now as the guy that owns this pen wants to write too.

Take care of yourselves now and have a good time as long as you can't work.

I'll write tomorrow.

Your Loving Son

Bob

Aug 19

France

Dear Mom Dad,

I just wrote a letter to you last nite and it will go out this morning. I might not have time to write another tomorrow so I'll just drop a few lines so you can get mail more often.

It is about 9 o'clock in the morning now and it is very foggy. It looks like it is beginning to lift, but you can't be sure as the weather is crazy over here.

From what I read in the paper our troops aren't far from Paris. I suppose we will end up taking the city if it is too tough for the rest of the army. We usually end up doing all the dirty work.

I am going to write Hazel a letter and send it to you and you can give it to her when you see her. It seems to me she wrote to me some time back and I never did answer.

I got a letter from Helen yesterday but I answered it before it got here.

It is starting to rain now, after all this swell weather we had I hate to see it rain. We are getting into the beautiful part of France now. It is hilly and you can see for miles on a clear day. Every house has a beautiful flower garden. You would really enjoy seeing it. I never seen any more beautiful flowers in the States. The fog is getting worse now. It isn't raining so hard though.

Well I hope I get orders to take my tank to ordinance and get a new engine today. I sure need one. The one I have now is just about shot. She carried us through many a battle so we have no kick with it. You asked what name we gave the tank. Well we never got around to naming it. It is too much trouble to paint a name on it.

Well I guess that's about all the news for today, so I'll close now and try and write tomorrow.

Love to all

Bob

P.S. Going to ordinance for new engine no mail for a few days.

Aug 22, 1944
France
Dear Mom Dad,

Don't think the mail service is bad or that I don't want to write, it's just that you can't write and drive at the same time. We have been going like mad this past week. I have driven day and nite trying to catch up with the front line. I haven't driven this much since maneuvers back in La. I guess you can see by the papers just how we are doing. I guess the boys just wanted to show the Russians, they weren't the only ones that could pick up their feet and move.

The weather has been rotten these past few days. It keeps our planes on the ground and gives the enemy the chance to sneak out of our traps. We are doing alright though, 600 more prisoners just marched by our tank. That's the 3rd bunch of 600 each that passed us today. I'll tell you more about them in a few days.

I haven't received any mail in the past three days as we have been moving too fast. Well Dad I hope you feel better by now. You have had almost as much time off as Grand Pa in the past mo. You earned the rest though and I'm glad you weren't too sick to enjoy it. The hell with the money you lose. You can make plenty more later.

I'm glad they haven't called Roy yet. He must be having a good time according to your letters.

Joe has not been able to get in touch with me yet, as I said it will take at least 20 days.

I am in my tank now keeping dry as it is raining very hard now. It will be 2 or 3 days before this letter gets mailed, so I have no idea when it will reach you.

I'll close now and get a little sleep before we have to move again.

Your Loving Son

Bob

(Aug 24)

Hello again.

The mail hasn't gone out in a few days so I thought I would add another page before it does. I got some good news about Joe yesterday. One of the men in his crew came back from the hosp and he seen Joe. He said he will be alright. He won't be back in the war but in a few months he should be up and around as good as ever. I can't wait to hear whether he is going back to the states or not. I hope he does.

It rained all nite but it is clear and warm today. That's all the news from here. I'll write tomorrow or the next day if possible.

Aug 24,

Dear Mom, Dad.

We are in reserve again and taking it easy. I haven't heard a gun go off for 4 days. It sure feels good to be away from all that noise for a while. We have been taking prisoners by the thousands. We passed a group of 8 thousand the other day and they were so crowded in they couldn't move.

We are on a very large farm or pasture land. There are cows running around all over the place. We caught about 15 horses that did belong to the Germans. We are riding them bare back all over the place. I fell off twice yesterday. The first time I jumped on his back and fell off the other side. Later I was riding and the horse started running and I wasn't ready and you can guess the rest.

I haven't had any letters this week but they say mail should come in today. You see the post office is over 100 miles back in St Lo.

It looks funny to see all the captured German jeeps and motorcycles and trucks going back and forth on the highway. We fix them up and use them to carry dead Germans to the rear.

There is nothing new, just the same old stuff over here. It is starting to rain so I'll close until tomorrow.

Your Loving Son

Bob

Aug 28

Dear Mother, Dad,

The last time I wrote to you I was over one hundred miles from here, so you can see the reason for the delay. We have been going day and nite. The country here has changed. The first big change is the women, they are really good looking in this part of the country. There are plenty of them too.

The day before yesterday we drove over 40 miles and every time we stopped the people would run up and give us a drink of wine or cider. One old man came out with three bottles of champagne. When he opened them up, I got a bath. It went all over everyone. Another fellow came up with 15 eggs, we gave him 4 packs of butts for them. Then another guy gave us about 2 lbs of butter. Later we got apples, pears, tomatoes. We did alright that day.

I just got a haircut from Omid Ben Kassam the Indian. I sure did need it too. It is the first one since I got that baldie in Eng. It is well over a week now since any mail came in. We keep getting further away from the post office.

I'll tell you all about Paris when I get home. Right now I have to do some more work on the tank before we move out again.

I'll write as soon as I get chance to but it may be a long time, so don't worry about me. I am in good health and having the time of my life.

There is no news from Joe yet. Love to all Bob

9/2/44

JERSEY SOLDIERS GET BRONZE STAR

WITH THE 29TH DIVISION IN FRANCE-
THE BRONZE STAR FOR "MERITORIUS ACHIEVE-MENT" IN MILITARY OPERA-TIONS AGAINST THE ENEMY HAS BEEN AWARDED TO 68 OFFICERS AND ENLISTED MEN OF THE 29TH IN-FANTRY. FAMOUS BLUE AND GRAY DIVISION. THE FOL-LOWING NEW JERSEY MEN RECEIVED THE AWARD:..
SGT. RYNIER R. CADMUS, 10 GRESER AVE.

Aug 30
Dear Mother Dad,

I have a few hours to myself so I took off to the woods where it is quiet to write a letter. We are in a big woods outside of the big city. It looks like a park as there are small dirt roads running all through the place. Every hundred yds or so there are park benches made from logs. I am sitting on one of them now.

We traveled about 15 miles yesterday and passed through many towns of all sizes. The people were all out waving to us as we went through. In some places there were so many you had to stop the tank. Young and old were all alike. They were going nuts. They were throwing us all kinds of fruit and vegs. One old man got out in front of the tank and made me stop so he could give us a basket of tomatoes. Once you stop you're done. They crowd around you so that you can't get away. I seen one old woman she must have been at least 70 years old, jumping up and down and waving both arms at once. Boy what a difference from Normandy. Up there was the most rotten looking country in the world. The girls were ugly and the people did not like us and many of them fought against us. All this part of the country is beautiful. I never seen any better, any place in the states. Even the girls are better than a lot of places in the states.

There are very large farms around here. They keep them in very good condition too. You ought to see the pumpkins and tomatoes. There are fields and fields of them.

The weather is even beautiful. The sun shines most every day. It gets pretty hot too once in a while. The other day my face got so sun burned I could hardly stand it. My eyes were sore and watering so bad I couldn't drive for a while.

Well it is about time Joe's address should be coming in. I can't wait to hear where he is. He is probably somewhere in England but there is always a chance he is in the U.S.

I haven't received any mail in almost two weeks now but some day it will all come in at once. I guess by now you are pretty hungry Dad. That is IF you stuck to your diet. Well I'll close until tomorrow when I may have some more news
Your Loving Son
Bob

Sept 1
France (yet)
Dear Mom Dad,

Well I am going to try again to write a long letter. I don't know how far I will get but at least I have good intentions. I received your letter of the 11th of Aug this morning just before moving out. It was the first letter from you in about two weeks. You asked bout Sid Craig. I thought it was about time for you to hear about that. You see we are not allowed to mention deaths until after their families are told. He was killed just outside of St. Lo. An artillery shell landed almost on top of him and did a fast job. Joe Skelly seen it happen, and got out of his tank and dragged Sid's buddy who was wounded by the same shell, under his tank about 200 feet away. They were also under heavy mach gun fire. That was how Joe got the Bronze Star. I was up ahead about 200 yds in the spearhead when it happened, and didn't hear about it until that nite. It was just his time to go and he died in the battle that was the beginning of the end. You won't remember him as a man, but as a wise guy that used to cause nothing but trouble, but he was one of the best soldiers and well liked by the battalion.

You asked about Paris. Well I was there alright <u>but</u>. It was 3 o'clock in the morning, it was raining so hard you couldn't see, and we never took the tanks out of 5th gear all the way through. You will have to ask some 4F from the MP or one of the million pencil pushers that follow up the fighting army. If we stopped to go sight seeing we never would catch up with the Germans. I did see the tower though. It was a long way off, but I did see it.

I haven't heard any news in the past couple of weeks but I know by the way we are going that it must be good. What did you think about the big pocket at Vire. That is the one we made when Joe got hurt. There were thousands of dead Germans laying all around the place. It sort of made up for the boys we lost at the beach. I never seen so many prisoners in all my life. They were a surprised looking lot.

Well it is raining again so I will have to close very soon now. Thanks for the offer to take me with you on your tour of the country but you will enjoy it more without me. Besides I seen enough to last me a while.

I'm glad to hear you are able to work again Dad. I guess that long rest did you some good.

Well Roy good luck in your new job and learn all you can. It pays. I'm glad you had such a good time at the beach Mom. I sure wish I could go swimming with you. I know you don't like to go in alone.

That is about all the news from here so I'll close now and check on the tank before we move out again. Don't worry about me when you don't get mail. It may be weeks in between letters. Even when we do get time to write we can't always mail them.

I'll write you as soon as we reach Berlin for sure.
Your Loving Son
Bob

Belgium
Sept ?
Dear Mother Dad,

As you can see by the top I have lost all track of the time and date. One day seems to run into another. Maybe it is better that way as the war might not seem too long. We had a little excitement yesterday just after I finished my letter. No one was killed though. As soon as it got dark we just dug in and held the ground we had taken. We got some eggs and opened a can of bacon and had a swell supper. We slept outside of the tank on the ground. It got very cold towards morning and when I woke up my feet were sticking out of the blankets. They had frost on the toes. I haven't been able to get warm all day. About 9 o'clock we led the spearhead on to our objective. It is now about 6 o'clock and we just finished eating supper. 4 eggs and 8 slices of bacon apiece. We enjoy eating 1 egg as much as we used to enjoy eating 1 qt of ice cream.

I am sitting in a straw pile in a farmer's back yard, with the late afternoon sun shining down on me. It is the warmest I have been in two days, and still the wind is cold.

It gets dark real early now, by 9 o'clock it is dark. That means we stand two hours guard instead of one, like we used to.

I just heard some good news. My tank is ready to roll so tomorrow I will probably go back to France and get it. I will also probably get a chance to mail this letter. The people here don't seem to be any the worse for the war. They have plenty to eat, even meat. They also have good shoes, and some very good homes. I think the Germans must have liked these people or something. They are glad to see us but do not act like they really cared. In France when we freed a city or town the people would go crazy. Some even cried. They would climb on the tanks and you had to kiss every last man, woman and child in the whole damn town. Thank God that is over, but in a way it is a wonderful thing to see how happy they are when they see the first troops roll into town. That is one thrill no one in the world can get except those that are there. My tank is the lead tank and we have been first in hundreds of cities, towns, and small villages. Just seeing the people make you want to keep on going until the world is rid of them that might spoil it.

Well I'll close for now and write some more before I mail this.
Bob

Sept ?
Luxemburg
Dear Mother Dad,

Well we didn't go back to France after my tank after all. Instead we kept on going in the other direction. It looks like Germany is next on our tour of Europe. I hope it doesn't take too long to get there as I am anxious to see what Berlin looks like. Last nite was very quiet. Nothing happened except for a few planes looking for us once in a while. I slept in a hay stack. The nite was very cold but I kept warm under three blankets and about a foot of straw. There was no frost this morning but it was still too cold to enjoy getting out of bed. The sun is out today and there isn't a cloud in the sky. Every once in a while you can see clouds of silver specs (our bombers) heading towards Germany. It is a wonderful day for flying. I understand the mail is going out today or tomorrow so I'll put this letter in with the others and have them censored.

Sept about 3 days later
Sorry but the orders were changed and I still didn't get a chance to send the letters off.

Sept 8

Dear Mother Dad,

I suppose you have been worrying and wondering what the trouble has been to keep me from writing. There has been no time to write or even sleep in the past few weeks. We have been far into the front lines and away from anyone who could mail our letters for us. The rest of the army has finally caught up with us, now we may be able to get a few letters out. Our mail finally caught up with us last nite. I received 7 letters from you, 1 from Helen, 2 from Kitty, 1 from Grand Pa, 2 from the Lakes, 3 from Dot in Texarkana, and 2 from Hazel in Texas. It sure was a long time to wait but it was worth it.

I am in a concrete pill box now keeping out of the rain. It has been raining for three or four days almost continuously. Last nite we slept under the tank for a few hours and the water came in and flooded us out. We then came inside of the tank and sat there all nite with the water running down our necks. It was a rotten nite and I am glad it's over.

We went into a small town the other day to hold a very important bridge. We parked on the main street and stayed there for two days. I met a girl that could speak some English. She invited me to her home to eat dinner. When I got there I was surprised to see a very nice little home. It had modern furniture and even a radio. I can't tell you very much more now as it is a newly captured town and the censorship regulations are not too easy to get around. There is a long and interesting story about the town that I will tell you as soon as I get home. I am going to send you pictures in a few weeks of the town and bridge we were holding.

Well Roy is gone by now I guess. I am sure he will not like it but it will do him a lot of good. Let me know what he writes in his letters.

I am glad to hear you are all in good health again. You know me I am always in good health. I guess this life agrees with me. I will have to close now and do some work on the tank.

Your loving son

Bob

Belgium

Sept 10

Dear Mother Dad,

This is a funny time and place to write a letter, but I couldn't write for a few days and I thought you might be worried. We are leading a spearhead into Germany and right now we came across some enemy opposition. The tanks are firing and the infantry are advancing. My tank is on guard against a counter attack from the flank. I am sitting in the driver's seat trying to keep awake, as we didn't sleep since the nite before last. I could only find this one piece of paper and nothing but a K ration box to write on. That's why I had to fold this paper this way. Belgium is a very nice looking country, and has good roads. The people are very glad to see us and hang out their flag and the American flag as soon as we reach town. Many of them like the French have guns and are fighting along with us. I don't see how the war can last much longer over here. We are cutting the German army to ribbons. Every life lost now is for a lost cause.

The women here are not as pretty as those in France but some are not bad at all. The people here seem to have plenty to eat. The only thing they seem to need as in all the rest of Europe, is shoes. Most of them have wooden shoes or no shoes at all. I haven't had time to get out and meet anyone yet but they seem to be very nice people. Enclosed is a picture of a bridge. Keep it and I will tell you a very interesting story about it when I get home.

I can't figure out why the Lakes treat me so good. It was sure nice of them to send you that package. I just can't write to everyone at this time Mom. It is terribly hard for us to get any time to ourselves. When we do write it often takes days to find a place to mail them. I will write to Kitty as soon as it is possible. I can never think of anything to write her. All she writes about is her garden and the weather. I know that is all she has to write about but it gets awful tiresome reading the same things all the time.

I am dying to hear how Roy is making out and where he is. I hope he gets in a good outfit. You be sure you do what the doctor tells you Dad. It will pay in the end. I'm glad to hear your knees are all better anyway.

Yes Mom if the weather is anything like we are having it is time to quit swimming until next year. It is darn near winter over here. I was so cold this morning I was numb all over.

I haven't heard from Joe yet and it is almost a month. Of course I have been traveling so fast word is slow catching up.

We have traveled so much I wore the tracks off my tank. The ordnance is putting nice new ones on now. I have the Major's tank to use until mine is running again.

We are about ready to resume the offensive as they have stopped all shooting. I'll close now and mail this the first time I see the mail clerk. Perhaps I will put in another letter with this one before then, who knows?
Your Loving Son Bob

Germany
Sept 12
Hello Folks,

According to the mail from home I suppose you're in Atlantic City at this time. I hope you didn't get in the big storm that I read about.

Yes it has been a long time since my last letter but you can see by the top of the page the reason for it. We haven't been letting any grass grow under our feet. My tank was the first American tank to enter Germany. It wasn't my fault either.

I had a gun in my back. Yes we were fighting in Germany when Patton (Guts and someone else's blood) was still in O.C.S.

The only letters I have written in the past mo. were to Mother. I figured she would tell you the news and that would give me some much needed sleep. Back in Belgium I wrote a letter to you but couldn't mail it and it finally got lost.

I hear both Eddies are still on their Islands enjoying their vacations. Tell them not to worry, we will be over there in a few months and show them the rest of the way to Tokyo. By the way this is a great day in Naval history. They landed the See Bees at Chendburg.

All jokes aside the first thing I seen on D Day was a group of See Bees with a bulldozer clearing the beach under heavy fire. They did a great job.

Well how are the Saturday nite party games coming along? Is Uncle Bob still cleaning up all the pennies? You ought to see some of our party games. French, Belgium, and English money all in one pot. It sure is a good way to get rid of it fast.

Your letters haven't been coming in very often lately. I guess they can't catch up with me. I got one letter from Helen when I was back in Luxemburg. Thanks for the letter and the cartoons Helen, we always get a laugh out of them.

Well it's almost time for chow so I'll say goodbye until the next time we get a chance to write. (Berlin no doubt).
Your Loving Son, Bob

Sept
Germany
Hello Mom Dad,

I'll bet you are surprised to hear I got into Germany so quick. Well you're not half as surprised as I was. We had orders to go back to our btn the other day. Just as we were about to leave new orders came through. We left early the next morning and headed east. We met a btn of infantry farther up in Belgium and kept on going. The (crossed out) rode on the back of our tanks. We started out along the roads and met quite a bit of mortar fire and mach gun fire. After we broke through the resistance, we followed German tank trucks for miles through the woods. Finally they went down a steep hill and across a small stream. The other side of the stream was Germany. We crossed it and were not 30 feet across when three shells landed in front of us about 40 feet away. It was too late then to stop us. We went up the hills to high ground and as we reached the top we seen the German tanks. Johnny fired the 75 at it and my asst driver fired his mach gun at foot troops that were with it. Boy were they surprised! From the top of the hill we could see for miles on all sides. We shelled convoys of German equipment that were heading for the Siegfried line. A piper cub observation plane come over about that time and directed artillery fire on a tank that was out of our range. After about 4 shots a shell landed on the German tank. It was the best shooting I ever seen. Down in the valley on the other side they spotted a mark IIII tank. All our tanks opened up on it. After a few minutes it burned up and nothing left but smoke could be seen.

We held the high ground all nite and were relieved by more troops in the morning. We then came back to Belgium and are now waiting for orders.

I just went down to a small stream and washed up for the first time in days. It is too cold to shave so I'll wait until tomorrow. I have no idea now if or when I will be able to mail these letters.

Maybe I had better wait and deliver them to you myself. I'll just put this one in with the others and mail them all at once some day. Well I'll close and maybe write some more tomorrow.

Your Loving Son
Bob

Sept
About 17
Belgium
Dear Mom Dad,

Yes I am back in Belgium after a couple of hot days in Germany. We did most of the dirty work of crossing the border and establishing a foothold. They pulled us back across the border yesterday to repair our tanks. We got the best break we ever got too. We are in a millionaire's mansion. It was built by the Tobacco King of Belgium. It looks about 10 years old. It was built of stone on the outside, and resembles a castle. There are two towers and at least 15 chimneys. As you come in the front door there is a large marble doorway. It is on the order of something you would see in Radio City. The first room is about the size of our house.

The floor is marble (orange and black). The walls have oak panels up about 5 feet and from there up is the most expensive wallpaper I ever seen. It is thick paper with metal designs (gold) all over it. The ceiling is polished oak, finished like a hardwood floor. Each room has a large marble fireplace. They are the finest pieces of work I have seen. One of them wouldn't even fit in our house. The building has steam heat, electric lights, telephones from one room to another, bathrooms every 15 feet. It is 5 stories high and I haven't any idea how many rooms. The place must have cost millions to build. Everything is marble or oak. Our whole company is sleeping in it and we never even see each other. I will have to tell you about it after the war. I believe we will move out by tomorrow though, they need us up at the front. Our tanks will be ready to roll tomorrow. Oh yes, there is a beautiful lake just outside. We have been fishing for the past day and a half. I received most of my back mail today. Your letters were of the 26-27-28-29-30-31-5. I mailed 6 letters to you today that I wrote up at the front.

In a way I am glad to see Roy in the army. It will do him a lot of good. I just hope he doesn't have to see action. I wouldn't wish that on anyone. It is hard at first but he will get used to it. If he is in the infantry as he thought he is in for a tough time but in the long run it is going to help him. I would like to transfer to the infantry if I could but that is impossible. I like the way they fight.

I don't want you to get your hope up about me getting home by Christmas. That is out. There isn't a chance in the world of that. We are now in Germany and there is no sign of them giving up. And there is Japan. We have to beat them too.

It has been raining the past two days but we don't mind, and besides the sun is coming out now. I'm glad to hear you're on the job again Dad. I thought you were going to retire. Well I can't think of anything more to write so I'll close for today.
Your Loving Son,
Bob
PS There is no word from Joe yet. Thanks for sending him the cake as well as me. One of the packages came a few days ago with cake in it. It was swell. Thanks a lot Mom.
Bob

Sept 23, 1944
Germany
Dear Mother Dad,

It's a beautyfull morning and at last we have a day off. The first thing I promised my self to do on our break was to write you a letter. Another package came last nite. It was the one with the shrimp, pen, cookies, and taffie in it. This is the pen you sent me, I am using it now. I think I better send it back to you and use pencil. I just borrowed another pen and this is a little better. I just filled the other one with ink too. I never did have any luck with a pen anyway. I'll use pencil from now on and never use a pen as long as I live. Roy had the best idea when he sent these pencils along. I got so mad at that pen I don't want to write any more now. I also received two letters from you of the 5th and 6th. You said you weren't getting any mail from me. Don't I know it. I went for weeks without writing. It was just impossible to get the mail out. We were so far in advance of the regular army. I did try to write once in a while though. I have Joe's address now and will put it in this letter. He said he has a good chance of going back to the states. You keep talking about me coming home soon. We were figuring it out last nite. If we don't have to go fight in China (witch we probably will) we will be lucky if we will be home in a year from Christmas. If we do go to China, it will be at least another year if not more. So don't even think about me coming home any more. I have loads of work to do on the tank and it has to be finished by morning so I will have to close pretty soon. I sure wish Roy all the luck in the world and I also hope he is not sent into battle. He is not the type of guy to fight. I'll get Joe's address now and put it in so you can write to him.

Sgt Joe Skelly
US Army Hosp.
Plant 4173 APO
121
C/O P.M. NY.
NYC
Your loving son,
Bob

Sept 24
Germany
Dear Mother Dad,
Well their was no mail today again. I have been waiting all afternoon for it, but it looks like I will have to wait until tomorrow. We went out this morning in the rain. It was the most miserable day I think I have ever seen. I got soaked to the skin and almost froze. They halted the attack about 11:30. I led the way back to the camp and drove as fast as that old tank would move.

(ABOVE) NATIONAL ARCHIVES PHOTO NO. 111-SC-237340
MEN OF THE 747TH TANK BATTALION ATTEND CLASS DEMONSTRATING USE OF THE E4.5 FLAMETHROWER IN A BATTLE SCARRED CHURCH IN SCHLIEDEN, GERMANY. THE WEAPON IS AT LEFT BY THE HOLE IN THE WALL.

I got mud all over my face so thick I had to scrape it off. It took all afternoon to get my clothes dry over a fire. I felt so rotten I wasn't going to write today but after supper the sun came out and that changed things.

Just a few minutes ago another package came in with more shrimp. That is three nites in a row I have had shrimp. Boy do I enjoy that. There is also a bottle of catsup to go with it. I just had tuna fish and the jam you sent me for breakfast. We ate the candy while on guard last nite. I'll heat up the hot dogs tomorrow while we are not in trouble at the front. I can't thank you enough Mom for sending me such swell packages. You have no idea how much we enjoy them. In our tank we average 3 or 4 packages a week. This week we have already gotten 11 packages. It sure tastes good after K rations for so long.

It is almost dark now and it is only 6 o'clock. When we first came over here it was still light at midnite. Now we have to stand almost 3 hours guard each nite when it used to be 1 hour each. There is nothing new to write about except I made a mistake when I said the pen you sent me was no good. I got to thinking you wouldn't send a pen that wouldn't write so I took it apart and cleaned it and it writes good now. It had dried ink stopping it up.

I can imagine just what Roy is doing now. I often think of him during the day and laugh out loud. I can just see him hurrying or starving, working or getting KP for not working. Doing what he is told or getting a rack over the head. I know it is tough on him but I know he can take it.

Good nite and God bless both of you until I see you again.
Your loving son,
Bob

Sept
Germany
Dear Mother Dad,

It was only last nite that I wrote you a letter, but I missed so many days in the past that I think I should try to make up for it. It stopped raining last nite while I was writing your letter but an hour later it started again. It hasn't stopped since and it doesn't look as if it is going to. I am sitting in a jeep next to my tank trying to keep from getting wet as yesterday.

I had no sleep last nite as the water kept dripping down inmy face all nite. The last of my blankets are wet now too. Unless it stops soon I am going to go nuts.

Yesterday afternoon I changed my class E allotment from $15 to $50 per mo. It won't go into effect until next mo so don't expect it for a while. By now you should have received three checks from France. The first for $75, $50, $50, after that there should be another $45. (I lost the other $5 in a crap game). Please write and tell me when they come in so I can keep track of them.

I think they are going to have hash for dinner so I am going to cook up the hotdogs you sent me. I still have a half bottle of catsup left to go on them. We had French toast, bacon, coffee for breakfast. It was good too. We were talking about how funny it was when we were back in warm barracks at Camp Swift and some one was always sick and going to the hospital, and now when we live in mud and rain and are wet to the skin all the time we never get as much as a cold. Many of us would love to get good and sick, or break a leg just to get back in a warm hospital where it is safe and dry.

One of the boys shot himself in the foot by accident the other day and we all stood around wishing it could happen to us. We laugh at our gunner as he fell off the tank one day head first and wasn't even lucky enough to break an arm, but scratched hell out of himself. Oh well it can't last for ever and if the Germans can stand it I guess we can too.

I hope some mail comes in today so I can find out what Roy is doing. I would laugh if he ended up in Texas. I'd laugh and at the same time wish I was there too!! Wait till he gets on one of those 25 mile hikes with full field pack. I only hope he doesn't get into the tanks. There isn't anything worse than a tank in the winter. I don't believe he will see any action in Europe, and the Pacific is a racket. The Japs don't have the brains nor equipment of the Germans. I believe I will be in the Pacific before he will anyhow.

Boy are my feet cold. One of these days I will have to take my shoes off and put on a dry pair of socks. I still have no shoes except the pair I had on when my tank was hit. I don't believe I have walked 10 miles since D Day but wearing them day and nite wears them out fast. My new ones are being made back in Boston and should be here any mo now. They ordered 6 new pair the day I lost the others. Last week they ordered 6 more for me as they figure by the time they get here the first 6 which I am waiting for now will be worn out. I'm such a problem with supply I don't see why they don't just kick me out of the army.

I wrote cousin Kitty a letter yesterday so that should hold her for a while. I also wrote letters to everyone else I write to for the first time in a week. Well I guess that is all there is to write about for today so I'll close and see what I can do about getting warm.
Best of health and good luck from your Loving Son
Bob

Sept
HOLLAND
Hello Mom Dad,

No you're not half as surprised as I am about being here in Holland. There we were fighting in Germany and minding our own business when all of a sudden bang! We are in another country. So far I have seen nothing of the country, so I will tell you about a trip through Belgium in a 1 tank convoy. We started out the other morning about eleven o'clock. It had just started to clear up after all that rain I told you about. We were driving through the mountains on a highway somewhat like the Storm King. The sun was just coming through the clouds and looked very beautiful shining on the river below. I sort of forgot I was driving and was just taking in the view when up popped a sharp curve with about a two hundred foot drop on the other side of it. Half my track was over the side but God was with us and we made it. About 5 miles further down the road we got a 10 minute halt. I got out and found a lot of bad connectors in my tracks. By the time we changed them the rest of the btn was long gone. From there on we were all by ourselves. I drove in 5th gear for hours trying to catch up with the column. We finally found out we took the wrong turn and were 5 miles out of our way. I turned around and finally got back on the right road. We stopped and tried to get another tank out of a ditch, but without success. That put us another hour behind the btn. About 6 o'clock that nite the luckiest thing in the world happened to us. We ran out of gas. And right in front of a group of houses. We no more than stopped when as usual we had people all over the tank. People came running out with everything from Dry Gin to pure alcohol. Baskets of tomatoes, pears, plums, grapes, a jar of jam, and an apple pie. As soon as they seen we were staying, two and three families at a time would ask us up to their house for supper. You know how I hate to eat, but I did accept an invitation from an old man who could speak some English. He was so happy to have us that he fell all the way up the steps to his home. He had a grand wife, she was 61 and he 62. She gave us apple pie and coffee (tea) and then black bread and jam. She made me promise to write her after the war and let her know how I made out. I am sending address home so I don't lose it. I left them at about 9 o'clock and went down to the tank. I no more than reached the tank when a young boy and girl took hold of my arms and took me down the street and up at least 100 steps through a beautiful garden.

When I finally got to the top I saw before me a beautiful home. It is second only to Buckingham Palace. We went in the door and there stood a woman of about 50 and a man about 55 years old. Both were very well dressed and I was surprised more than ever when the woman said "Good evening, come in and be seated.", in perfect English. Well you can bet I did go in. The woman (Mrs Parlat) did all the talking for her family and I just answered questions for about an hour. Then Mrs Parlat gave me a big cigar and a drink of gin, which you must drink whether you want to or not. Later came the eats. Lets not go into the eats yet as it will only make me hungry and breakfast is a hell of a ways off.

Claire asked me (Clair that's the young girl, age 20) if I wanted to wash, I said Yes I would be very happy to have a chance to get cleaned up. Just then the old man led me up to a real United States bath tub. There was plenty of hot water and boy did I enjoy that. I came down and we talked and listened to the radio for a while. The two old folks went to start packing for a trip to Brussels in the morning. Then the two servant girls (both red heads) came in. That made 3 girls (all good looking) and me. That was too much so I went and got my asst driver and gunner. We had music straight from NY on the radio, (Ozzie Nelson orch). It sure was swell. We gave the girls chewing gum and it is a riot watching them chew and play with it. They usually end up with it stuck all over their face. All you have to do to get yourself a girl is to pull out a pack of gum and they start beating them off with a club. It reminds you of 'Sadie Hawkins Day' in Little Abner.

We got back to the tank in the early hours of the morning. We turned down a dozen offers to sleep in a bed as we had to guard the tank. We got a couple hrs sleep anyhow. About 7 Claire was down to the tank after me. She said the cook was waiting for me to come for breakfast. So off we went. I had a breakfast of coffee, two eggs, sliced tomatoes, toast and butter. It was swell. We then listened to the radio and heard the US forces network which had all popular songs and re-broadcasts of Bob Hope, and many others. Also the Hit Parade. Say that is some song #4. I believe the name is 'Milkman Keep Those Bottles Quiet' or some such thing as that.

We later went out in the garden and set up a target for some pistol practice. I let Claire shoot 1 clip and she got a big kick out of it. I did a punk job but it looked good to her as I did hit the target once in a while. She said she had to go to her father's factory for a little while and asked me to go with her. Of course I couldn't say no so I rode her father's bicycle and she rode hers. You should have seen me ride. It was the first time since I was about 16 years old. I was all over the road but I made it anyway. I found out then where they got all their money. Her father owns a large steel works, and is a millionaire. She introduced me to all the office workers and the General Manager.

Two of the secretaries spoke fairly good English. One of them asked me how I liked the ice cream in Belgium. I almost died. I told them I haven't even heard of it since I left the States. Just then, three of them pushed me down in a big office chair and one of them ran out and was back in a few minutes with a ice cream sandwich. Boy did I enjoy it. It was really good too.

Clair then told them about how she fired my pistol. Then the manager got all excited and wanted to shoot it too, so we went out in the paint shed and set up a 1 gal oil can for me and the Manager as a target. He shot a few rounds and they all went wild. I then got 4 out of 5 hits and each time I hit it all the workers cheered. He got mad then and fired the last two shots and got a bull's eye on the last. He was so happy he jumped up and down. I had to turn down about 10 or 15 invitations for supper before I could leave. Riding back was all up hill and I got so tired I could hardly pump the bike. It is more work than I have done in years. When I got back there sat the gas truck next to my tank. We were all heart broken. We decided to move out at 1 o'clock but all the neighbors had pooled their food and were cooking up a spaghetti dinner for us. I had better not tell you what happened as I would get busted down to a private by morning, but we had the dinner and it was swell. We had to leave though as there is a war going on. Mrs. Parlat made me promise to write and she said she was going to write you as soon as mail goes out to America again. Well that is about all there is to that story, except I think I should have dug a hole and buried the tank and married Claire and lived like a king on her old man's dough. Well I'll write tomorrow Mom so don't feel bad about not getting anything but news.
Your loving Son
Bob

Sept 30
Holland
Dear Mother, Dad,

This is the third straight day that I am writing a letter to you, so your mail should be coming in pretty regular now. It is a week since I have had mail, but I know you are writing. It is the same every time we go from one country to another.

Well the weather isn't quite as bad as it was, but it still rains almost every day. It is a little warmer now so we don't mind it too much. I met some Dutch people yesterday and they were very nice and the best part is I can understand their language. It is part french and part german. About every fourth word is English. With all the motions and some of the words I do know we get along swell. I took a walk out on a farm and I met 2 girls digging potatoes. We talked for about 2 hours and got so we could understand each other perfectly. They invited me up to their house for supper. While we were waiting for supper I met the rest of the family. Their were 7 sisters and one boy and their mother. The father was killed by the Germans. None of the sisters were married so I had plenty of attention. Just as supper was being served I heard the tanks start to move out so I had to run off with out eating. They do wear wooden shoes but they do have leather shoes for good. It is also true that they are very clean. They only wear their shoes in the kitchen and not in the rest of the house. Their houses are just as modern as ours in the States. Most of them are even better, as they are built of stone. My sight seeing days are over though. We got orders today forbidding us to enter any house or town from here on. It is because of a new general we have. We also must wear a steel helmet at all times with the chin strap down. We must wear leggings at all time plus pistol belt, clean clothes, clean shave, and hair cut once a week. We also must wear our stripes or be busted. All non commissioned officers must also paint a white stripe on the back of any helmets. It is a beauty full target. Here is the best part. We must wash our tanks at every stop in between battles. We washed it with water and brush today. It makes it easier for the enemy to see us. Hear is another good one. We can not smoke in the tank either behind the lines or in battle. If the general will come in battle to watch us to see that we don't smoke, I am willing to quit. ha. ha. So if you see Pvt Cadmus on the envelope one of these days, you will know the reason why. Every time I go into battle I smoke at least 4 packs of cigarettes a day and so do the rest. I would like to see them stop us. If the war doesn't end in a few days I will be busted for sure as it is impossible to do what they order. I am anxious to hear about Roy. It will be swell if he can be stationed near home. It would be just his luck to be sent to Fort Jay or Monmouth. I see by the papers the war has slowed down. I guess we are in for some tough fighting. I seen my first flying bomb yesterday. They are a joke. They hit in the fields and roads most of the time. A family was standing near where one hit yesterday. He got a little cut on his arm. They break a lot of windows but that is about all. Boy would I like to own a glass factory over here. Well how are the ships coming along Dad? I read in the paper that two more destroyers were launched in the Pedral. Are you still putting out 1 a month? You ought to see the American cars over here. Their are 1936 Chevrolets, 1940-41

Buick, and others from Model T Ford to Cadalack. I haven't heard from Joe since that first letter. I guess it is the mail system or maybe he has been sent to the states. I got a letter from John Keiffer in England and it took 7 weeks to reach me. Well I'll close now as I can't keep my eyes open. Good nite, and love to all.
Your son
Bob

Oct 1, 1944
Holland
Dear Mother Dad,

Another day and more rain. It has rained at least once a day for the past three weeks. At least it is a little warmer. We are getting two more blankets, an overcoat, and wool underwear, and overshoes. I guess we will need them as we are pretty far north. It gets dark at about 6:30 now instead of midnite as it used to back in Normandy. I remember back in Scotland, in February it didn't get light until 10:30 in the morning.

Well I guess you can see by the paper that the war isn't over and probably won't be over before 1945. The Germans have short supply lines now and the weather is in their favor. Even the people will be against us from here on in. We are not allowed to talk to anyone or go to any town, or in any house now. The war is bad enough but why we can't have any fun in between battles it is almost more than you can stand.

The rain is dripping down on this letter and making it almost impossible to read. There is nothing I can do to stop it so it will just have to get wet.

There is still no letters from you. Only 2nd class mail is coming in. I got a package of cake from you this morning. It was swell. One cake was in perfect condition but the other was just crumbs. We enjoyed them very much though.

I have to go on guard from 8-9 so I will write until then. I don't think I will be able to write for a few days so I will try to give you all the news in this letter.

I finally got most of my clothes dry but my shoes are still wet. It took a week to get my blankets dry. Wet blankets are warmer then dry blankets but it gets pretty miserable sleeping in them.

I guess you told Roy all the news so I won't bother to write to him until I receive his address. I was going to write a letter to him and mail it to you but now I'll wait.

All there is to do for enjoyment over here is dream about the day we will be able to come home. That is about all we talk about now. We didn't mind it before when we could go to the towns and villages and have a good time with the people. We didn't mind fighting so much because after each town we took we could see all the people happy and see the good we did. Now when we take a town there is nothing. The people hate us and we hate them. You can't stick your head out of the tank for fear some civilians will put a bullet through it for you. Ah well, some day it will have to end and until then we will just have to fight it out.

I will have to write to the Lakes soon. It has been quite some time since my last letter to them. They write every week but the mail is so long getting here, their letters come three at a time. Yesterday I got the Hobo news from Grand Pa. We get a kick out of reading it but I would rather get letters any day.

Well I guess by now Joe is on his way back to the States. I hope he is anyway. I would gladly trade with him. In this war the man that is wounded is the lucky one. I am only sorry he didn't get to have all the fun of chasing the Germans across Europe. It was like a Coney Island shooting gallery. He would have loved it. You will probably hear from him before I do on account of the mail system here in Holland.

I got a new pair of pants today. They fit good around the waist but are a little too short. They are size 34-31.

I understand Roosevelt will be elected again. According to the papers Dewey doesn't have a chance. The people of France all asked me who I thought would be elected. I got a kick out of it. You see they read Gone With The Wind and think the elections are just a battle between the north and the south. Of course they want FDR to be elected. They think he is just grand. In our outfit most of the boys want him too.

Well I have seen quite a lot of Holland now and it looks like a very modern country to me. The roads are just as good as ours, they have our cars, new ones too. Their schools are operating now even with the bombs and fighting. The houses are beautiful. New, and built well too. They are built of stone and had glass windows much larger than most of ours in the States. Of course they have the poorer sections too. But even the poor people have nice clothing. They are very clean too. That is more than I can say for some places in the States.

Well I have twenty minutes left before I go on guard so I'll have to finish up now and get my rain coat on. I hope you are still having lots of fun Mom. I guess you must have seen every show going. Take care of yourself Dad and don't get sick again.

I'll try and write again soon.

Your Loving Son,

Bob

Oct 3

Holland (yet)

Dear Mother Dad,

Well the mail has finally started to come in. I got only 1 letter but it was worth waiting for. I couldn't understand a lot of things as the letters you wrote before this one haven't arrived yet. You said Roy is in Texas but I don't know what camp. You also said Dad wrote a letter and it hasn't come yet. I can't imagine what is wrong with your back. I guess you must have fallen on it or something. I hope it doesn't bother you very much. You said Helen was there with you too. I hope she can get rid of her cold so she can go out with you.

It has been a beautiful day today up until now. As you can probably see by the paper it has started to rain. Last nite after I finished writing your letter I went outside of the tank and went to bed underneath the tank. About midnite there was an air raid but I did not wake up. No everything was quiet until Lt. Lo, the last of the three puppies got in bed with me and started licking my face. It scared hell out of me too. I reached for my pistol and was ready for action before I realized what it was.

Early this morning the 155mm guns opened up and that was the end of all sleeping. After they got done the whole damn air force came over and bombed hell out of the Germans up the road. Well I didn't want to sleep late anyway.

We had breakfast about 7:30 and have been just taking it easy all day. I guess they are not going to send us up front today at all (I hope). We had roast beef for dinner and I found a few ears of corn in the next field to fill me up. The corn was tough but I enjoyed it as it is the first since I left home.

Well there isn't anything new to write about but I just wanted to let you know I am alright and having lots of fun. (Oh goody) The sun just came out and here they come again. About 500 more B:17 flying forts. It is funny, just as they came over all the machine gun fire just stopped.

I am writing early today so I will have time to write to some of my friends tonite. I guess they think I am dead or something as I haven't written in quite a while.

I cleaned my pistol today for the first time in over a week. It was starting to get rusty from all this rain and damp weather. I don't want it ruined until after war anyway. You can never tell when you might need it.

Well I'll close now and write again tomorrow if things aren't too hot.

Your Loving Son,

Bob

Thursday Oct 5th 1944

Dear Son Bob, This is your other old man writing to you, old man Pop Skelly. Your father wrote us a nice letter asking how Joe was making out. We wrote back and told them all the news that we had about him. I think your Mom has sent you a letter by now and she will probably send his address along with it. Well Big Boy, Socks is getting along O.K. now, about Sept 23rd the doc let him up out of bed for the first time, also his arm seems to be O.K. now as he is writing his own letters to us. How are you doing yourself? I hope that everything is O.K. with you anyway. I am praying like hell for God to take good care of all you fellows over there and a special one for the 747th. I wrote a letter to Dave Atien yesterday and told him to give you the news about Joe also that I was asking for you. You know Pal I did not know your address, but got a letter from your Mother and she sent the address to me, if I would have known where you were I certainly would have sent a letter to you long ago. Here is a little tip on your mother, Bob she is some woman, whenever we get a letter from her, it is good and cheerful and no weeping or crying in it, so hats off to Mom Cadmus.

See your brother Roy is down in Texas. Well the best of luck to him and I hope he makes out O.K. By what I read in the paper you fellers are keeping your-selves very busy and I hope that those german _____ (cut out by censor) fold up very soon. Do you get any baseball news or other entertainment where you are, but what a dopey question to ask when you guys are fighting like hell over there. Well Toots the St Louis Browns beat the Cards in the 1st game of the World Series 2 to 1 and a nice rain storm thrown in with it. Do you grin for baseball or would you like to be having about a dozen nice big lager beers with me and having a bull session. There's one thing me lad we have a date, when this damn thing is over, and it will be my pleasure to buy anything you care to drink, beer or the other stuff till it comes out of your toes. Well so long Bob and take good care of yourself, I can't write very much because I told Dave Atien most of the news yesterday. We will keep in touch with your Ma from time to time and tell Dan & Dave and the rest of the boys that Mom and Pop Skelly send their best wishes & love and God take care of you and all your buddies in the 747th.

I am your other old man
Pop Skelly
God bless you all.
I don't know whether you know where Joe got kissed by the jerries. It was his right ____ (other side of the page where the cut was made by the censor) and right leg and by what he writes to us, he is coming around very good and get-ting very good treatment and care, also there are a bunch of pretty nurses where he is and they are all a swell bunch of gals. Woof Woof you wolves
Pop

Oct 6, 1944
Germany
Dear Mother, Dad,

Boy isn't this a laugh. Just after I finished writing to you on the 3rd, we moved out and are back here in Germany again. I thought things were getting too quiet back there. It isn't too bad here today, we are just defending a town. The weather is still the same, it rains for a while then the sun comes out for a few minutes. It is cold again and are we feeling it. My feet haven't been warm in three days. I picked up a few things yesterday that I could have used a long time ago. I got three fountain pens and a wrist watch. The watch is pretty good but not valuable enough to bother sending it home. I am trying out the pens now. This one writes pretty good. I am going to try another one now. I heard yesterday that the mail is in but there is no way for them to bring it up to us. I guess we will just have to wait until we complete our mission and go back.

I have nothing to write, but this helps me to pass the long hours away. I will put this letter in with the other of the third and mail them as we get back of the lines. I had a hot cup of bullion and a can of pork and beef for breakfast. We felt a lot better after getting a hot drink in ourselves. Well the World Series is going on now and we sure would like to be listening in on it and much rather be seeing it. Maybe in a few years when the Yankees win the pennant again I will be able to make it.

I can't think of another thing to write so I guess I better close for today. I'll write as soon as I get back to the area, and get my mail.

Love to you both

From your Son

Bob

Oct 6

Hello again, I just finished a letter to you about 3 hours ago, but since then a fellow came up and handed me three letters. I got yours too Dad, and 2 from you Mom. It was swell to hear from you again. I could hardly believe you worked 30 days straight Dad. I'm glad to hear your knees are better then they were.

I am sorry to hear the mail has been coming to you so slow. I try my best to write as often as possible. Things happen so fast around here. I completely forgot your birthday Dad. Happy Birthday anyhow, even if it is 2 months late. Happy Birthday to you Mom too. I think you have one coming up soon too.

I wrote Roy a long letter just after I got his address from you. I gave him a few good hints but I doubt if they take effect. He will probably have to learn the hard way as I did.

Well good bye again for today.

Your Loving Son, Bob

Letterhead

Martin Heffels

address censored)

Oct 9, 1944

Germany

Dear Mother Dad,

We are back of the lines for a day or so of much needed rest. The sun is out and it is just like summer. Our air force is having a field day. The sky is full of bombers and fighters. Off to our left a group of P47 fighter bombers are bombing hell out of something. They circle around and dive down on a 60 degree angle and strafe with their 8 fifty cal machine guns then come up and go back and dive and let go with the 500 lb bombs.

I am going after a shower at 2 o'clock. They take us back about once every 5 or 6 weeks for them. I just put 3 letters in the mail for you this morning. They were written on the 3rd and 6th but this is the first chance I have had to mail them. I sent 1 to Roy and another to Hazel.

There is nothing going on that I am allowed to tell you so I will close now and try to write tomorrow again. The pictures in these letters are captured from the Germans. I thought you might like to see what they look like while they are still alive. When we see them they are only alive for a second and then all we can see of them is br_____ ((*other side of the page of what was cut out from letterhead address*)) meat. The mail just came in and there was no mail from you but I got a letter from Joe. He didn't say very much but he did tell me he is able to hobble around a little. His one leg is pretty bad yet. His hand is just about well enough so he can write a little. I am glad he got away with all his legs and arms. He was so badly hurt when he left here we didn't think he had much of a chance to live. He was full of shrapnel from head to foot. He just had what it takes to get well.

Kitty wrote the same old story. The apples are ripe etc. Well that's all for today. This is the first chance I have had to mail this letter. Oct 13.

Oct 14
Germany
Dear Mother, Dad,

It is a beautiful day in Germany today. The sun is shining and it is not too cold to enjoy laying around. We have been taking it easy for the past couple of days, just doing odds and ends and getting plenty of sleep.

We spent all day yesterday digging a big fox hole. It is big enough for 12 men. The roof is made of pine trees covered with 4 feet of sand. We sat up until about eleven o'clock last nite in it and played 500 rummy.

Today we went out in the woods and had target practice. We had two teams, the team that had the lowest score have to serve us our breakfast, dinner, and supper, and wash our mess kits all day tomorrow. I didn't do bad but my hand isn't as steady as it was in the states. I got a score of 21 out of a possible 25. The average score was about 16. I spent the rest of the afternoon cleaning my pistol.

Last nite for the first time in almost a week I received a letter. It was from you Dad. It's swell to hear from home once in a while. The weather is bad for flying over the Atlantic. That is one reason for all the mail coming so slow.

You better not try to work too hard Dad, you will only get sick again if you do. This war is only a political war now anyway so there is no sense in you hurting yourself. Maybe if Wallace, Morganthal and Hershey would keep their big mouths shut we could get this thing over with.

Helen is right again. She can figure out just about where I am by the radio almost all the time. We got some more men today fresh from the States. I went over to one and he said he was from Garwood. He went to Cr. High in 1932. He was also a good customer of ours. He was home just 1 month ago, boy was he lucky. There is another from New Brunswick and he went to school with one of our boys.

I'm sorry about the mail Mom. I can't write every day and that is all there is to it. I wish you wouldn't worry so much about me. Sure I'm having a tough time, but remember so are all the rest of the boys. I am better off than a lot of them. I can stand as much and more than most can. I don't think we will have to fight so much any more as there are plenty of other troops to fight here now. This isn't bad compared to that first week when we were the only troops here, and didn't have enough ground to turn around on. After that nitemare nothing can be too bad.

I am going to try and mail this letter tomorrow. It should get to you about 3 days from the last one I wrote. Maybe the mail will get straightened out soon so we can both enjoy 'mail call'. Don't feel too bad about Roy being in the Infantry, Dad. It is a great outfit to be in. It is the Infantry that wins wars. He will be a real man when he gets home. He is man enough to take anything they give him. Sure he will complain about the hard work, (and it will be hard too,) but don't we all? He will have it one heck of a lot better than I did. I was glad to hear he didn't get in some tank outfit as I don't think he would like it.

Well I hope you both enjoy the play you are going to this week. Sure would like to have had that big shore dinner you had, you made me sick all over by telling me about it. I had a can of beans (cold) the day I got that letter.

Well it is time to chow up so I'll have to close for now. Hope you are both in as good health as I am.
Your Loving Son
Bob

Germany
Oct 17
Dear Mom, Dad,
Last nite I received a letter from Pop Skelly. He said Joe is coming along fine. I just finished answering his letter. There is still no mail from you. About once every 4 or 5 days I get 1 letter from home. I don't know what's holding it up, but I'll be glad when it gets here. The box of chocolates you sent me arrived yesterday. We had a poker game going and ate while we played. It was delicious.

There is nothing new here. It's raining yet, but is not so cold.

Oct 18
Dear Mom Dad,
I couldn't finish this letter yesterday as my morale was way low and I just can't write when I am that way. Today things are different the sun is shining, we had pancakes for breakfast, I had shrimp for a midnite snack, and everything is going along swell.

Last nite another of your packages came in. It had shrimp, candy, taffy, sauce for the shrimp. It was swell. I enjoyed it more than ever.

I got a letter from a girl in France, she was the one that had me up to dinner when my tank was parked in front of her house guarding a bridge. She sent along a few pictures that she took while I was there. She could not use regular mail as it is not running yet in France, so she gave the letter to a soldier to mail to me. The soldier put in a little letter of his own too. He asked me to write to him and let him know how in the hell I had time to meet these girls when fighting was still going on in the city.

There is a very interesting story about this town and the people I was with while there. The family in the picture were members of the F.F.I. This is the town where the 3 American fliers jumped up on my tank when I rolled in and said 'what's cookin mack'. They had been hiding in this town for 7 mo. I will tell you the whole story when I get home. Jean L'Hoste that is one of the girls, speaks English. Not very good of course but you can understand her. You should see the letter she wrote. It is really funny as she don't know what words to use. I would send it to you but I don't think the censor would pass it. He would think it was a code or something.

Well Dad keep up the good work. I guess you are making money hand over fist. It takes me a month to make what you make in a week. I'll bet I save more than you though. By the way how about counting my bonds when you get time and let me know how much I have sunk into them. Also let me know how much I have in the bank. I must have enough to buy a jeep with by now.

Well I guess I'll close for today and write to the gang. I owe everyone a letter. I wrote a letter to Grand Pa but never had a chance to mail it so I finally burned it. Tell Roy I was asking for him and tell him the first 100 years in the army are the worst.

With all my love
I remain
Your son Bob
If you want a good laugh look at the letter I got yesterday. Save it for a souvenir:

Docteur Jean L'Hoste le 26th of September 44
Montherme
(Ardennes)   That is the name of my husband and the address
My dear Bob (I do not think it is very polite to call you by your name, but I do not know what I must tell. ...perhaps, Master? I do not know if you remember myself. I am the wife of the doctor who lives in Montherme Ardennes. I think to you very often and my husband also. We speak of you nearly every day. And today I send you the photographs (do you understand? I mean: the cards).But as we cannot send or receive letters I am going to try to speak with an American et ask him to send you this letter. But it is a little difficult because now we have no Americans in this country.

When I shall have again photographs I shall send you some for your mother.

I wonder where you are, and I should be very glad if you could write me a little. I hope you will understand what I mean et what I write but I am not quite sure. Now I am going to finish my letter. But I do not know what to say at the end. I leave you telling I think to you very often and I shall be very glad to see you again.
Amie L'Hoste

Oct 19
Germany
Dear Mother & Dad,

I already wrote one letter to you today, at least I finished writing one to you anyhow. I started it yesterday but didn't have the ambition to finish it then.

The package with the pepperoni, shrimp, paper, envelopes, candy came in a little while ago. We were just sitting here talking in our fox hole when it came. The pepperoni was delicious. It was better than the wops get themselves. We put the hot sauce on it and that even made it better. I had to drink cold water with one hand and eat with the other but I enjoyed every bit of it. I am saving the shrimp until the crowd goes home to their own fox holes as there is not enough for everyone. This is two nites in a row that I have had shrimp. It seems to be that way every time.

Boy I am in a heck of a position to write. The boys are playing poker and are sitting all over me. One guy has his feet about four inches from my face. The reason so many fellows are in our fox hole is because it is the only one with electric lights. It doesn't leak and there is lots of room. The darn lights run down my battery every nite and I have to run the gasoline generator all morning to get it up again. Today I never left my home except for dinner. I just slept all the time. They had hash for breakfast and hash for supper so I just stayed in bed. Dinner was good for a change. We had meatloaf, dehydrated potatoes, canned peaches. One meal like that sure helps out a lot!

I had a funny thing happen to me the other day when we were working on the fox hole. I walked about 300 feet to a hay stack to get some bedding. I stopped there to watch a few P47 dive bombers go to work on the Jerries. They did a beautiful job by the looks of the smoke that came up. They headed over our camp and I was just thanking God they were our planes when I seen what I thought was an aux fuel tank which looks like a bomb. It came over and whistled just like a bomb and hit the ground about 150 feet away from me in the woods near my tank. By then I knew what it was and hit the ground. Nothing happened so I started to get up when she let go. Man did I go down again!! I then started to get up again. Just then down came the rocks, stones and shrapnel. Down I went once more. I was fairly sure everything was OK before I got up again. It was a miracle all the way around. What happened, the bomb got stuck on the hook and couldn't be released. Then as the plane started back to its base it jarred loose. Then it only had about 100,000 sq miles to drop in and it had to pick on my home to land. The best part and the thing that saved me was the darn fuse didn't go off when it hit. She buried herself 20 feet in the ground before she exploded. When she did go it blew straight up. It blew a hole about 15 or 20 feet deep and 40 feet in diameter. The trees 10 feet from the edge of the hole didn't even have the leaves blown off. Here is the payoff. If I did get hurt I wouldn't even have gotten the Purple Heart as it was our own bomb.

The happiest moment I have had in the past week was about 3 hours ago when a guy stuck his head in and called mail for Cadmus. It was the first letter in a week. It was your letter Mom of Oct 5. Now I feel better knowing everything is alright at home. I caught up on all my letter writing today. I wrote to Pop Skelly, Joe Skelly, Grand Pa, The Lakes, a girl in Belgium, a guy in the engineers, Pvt Roy Cadmus, Mrs Mr O.H. Cadmus, Hazel from Texarkana, and last but not least Sadie from Brooklyn. I did forget one, it was Kitty from Chester but I'll get around to that tomorrow.
Good nite and God Bless you both.
Your Loving Son,
Bob

Oct 19,
Germany
Dear Mom – Dad,
I don't know how in the world to write a letter when we aren't doing anything or going any place. I know you will worry if I miss a few days so I will try to fill in a couple of pages somehow.

It is raining out now, and has been for the past two days. I don't mind it though as I don't have to get out of my fox hole except to eat, and turn on the generator when the light starts to get dim. I read a book since yesterday at this time. It was called 'Skin and Bones' by Thorne Smith, the same guy that wrote Topper. It is the same kind of a book except in becoming invisible he turns into a skeleton every once in a while, and at the darnedest times. I think it was way better than Topper. I am going to read 'February Hill' next. It looks like a good book.

Well by this time I guess you have taken another vacation Dad. You earned it anyway. Say I wish you would quit telling me about those wonderful dinners you are always getting. Every time you mention food I dream about it for a week. The other nite I dreamed about eating steaks with onions and woke up hungry as heck. I then broke into my last chocolate ration and finished it up. Say, that bottle of hot stuff you sent me will sure put hair on your chest. It's the hottest darn stuff I ever ate but I liked it. We finished it up today on our dinner. It helped take the taste of that slop away so we could eat it.

I'm worried about the roof of our fox hole. It is sure to start leaking soon if this rain keeps up. We have about 4 ton of sand on top and it is bound to start soaking in sooner or later.

Well, I'll have to close now as there isn't another darn thing I can think of to write. I'll try to write again tomorrow, maybe a Vmail. Until then so long
Your Loving Son
Bob

Oct 22, 1944
Germany
Dear Mom, Dad,

We are in the same place yet and not doing anything much. I had the funniest thing happen to me today. We were standing around talking when 4 deer came running up and tore through a barbed wire entanglement. We only had our pistol with us, and they were far gone before we could get a shot at them. We ran back for rifles and then started hunting. Here is the part I will never live down. I was standing in a clearing when one ran up and stopped about 150 feet from me. I took good aim and pulled the trigger. Nothing happened. The safety was on the gun. By the time I got it off he started to take off. I fired one shot and missed. Then another jumped in the same clearing right in back of the other. He was going like the wind but I got two shots at him. One shot got him in the rear end but he kept going and right into the enemy lines. I was the only guy that got a shot at them and I missed. I'm getting it from all angles now. Every time I turn around someone is kidding hell out of me. I put the gun down and ate supper and then went out after squirrels. That finished me. There was a squirrel up in a tree and I aimed at him and pulled the trigger and once more nothing happened and another guy shot and the squirrel dropped dead at my feet. The owner of the gun had removed the bullet from the gun chamber when I was eating so he could look at the barrel.

Well I just got two letters today of the 12-15 of Sept. It was old news but I still was glad to get them.

We are playing rummy in the fox hole now and it I my turn to get in the game so I will close now.
Your Loving Son,
Bob
P.S. It has stopped raining.

Oct 25
Hello again,

I didn't get a chance to mail this letter yet so I'll just add a little instead of writing another. I have been deer hunting some more but haven't been able to get in another shot.

Last nite I got two letters from you from Virginia. Gosh I'm glad you are having such a good time. You seem to like it down there more than you do in Jersey. I know it is very beautiful country down there. They also have some very beautiful homes too.

There was a letter from the Lakes too. They said they would like to write you in N.J. after the war. They said they have mailed 3 packages to me. I can't wait to see what is in them.

I have no mail from Roy yet. It should be coming in, in a few days if he has written to me.

Kitty also answered my long letter that you asked me to write. And she even wrote me a long one.

Well there isn't any more news from here so I'll sign off til tomorrow.
Your Loving Son
Bob

Oct 27
Germany
Dear Mom, Dad,

There is nothing new to write about so this letter will be plenty short. I washed out a few clothes and took a long walk in the woods today. That's about all. I just finished a short letter to Bayonne. When I finish this letter I'll be all done writing for another week.

It's almost time for supper so I'll finish this mess tomorrow.

Oct 28
Hello Again,

It is about midnite and the four of us just finished a game of hearts. It was the first time I played that since I played it with you years ago. Earlier we read the home town newspapers of the other two boys. I get a kick out of them. One is named the 'Kickaboo Scout' from Soldiers Grove Wis. The other is an Oklahoma paper. We were just talking about what we were doing a year ago. One year ago tonite Joe Skelly's tank turned over in Louisiana. Remember? We remember it as Mack in my fox hole partner received a telegram that nite that his wife had a baby, and he is 1 year old today.

Last nite after I finished writing the first half of this letter we had a hell of an air raid. None of the bombs landed very close but it jarred all the dirt from the roof down in our hair. We played rummy all through it. I looked outside once just in time to see one of their planes come down in flames. During the raid I got a rummy hand dealt to me and we put our partners 100 in the hole. About 4 o'clock this morning a lone Jerry plane came over at tree top height. That was all for last nite. Tonite all is quiet so far. All you can hear is an occasional burp gun, and a reply from our machine guns. Now and then you can hear a shell from a long gun whistle going off but the gun is so far back there is no explosion to be heard.

I go on guard from 4-5 in the morning so I guess I'll miss breakfast and get some sleep. Maybe I'll crawl out of my hole about 11:15 in time for dinner.

I got a swell letter from Mrs. Lake yesterday. She said she has shrimp and fruit cake on the way. I didn't ask for any of it but she said she did not need a request.

Well I hope you had a good time in Virginia. After 50 days of work you earned it. Even if you didn't you would have gone anyway. Lets have a few letters once in a while Dad. You have more to write about than I do. All I do is look at 4 walls of dirt day and nite. I sure would like to hear from Roy once in a while too.

Well I'm going to get a few hours sleep so good nite and God bless you. Your Son,
Bob

Oct 28
Germany
Dear Mom Dad,

Things are quiet as usual today. I am writing mostly to let you know that my A.P.O. has changed from 230 to A.P.O. 339 c/o PM NYC. I don't have any idea why the change.

Well it started snowing along part of the front today but we didn't get any of it (yet).
I got a letter from Roy today and he seems to be doing O.K. There was no mail from you as usual. Maybe tomorrow it will come in.

They took us back in trucks today to get showers. It sure feels good to be clean for a change. We are going to play some cards now so I'll close for today. Please tell everyone about the change of address.
Your Loving Son
Bob

We have just finished two games of 500 rummy. It's about midnite but I am not sleepy so I thought I would write another page or so if I can think of anything to write about.

The moon is out tonite and for the first time in a week you can see your hand in front of you. I heard some swell news tonite about a good friend of mine. His tank was knocked out some time ago and I seen him get out before it blew up. However we could not bring him back with us as things were too hot to wait for him. We were afraid he was killed all this time but just found out that he is a prisoner and doing fine.

I don't go on guard until 6 o'clock in the morning so when I do get off it will be time for breakfast. After breakfast I'll go to sleep until dinner. By that time it will be time to start another card game until tomorrow nite at this time. So you see we are having to lead a very dull life here with nothing to write about.

Our new quota of books will come in either tomorrow or the next day and that will keep me busy for a while. I read all the good ones that came in last week. The last one I read was The Life of Davie Crockett. It was good too. The Readers Digest will be in any day now and that will pass some more dull hours. The army newspapers help to run what little morale we have left to the dogs. Every day they say when you get done here we will have to go to the Pacific. They said today that all our (Army) tanks will go to Pacific.

Oct 29
Hello Folks,

It looks like I never will get this letter in the mail. Another day has passed and nothing new has happened as usual. It is only about 9 o'clock and it has been dark since 5 o'clock. We just finished a game of pinochle. They just taught me to play it. I think it is a rotten game. I just can't see any sense in it. Some of the officers just left on 7 day passes to Paris. They need it more than we do of course. The only passes we get are the ones we take when no one is looking and take a chance of getting 20 years in the joint if we get caught.

Well I'm going to sleep early tonite as we have to get up early tomorrow for an inspection. I'll try to get this in the mail tomorrow for sure.
Your Loving Son Bob

Oct 30
Germany
Dear Mom, Dad,

Well I am not in my fox hole tonite as I have been for the past week or so. We moved this morning. I sure did hate to leave. That fox hole was the next best thing to living in a hotel. We worked all afternoon on another but could not finish it before dark so here I am sleeping in the old stand by A-1. A-1 that's my tank of course. By the way my tank commander just made captain. He is the new company commander.

I am having a great time while writing this letter. A bunch of German airplanes are flying around trying to find a target to bomb. Every time they get near us a solid wall of orange tracer bullets go up after them. It is really a beautiful sight. There is a full moon and you can see the bullets all around the planes. They haven't brought any down yet but I expect to see one any minute. I am looking out of the periscope of course as what goes up must come down and I'm sure I don't want to divot up my new steel helmet.

The mail should come in tomorrow noon. I hope for once I hear my name called.

Winter is here now! I'll bet the temperature is no higher than 40 degrees now and will go down lots more before morning.

We got our battle ribbon today with 3 stars on it. One star is for Normandy, another for Central, eastern France, and the other for Belgium, Luxembourg, Holland, Germany. We can't send them home in a letter so I'll just hang on to them until I can bring them home myself along with the rest of my junk.

Well it's getting late and I am very tired from digging. Tomorrow nite I should have my fox hole finished and the light hooked up. If so I will write again tomorrow nite.

I hope you're all in good health and not working too hard.
Your Loving Son
Bob

Nov.2

Hello again,

Maybe some day I'll get this letter in the mail. I just found it in the tank where I left it the other nite. We worked all day yesterday on the hole. We just finished it last nite as it was getting dark. I was so cold last nite I could not write. The hole is now about as large as my room at home. We have oak logs split for rafters. On top of the logs we have a foot of straw (to take up rain). Then there is 4 feet of dirt on top of that. We have lots of branches and leaves for camouflage. We have a foot of straw on the floor and about 40 blankets over that. For light we have a truck headlight hooked up to the tank. It is a little cool in here now, but not to cool to enjoy a little card game. We get paid tomorrow and that means poker for a few days until one guy gets all the money. We get paid in marks over here. One mark is 10 cents. It's German money but made in USA.

I received one letter from you tonite, it was dated Oct 16. I also got a package of nuts from Grand Pa.

Well my hands are getting so cold I can't push this pen around much longer.

Well good nite and good luck til tomorrow nite.

Your Loving Son,

Bob

Nov 3

Dear Mom, Dad,

This is about the fourth letter I have written to you in the past week and I haven't mailed any of them yet. I have a big one in my pocket that will probably need two stamps to mail it. Tomorrow morning I will mail them for sure. I didn't get out of bed this morning until after the mail had already gone out.

There has been no mail coming in in the past few days. I am starting to get disgusted with it.

It is getting colder every day. I almost froze yesterday out in the tank. You see I can't put on a coat as I wouldn't be able to get out of the tank fast enough. I'll just have to freeze it out til summer.

My shoes are going fast. The heels are gone and the soles are starting to come off. They can't get any new ones no matter how they try. Every week they put in an order but no luck. They have been doing that ever since June 12 when I lost my others on the tank. My arch supports are still in good shape. I only have one pair left as the others were with the tank. I have a good idea though, the next time the General comes around I am going to run up in my bare feet, click my ankle bones together and report. If he don't get me shoes I miss my guess.

Well they gave us two more needles today. I get so I don't mind them so much any more.

The boys are playing Black Jack here and making the usual amount of noise so don't mind if the letter sounds crazy as I can't keep my mind on it. I owe everyone a letter but I can't write to them at present so they will just have to wait. What ever happened to John Keiffer? Is he going overseas again? I was just wondering if Mrs. Daktar is still working day and nite as she was. Tell her I was asking for her the next time you see her.

The shipyard must be getting cold now isn't it Dad? Don't let it get you down. At least you have a nice warm house to come home to every nite.

Here comes the first Jerry plane of the nite. I can hear him flying overhead now. We are pretty well hidden here so I don't think he will find us. They will be flying around all nite, or at least until they get shot down. I haven't seen one of them up in the day light in some time now. I guess you are wondering how we can tell they are German planes when it is so dark. They sound just like the old public service busses used to sound. You can't mistake them. In a little while some of our P61 (Black Widow) nite fighters will come and chase them. They are bombing now. It sounds to be about ½ mile away. They must have spotted something. That stuff used to scare hell out of me when I wasn't used to it. Now they can bomb til their hearts content and I never wake up.

Roy has finally come across with a letter. He only wrote about a page and a half, but I was glad to hear from him. He is already looking forward to his furlough. He is finding out how easy he had it. When he gets over here he will find out what a swell country he came from. Yes this army teaches you plenty. I'll never regret any of it. It's a hell of a way to learn but when you learn it this way, it can never be forgotten. You are probably getting tired of reading by now so I'll close now and wrap up in some blankets and try to get warm.

Your Loving Son

Bob

Nov 8

Germany

Dear Mom Dad,

I just got back from a 48 hr pass in Holland. I had a good rest but that's about all. Your letters just came in, 2 from you, 1 from Joe, 1 from Kitty. That's about the first mail I have had in almost two weeks. I got a laugh about Ed R. getting shot at with an 88. Wait until he gets into some action. I wonder how he would feel if he had them shoot at him for 3 or 4 months day and nite.

Two buzz bombs flew over our heads while we were on pass. We all sang 'Praise the Lord and Keep the Engine Running'. Well I'm just as glad to be back here in my fox hole. That town was about as wild as Clostes on a Sunday afternoon.

Joe is going back to the states, pretty soon I guess. You will be able to visit him there if you want to. He said he enjoyed getting your letters very much. He also got one from Roy. I'm glad to hear Helen is feeling better again. I was worried about her with all the cold weather coming in. I am going to put a Holland dollar bill in this letter so you can see what they look like. They are printed in the USA.

It is getting colder every day now. We will probably have snow within a week or two. The sun is shining today for a change, but it will rain before the day is over. The mud is getting bad. It will hold up the war to a great extent. Maybe next year we will be able to finish this job up. I was hoping it would be over before Roy got here.

No Mom there are no places over here to have your picture taken. I haven't changed a bit so the pictures you have are good enough.

What's this I hear about you losing so much weight Dad? I hear you are down to 240. Keep up the good work. Well I have 5 more letters to write today so I'll close now wishing you lots of luck and good health.

Your Loving Son Bob

Nov 9

Germany

Dear Mother, Dad,

I haven't mailed you the letter I wrote last nite yet but as long as I have nothing to do I'll write another. We played poker all nite tonite and for a change I won a little. I'll put it with what I draw at the end of the mo. and send you about $60.

We had a little excitement today. About 6 planes came over and strafed, and dive bombed our lines. No one was hurt and it was fun watching our guns go to work on them. They bomb every nite but very seldom during the day.

The mail is rotten. Only 20 letters came in today for the whole company (none for me).

We had a hail storm today, the hail stones were about as large as marbles. It only lasted a few minutes, but was enough to cover the ground.

I'm going to write Joe now as I fell asleep last nite before I got to him. Well good nite and God bless you.

Your Loving Son

 Bob

Nov 10

Germany

Dear Mom Dad,

At last some of the mail came in. That was a swell letter from you Dad. I want to get lots more just like it. The pictures you sent were really swell. Some of the others you sent weren't so hot. It's about 10 o'clock now and we are all sitting around looking at each others' pictures. This goes on about every three weeks or so. We will talk about home now until about three or four in the morning. I guess the whole army is the same. We are making big plans about what we are going to do after the war. The subject goes from fishing to squirrel hunting. A buddy of mine here has it all planned how he and I are going to live in a little log cabin for a week, far back in the hills of West Virginia and do nothing but hunt and fish. Another from Oklahoma has it all set for us to go coon hunting for a week or two. Well we have a swell time talking about it even if we never get the chance to do it.

Boy it is really getting cold now. We had our first snow yesterday. It is going to be one tough winter if things keep going like they are now. This morning I got so cold I was numb. I don't believe we will be able to do much driving without getting sick. I just hope I am lucky enough to break a leg or something and spend the winter in a hospital. No kidding though, I'll be glad when this winter is over.

<u>2 hrs later</u>

Well I'm going to finish this letter tonite yet. I got so interested in the bull session I could not keep my mind on the letter. Say, send me a picture of Roy in his uniform as soon as you get one. That was a swell picture of him in civilian clothes.

The subject just in case you're interested, has changed to apple pie. You can bet I put my two cents in about your pies too Mom. I just went outside and it's raining hard. It has gotten a little warmer, though.

Well I'm going to try and get some sleep now as I have to get up by 9:30 in the morning.

Take care of yourselves now and don't work too hard.

Your Loving Son,

Bob

Nov 18

Dear Mom, Dad,

This is the fourth nite in a row that I have started to write to you. Each time I managed to write half a page but could not think of anything else so I tore it up. I wouldn't doubt but what the same thing will happen to this one.

It has been raining for the past month and now it has changed to snow. It melts as fast as it hits the ground but it is still cold. The mud is over your shoe tops now. My shoes haven't been dry in over 2 weeks.

I just came off guard and am about frozen. I go on again from 12 midnite until 2. I am trying to dry my shoes with a candle but without much success. The best I can hope for is a good case of pneumonia. They have overshoes for most of us but the guys with the big feet are just out of luck. I sure wish the big push would start. We are thinking more about it than we did hitting the beach. If Roos..... and his gang would keep their big mouths shut about what they are going to do to the Germans after they are licked, maybe they would give up. Well I'll either finish this tomorrow or rip it up and start a new one.

Nov 19

Germany

Dear Mom Dad,

One of my old buddies that was with me when I lost my first tank, just came back from the hosp. I sure was glad to see him. He was full of holes when I found him back in June. I thought his back was broken but they found a 22mm bullet under his backbone which was the source of his being paralyzed. He was caught by the Germans the day I almost got caught. They thought he would die in a few moments so they just stole his cigarettes and left him lay. That nite about midnite when I was making my getaway I found him in a hole. I got him back with me and that was the last I saw him until today.

We went to take showers this morning back in Holland. There are swell showers in a cold mine, that we use when ever we have a little time off. On our way there, we saw an accident. We were on a truck and a little girl about the same age as Janet Schneider waved to us and stepped into the road. Just then a truck came along and run over her. It killed her instantly. I don't mind seeing a soldier getting killed but I hate to see little kids get it. That is the second one I seen get killed the same way over here, only the other one was a boy about eleven years old.

Capt. Bulvin went to the service company to see about my shoes today. They told him that the whole division is the same way. None of the extra large sizes are available. It was repeated to General Ike the other day when he was on his visit to the front. I'll bet it won't be long now before they come across with shoes and overshoes.

Last nite 2 of your packages came in together. One of them had the sweater (just what I needed), pepperoni, shrimp, candy, figs, pens, and everything else I could have hoped for. Thanks a lot. We sure do appreciate those packages.

I got a letter from Roy today, (1 page). He seems to be getting along OK. I told him to go to the hosp and make them take care of his back. If he does he has a good chance of getting in another outfit. You keep on him to go, in your letters and I'll do my best from here. I don't want him over here, and if he does what I tell him he won't be. Well the weather has finally cleared up and the air corps are making the best of it. In the past weeks we have had hail, snow, sleet, rain. This morning the mud puddles had ice on them. It is getting colder all the time. Well I'll have to close now and get some sleep as I have to go on guard about 3 in the morning and it don't pay to sleep on guard.

Well good nite and God bless you both.

Your loving Son,

Bob

Nov 23

Thanksgiving

Germany

Dear Mother, Dad,

About eight days ago we made an attack and have been going day and nite ever since. It rained every day and the temperature never went over 50 degrees.

Yes it was rotten, in fact it was about the worst eight days of my life. Last nite about 10 minutes after we were relieved I ran into a bomb crater. The mud was terrible, it was over our shoe tops. We had to leave the tank and come back behind the lines in another tank. This morning I went back and got it out with the help of two tanks and two wreckers. As we pulled it out a track came off and that was about 4 hours more work. My shoes and clothes haven't been dry since we started. Today it rained hard all day and to top it off I had to crawl under the tank in the mud to fix that track. All during the day enemy shells were falling and we had to dive in a hole full of mud about every 10 minutes or less. This afternoon we were standing around waiting for a new cable, and an armored car rolled up loaded down with turkey for the infantry. I was starved so I pulled out a K ration and just took a bite of cheese when a guy called us over and gave us a turkey dinner. (The cheese was bait.) Well we finally got out of the hole and the engine wouldn't run. They pulled me all the way back to the Btn area. When we got here, Walter Knoles the only good cook in the co., had about three quarters of a 20 lb turkey ready for me. I polished most of that off and gave the rest to a couple of foot cloggers that were passing by.

Then the mail clerk had another surprise. He handed me a letter from you (the first in 12 days) then came two packages, one from Grand Ma, Pa, and the other from Fritzie. We put a good dent in them already and will finish it off tonite. So although it wasn't as good as last year or the years before that but it is, I suppose a lot better a Thanksgiving than some had. The boys that weren't fighting today took turkey dinners in the tanks up to the front for the others.

Tomorrow morning I am taking my tank back to Holland to an ordnance Btn and get a new engine, gun, clutch, and repair wiring. I am hoping it will take a few days or even a week but it may be finished in a day. Here's hoping anyway. I put eleven hundred miles on that last engine since St. Lo or was it Vire. I can't remember now. It seems like a hundred years ago.

Well I haven't shaved or washed in 10 days so you can imagine how I look. I'm going to wash now and shave tomorrow.

How about writing once in a while even if I can't answer them but once in a while.

Love to you both and take good care of yourself. Don't work too hard Dad! HA HA.
Your Loving Son, Bob

Nov 30
Holland
Dear Mom, Dad,
I know it has been weeks since my last letter to you but it could not be helped. I wrote a letter to you Thanksgiving Dad, and explained everything but have been unable to mail it yet. It is now back in camp and it will be at least another two weeks before I get back there to mail it.

My tank finally went to the dogs and I am back to ordnance having it repaired. I have my choice of getting a brand new 45 ton tank or having the old baby fixed up. My crew and I have come out of many a tight squeeze with her and don't like to give it up. It has never failed in a pinch. So we are getting a new engine, and having it rewired, plus a few other odds and ends. A guy that I used to go to school with is doing the rewiring. His name is Warren Corelson. He used to live on Orchard Terrace. Roy knows him.

While I am here I have nothing to do so I go to the movies twice a day. There are two shows. This morning I met some very nice Dutch people. The lady invited me in for coffee and ginger cookies. She owns the local bake shop. She made me promise to come back this afternoon, so here I am sitting in the parlor writing letters. She also has a very pretty girl working for her. I have lots of fun with her and have a date with her for tonite. Her name in English is Catherine (I think). She took up English in school and with what Dutch I already know, we get along fine.

In this room I am sitting in now, there is a cuckoo clock exactly like the one we used to have. It works too. There are three rather large pictures on the wall. One of a small Dutch village in the background and an apple orchard in the foreground. The orchard is flooded and the water is washing away the trees. There is a piano here too. It looks something like ours used to. Over in the corner is a Singer sewing mach. There are a few clay pipes on a rack. They have a stem about 1 ft long. A fireplace made of white marble is burning brightly in the corner. It is just nice to take the dampness out of the air. This house as well as all Dutch houses is spotless. They wash all the windows at least once a day and scrub the sidewalks until they are clean enough to eat off them. They even keep their streets clean. You can't even find a cigarette butt or match stick on the streets.

These people don't think much of the French. They are too polite to come right out and say it but they think it is a disgrace the way they come out and ask us for candy and cigarettes. They also were shocked when they heard how the French girls in Paris kissed every G.I. and acted like we were all Frank Sinatras. To tell you the truth I was shocked myself but damn if I minded it.

The lady just brought me in a cup of hot chocolate as she heard me coughing. She said it will stop it. I'm just getting rid of that cold I got up at the front,. If I had to stay out in that cold and wet one more day I would have had pneumonia.

I showed them the pictures I have of everyone and you should have seen the fun. She first seen the one of Grandma and Grand Pa. She said they were very good. Then came you and Dad. She looked at me and said 'You double rations, Mama and Papa double rations'. Meaning we all eat twice as much as anyone else. I laughed until I thought I would die. Roy came next in his graduation costume. They had never seen anything like it and laughed until they cried. The little boy said his hat looked like a bird house. Catherine said he looked like a scare crow in that outfit. Hazel in the grass skirt came next. They all laughed and mama says 'Picture nix good'. She then put a paper over the picture and left just the head showing and said 'Now good'. She told me I have a very good looking mother (as if I didn't know it).

There was a wedding this afternoon. You should have seen it. Along came a whole line of coaches and horses. The drivers were full dressed with high silk hat and all. The bride and groom were in the last coach. It looked like something in a movie.

Well I got a lot of packages from different people and I have to write and thank them so I'll close for now wishing you all a Merry Christmas, and God bless you both.

Your Loving Son

Bob

PS I forgot to tell you that I had a date with a real American girl yesterday. I took her to church in the morning and the movies in the afternoon. She was a Red Cross Club mobile worker. Frances from S. Carolina.

One mail thing- I have received exactly 1 letter in three weeks.

December 7

Dear Mother Dad,

I hope you haven't been worrying about me in the past mo or so. I have been very busy and unable to write. I am alright and doing fine, so don't worry. The weather is a little better now. We still have lots of mud to keep us busy though.

I hope you all have a Merry Christmas. Maybe Roy will be lucky enough to get home and spend Christmas with you. I have had exactly 2 letters in about 7 weeks. One was from you Mom and the other from Dad.

Well there is nothing new so I'll close for today.

Your Loving Son,

Bob

Dec 10

Dear Mom, Dad,

Today was a great day as far as my mail was concerned. I got five letters, and was glad to get them. Thanks for the picture of Roy. Don't worry about him. The more he hates the army the more good he is getting out of it.

Well there isn't anything new here. Just the same old grind. That five days I spent back at ordnance did me a lot of good. I feel a whole lot better now.
I received packages from Grand Ma, Fritzie, Mrs. Lake, Maxine. I haven't had the chance to answer or thank them yet. They were swell packages too.

Well that's all the news from here so I guess I'll sign off. Take good care of yourselves you two, and don't worry about me. Have a good time Christmas and you can bet I will too.

Your Loving Son,   Bob

Dec 11,
Germany
Dear Mother Dad,

I wrote to the Schneiders and the Lakes last nite as it has been months since I wrote to them last. The mail has started to come in a little better now, I got 5 letters the other day but none since.

This morning I stayed in bed until 10:30 and just got up in time to go to church. We had a swell turnout. There wasn't enough room for all in the place we have been using, so we moved to a larger building. We have a swell chaplain. After that last trip to the front we have guys going to church that never went before in their life. I don't remember whether I told you or not, but I ended up getting a new tank. It's an M4-E2 with a 550hp ford V8 engine. It weighs 42 tons. It has all the modern conveniences too. Plenty of lights to read by at nite, duck feet for mud, and plenty of extra armor. It also has a big hole where the driver gets in and out. I can drive with an overcoat on now. Capt Bulvin wants to name it the Ambulance as we have brought back dozens of wounded soldiers on it, when things were too hot for an ambulance. We even brought back a wounded German soldier one day. He was a Polish fellow who was willing to give us some information so we loaded him on the tank and brought him back.

I get a kick out of Roy hating the army so much. I have to laugh every time I think of it. There is a lot of crazy ideas pop into the heads of some of those officers but you just have to overlook it. (That includes you too, Capt Bulvin). Don't worry about him Mom, as long as he stays in Texas he will be alright. I got a new pair of shoes yesterday. I had to go all the way to 29th supply house for them and it was the only pair they had. I got a new overcoat and G.I. sweater too. This is the first I have been warm in months.

Madame Hogedoren made me promise to come to her house for Christmas if it is possible for me to get some time off. If I can make it, it will be the next best thing to being home. So don't worry about me having no fun at Christmas. Did you know that in Holland they celebrate Christmas for 3 days in a row? No one works for the three days, they just have big parties and have a good time. The children celebrate Christmas on Dec 9, that is when they receive their presents. The adults celebrate it starting Dec 25th same as us.

Well I'll have to close now and get some sleep.
Your Loving Son,
Bob

Dec 15
Germany
Dear Mom, Dad,

The mail has finally started to roll in. I just got all your old mail. Oct 28 to Nov 11. It sure is swell to get mail from home once in a while. Kitty sent me a

Christmas package and it was swell. I just got a letter from her too. I am going to write to her as soon as I finish this letter.

Roy hasn't written in the past few weeks but I can understand that. I never had anything to write about either. I know just about what he is doing anyway. Helen says they haven't heard from him since he left for the army. I wrote to him last week but I don't expect an answer.

Well it is still raining and it doesn't look as if it will ever stop. We had a good freeze last nite and this morning all the mud puddles had a good thick layer of ice on them. One of these days we will get a good snow storm, perhaps by Christmas. I went back to visit Mrs. Hogedoren the other day and she made us a big roast beef dinner. It was really good. We had apple pie and cake for desert. Papa sure can bake good pie and cake when he wants to. They made me promise to come and stay for a few days around Christmas. If we can get a pass you can bet I'll be there too.

Joe Skelly will be home by the time you get this letter but I don't want you to say a word about it. No one knows about it yet. He will get in touch with you when the proper time comes. He is going to have a hard enough time with his folks for a while. Be sure you don't say anything to anybody about him coming home until he comes to see you. It may take him some time but I am sure he will be over to visit you.

You asked me some questions that I am not allowed to answer but you will find the answers by reading the newspapers. You see our outfit is still on the secret list. No, the paper wasn't wrong, things have changed over here.

Well Dad I hear you are doing good on your diet. That makes 2 lbs you have lost since I left home. Keep it up and in about 80 years you will be back to normal.

Well that's about all the news from here so I'll close now and try to write a few lines to Kitty.
Your Loving Son, Bob

12/44
Dear Mother, Dad,

Your mail is coming in very good. Keep up the good work. I'm glad to hear you are working regular now Dad. How about a letter from you, and maybe Roy if it's not too much trouble. Our work has started at last. We have our XXXXX and they XXXXXX of XXXXXXXXXXXXXXXXXXXXXXXXXXXXXXXXXXXXXX ((*censor blacked out the words where the X's are*)) and we walk to them each morning and work on them and walk all the way back each nite. It is rough training but it is the best thing in the world for us. We still get chicken 3 times a week and the rest of the meals are good too. I go on guard tonite so that will get me off the hike tomorrow. Thank God!! I got a letter from Kitty yesterday.

It was the only one yesterday but I had 20 letters in the past week. Hope to hear from you soon.
Your loving son,
Bob

Mr. R. Milden
16E 44th St.
Bayonne
New Jersey

Dec 15
Hello Folks,

I hate to write a Vmail letter, but I want it to reach you soon, so you will know I am ok. I will write a regular letter tomorrow but it will probably take months to get to you.

As you can see by the papers they have been keeping us very busy, and we have had very little time to write.

Your package arrived on Thanksgiving day, along with another from Fritzie. God they were swell, it helped a lot of us to remember what we have to be thankful for. I received your letters Helen, and also one from you Grandpa. I am always glad to get mail from you and look for your letters at every mail call.
Well I am doing fine and hope you are all in good health too. Merry Christmas to you all.
As ever
Bob

Germany
Dec 20
Dear Mother, Dad,

I hope by now you are receiving my mail once in a while. I have been writing quite regularly in the past few weeks. My new tank has been acting up on me so I am back at ordnance having it checked. I have been here for three days now and have done nothing but sleep and eat. If I am still here Christmas I will go down to Holland and celebrate.

The last time I was up the front, I found a German dress sword. I was going to send it home for a souvenir but before I got a chance to mail it a guy offered me a Mausser pistol for it. It was a World War I German Calvary pistol. The barrel was about 9 inches long. I tried it out by shooting at a sparrow that was in a tree about 35 feet away. Well you guessed it, there was a cloud of feathers and not much left of the bird. A buddy of mine seen me do it and decided he wanted the gun. So he gave me a Belgian automatic pistol plus $10. I brought the Belg gun down here to ordnance with me and a guy offered me $75 for it, so the gun now belongs to him. That got me $85 for nothing. Pretty good if I can keep it up, how about it!

I just sent you $70 for my other pistol did you get it yet? I will send you about $100 the end of this mo. if I am lucky enough not to lose what I get now.

I don't see why you want to put my picture in the paper. The guys you read about in the paper are the ones that deserve it the least. They like to see their names in print to convince themselves that they are good. If you do something good the paper will hear about it and print it without you asking them too. That is why they have reporters.

I hope you had a good time in NY with Kitty and Mrs. Zulik. I sure would like to have been around over there for a few days. I did get the jump on Radio City though. Right here in Germany, too. The 29th Inf and attached units were the first to see the new picture 'Saratoga Trunk' with Gary Cooper and Ingrid Bergman. I seen the world premier. It was a swell picture too. I would like to see it again. I was one of twelve in our company to go see it.

Well Dad you're down to 239 now. What did you do, run around the block or did Mrs. Daktor run out of ice cream some nite last week? Keep it up and you will be able to see your feet again before you know it. I lost about 5 more lbs yester-day. It wasn't from not eating either. Jerry sent over a bunch of bombers and I shook it off.

The rain has stopped at last. It hasn't rained in the past two hours. We haven't had any dust storms yet, but you never can tell.

Pop Skelly sent me another letter. He sure is a grand old guy. He is always full of fun just like Joe. He is worried about Joe but he tries not to show it. He has a cousin in the WACs and she went to see Joe in England. She wrote and told him what was wrong and that was plenty. I don't think Joe ever told him how bad he really was. I was plenty worried for a while myself. I never though he would live until he reached the hosp.

Did I tell you Kitty sent me a Christmas package? Well she did and it was very good. It even had a can of chicken in it. I wrote and thanked her for it the other nite. I got another package from Mrs. Lake and it had the shrimp in it. It was in perfect condition. She had it packed in a tin box with plenty of packing around the jars. Boy I made me a real meal out of it.

Marge and Bob also sent a box of candy which was very good. I haven't writ-ten to them yet. I got a card from my long lost Uncle Ed. It had no writing on it and was just signed 'Ed'. (What is he kidding?) He is worse than the person who writes a Vmail and expects a letter in return. I gave my mail clerk orders to put all Vmail addressed to me in the nearest latrine. The same for Christmas cards. If a person is too lazy to write a regular letter I would rather not hear from them.

How is John, and Mrs. Zulik and Catherine coming along? Is John still work-ing? Remember me to Mrs. Riley and partner next time you see them.

Well your mail is coming in now so I have no kick coming on that score. Of course those Lakes in Texas seem to get about three letters a week through the mail, but I want mail from you and not them as much.

Do you know what June did? She sent me a package with a box of chocolates, a whole stack of envelopes (air mail) all addressed to her. Here is the payoff. 1 G.I. neck tie. What the hell does she think I want with a necktie? If it wasn't for the candy I would have sent the tie back and told her to wrap it around her neck and use it as a tourniquet. Ah well I guess she meant well anyway. I'm all out of paper so I have to sign off until I get back with my outfit. I hope you had a good Christmas as I am sure I will. I have a camera and two rolls of film so you can expect some pictures in about two or 3 months.

Your Loving Son

Bob

Dec 24

Germany

Dear Mom, Dad,

As you can see by the papers, things over here are in one hell of a mess. Maybe by the time you get this letter we will know about how much longer this war can last. This battle looks like the showdown. If we can whip them this time maybe Roy won't have to come over. I am praying for it to end before he can be shipped into it. I am no longer in the first army as you have been thinking. We are now in the 9th Army, 19 corps. That's all I can tell you about it at this time.

This is Christmas Eve, the nite we usually spend together. Back where you are it is still early in the afternoon, but before I finish this page it will be Christmas in Germany. I can't help wondering what you are doing now. Preparing the supper for the party, out doing your last minute shopping, or just finishing up on the tree. Whatever it is, I would give anything in the world to be there doing it with you.

Things didn't turn out over here the way I hoped they would. Everything broke loose at the wrong time. I had hoped to be able to get away for a day and spend Christmas with my friends in Holland or Belg. That's out, so we will do the best we can here in our area. I am going to church services in the morning, after that we have a big chicken dinner coming up. We put up quite a few Christmas trees around in the different houses. We found lots of decorations for them in some of the places that haven't been completely destroyed.

We have a radio here in our home hooked up to the tank. We are listening to the Christmas programs from the States.

Well I got my sleeping bag today. It looks good, but I'll let you know how warm it is after I try it out. I have two pairs of shoes and a pair of overshoes now, so the cold weather and mud don't seem so bad any more. It sure is good to have dry shoes.

I haven't heard from Roy in a mo. or two. The last time he wrote he didn't say anything anyway. I'll answer his letters if he ever writes again. Well I'll close now and get some sleep as I have a little work to do before church in the morning. Good nite and God bless you.

Your loving Son,

Bob

Dec 25

Germany

Dear Mom, Dad,

Christmas has come and gone and I am still over here just as I told you I would be. Lots of the boys used to think they would be home for Christmas, but I had no hope of it, so it didn't bother me too much by being away.

We had a beautiful day today, in fact it was the best day we have had since we have been overseas. It was cold all day, but the sun was out and there wasn't a cloud in the sky. The ground was frozen and the frost didn't melt all day.

We had a few German planes come over but they didn't bother us. We had a swell turkey dinner with all the trimmings. I had all I could eat, (and that was plenty).

I had a roll or films and took some pictures, but somehow the film got spoiled and I ended up by throwing the whole works away, camera and all.

The Red Cross gave out packages to everyone. I got two packs of cigarettes and some other junk. I also got two packages from Hazel and Mrs. Mallander. I would much rather have gotten a letter or two.

Well I have to write to some friends so I had better close and get busy.

Good nite and God bless you both.

Your loving Son, Bob

Dec 29

Dear Mother, Dad,

Today was the first cloudy day we have had in four days. When I woke up this morning it was snowing. It was only a light fall of snow but it looks as though it will stay for a long time. The temperature has not gone above freezing for the past week. The air is dry so you don't feel the cold as much as you would at home.

A few miles back the Dutch people are ice skating on the rivers and ponds just as if there was no war going on. I went to the movies today and seen a third rate picture with a first rate cost. It was 'The Open Road'. Charley McCarthy, W.C. Fields, Bonita Granville, Sammy Kay were a few of the stars and they all <u>stunk</u>.

The boys are making up a pot of soup out of some C rations. Three cans of stew, two packages of bullion powder, and about two quarts of water makes a pretty good pot of soup. At least it warms you up after a couple of hours of guard.

The mail is not coming in any more. We have had no letters in about two weeks. Just packages and more packages are all that's coming in. We like the packages but we also like a letter once in a while. The last time I did get mail the letters were two months old. I have to write to Pop Skelly one of these days. I never did find time to answer his last one. I suppose I will have to drop a few lines to Mrs. Mallander and thank her for the package. Mrs. Lake sent shrimp, pickles, cookies, cake and I don't know what all. Everything arrived in perfect condition as she used tin boxes and lots of packing. I am going to write to her tonite.

Well Dad how is the Shipyard coming along? I'll bet it's cold as the devil. Guess what! I'm putting on the weight again. I wear size 38 pants now instead of 34. I guess this kind of life agrees with me. The reason I lost so much weight is because I was so scared I couldn't eat for 3 or 4 days at a time. Now it's the other way around. The more danger we are in the more I eat. It seems like the other boys are the same way too. John Naige my gunner is darn near as fat as when he came in. Another thing that helps is, we are getting fresh food now. We get meat every day and lots of fresh potatoes. We have plenty of fresh bread too.

Well the soup is about ready so I'll close soon and eat. I got two more letters to write yet, and by that time I will be ready to climb into my sack.

Well good nite until tomorrow and write whenever you get time.

Your Loving Son,

Bob

LETTERS FROM 1945

Jan 1 1945
Still doing ok.
I got a card from Roy today. It said 'Hi Bob' signed Roy
I guess that's the news from Texas and Germany.

Germany
Jan 8, 1945
Dear Mother, Dad,

Well it's about time I start to write a few more letters, so the first one is naturally going to you. I got a letter from you Dad yesterday and one from Mom today. It's the first mail in weeks.

There is nothing new going on over here, it's the same old stuff over and over. I just finished cleaning up the hole that I live in and it sure needed it. We carried out about one hundred lbs of cigarette butts alone.

We had a little more snow today, but it melts as soon as the sun hits it. It is pretty cold out now, but we have a good fire going in the stove so we don't mind it.

Supper wasn't so good tonite and there wasn't much of it, so we are cooking up a couple of chickens on the stove. They should be done in about an hour. The French fried potatoes are just turning brown. I wish I had some catsup to go on them but they will be pretty good without it. You should have seen the fun when we were trying to catch them chickens. We chased them all over town and could never corner them so I got disgusted and shot them with my (new) 45 pistol. I shot one in the back and the bullet did a good job of cleaning it. It didn't spoil it altogether though. The other one just got its head shot off. They were the last two chickens left in town so this is our last chicken dinner for a while.

I got a new pistol the other day. It's a lot easier to carry than a submachine gun. I found it out on the edge of town, near an old machine gun nest.

I don't blame the doctor for being disgusted with you Dad. You been on a diet for about 3 months and only lost 5 lbs. Oh well. Maybe some day they will stop making ice cream.

There isn't anything else to write that I can think of so I'll close for today. Please write when you have time as I am always looking forward to your letters. God bless you both

Your Loving Son

Bob

PS I got a Christmas card from Roy. At least I know he didn't break his arm.

Jan 10

Germany

Dear Mom, Dad,

The mail is coming in almost as good as ever now. I got 2 letters from you yesterday. You said the flowers came on your wedding anniversary as well as Christmas Eve. Well that is the way I wanted it. You see that is one occasion I can remember.

We had a small blizzard last nite. Four inches of snow in one hour and a half. It cleared up a few minutes later and the stars came out. Today we got another inch in about an hour. In a few weeks at that rate we will be snowed under.

I got a letter from Kitty today and I just finished answering it. She seems to be getting lonely up there by herself. She said you invited her down for Christmas and she though the change would do her good. Did she ever get down for Christmas or was the weather too bad? She said that you came up to see her one day and she was so glad to see you. She always tells me how glad she is to see you.   So go up and see her whenever you can.

I still haven't gotten any mail from Roy. Just a Christmas card with no writing. I get all the news about him from Kitty. I think I'll write to June and have her visit him. I'm sure he would like her. She can show him around down there. I wish I could get some of the warm weather he is getting down there. The wind goes right through you over here.

In your last letter you said you were going to use Vmail. If you use it so will I. I would rather not get any mail than to get one of those things. They take as long to get here as the others do anyway.

Is Roy still a private? He should be making some kind of a rating by now. What's this I hear about going on maneuvers?

Well I got to go to work for a while so until I write again good bye and good luck.

Your Loving Son,

Bob

Jan 14 1945

Germany

Dear Mom, Dad,

You are probably surprised to be getting so many letters in the past few weeks, but I figure maybe it won't be long until it will be impossible for me to write every day. So I am making up for it now.

I got two more letters of yours today. They were 7 weeks old, but I enjoyed reading every bit of them.

We discovered something new here yesterday. We can now make ice cream. It isn't Breyers, but it is some treat for us. We melt our D ration chocolate bars, add sugar, milk, and then mix with snow. If you make it right it tastes as good as Lampkins. We also make lemon, pineapple, orange. The best so far was the pineapple. I had a gallon of it today already and the boys are making up some more chocolate now. It only takes 5 or 10 minutes to make all you can eat. The weather is still very cold, in fact it hasn't gone above freezing since Christmas. The day before yesterday it was two below zero. It snows almost every day for an hour or so and then the sun comes out for a while.

You asked me if we are getting enough cigarettes. Yes we now get 5 packs a week. For a while we went weeks without any. That is except for German cigarettes that we take from Germans that don't need them any more. By the way did you get that last money order I sent for $70? I have another hundred here that I will send as soon as I find out whether or not the first one came.

Well they got me on guard from 3 to 5 in the morning. That is going to be a humdinger. I'll bet it is zero out now and it is still getting colder. It sure will be swell when a guy can go to sleep and not have to worry about guard. Most of the boys are in bed already so I better finish up this letter. I still have to wash and shave yet before I can go to bed. I am going to church tomorrow and the dentist Monday , and the barber Tues..

A Christmas card came today from Mrs. Zulik. Thank her for me and that will make us even. I got a letter there that I wrote to Pop Skelly a month ago and I can never think to mail it. I'll have to mail it tomorrow for sure.

I think I'll write to Roy just once more, and if he doesn't answer that, the heck with him. Maybe he just hates sergeants. I can't keep my eyes open any longer so I'll close now and get ready for bed. Your Loving Son, Bob

Jan 18, 45
Dear Mother, Dad,

It's now 4:30 o'clock in the morning, I just came off patrol. I went to bed early last nite so I am wide awake now and can't even hope to go to sleep before breakfast.

It sure is a dark nite, you can hardly see your hand in front of your face. I fell into a fox hole full of water before and I am not warm yet. We got a pretty warm day yesterday, it made a lot of the snow melt and made things nice and sloppy. It froze up again last nite though and there is a strong wind blowing now. The fire went out last nite and I just built a new one when I came off patrol duty. The stove is red hot now and the hole is starting to warm up. It will be nice and warm when the boys get up for breakfast. I got a pot of coffee on now, it should be ready in a few minutes.

The old mail is starting to come in now, I even got a letter from Roy (Nov 2). Also the one you wrote about taking cousin Kitty to the show in NY. I got another one of your letters Dad, (Dec 30). I am sorry about the mistake I made in one of my letters. I thought you lost 2 lbs, but I guess you gained 10 before you started on your diet.

Well by the time you get this letter Roy should be home on his furlough. He said in his letter that he almost went to the Tank Destroyers in Camp Hood. If he ever gets another chance to go, see that he goes will you Dad? It's the safest combat unit there is. I would give anything to be able to get into it myself. I am going to write and tell him but you know Roy, it will take both of us to talk him into it. I was the same way as he is but believe me I know what the score is now. I can see what Tom Albains was talking about now, and he didn't put it half bad enough.

Well the coffee is done so I'll open a can of cheese and go to work on it.

I'll write again soon.

Your Loving Son,

Bob

Jan 25

Germany

Dear Mother Dad,

The first bunch of letters in over a week came in today. No, I as usual didn't get any, but it at least looks promising anyway. The same old stuff is going on here. We haven't even had a good air raid here to liven up the joint.

Looks like the Russians really mean business this time doesn't it. Well more power to them.

Dad you asked me one day whether or not it is true about the Germans killing the prisoners they took during the big counter attack. Well I have no reason to believe one way or the other. I never seen it done nor do I know anyone who has. Of course it is possible in a push of that kind as it would be very hard for them to transport the prisoners back to the rear lines. In any case don't worry about it as here is one guy that doesn't figure on being captured.

Well it's getting colder out again. I wouldn't be surprised to see a good snow storm before morning. We have had snow on the ground ever since New Years.

I seen a funny thing the other day in a town near here. An artillery shell land-ed in a cow pasture and killed one of the few remaining cows. A few minutes lat-er three infantry boys were busy cutting up the remains. I went over a little later and all that was missing was the steaks. Talking about food, some of the boys dug some loose bricks out of a house near here and found five dozen eggs in salt brine. Also all the house hold articles that the people could not take with them. We find all sorts of canned foods buried around the houses. In the house I am in we found twelve tires, a case of soap, ten lbs of sugar, and about ten sets of dish-es. Almost every house is the same, all you have to do is look for it. We even used a mine detector but were fooled by nails and other metal objects so much that we gave up the idea. I found 6 bottles of wine hanging by a wire down the well.

In the houses you can find Singer sewing machines made in Elizabeth NJ. Once we found an electric ice box made in Ohio. Their cars have Ford engines in them built to burn cheap fuel, and get about 30 miles to the gallon. The engine is just a little larger than a motorcycle engine.

The Tiger tanks you hear about have 12 cylinder Ford V engines. The oil they use on their machinery is mostly Wolf's Head Pennsylvania motor oil (the best we got).

The houses are all brick. The cement they use is so bad you can practically tear a wall down with your bare hands once you get it started. The roof is gener-ally made of clay shingles, the same as in France. The furniture is built very well, and is on the same style as in the U.S. The drawers even stick like ours. Each house either has a bomb shelter built under the house or the ceiling in the cellar is about two to three ft thick. Their roads are very good. They are as slippery as glass when wet though.

The wild game over here is really something. The deer though small, are plentiful. The rabbits are three times as large as ours and the jack rabbits are enormous. Pheasants are also very numerous, and are exactly the same as the ones in the States. They also have quail, grouse, wild pigeons, red squirrels, and we even seen a very large flock of geese. Fishing is even good in the streams that I have seen. I know they have trout but whether they have bass or not I do not know. Well that should give you a fairly good picture of the place and as soon as we get rolling again I'll tell you about the rest of Germany.

Mom you don't have to worry about me carrying my gas mask. I have it with me where ever I go. That is one thing that I am really afraid of and besides I learned my lesson way back in Normandy. One nite just after D Day there was a very sweet smell in the air and the gas alarm was given. Well that was a heck of a time to start hunting for a gas mask but that is just what I had to do. When I did find it, I almost had to shoot my asst driver as he couldn't find his and thought I had it. Well those were the days when we thought we knew it all. Believe me things are different now.

Well it's getting late and I have to get up early so I'll close now and hit the old sack. I'm in good shape as usual and hope you two are the same. Please

don't worry about me as everything will be alright I'm sure.
Your Loving Son,
Bob

Jan 26
Germany
Dear Mom, Dad,

I just came off patrol duty and am half frozen, so while the water is getting hot for coffee I'll write a few lines to let you know I'm doing OK.

The moon is out and you can see for a long way now, but when I went out it was snowing and so dark you had to feel your way around. Yesterday we had to finish up a little work on the tanks in the morning but had the afternoon off. I went to church at 1 o'clock and then went rabbit hunting in the afternoon. We had lots of fun but the rabbits made a fool of us. We were tracking them down in the snow and when we thought we were near him he would pop up way across the field. After hours of that sort of stuff we discovered it was two rabbits instead of one. Well anyway we ended up with wet feet, no rabbit, and dead tired from tramping through the snow. The day before yesterday we spotted an eight point buck. He was too fast for us and got away before we could get a shot at him.

Well last nite I had a Coca Cola for the first time in a year. They have a Coca Cola plant in Belgium some place and we got our first ration last nite. It was ice cold and exactly the same as you have at home. I sure did enjoy it.

The mail has stopped almost completely again. I imagine it is caused by bad flying weather across the Atlantic. It is bad this time of year. At least it was last year at this time.

Well my shoes are rolling fast now, I have three pair. So are all the other odd sizes. Even the large size overshoes that used to be impossible to get are coming in. I guess that visit by General Ike did some good after all.

I received the package you sent with the candy in it a few days ago. We all enjoyed it very much. I am looking forward to the one with the fruit cake. I been wanting a piece of cake for a long time. The boys haven't' been getting many packages, the most of them were lost in the counter attack around Christmas. It's a good thing mine were all mailed early. I got all my packages before the attack started. So far as I know I didn't lose one. Well I can't think of anything more to write so I'll drink the rest of the coffee and get an hour's sleep before breakfast. I hope you are all in as healthy a condition as I am. And that's tops.
Your Loving Son, Bob

Jan 27
Germany
Dear Mother, Dad,

Today was a great day as far as the mail was concerned. I got your letters of Dec 12, 13, 14, 15, 16. It's about time it came in, I was beginning to give up hope of ever getting mail. With the letters came 3 packages from you. One had the socks, another had shrimp, figs, chocolate. The last had cookies. We are making a feast of them tonite. You will never know how much I appreciate the socks. I really need them now. I always like to get packages but would much rather get letters regularly.

In your letter you gave me some very bad news. I have been expecting it for some time, but always had hopes of this war ending first. As you already know Camp Meade is Roy's next to last stop in the US. He is probably gone from there by now. When this letter reaches you he may be on his way over here. If he gets assigned to the same outfit here in Germany I'll go see him if possible. If he only did what I told him, he never would have to come over here.

Yes I remember seeing Warren Erickson back in Holland. I seen him twice since then. He is in the ordinance that takes care of our tanks. He has a swell job back there. Plenty safe too. He doesn't have to do anything but rewire tanks and fix the radios. He gave me a swell pair of earphones the last time I seen him.

We had a swell time today riding a German track motorcycle. It has a Ford engine in it and goes about 45 miles per hour cross country. We rebuilt the engine in our spare time. After we use it a couple of days we are going to use the motor to drive a generator so we can have regular house lights.

I am going to write the addresses of a couple of buddies of mine down so you can keep them for me until after the war. Put them where I can find them when I get back.

Mr. W.R. Burns
719 9th Ave
Brackenridge Penna

Frank Quinn
50 Rochester St
Port Byron NY
Sup. Of Tracks Lions NY

Well there is nothing new yet so I'll close until the next time.
Your loving Son,
 Bob

Jan 28
Dear Mom, Dad,
Well here I am writing a letter again tonite and there isn't a darn thing more to write about tonite than there was last nite this time. It's really hard to keep writing when you are not allowed to write what you are thinking. They tell us we must not break down the morale on the home front. We must not tell you how much we hate the English or why. In fact there is nothing much we can say except that we are in good health and still kicking. So if just hearing that I am still

alive makes you feel so much better, as you say it does, I'll keep writing the same old stuff even if it does get tiresome. I got five Christmas cards today. I heard I had five letters and when I saw they were only cards I felt worse than if I had received no mail at all. I suppose the proper thing to do is thank them but I'm afraid if I do they might send me more of the blasted things next year. You really ought to see some of them. One from Ed Reinhart, way down in the S Pacific and all it had on it was two letters. "Ed" The same came from Roy only his had three letters.

I found a cartoon laying on the floor here that makes me laugh every time I look at it. It shows exactly how I feel about this war. Nothing but a pain in the neck. It sure is exciting at first but after you see it all, it's just another rotten job.

We sure are having our troubles with the fire in the stove tonite. The wind comes down the chimney instead of going up. As a result I feel like a smoked ham. It ran us out of the hole twice tonite already.

I dug up a picture of some of the guys that have been with the outfit ever since the beach. They are still with us, all except the guy in front. He got disconnected with this world back in Normandy.

Say hello to everyone back there for me, will you? You know, anybody that might happen to be interested. Well I did manage to fill up four pages at that. I got to get up early so I had better turn in as it's after midnite now.

Your Loving Son,

Bob

Jan 29

Germany

Dear Mom, Dad,

I didn't get time to mail my last letter yet so I will enclose this one in with it.

I just came off guard and it is snowing like the dickens out now. About four hours ago when I first went on guard the moon was out (full moon) and it was light as day. It only takes a few minutes to change from cold to hot, or clear to stormy. It snows at least for a half hour every nite without fail.

I spent about two hours earlier tonite cleaning my guns. I have two pistols and an M3 submachine gun. They keep me busy keeping the rust off them. I am going to sell my German pistol the next time I go on pass or go back to ordnance. I should get around one hundred bucks for it. The gun isn't worth 25 dollars but those 4F's back there will pay anything for a souvenir. It is cheap at that, at least they don't have to fight to get them like we do.

Well there isn't very much work to do tomorrow. I have to pile sand bags on front of my tank in the morning (anti-Bazooka). In the afternoon I will go to church and then take it easy for the rest of the day.

We ate the shrimp last nite and it sure was a treat. Frank and Bill enjoyed it as much as I did. The rest of the stuff was equally delicious.

I have Roy's picture up on the wall along with some of the other pictures you sent me. I have a swell collection now. John Kieffer sent me a picture of himself and Alice. I really do enjoy looking at them all. I still have the pictures you sent me way back at St. Lo. Some of them have been wet and dried a dozen or more times but are all good yet. Ever since I lost that first bunch, I keep them in my bible in my shirt pocket where they can't get lost. Keep sending pictures when ever you get a good one. Every time I meet people they want to see all the pictures. Even the boys pass around all the pictures at least once a week. We all know what each others' families look like and their whole life history.

I got a letter from cousin Kitty today (Vmail). Ah well: she means well anyway. She really has nothing to write about. She seems to enjoy getting letters from me so I keep knocking out one or two a week. She was disappointed because her package arrived a month early. I got it Thanksgiving day and was darn glad to get it as that was the worst day I think I ever spent in my life. I'll tell you about it after the war.

Well Capt Bulvin should be home about now. He left about the 10th of Jan on an emergency furlough. I am still driving the same tank but for Captain Stewart.

Mom I wish you would stop expecting me home on furlough. The only time I will be home is after the war is over and not one minute before. In the first place I am not an actor nor am I a General's son. And I don't want an emergency furlough. So let's forget it, huh?

I have been thinking about Roy again and the more I think about it the better it looks. With the Russians pushing like they are and our army's all on the move it might be over before Roy gets in action. And by coming over there he might be saved from going to the Pacific. Well all we can do is pray for him and let God handle it as he sees fit.

Well it's getting late and my eyes are playing tricks on me so I had better cut the gab and hit the hay.
God bless you both.
Your Loving Son,
Bob

Jan 30
Germany
Dear Mom, Dad,

Well I just finished reading the Stars and Stripes and the news still looks pretty good. Of course it's just another newspaper and you read the news they want you to read and nothing more.

Little Abner is still in a jam as usual. At least things look a little better for him this week than last week. There was no mail today for anyone as usual. I sure hope my letters reach you faster than yours reach me.

Pat seems to be in the same fix I am in. He has been sitting here for the past hour trying to think of something to write to his wife.

What are you doing with all your spare time Dad? I hear you have Sundays off. Gee every Sunday plus three or four days you take off anyway should give you plenty of time to take in all the good shows, and steakhouses in Jersey and NY.

You said you were going to buy a new car after the war. What kind are you going to get? I'm thinking of getting a new Chevrolet myself. But not until about 3 years after the first new cars come out. The first ones are going to cost a small fortune. Roy will by that time, have enough for a new Packard if he keeps his lawyer on the ball. I wonder who is going to be his next victim.

I'm glad to hear you are such good friends with the Lakes. They really are swell people. We will all have to go and see them after the war.

I got a letter from Roy the other day. It was an old one sent from Texas. He told me all about his first nite sleeping out on the ground. Boy has he got some surprise coming when he sees how long he has to sleep over here, that is if he gets time to sleep. He said he had three or four blankets, two comforters and a pup tent padded with leaves, plus a fire. Why he couldn't have been more comfort-able if he spent the nite at the Hotel Astor. Well anyway he is a strong kid and this life won't hurt him physically but he will be a different Roy when he gets back.

He also said he stayed at the USO in Ft Worth. I got stuck one nite and had to stay there too.

Well I don't have to go on guard tonite but I do need a little sleep so I'll sign off for now and drop you a few more lines tomorrow nite around this time.

Your loving Son,

Bob

Feb 1 1944

Dear Mom, Dad,

I am writing you a vmail just in case the other mail isn't getting through. Everything is still the same, except that it's raining now instead of snowing.

Your old mail is starting to drift in once in a while now. Also a few old letters from Roy when he was still in Texas. I wrote to Helen tonite also a few other people I have been putting off for a long time. I haven't heard from Joe since be-fore he left England so

don't ask me how he is making out as I don't know. Well I'll write a regular letter tomorrow.

Your loving Son,

Bob

Feb 6

Germany   mailed Feb 10

Dear Mother, Dad,

Gee Mom your letters are really coming in now. I got six of them today and one was from Jan 23. Gosh I feel a lot better now that I know how you all are. We were all feeling kind of punk lately. No mail, bad weather, and everything seems to go wrong at once. I don't know if the letters did me any good or not. I feel kind of homesick now. I have been looking at your pictures for the past hour or so. They are getting kind of worn out from looking at them. Some of the ones you sent me way back at St. Lo have been wet for weeks at a time. You see I carry them in my shirt pocket all the time. Lots of times when the going gets kind of rough I pull them out and it almost makes me feel as though I am back there with you.

Maybe Roy will be lucky enough to stay in a replacement center for a month or so. By that time I think we will have the Germans on the run again and then it will be a little easier on him. If I can get to see him over here there may be a way for me to make it a little easy for him.

You were saying something about a board of some kind that told you I would be home by March 9th. I hope you are wrong about that, as the only way for me to get home that quick would be to get shot up pretty bad. Somehow I always get scared when someone shoots at me and do something about it. Mostly run like <u>hell</u>. Of course it is possible for me to get home by March 1946. It's a slim chance but I do have hopes of it.

You said something about marrying some girl in Texas too. That is a crazy idea all the way. I would never dream of marrying a rebel.

Boy am I putting on the weight this winter. I'll bet I gained 25 lbs in the past three months. You asked if I would like spaghetti in a package. The boys all get it from home. Every time someone gets some we put it in a big box until we have enough for a big dinner then we cook it up and have a grand time about midnite. This happens at least once a week. We got some real wops here to cook it too. You are so good to me sending so many packages that I hate to ask for anything. You always send swell packages, too. They are the best ones in the company. We have a package almost every day in our hole. It helps us to forget our troubles and we love the stuff. I have had more candy and cake over here than I ever ate at home.

I don't need any more razor blades as I have thousands of them now. Those Jerries sure do carry a bunch of blades with them. I got seven or eight razors and about three of the best brushes I ever seen. I use two blades with every shave. Boy that's living high isn't it Dad? When the razor gets dirty I throw it away and use another. They are good ones too. Boy you're going to have a heck of a time with me when I get back.

Well it's getting late so I'll close for tonite. Oh, I got the package with the chocolate in it. I almost forgot to tell you. I thought I told you in the last letter but remember now it only came in yesterday.
Your loving Son, Bob

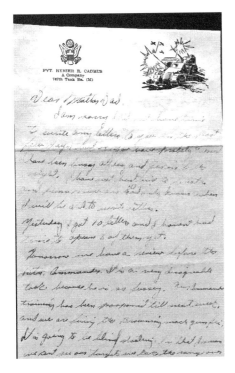

Dear Mom, Dad,

There is still a few minutes left before I have to go out on patrol, so I will just say hello and good bye tonite, and write a real letter tomorrow nite. I got an old letter from you yesterday. I sure hope the new ones will start coming in soon. I went to the dentist yesterday and had 1 tooth pulled. That finishes me up with him for a while. The dentist is the same one we had back at Camp Bowie and he told me to look him up as soon as we get relieved and he will make me a tooth for the one I lost in England.

Don't get any funny ideas about me coming home on furlough. That is only for men with plenty of pull, so that lets me out. I'm feeling fine and still putting on weight so don't worry about me.

Your Son
Bob

Feb 13
Dear Mom, Dad,

There is nothing going on here yet, as you can see by the papers. The weather is rotten, nothing but rain and more rain. The temperature is high and that naturally means gangs of mud.

I'm feeling fine though, can't even get a head cold or nothing. Boy I got the scare of my life just now so don't mind if I write a little shaky. There was a big explosion and it blew the windows out and glass showered down all over me. I thought it was a large bomb but found out the engineers just blew up the house next door. They needed bricks to build a road and they sure got them in a hurry as that's all that's left of the house, just a pile of bricks. I'm still a little shaky but didn't even get a scratch. The plaster on the ceiling also fell down but didn't hurt.

If I am still around here tomorrow I will write a long letter, if not I'll drop another vmail.

Your loving Son, Bob

Germany
Feb 14
Dear Mother, Dad,

I'm back in the same house that I was in last week this time. I got in about noon today. There was a package from you and three letters dated Feb 4 – 5. The package had the spaghetti, it didn't take long to get here did it? I started to cook it up about two o'clock and we ate it tonite about eight. I found lots of onions and fried them with some meat I got for dinner. After they got good and brown I put in the tomato sauce, plus two quarts of tomato juice, and a bowl of tomatoes that we had for supper. I let it cook for hours on the kitchen range. It got good and thick, in fact you could eat it with a fork. Then I cooked up the spaghetti and we ate until it came out of our ears. There was plenty for the six of us.

I took a good hot bath again today, and did I leave some swell rings around the tub. We have to carry the water upstairs (2nd floor) as there is not enough pressure to make it reach the second floor. Mack dumped about a gallon of ice water on me, and I almost froze but I put up a good fight. Just wait until he takes a bath.

A buzz bomb flew over a few minutes ago, and were we glad he flew over. I was sure worrying about it coming down and busting the windows out of our house. The only house in Germany with windows in it. We have an electric washing machine running in the kitchen now. I have all my clothes in it and am sitting here writing in my long handle drawers. I will hang them next to the radiator before I go to bed and they will be dry by morning.

As soon as I get Roy's address I will write to him but there is no use of me using his old one as it would take months to catch up to him.

Well guess what! The sun came out today for four solid hours and it was so warm you didn't need a coat or nothing. The wind is getting strong now though and the temperature is beginning to drop. I suppose it will snow tomorrow to make up for today.

You asked about the money I got for my gun. Well I sent $70 to you in a money order in a letter about the first of December and you have not received it yet or you forgot to tell me if you did. I have another hundred in my pocket but will not send it until I hear that you received the other.

I haven't heard from you in some time now Dad. You were doing good for a while and then you stopped again.

I haven't written to Kitty in quite a long time so I think after I finish this letter I'll drop her a few lines.

I guess Ray Daly is proud of himself with that job he has. I didn't think he would ever stoop so low as to take that job. In case you don't know it, that is the lowest thing a soldier could do. I don't know how he will ever be able to look some of these men over here in the face when they get back home. If Roy ever did that I would never talk to him for the rest of my life. Maybe he intends to move to some other state after the war, where no one knows him.

Well it's getting pretty late and I still want to write to Kitty tonite so I'll sign off for now.

Your Loving Son
Bob

PS. I got the pictures and they were swell. You both look fine. The old house sure looks good too. I almost forgot what it looks like.
Remember last year this time? I was on the boat and you were having a snow storm.

Feb 18, 1945
Germany
Dear Mom, Dad,

I'm sorry I did so much complaining about not getting any mail. Today thirteen letters came. Your letters were of Jan 22 – Feb 5. Guess what: Roy is in Paris or near there anyway. I got a letter from him today, dated Feb 8. His censor cut out a lot of stuff but I could tell exactly what he wanted to say. He had a long train ride in France and didn't like it. I wonder if he realizes his future buddies had to walk across France. Oh well he will learn. I am not going to write to him until I receive his new address as if I write now he will be months getting the letter. Don't worry about him Mom, he will get along alright. If I possibly can, I will go and see him as soon as I learn his org. He is just like me (I mean as I was); he just can't wait to start shooting. He will as I did, learn there are guys shooting back too.

I got your letter Dad. That's swell bowling Roy did, but are you sure you didn't help him along? I hear you are going to buy a new suit when you hit 225. I know where you can find a big barrel to hold you over. Say, those pictures of you are swell. You look fine too Mom. In fact I never seen you two look better.

Just in case you forgot that was Elizabeth Station and not Cranford Dad. You see I remember it better than you. Some day in a few years I'll call you on the phone about three o'clock in the morning and ask you to come and pick me up at Elizabeth again.

Mom you asked me what kind of a dump I am living in now. Well I just got back today to the house I told you about with the lights and running water. Kitty's letter came today too. I answered it just before I started on this one.

I started reading a mystery book last nite with a flashlight and couldn't gain much headway so tonite, now that I have lights I am going to finish it or bust. You would like it Mom the name is 'Red Harvest'. I don't like those kinds of books but there was nothing else so I had to read it. Now I'm interested and can't stop. Dad I got a book you would like. I laughed until I was sick when I read it. The name of it was Skin and Bones by Thorn Smith.

I haven't seen a movie in a couple of months. I had a chance but was too lazy to walk to the joint. You can't enjoy a picture over here as there is always light in the room and something is always going wrong with the projector. The boys are going to bed so I will be able to read in peace. I don't go on guard until 7:15 in the morning.

I heard from Joe. He is in Penn. and doing fine.

Your Loving Son, Bob

Feb 20
Germany
Dear Mom, Dad,

I just came back from a movie, in a town near here. It was a real theater and the projector was in good shape. We didn't know what the name of the picture was until it was flashed on the screen, and what do you think of this. The picture was named 'The Bridge of San Luis Ray' and I just finished reading the book of the same name about two hours before. I didn't even know there was such a picture until tonite. I thought it was a wonderful picture. Maybe because of reading the book, or maybe it's because it has been so long since I have been to a show. I don't know, but if you get a chance to see the picture write and let me know how you like it.

I received an air mail letter today dated Feb 8th, from the Lakes. It made better time than yours. The latest one from you (yesterday was of the 6th of Feb. I haven't heard any more from Roy yet, but will let you know as soon as I do. His letters will take 6 or 7 days to reach me even if he gets stationed in the next house from me. I hope he don't though, not because I don't want to see him, but I don't want him in this army.

Yesterday I read two books, 'The Invisible Man' (rotten) and "Mutiny on the Brig'. I guess you are wondering why I am reading so much lately. Well I guess that you heard that the hardest part of war is waiting, and that is true to the letter. Reading helps, and helps a lot.

I can't get over how much better you look in that picture you had taken Christmas. I put it next to one of your other pictures and you look swell. I can see you lost weight especially in the face Dad.

We had a beautiful day today believe it or not. It was warm and just like summer. Tonite the stars are out and all is quiet along the front.

Well good nite and God Bless you.
Your Loving Son,
Bob

Germany
March, 3, 1945
Dear Mom, Dad,

You haven't heard from me in quite some time now as I have been kept pretty busy as you can see by the papers. We have a few days break now and are spending it in style. I'm in a swell house with all the comforts of home. We even have electric lights. I just found out how to make this darn thing write in black so I will use it.

I haven't heard from Roy since he was near Paris and am still waiting for his new address. Your mail is getting here in about 9 days. (air mail). The v— mail takes

232

about twelve days. I am in perfect health as usual. Not even a head cold. Things were pritty rough for a wile but everything is under control now.

I got a letter from Gr Pa. yesterday and one from Kitty the day before. They are all Ok. from the sound of there letter.

Your letters and pictures are a great help in keeping up my moral when we are up the front, so please keep up the good work. All I have to worry about now is weather or not I am going to get mail every day. I found to real good cigarette lighters to day so that solves the match situation. We had a heck of a time getting matches for a wile.

We are having real spring weather, rain one day and clear the next. It has been extremely warm except for today's Snow, rain, hail, and the most beatutyfull sun-shine you ever seen. The sunshine does us good for a change. That rotton weather gets you down in the dumps when you get to mutch of it.

The lights went out a few minutes ago, so we lit up a few candles and I played the harmonica for the boys until they came on again. They wanted me to keep on playing but I made up my mind I was going to finish this letter to you. I found the harmonica a few days ago and they have me play it day and night. I can thank you for teaching me how to play it, remember how you use to buy me one every year in hopes that I would someday take an interest and learn how to play. Every once and a wile I come across a guitar and play it until it gets shot full of holes. You see I have to carry it on the back of my tank and that usually finishes it up toot-sweet. Looks like those lessons weren't wasted all together huh?

When you write to my friends tell them I am busy and will write as soon as possible. I actually am not as busy as all the but I don't feel much like writing just yet. I will write to you as often as possible and only you.

Well what do you think of our last attack Dad? I guess you thought we were laying down on the job for a wile didn't you?

Well that is about all the news fit to print from over this side the world so I'll sign off and wait to here from you all. (Get that you all stuff)

Your loving son

Bob

March 5, 1945

Dear Mom Dad,

I received three letters from you to day but they are all v mail and plenty old. I sent a letter to you yesterday by regular air mail so it should not be to long be-tween letters for you. The black tape is all worn out so I will use red. Their is nothing new here except the weather has changed to rain and cold. I new we would have to pay for the few clear days we did have. Kitty's letter came today also. She said you were up to see her the other day and she was very happy to see you. She says she has to use a cane when she goes down town. I guess she is start-ing to feel her age. I just helped carry about half ton of coal up three flights of stairs to our room and now I can hardly stand up. I'm not use to work any more I guess.

We got a radio working today and all we could hear was German propaganda. They are trying to get us to feel sorry for them. I wonder if they think we could ever forget what we seen them do in France. You ought to hear them cry the blues now. I really enjoy hearing them cry, it shows we are making them wish they never heard of Hitler.

Did you ever tell Mr. Siefile *(illegible)* I received and enjoyed the candy he sent me? You asked me if I ever received the socks you sent me. I told you I did in one of the other letters but I guess you never received the letter. I am wearing them now.

No news from Roy yet. I guess he is to busy to bother writing to me. Of course you have to realize he will not have the opportunity to write as often as I do. You see I take my home with me and he has to build his at every stop.

I found a pretty good gold watch this afternoon. It keeps good time so I will keep it for a wile. At least until I can get a good traid.

Well I guess you are getting tired of listening to my chatter so I'll sign off for tonite.

Your loving son Bob

March 6, 1945
Dear Mom, Dad,

I am still in the same place as you can see by the typewriter. There is nothing new. I am just writing a few lines to let you know everything is alright.

It was cold and rainy all day but it has started to get a little warmer tonite.

We had a swell supper tonite. Chicken, corn, mashed potatoes, fruit salads, butter bread and jam and lots of coffey to wash it down. I had three helpings of chicken and was still growing strong when they closed the kitchen.

Their is a line waiting for the typewriter so I am going to end this letter and give them a break.

I'll write tomorrow so don't worry about a thing.
Your loving son Bob

Holland
March 8
Dear Mom, Dad,

You are no doubt surprised to see that I am in Holland again. You are no more surprised than I was when they brought us here. I am not here for a rest this time either. I can't say what I am doing until after it comes out in the papers. You can never guess what I am doing so don't bother to try.

I am going to enclose a money order for $45. I hope this one doesn't get lost like the last one that I sent back in Dec. I guess it got lost you never said anything about it in your letters. It was for about $70. By the way I lost the receipt.

We are living in a farm house with a family of 14. We have a spare room to ourselves. At least it was spare. Now you can usually find about eleven pair of tiny wooden shoes outside the door. The kids aged 1 to 16 are always in here bumming candy or gum from us. They keep the place clean for us and take care of the fire so it is worthwhile having them around. Some of them never seen candy before so we get a kick out of giving it to them.

They are Catholic and say their prayers every nite from 7 to 10. They all pray together in Latin (Mother, Father included). For two hours it sounds like a fleet of bombers going over.

I haven't heard from Roy since Feb 8 and still haven't got his permanent address.

It got clear and warm this afternoon for the first time in a week. The Air Corps are having a holiday. Thank God for that.

The people back here don't have blackouts any more. Even the army trucks are allowed to use headlights again. This is the first time in over a year I have seen headlights. I don't like them either. They all but blind you.

I was over to see Mrs. Hagadorn last nite and they are all doing fine. She cooked up some ham and eggs for midnite supper. Pop had a swell apple pie in the oven an hour after I arrived. They were very glad to see me. They thought I had been killed or wounded because I hadn't visited them for so long. Her brother and his family lost their home a week ago by a buzz bomb and are now living with them. Two nice daughters too. 18 and 19 years old.

Ah well the kids just came in and this place is now just short of a mad house. Betsy the next to the oldest and Joie the next to the youngest just got a fruit bar from some of the boys and the whole mob came in trying to get a bite. I know about seven of them by name and the ones that I forget are highly insulted.

Some dirty bums blew up the bridge and power house so we have no electric lights. I have one candle so I will write until it goes out.

Greta pronounced Grada in Dutch just wanted to say hello. I told her you would understand. Maybe you can (I don't know). If you can't Helen can. She is 16 and will be 17 on the thirteenth. She is very pretty, I think if I meet Roy over here I will give him the address.

I am Sgt of the guard tonite and it is about time I made a check to see if they are all awake. I'll write soon, don't worry, and be good to yourselves.
Your Loving Son   Bob

Dear Madam,
   Your son has a room with us. He is a real good boy. We all like him and are good friends. He told me that you could understand Dutch and that I should write you something and that is what I have done.
   Receive from all of us Best Greeting
Family Schmeits

Beste Mevrouw, uw zoon is bij ons ingekwartierd. Het is en echte goeie jongen. Wij zijn allen goed met hem bevriend. Hij zei dat uw Hollands verstaat, en ik moest uw uw schrijven. En dat heb ik maar gedaan. Ontvangt van allemaal vele groeten,

Familie Schmeits
Ohe 88
Ohe in Laak
Limburg
Holland

March 9

Dear Mom, Dad,

This is Sunday but not exactly what you would call a day of rest. We got up at seven o'clock, had pancakes and bacon and then put in a long day of training. Seems like a funny time to be training doesn't it? Well you will understand some day when I am allowed to tell you what this is all about.

I didn't have time nor chance to go to church today. They never tell you when or where church is to be held until a few minutes before it starts. Then you have to hunt for it and by the time you find it, it is all over.

All the civilians were dressed up in their best clothes and were off to church bright and early this morning. Some even had leather shoes on, the rest had brightly painted wooden shoes.

Tonite after supper we loaded onto trucks and went to the movie. A murder picture was playing as usual. That makes you feel a lot better seeing a good murder picture after coming back from the front where you see all the <u>beautiful</u> things in life. Maybe some day they will wise up and send us something we can laugh at.

Tonite we were invited to supper with the family in the other room. They have supper at eight o'clock by the way. We didn't eat but sat and kept them company. They have black bread for supper. That's all, just black hard bread. I'll never understand how they stay so fat and healthy. They pray before they eat too. Maybe if some of the people in the States would sit down and eat with them a few times they wouldn't mind doing without butter and meat once in a while.

We got our home made power plant hooked up tonite and the houses are all lighted up like Coney Island. Tomorrow Ed ((*Gunkle*)) will hook up the voltage regulator and we will be able to hook up a radio. The news that comes in here now is nothing more than rumors. We hear all kinds of them, everything from the day the war will end to who will get the next pass to Paris.

Our mail plus the Stars and Stripes our only newspaper is lost en route I guess. The grease you see on this paper is from the bacon we are frying on the other end of the table.

Well that's the news for now I guess so I'll sign off and climb into my sleeping bag. Those sleeping bags by the way are really something. They don't keep you warm, but you get so hot and sweaty getting in, it takes you all nite to cool off. Your Loving Son,
Bob

Germany
March 18
Dear Mother, Dad,

Well we moved again and for a change it was for the better. We have a farm house all to ourselves. Plenty of fresh milk and eggs. I have been eating eggs since early this morning. I ate four goose eggs which are about five times as large as chicken eggs, plus about ten or eleven chicken eggs. I also had about four chickens fried in butter throughout the day. It sounds nice but it sure is work taking care of a barn full of cows, chickens and horses. If we stay here more than a week I'll be up to about 280 again. There are no electric lights here yet. I think they are going to bring up the generator tomorrow. Now we use lamps and are they causing trouble. We ran out of fuel and started using gasoline. About an hour ago the one in this room exploded and the whole room was on fire. We got it put out in a few minutes but it was some battle. I got a small hole burnt in my sleeping bag but not enough to hurt it.

I was out riding a bike today for the first since we were in Texas. I can't take it any more, my legs are so stiff and sore I can hardly walk.

I received your package of shrimp and nuts last week. They were very much appreciated as always. I just mailed you another money order the other day before we moved. I had two so I put one in your letter and one in a letter to Helen. I didn't want to put two in one letter. She will give it to you when you go to Bayonne next.

There was just a slight pause for a quick trip to the cellar in my bare feet. A German plane just tried to fly down our chimney. So if the writing looks a little shaky you will know the reason why. That is the second time today. This morning somebody yelled "Down the cellar" and I was sound asleep but managed to get down there first. I ran so fast I lost the seat of my long johns on the way.

I heard from Roy yesterday. His mail takes about 5 days longer to reach me than yours does. It was dated Feb 28.

I'll write again tomorrow Mom so don't worry. That plane made me forget all I was going to write.

Your Loving Son,

Bob

Germany

March 19

Dear Mom, Dad,

This letter was going to be a very short one but after looking over the size of the paper it looks like I am going to have to stretch out the story to fill in the space.

The situation hasn't changed since my last letter but we are getting tired of fried chicken and fried ham. I guess we should be by now, after 12 of us polishing off six smoked hams and dozens of chickens and by-products. Today we had a little extra to go with it after me finding two hundred lbs of fresh butter, tons of potatoes, and hundreds of jars of pears, cherries, plums, and jam.

I had to change my pants today, the old ones won't fit any more. It's a good thing you aren't here Dad, your 13 lbs would be all shot to hell in no time. There is a German police dog here that is even bigger then Wolf. He eats more and sleeps more than Wolf did but otherwise they are a pair. He opens and shuts the doors as well as we can and isn't bashful about it either. Last nite I fed him some raw ham before we went to bed and he went in and out of our room about 25 times after water during the nite. He sleeps with Nostrury and I. The poor dog is shell shocked even more than we are (if possible). Last nite we had a hot time for a while and had to run for the cellar and darned if he didn't beat us all down there.

One of the milk cows got in the house tonite and before we could get him out he knocked over both our lamps, upset the kitchen table, and got red paint all over my new shirt. You are no doubt wondering how he got red paint on me. Well it's like this, there are gangs of cows around and we only milk four of them. We paint a red stripe around their bellies and horns so we can tell them apart.

There are all sorts of headaches to this farming. The rabbits get in the fields, the little pigs steal the spuds and our Billy Goat insists on coming in and looking around once in a while. Why the chickens even hide their eggs on us.

Today was a swell summer day and lazy as I am I had to go out and enjoy it. I got four flat tires on my bike and finally busted it all together, when a shell came over and I dove off the bike into a hole. I must of kicked my foot through the wheel. Busted open a cut on my hand that was just healing up from the air raid the other nite. Went through a door without opening it and got a swell slice on the mitt from it.

Got a letter from Joe the other nite and he jumped all over me for not writing to you and him often enough. Well I'll try to do better but it is hard to get mail answered when you move around so much. Sometimes I carry a letter in my pocket for a week before I get chance to mail it. He must be doing OK up there with all those pretty nurses. At least he never complains of being lonesome.

It's past ten o'clock and I am finding it very hard to keep my eyes open so I'll finish this letter up in the morning.

March 21
Dear Mom Dad,

Last nite I wrote you a long letter so I'll just drop you a few lines tonite to let you know I'm alright.

Something is holding up the incoming mail again. It happens every time we get switched around.

I just heard the news over the radio and Roy's Army is going great. No opposition and all kinds of prisoners giving up. Everything is quiet here today. That is all except for our bombers taking advantage of a beautiful day.

Your Loving Son,
Bob

March 26
Germany
Dear Mom, Dad,

Well the job for which we were trained has been completed. No one made any complaints so I guess it was done to everyone's satisfaction. You no doubt read all about it but had no idea I was in on it. After a week or two I think we will be able to tell you all about it.

Last nite a couple of the boys and myself set up the 50 caliber anti-aircraft gun and got plenty of chances to use it. I (as usual) pulled a fast one and shot down one of our barrage balloons in flames. I'll never live it down if I live to be a hundred. The plane flew right in front of it and before I knew it there was a hell of a big fire and it wasn't the plane. Wait til Joe hears about it. I can just imagine what he will say.

((A **barrage balloon** is a large balloon tethered with metal cables, used to defend against low-level attack by aircraft by damaging the aircraft on collision with the cables, or at least making the attacker's approach more difficult. Some versions carried small explosive charges that would be pulled up against the aircraft to ensure its de-

struction. Barrage balloons were only regularly employed against low-flying aircraft, the weight of a longer cable making them impractical for higher altitudes.))

The news that just came over the radio is wonderful if true. Judging by the prisoners coming down the road I wouldn't doubt it either. It said the German 14th Army surrendered. You can never tell whether it's the Germans or the Americans on the radio so you have to be careful what you believe. At any rate I really hope to be home or on the way at least in a very few years now.

Well for about the fifteenth day in a row the sun is shining and there isn't a cloud in the sky. I never seen any more beautiful weather even in the States. The air corps is in their glory. I have seen more planes in the past two weeks than I have in all my life put together, including the 3000 plane St. Lo raid. The day before yesterday I seen 500 heavy bombers all at once. The sky was almost black with them. I hear Roy's Army is going like mad. If they keep going it just can't last long now. Everything is going in our favor.

Well tomorrow I will have spent my third birthday in the army and my second overseas. I feel just as young as I did when I left home. Maybe just a little bit wiser in a way but still the same old Bob.

Thanks for buying Grand Ma the flowers for me and Roy. I can never remember dates and even when I do it is almost impossible to send presents. Helen said she really enjoyed receiving them.

Well Easter will be coming around soon. It has kind of got me worried. The first Easter Sunday I spent in the army was doing guard duty in the blazing Texas sun. The second was shoveling dirt off the roads in OakHampton, England after our tanks got them all dirty. Maybe this Easter it will be different (I hope).

We haven't been able to go to church in the past few weeks as the outfit has been moving too fast for any chaplain to keep track of us. I was in three different countries in one day, a week or so ago.

Well I think I'll go out and get some of that sunshine. I don't think it will last much longer. It just isn't right for the sun to shine in Europe.
Say hello to all of the neighbors for me and thank Mrs. Mallander for the letter she sent me.
Your loving son, Bob

The mail just came in and so far I got a package from Maxine Dunn and a Reader's Digest from Kitty. I think I hear my name being called for some letters now. _____
Here it is, 2 letters from you March 14, 17, also your pictures in wallet, one letter from Helen.
Thanks a million for the pictures. Bob
Germany
March 28
Dear Mom, Dad,

This has been a busy week and I haven't been able to write as often as usual but I'll try to make up for it one of these days. I received the fruit cake and the package of candy almonds, shrimp yesterday on my birthday. It was the only thing that made it seem anything like a birthday. Your birthday card plus a letter came today. Thanks a lot Mom. You'll never know how much I appreciate all you're doing for me. I got a letter from you Dad, it was an old one dated Feb 3, but I was darn glad to get it anyway. That is a rare thing for me to get a letter from you. I know just how you feel though. I never could think of anything to write when I was home either.

I'm sorry to hear Slim's wife left him but it must be his fault. If he can't hold his wife now what would he do when he has 11,000,000 more men around to compete with.

Mom I wish you would stop thinking about me being on my way home all the time. I am sure that I will not be home for at least two more years. If they don't send me to the Pacific I'll have to stay here as Army of Occupation. So please forget the whole thing. When you tell me you have a hunch I'll be home in a few weeks it makes me nervous as the dickens. I keep thinking I'm going to get wounded as that is the only way to get home that quick. Today is Good Friday and we were lucky enough to get to go to church. That is more than most guys got this year. We had a big turnout as usual. The crowd usually depends upon how the fighting is going. If things are bad or if there is a big push coming up you can't get near a church service unless you stand in line. Other times you just see the old familiar faces.

I am sure you will understand if you go a few days without mail from me. Things are going good over here but it takes a lot of work to keep it going that way. If we can keep pushing now we got them licked, but if we take it easy it will be the same old stuff of yard by yard.

I read something about Roy's division in the paper the other day. It said they were fighting in Koblenz. He is probably long gone from there by now. He got in the best Infantry outfit over here. I don't mean it's the best fighting outfit but it's the best one to be in. I was praying for him not to get in an assault division and my prayers came true. Until I received his new address I had crazy dreams of him getting in the 29th. Boy what a relief it was to hear he didn't get in it.

There are lots of things we are not allowed to do while we are in Germany. In fact we aren't supposed to do anything. So just because I don't tell you about what we do over here don't think we don't have a little fun once in a while.

I can't get over you getting yourself in all those clubs and things back there Mom. The first thing you know people will name you Eleanor R. That's a lot of work but if you like it more power to you.

Well that's the news from here. I may not be able to write for a week or two so don't worry.

Your Loving Son
Bob

Germany
April 5, 1945
Dear Mother, Dad,

Well here I am again, broke down and waiting for a new tank. Boy we really broke down this time too. The drive shaft broke and tore everything up. There is a slave labor camp near here that we freed last week. The laborers are still in it waiting for transportation to their homes. Next to it is a P.W. camp filled with Russian soldiers, French, Belgium, Polish, and half dozen other kinds of political and army prisoners. Each country has their own barracks but they all eat and work together. There are about fifty Russian girl snipers among them. What a tough looking bunch of girls they are! Some of them are bigger than I am and twice as strong. They are all between the ages of 18 and 25. I was over visiting them last nite about 6 o'clock and about five of the soldiers got me in a room to one side and made all kinds of excuses to keep me there for an hour or so. Then some of the girls came over and got me to go with them over to their barracks. While I was gone they had taken down all the partitions and moved the beds out and made a big dance floor out of the joint. There were about three hundred of them there and every one of them was talented. Some of the men played the guitar and mandolin while the rest danced and sang. It was just about as good a nite of entertainment as I ever had in my life. It took me a long time to figure out what these people did besides work but I think I am beginning to catch on at last. Well anyhow the thing went on until about 3:30 in the morning. When I left I could hardly stand up and I'm not sure yet whether it was because I was so tired or the vodka that made me that way. There is another dance tonite at the French barracks in my honor. I can't dance like they do in the states but I can hold my own in these affairs. It's more fun than a barrel of monkeys. At least tonite I will be able to get the drift of the conversation as I can understand a little French but that Russian lingo got me stumped. I can't get a word of it. It's a good thing some of them know a little English. There is a French girl here that lived in a town in France that our company captured. She has been a prisoner here for three years and was glad to hear about her home town. She was afraid the town was destroyed but as far as I can remember we had nothing but sniper fire there and no part of the village was damaged. She was so happy she cried a little.

Well I will probably catch up with the outfit in a few days and get my mail (there better be plenty of it too). I forget whether I told you or not but I received two packages from you before the push. (fruit cake, shrimp)

I didn't know Easter had come and gone until yesterday when I saw it in the paper.
Well, God bless you both and don't worry about me.
Your Loving Son,
Bob

Germany
April 8
Dear Mother and Dad,

I hope you haven't been worrying about me Mom, as there has been no need to do so. You see for the last couple of days I have been back here at ordnance. Yes they are giving me a new tank again. My other one was too far gone to fix in a hurry so they decided to give me another new tank. It is being checked today so I guess I will be going back to the outfit tomorrow or the next day.

We are staying in a three room apartment with lights and running water. We have a radio and are now listening to an American broadcast from NY. It is coming in pretty good now but up until a few minutes ago 'Dirty Girty' from Berlin was doing her best to keep us from hearing the news.

Today for the first time in over a week, the sun came out and stayed out. The air corps is making the best of it too. We could see fleets of bombers going over all day. The P47'our pals' were out dive bombing and strafing all day. According to the radio everything is going fine, in fact it is going better than we could have hoped for.

Roy hasn't written to me since he first joined the 3rd Army. He is probably busy as the dickens and doesn't feel in the mood to write anyway. When you first go into battle you can't write because you are too busy thinking. But he will get over it after he gets used to seeing a little dirty sights. I am not worrying about him as I think he can take care of himself. Maybe after things clear up over here we can get in the same outfit together for the Pacific.

Well my girl and I are getting along swell together, maybe it's because we don't speak the same language or something. She is leaving here tomorrow for the rear area where she will be sent home to Stalingrad Russia. I was thinking of bringing her home to the states and putting her in the ring against Joe Lewis. She could even get a job as a ship fitter or something and I could take it easy. Maybe you would be interested to know what she looks like. Well she's about 5 ft 9 and about 140 lbs. Twenty one years old and strong as a bull. She stands straight as an arrow and can stare a hole in a brick wall. She has pretty black hair and keeps it looking nice all the time. She spent two and a half years in the front lines as a scout and leader of a guerilla band. She was captured after she was shot four times in the shoulder and arm. Oh yes! Her name is Annie in English or Ana in Russian. Well I hate to see her leave but we did have fun for a while anyway.

Jimmy Durante just sang his famous song (a dink a dee a dink a doo) and told the joke about the waiter telling him to watch his hat and coat and someone stole his dinner. Now they are playing 'There's a Hot Time in the Old Town Tonite'. It really sounds good too. The Ink Spots are on next.

It's getting kind of chilly in here so I just built a fire in the stove.

Another fleet of about four hundred bombers are going over now. They aren't wasting a minute of this good weather.

Well Dad if I don't miss my guess, it's about time you were getting the urge to take a trip to the mountains or down to Virginia. I can see you now, looking at the tires on the green hornet and figuring how far you could go on them before they blow. Well go ahead and enjoy the country, that's what we are over here fighting for. The leaves are starting to come out on the trees over here and there are a few song birds out already. In another month everything should be beautiful over here. We pushed the clock ahead an hour over here and we have daylight from about 5:00 in the morning to 9 at nite. I hope it is the same here as it was in Normandy. Only 4 hours of darkness in June.

Well, Mom Mother's Day is almost here again and it looks like we won't be able to be together again this year. Well even if we are 4000 miles apart we still feel as though we were but in different rooms of the same house. As long as you and Dad are home waiting for me there is nothing can keep me from getting back. Well Annie is waiting for me so I better sign off for now and get going.
Your ever loving son
Bob

Germany
April 12

Dear Mom Dad,

Well it's been over two weeks now since we crossed the Rhine so I guess it's alright to tell you what we have been doing. We were back in Holland training as Alligators. Then we came up and took the assault troops across the river. That's all there is to it. Now we are doing another job that I can't tell you about yet.

I got back from ordnance the other day and I'm not a bit sorry as we are in a beautiful farmhouse taking it easy. The weather is beautiful and too warm to wear a coat or even a shirt. Today I walked about 15 miles through the country just like I used to do back home. It is hilly just like up on #10 highway. In fact I can't hardly realize I'm not in the States. There are plenty of deer and all sorts of wild game. The trees are all green and all the flowers are up and in bloom. It really makes me homesick.

Tomorrow I'm leaving here to do a little job and I may not be able to write very often so don't expect too many letters for a while. Don't worry as there is no danger to the job we are doing. The only way I could get hurt would be to stub my toe and break a leg.

When I got back from ordnance there were about eleven or twelve letters waiting for me. It was swell to hear from you after so long a time. There was also a package from Maxine Dunn. It was an Easter basket in a big round can. It had fruit cake and candy in it. The basket was really a work of art. I'll have to write and thank her the first chance I get.

Kitty wrote and said you were up to see her and helped clean up the yard. She really is glad to see you come up. I guess she gets lonely up there by herself. Sometimes she writes me a swell letter, and other times it's just about how she manages to get the yard cleaned up but I always like to hear from her. One day she said she had only written to me the day before but she just felt like writing again so she did. There is one thing I have learned over here and that is how to tell whether a person means what they say and do or whether it is just more convenient at the time to act the way they do. In other words some people write not because they want to but because they think it's just the right thing to do. You were saying the guys in the yard are afraid they might lose their jobs when the war is over Dad. Well don't say anything about it to them Dad, it won't do any good. As long as I know you aren't that way that's all that matters. Those guys are just like these farmers over here. They are never satisfied with what they got. The English kick because our soldiers have more clothes than them. The French always want something for nothing, and the Germans always want their own way. This Europe is just the biggest collection of ignorant people in the world all stuck together in a bunch. It's no wonder there are always wars over here.

If you think the guys in the yard are bad just listen to this. A Dutchman said to me one day "What are you Americans fighting over here for? We only fought four days and quit". Another said "If you Americans weren't making so much money on this war you would get busy and finish it." When a guy hears that kind of stuff you don't feel much like fighting. But you just have to overlook it. The whole thing is just a big rotten mess and all we can do now is finish it.

You asked about the conditions over here in the Allied Countries. Well black bread is the main meal. They drink hot milk in the morning with bread, dinner is black bread, and supper is potato peel soup and bread. The families live well and would just as soon have the Germans here as us, but the city folks are starving to death. These Russians that we have freed have had nothing but black bread and potato peel soup for four years. We gave a Russian girl a real dinner today and she couldn't eat it as her stomach just wasn't used to it. Yes things are really bad over here. You would have to see it to believe it. I had a side of bacon on the tank and gave it to the Russians the other day. They were so happy that tears came to their eyes. By the way they eat it raw. I gave Grada a slice of my pineapple when I was in Holland and it was the first she had ever seen. The younger children never seen candy in their life. It broke my heart to give my chocolate ration to them but it was worth it to see them go after it. I don't believe I ever ate my candy rations since we have been overseas. 4 oz per week when you get it.

Well one of the boys just got back from the states the other day. He said there were so many strings attached it took the pleasure out of it. Well that's the way the army is.

I got a letter from that long lost brother of mine yesterday. Don't worry about him Mom. Any guy that can find as many things wrong with the Army as he can is sure to be a good soldier. He was telling me all about how much he knows already. Wait till he finds out how much the Germans know and he will sing a different tune. Sure it's fun when you are doing the shooting but as for me I been shot at more than the other way around. The Germans are crippled now and he is cleaning up the gravy. When he gets home he will always believe there was nothing to this war. Well I just got a good laugh and let him believe he knows it all and thank God it is that way. There is no need for him to know what the boys before him went through to make it that way for him.

Well it's way past my bed time and besides, I've said enough for one nite.

God bless the best Mom and Dad any guy ever had.

Bob

Germany

April 20

Dear Mom, Dad,

It's another beautiful day in Germany, the fifth in a row to be exact. I am enjoying it to the fullest extent back here in ordnance again. I know you are wondering how come I'm back to ord again so soon, well I have been running into a little bad luck lately that's all.

We have a swell house to live in while we are here, electric lights, running water, and a good cook stove.

We have a swell radio now and we can get programs from the States instead of the BBC. In other words we can hear what the American armies are doing. For a while I was beginning to think the English were the only people fighting this war.

Bing Crosby's program is on now. He has the Andrews Sisters as guest stars. They are swell. They just sang the funniest song I heard in years. It is called "One Meatball". They also sang "Don't fence me in". It is the first time we heard those songs and we think they are swell. Jimmy Durante and his gang are on now. The guys over here think his program is swell. He makes you forget the war for a while anyway. He just told the joke about how he made a 4000 ft parachute jump from a flying fort. He said some wise guy wrote "Gentlemen" on the bomb bay door.

Well I have had more fun over here in the past week than ever before in the E.T.O. I can't tell you what I was doing til I get home, but you will die laughing. I couldn't help picturing Joe here beside me all the time as I know he would have had as much fun as I.

Well I heard from Roy but I just can't get around to writing to him. There is nothing to write that he doesn't already know. He has troubles of his own and I don't want him even thinking about me.

I'm glad you enjoyed the flowers I sent to you for Easter. Sometimes we get a chance to send flowers and things but not very often.

George Burns and Gracie Allen are on now. They are not so hot today.

Well I took a bath yesterday, it was in a river and the water was cold but at least I got some of the dirt off.

Gee I owe so many letters I don't know where to begin. Kitty will feel bad if I don't write so I guess I better get busy. I got lots of mail from you at my last stay with the outfit and I hope when I get back this time I will have another bunch.

There is no way for me to know how long this letter will lay around here before they mail it. I hope you have not started to worry about me again. You should know by this time that I can take care of myself.

God bless you both till we meet again.

Your Loving Son

Bob

April 30

Germany

Dear Mother, Dad,

Well this is the first time in weeks that I have had time to sit down and really do some letter writing. I suppose everyone is going to write and ask whether or not I broke my arm or something.

Well Roy wrote to me on March 16th and it just got here yesterday. There is no reason why his mail should take longer to reach me than yours does, but that's the way it is. He is getting along fine. I can tell by the way he writes, not what he writes. He still thinks the war is a joke and the Germans are dumb. As long as he keeps writing that way you know he hasn't seen a battle yet. The tanks are doing all the fighting down his end of the front so that only leaves the infantry a little mopping up in the towns.

We are living like kings now, plenty to eat and not much work. The hardest thing we do is wash and press our clothes and shave at least once a day. It looks like a good steady job too.

Dad I can't believe you are going to work while Mom is in Virginia. I'd be willing to bet you end up down there yourself in a very short time (the day after Mom leaves). Thanks again for the letter Dad, I know when you write there is plenty of effort in it. I can just picture you writing a letter (as much as you hate to do it).

I stumbled upon about one hundred and fifty eggs the other day and boy am I putting them down the hatch. I eat at least 30 a day. This morning I had twelve for breakfast and then six more after breakfast and six more before lunch and another six for lunch and I got an eye on about twelve more before I go to bed. I don't even go to the mess hall to eat.

Ed is out in the barn working on the generator and the lights are going bright for a minute and then dim. When he gets tired of playing around they will be back to normal.

Just because the war is about over in Germany don't stop building those ships Dad. One of them may save me from getting an unwanted bath in the Pacific ocean. Believe me those destroyers are great too. I seen one of them go within a hundred yards of the beach and shoot every gun they had at the cliffs where the Jerries were dug in. Those five inch guns really tore things apart on that beach. If it weren't for them we never could have landed on D Day.

I stopped in at an airport the other day and found hundreds of wrecked German planes, but the thing that was most interesting to me was a P47 Thunderbolt painted up in German colors. They have been telling us that the Germans haven't been using American planes but now I know that I was right when I said I seen P47's strafe and bomb our troops back across the Rure.

I got a letter from Joe yesterday. He is going to have another eye operation and then be transferred to another hosp to get some more shrapnel out of the rest of his body. The poor guy is going through hell but you would never know it to read his letters. To tell you the truth I never thought he would live to see the sun go down on that day back in France. He was full of holes from head to foot. He would have been left to die if he hadn't had the guts to climb into another tank before he passed out. Things were happening so fast that day it's a wonder any of us came out of it.

Well Dad I have been through a good part of Germany and I think it is the most beautiful country I have ever seen. The part I seen is made up of small mountains, hills and lots of fine trout streams. The woods are full of deer and all kinds of game. I seen more deer over here in one day than I ever seen in my life. The streams are full of fish. I caught three trout ranging from 1 to 2 ½ lbs each this afternoon and a three and a half lb pike tonite after supper. I'll let you know how they tasted in my next letter. You would really enjoy driving through the country over here. The highways are lined with trees that shade the whole road.

How did you enjoy your trip to Va., Mom? I'll bet you had a good time. You always do. You and I are about the same that way. We can have a good time any place.

The weather turned cold for the past two days but it is clearing up now so nice and warm tomorrow.

I am about all out of news so I'll close this letter and start on some others. I have to write to about five or six people tonite yet. June wrote her last letter to me the other day. She said she knew it took a long time for mail to come from Germany but not four and a half months. It's about time she caught on.

Well have a good time and don't worry about a thing.
I'll try to write soon.
Your loving son,
Bob

V-E-D + 1
May 9
Germany
Dear Mother, Dad,

Last nite your first letter from Virginia arrived. I'm glad to hear you are having such a fine time. The first thing I know you will be moving down there yourself. Some of your letters must have been lost as I don't know why you went down there. From all I can gather Fritzie must be sick or something.

I wrote to Roy last nite for the first time since he was put into the 87th. I didn't want to write until he found out what the score was.

John Huey and I went to a concert by Jascha Heifetz. He is one of the most famous violin players of our time. He was accompanied on the piano by Seymour Lipkin. I had a seat in the seventh row and could hear it perfect. There were only three men from each company allowed to go. General Charlie Gerhardt sat in the seat in front of me and all the 9th army brass could be seen floating around, if anyone was interested enough to look for it. They tell me that the seat I had would have cost about $25 in Carnegie Hall if I had enough pull to get it. Well it was very good but not quite $25 worth to me.

This pen you sent me is still working but you have to hold it sideways as it is worn down so much.

The weather isn't so good any more, in March we had beautiful weather but since then it is only half and half. But still it is the best weather I have seen since I left Texas.

I just got word that John Furze is back in the States. He was wounded at Julic. There are two more of my buddies home now also. They were captured the day I lost my first tank on June twelfth. The Russians freed them and they are now stationed at Camp Kilmore NJ (the lucky bums). We thought they were both killed for a long while.

We just heard that the German army in Italy surrendered. That's sure good news to us. I'll bet by the time this letter reaches you they will all surrender up here too. At least if they have any brains at all they will.

We were just out playing ball and I got a couple of fingers swollen up and had to quit. So I thought I had better write a letter and let you know things are ok.

I am going to press my pants as soon as John gets through with the iron so you will know the reason if this letter gets cut short. You see there is a waiting line on the iron. He is through now so I will finish this letter later.

You asked me if I received the pictures you sent me in the wallet. I told you I did but I guess the letter got lost. They are good pictures too.

No I don't mind if you write to Roy first. He can use plenty of mail. The same with the packages. We get plenty to eat now and I don't need anything extra.

I think I will write to Kitty this afternoon so I had better close this letter and get busy as it will be time for supper before I know it.

Your Loving Son
Bob

Germany
May
Dear Mother, Dad,

Some of your letters just reached me from Charlottesville Va. and one from Washington DC. I just got in last nite from a long long trip. After two and a half days driving I was too tired to write so I put it off until today. I did mail some letters to you last nite but I have been carrying them with me for a week or so, but never got chance to mail them.

VE day went by almost unnoticed over here. I first heard about it when I arrived in camp last nite. I didn't feel any different when I heard it as there is still plenty of our boys over in the Pacific. When we finish up over there it will be time enough to celebrate. We have been doing a little celebrating today if you can call it that. We had a full dress parade up to a little hill in the woods a few miles from here. It was in honor of our boys that didn't make it. The btn stood at attention for about two hours while the division chaplain said a few prayers and the executive officer read off the names of the boys lost in action. They had the 29th band there and they played taps when they were finished reading the names. I could hardly believe there were so many of my pals missing, but you get that way in the army. They come and go so fast you almost forget whether they were killed or wounded.

Another thing that made the day seem kind of not so important is the fact that at exactly three o'clock on VE Day I seen a G.I. get killed. I didn't know it was VE Day at the time and didn't think anything of it. In fact I had forgotten all about it by the time I hit camp. But when I heard the war was over I got a funny feeling in my stomach, just like when I seen the first G.I. get it on the beach.

General Gerhardt made a little speech at the gathering this afternoon. He gave us a fine speech or I should say a talk. He said when we took Isigny on June 8th we broke Omaha beach wide open. At the time we couldn't figure out why he wanted Isigny so bad that we had to make an attack on the city at two o'clock in the morning. You see nite fighting in a tank is just like lighting a match to see how much gas you got in your tank.

Today was hot as blazes but I loved it. This morning I went for a long walk in the woods by myself. Everything was so peaceful it was hard to believe there had

been a war on the day before. I came upon an airport out in the woods with a bunch of P47 Thunderbolts laying around. I went over to see the pilot of one and he had his plane shot down the day Joe got hit. He jumped out and landed behind the German lines but managed to escape that nite. I asked where it was and he said over the Vire highway. That morning at the same time I was going down that same highway in fifth gear with those white tracer shells whistling past me, and I said to Capt Bulvin (as a P47 went flaming across the sky) "There goes a guy that's even worse off than us." I was invited to go up for a ride in a two seater P47. They are very few and far between. I was tickled to death to get the chance and we started for the plane. I began to think a little and before we got there I said 'I'll be damned if I will'. It would be just my luck to get it after it's all over.
Later

Well we were just issued a glass of champagne, a half pt of red wine and three shots of cognac. I feel kind of shaky but that will wear off in a little while.

I'm sitting on a chair made of logs under a large oak tree, (it really isn't oak but oak is easy to spell). Well anyway it is a darn big tree, and it has plenty of shade under it. The house is about 20 feet away and we have a radio in the window which is on full blast. Bob Hope is on now and I am trying to listen to him and write at the same time.

There are hundreds of B17 flying fortresses flying over at about 1000 ft. I think they are taking food to some liberated country. I never seen them fly so low before. They all have a big V for Victory painted on the wings.

All of the eggs I had are gone now but I really did enjoy them wile they lasted. I had 14 for breakfast the other day. I'll have to go out and dig up some more.

I'm glad to hear the camera finally reached home. For a wile I thought some 4F mail clerk stole it. They usually do. There is another package too. It was mailed a day or so after the first two. By the way don't ask me where I get things. Don't give too much of that money away as some of it is good. I don't know witch is witch yet but I'll let you know. You can give the rest of the stuff away if you don't want it. Maybe the camera isn't any good but if it is it was worth the trouble of sending it.

Well the sun is going down now and it is starting to cool off. I'm pretty tired and I think that is as good a time to go to bed as any so good nite. I'll finish in the morning.

Thursday Evening

Today was even hotter than yesterday. I got up at about eight o'clock and started off through the woods for a walk. I never got tired so walked further than I should have. I came across a river with a nice sandy bottom and clear as cristal. I decided to go in for a dip and cool off. The water was ice cold but after you got to swimming around it felt good. After I was finished I walked along the river for a few miles and finally came across a few eggs. It was to hot to bother cooking them so I ate them raw. (Something I learned from the hill billies.) Well by then I was ready for another swim so in I went again. By the time I decided to start back I didn't know which direction to go. Well any way four hours of fast walking got me back in time for supper.

We just had a meeting and were told that we would get up at 6 every morning from now on. Be ready for excercises at 7:45 to 8:45. Road march from 9 to 10:30. Then classes on military courtesy and how to be a soldier until noon. 1 to 2 drill, 2-4 maintenance on tanks, 4 to 5:30 baseball. 5:30 retreat 6 supper and then we have all nite off to do nothing except stand guard for 4 hours. That scedual goes every day from now on. I like it too.

I said to myself when we were fighting that I would never complain about anything they make us do, even to fight, and then do the best I could.
Well good nite and God bless you both.
Your Loving Son
Bob

Sgt Joseph Skelly
Patient's Mail
Valley Forge G. Hosp
Phoenixville, PA

*Dear Mrs. Cadmus:
Received your letter
yesterday and I was
very glad to hear
from you. Now that
the war in Europe is
over we can look
forward to seeing
Bob, Roy, home
again. I will cer-
tainly be glad to see
them. As you prob-
ably know we are
really going to cele-
brate.*

*As you have no-
ticed I m not writing
this letter or any of
my letters but I have
a very very nice WAC
writing for me. I am
down again for the
full count. Had an
operation Tuesday
which as far as I
know will turn out
successful. I really
can't think of any
more to tell you, so I
will close for now and
I hope to hear from
you soon again.*

*Sincerely,
Joe*

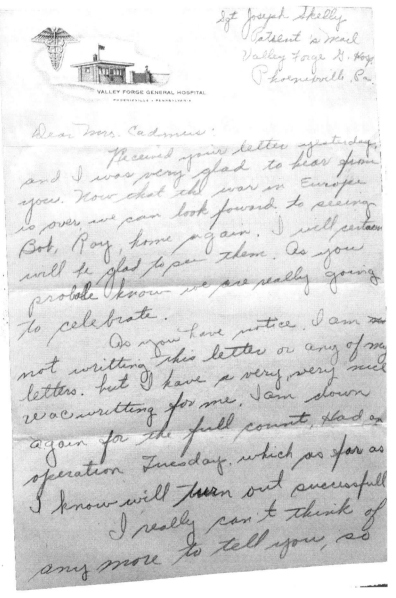

May 12, 1945
Dear Mom, Dad,

   Just a few lines to let you know I am alright and not working too hard. There was no mail yesterday or today. Everything is still the same, so there is nothing to write.

   Write and tell Kitty I can't write for a few weeks. Tell the Mildens the same. I'll try to write a few lines to you every other day.
Your Son,
Bob

May 15, 1945
Germany
Dear Mother, Dad,

   A few hours ago we arrived in this new area. It looks bad to me but I don't imagine we will be here for very long so it doesn't make very much difference. I was going to write to you on mothers day but we were on the move so it was impossible. We weren't even able to attend church but I was thinking of you all day as usual. I hope you received the flowers I sent you, sometimes they come late, but I'm sure you won't mind as long as they get there.

Well I suppose you are interested to know how many points I have to my credit. Here is the whole story, (a sad one at that) I have 28 months service, 15 mo over seas. That gives me 42 points. I have three campain stars, 15 more points. Five more for my bronze Star medal. That makes 62 altogether. Their is a chance that my (purple heart) medal may come through. I was put in for it on November 23 when I was hit in the leg by schrapnell. Some how the records got lost or misplaced and it didn't come through. I didn't want it anyway so didn't bother to track it down. Now the extra five points would probably save me from going to Pacific. Ah well that's war for you. I was wounded twice before and offered the

medal but was ashamed to take it for such small wounds, as lots of my buddies lost legs, eyes, and even their lives for the medal. have a few other things holding me back on points too. Each kid brings 12 points and that lets me out. Also combat men get no more points than anyone else. Most of the service troops have been over here for three years and the combat troops just came over before D day. So the service troops go home first. That's the only part of the system that hurts. We don't think it's fair.

The censorship has been lifted to a great extent I see by tonites paper, so I will give you a brief discription of what we have done.

We left Camp Shanks NY on Feb 11, 1943 landed in Glasco Scotland on Feb 22. Went by train to Fairford England (near Oxford). We drove our tanks their and got them cleaned up. Later we went to Oak Hampton for practice in gunnery. From there we went to Wales on the moors for maneuvers with the 29th division. From their we went to Plymouth England and water proofed our tanks. June 1 we loaded on an English L.C.T. and stayed in the harbor for three days. June 4th we started across, were brought back because of bad weather. June 5th we really went across. We were to hit the beach as soon as the anti tank traps under water were removed. We could not take the beach so the navy blasted it all D day and D day nite. We attempted to land again that nite but were unable to get in until five oclock in the morning. Read (Ernie Pyle's) (Brave Men) from June 5 to Paris for the reason why. He was their. We took Vierville that morning and on to Couvains, to St Clair, Trevieres and Isigny. Then on to 7 miles from St Lo where we were stopped cold. That was 14 days and nites of steady fighting. We then pulled back about 2 miles to reorganize and get replacements. Then on to St Lo. We were said to have made the main break through at St Lo. that was the day after I got the star. After the breakthrough we helped close the Argentan Falaise gap where we killed and captured the German seventh army. What a mess that was. We then took Vire on to St Germain where Joe got hit. Then the 29th went to Brest and we were attached to the 4th division and our tanks spearheaded to Sees, 86 miles in 16 hours. Then we went to Versailles near Paris. Then through Paris at nite in the rain on to (Dam Mortain) then on to (Bastone Belgium) we took the town. It was later destroyed in the Bulge in December. From there to St Vite. From St Vite to the German border on Sept 11th my tank led and was first to cross the border. We were then relieved and sent north and rejoined the 29th div. Then we cracked a hole in the Siegfried Line with the 29th. It was some line and hard to break. Dragons teeth and pillboxes (7 ft thick). We then were detached from the 1st army and joined the 9th army. North again to just above Aachen. We took two or three towns there and then went to within 8 miles of the Roer river. On Nov 18th we made the push to the Roer and made the 8 miles in seven days ending on Thanksgiving Day. That 8 days were the worst in my life so far. Every day I would say to myself (Well man you're $10,000 bucks richer.) We ran into every German tank that could fire its guns. We made it anyway (at least I did). We then pulled back a mile or so and dug in for the winter.

On Feb 23 we went across the Roer and took a pile of bricks called Julich. It was even worse than St Lo if possible. Julich to Munchen Gladbach. Then we were relieved from the 29th. They got a rest and we went with the 30th inf div. Back to Holland and the Maas River for Aligator training. Then up below Wesel for (8 day). We got a 1400 gun artillary barrage starting at 1 oclock in the morning at two oclock we started across loaded down with dough boys. Black as the inside of a boat but across we went. How I ever found the last bank I'll never know. Well I did it and made 43 more trips that day. We then went back to Munchen Gladbach and got our tanks. Up and over the Rhine bridge and thats as far as I can go under the censorship laws.

Say hello to every body and take care of yourselves.

Your Loving Son

Bob

May 17th

Dear Mother and Dad,

Your package arrived last nite, that's the one with the cookies, peanuts, tamales. Thanks a million, it just came in after I missed the truck to supper.

Well I went down to the office and raised hell about the Purple Heart I was put in for and never got. The Captain wrote out new forms and if the division approves of it I will get it. I am trying to get all the points together that I can. If I knew it before, that is, how important they are, I would have turned myself in each time I was wounded and would have had three oak leaf clusters by now. I think I have done enough over here by not missing a single day of combat with the Btn since D Day. Each time I was in ordnance the outfit was in reserve so I didn't miss any action. From now on I'm all out for myself. If I can get a soft safe job back of the lines I'm going to grab it. I'll continue on another vmail.

Part II

Hello again,

My back and knees have been bothering me for the past few weeks. Yesterday I went to the medic and seen the doctor. He said as soon as we move to our new area (permanent) he would take me to the hosp and get me x-rayed. I'll let you know how I make out as soon as I can. Right now I am taking it easy and not pulling regular duty. The rest is doing my legs good. In a few days they will be back in pretty good shape.

The mail just came in but they haven't given it out yet, so I don't know whether or not I have any. I'll go and see before I finish this letter.

No mail for me. Well it's raining out now and I really mean raining. Thunder and lightening too. It feels good not having to duck when you hear the noise.

God bless you both.

Your loving Son,

Bob

Germany

May 22

Dear Mom, Dad,

Your letter of May 12 just came in and either you were drunk when you wrote it or else you have a lot of things mixed up. In the first place what's that bologna about Maxine Dunn? Who said anything about getting married?

She is only a kid. Her father invited us for dinner one day and I wrote and thanked them for it. Maxine wrote a letter asking about the army and stuff and I had to answer. Well she just kept writing and sending packages so I had to answer them. That's all there is to it. Now if you or she has any other ideas you can forget them.

You wanted to know how many points I have, well I told you in my last letter but just in case you didn't understand here it is again. 44 points for service. Three campaign stars France; Belg/Holl/Lux; Germany. That makes 15 more points. 5 more for the Bronze Star, 5 more for the purple heart if it is approved by the 29th Div. So I have 63 or 68 depending on the Heart. I don't know how you figured 75 but anyway it's wrong. I may have a few weeks or more before going to the Pacific but unless something turns up I'll be heading for the east very soon. I think I will volunteer for the Infantry as I have had about all I can stand of these tanks. It wouldn't be so bad if we were in an armored Division but being in an Infantry Division we get all the dirty assault work and after we break through the defenses the Armored Division rolls through and gets the gravy. If I could lose about thirty lbs I could make the Paratroopers and have it made. They make a jump and as soon as the rest of the army breaks through they are relieved. We just keep going until we can't fight no more and then we have to beat off counter attacks until the Germans give out and then we push off again. It's too tough for me so I am getting out into an easier outfit if I can. You asked me once before not to join up with them but believe me it's the easiest fighting outfit going.

Well the weather is fine over here. More warm days and only an occasional thunder shower. Of course we still have hikes, classes on gunnery, classes on tank care, more classes on how to be a soldier. All these classes are of course by officers that are fresh from the States. I said I wouldn't kick about anything we had to do but I can't help but want to go to the Pacific as soon as possible as long as we have to go. Not only to get it over with but to get rid of some of these jerks that tell us how to shoot and abandon our tanks in a hurry.

You asked me how many tanks I have had over here, well I just figured it up and since D Day I have had 7 tanks. Not all of them have been destroyed altogether. The average tank that gets knocked out has one man killed and one man injured. Sometimes no one is killed and sometimes they are all killed. God must be on my side as I have only been wounded three times and none of them serious. One buddy of mine from New Brunswick broke his back getting out after his tank was knocked out.

I received another package from you last nite, it had spaghetti and cheese and crackers in it. I had the spaghetti tonite for supper and it was swell. I put some onions with the meat and browned them before making the sauce. Well I think I shall eat another dozen eggs and then go to bed, as I have to get up real early and learn how to fight a war.
Your Loving Son Bob

Germany
May 22
Dear Mom,

Please have some copies made of this picture. About 10 ought to be enough. I think Joe will want one, if he does he will write and ask for it.

Out of the eleven of us in the picture there are only 4 of us left so ask the guy to try to do a good job as it is the only picture I have of Harry Clark. That's the tall skinny guy third from the right in the back. He was killed right near me when our tanks were knocked out together. The picture was taken in the US I think in Camp Swift.

Well I wrote you a letter last nite so I'll just close for now and get to work on my pistol as there is plenty of rust gathering in the barrel since we stopped the shooting.
As ever
Bob
Send copies as soon as possible as some of the boys are leaving the outfit and want one.

Germany
May 25
Dear Mother Dad,

The days of censoring are over so now we can write what we want to without having to worry about our platoon leader (the censor) finding out all about what we have done that we shouldn't have. Capt Bulvin has been my platoon leader since June 20th. He very seldom read my letters so I was able to write a lot of things that might not have been passed by another censor. I had to be reasonable though to keep him from getting into trouble. He left for home back in November and isn't back yet but he is over here on the continent. He should be back here soon. When he left I took another job driving the tank dozer until he gets back. The tank dozer is a regular tank with a 4 ton blade in front for covering up pill boxes, clearing road blocks, and filling in bomb craters and breaking through hedgerows in front of the tanks. It is the worse job there is, as the dozer has to make paths before the rest of the tanks can move. I had to go across the Ruhr with the dozer so I could fill in the bomb craters. That is why my tank was first to get put out of action on the east banks of the Ruhr. Two days of hard work got her into shape again and away we went.

What really makes you nervous is the fact that there are SS men that would go on suicide missions to get you in particular. I seen Cook the guy that lived in back of the community house get killed just that way. It was on the Siegfried line. Our whole battalion was being held up by one pill box. Fifty of our tanks pulled up in line and all fired at once at it. We couldn't even scratch it so while we fired we sent the dozer from B Company up to bury it. Just as the dozer got up close to it an SS trooper jumped out of the pill box and hit the dozer with a bazooka. The dozer blew up and they all died in it. My gunner hit the bazooka man in the guts with a 75 HE before he could duck his head. Well he was blown into powder but still he did his job and our tanks were held up for days. Don't say anything to anybody about Cook as I wouldn't want his folks to hear how he died. Well that should give you an idea of how you feel over here after a battle. You don't feel much like writing any letters or doing anything. It wasn't because I was too lazy or because I wasn't thinking of you but just a little sick mentally to write. It's hard to sit up there and watch the best guys you ever knew get killed right in front of you and not be able to do anything about it. Maybe you can see why I want to join the Infantry if we go to the Pacific. I want to be able to get down in a hole when they start shooting and not have to sit up there like a duck on a pond. Enough of this stuff could ruin a guy. So please don't make me promise not to join another outfit.

You asked me who the girl was in the picture I sent you. Well she is a friend of mine that I met a few months ago. She is 21 years old and her name is Elizabeth. Thad Weinmeyer, Joe's and my buddy goes with her sister. Some day I'll go back and see her.

We are on our honor not to tell the exact location that we are in while in Germany, so I won't tell of course. The weather is cold and that North Sea air goes all through your bones. It had been a long time since I smelled salt air. They tell me Bremen is in real sad shape. The British bombed it to the ground. In fact one of our trucks ran into a bomb crater just the other nite right near here. Roy's letter arrived after a 6 week tour of the Eto. He seems to be doing fine. He says the tanks are doing all the work down there and the foot troops are just cleaning up the remains. God sure is doing a fine job on my prayers so far.

Today we signed up for school. We have a list of subjects to choose from. I took arithmetic and railroad operating to start. I have a friend that says he can get me a good job with the NY Central RR. I sent the address home to you and I hope to God you don't lose it. I don't know when the school starts but I am going to get all I can out of it. If I can stay here for a couple of years as Army of Occupation I will really get a chance to get some schooling. I am going to take a course in English also, God knows I need it. Later if things turn out alright I am going to take up Spanish. I was thinking of working for an American company in Brazil after the war and the use of the native language would no doubt come in handy if I decide to take the job. I can't make up my mind yet as to what I am going to do but time will tell and a little extra learning won't hurt anybody. I am getting along fine with the German lingo. In fact I can almost carry on a regular conversation now. I have a pretty blond teacher.

Well I suppose you wonder at times what I look like now. It's like this 6'3 tall 13 ½ EE shoes. 36-33 pants, 16 ½ 33 shirt. One tooth missing in front, hair brown and 1 ½ inches long. A few gray hairs but not many. A little nervous and very very sensitive to backfires or door slamming. In fact I was washing up today and somebody scratched a match on the wall and I ended up with a bump on my head where it connected with a bed post as I was sliding under.

This morning we got up at 6:30 and stood revelry and ate pancakes for breakfast. Then we went to work on the tank. We worked on the inside cleaning it up until noon. We had meatballs and potatoes etc. for dinner and then went back to the tank where I discovered 10 bad blocks in my tracks. We broke our backs changing them and ended up missing supper (they had chicken) and finding out that I was Sgt of the guard. Guard mount went at 6 o'clock and I posted the guards and came back to grab a little rest here in the guard house. It wasn't five minutes before they called me to draw my rations for the week. 7 pks of butter, 1 pk of gum, 1 cake of soap, and 7 chocolate bars. They are all free. But next week we have to start buying our rations. Since D Day I haven't spent $10 on myself. It will be hard parting with my money now as I am out of practice. I'm sure a pass to Paris would get me back in practice though. Speaking of passes I'm due for a pass to the Riviera in southern France for 7 days plus traveling time. When I will get it no one knows. Well anyhow back to the guard house. I came and two minutes later the officer of the day was around to check the guard and he caught one of them off his post and gave me hell. Next the mail came in and away I went to get the guards' mail I was lucky and got a letter from Fritzie and a box full of delicious candy from you. I got a bunch of hungry guards around here and they made quick work of the candy but I managed to get my share. Thanks a million Mom.

Well I'm going to try to keep them from cutting out my allotments but if I get a pass once in a while I'll either have to take a staff Sgt's job or cut the allotments. I hate to do either. I have $60 now and I am going to see if I can't make it grow. My main source of income is shot. The price of pistols has gone to the dogs. I sold a Czechoslovakian pistol yesterday for 20 bucks and a month ago they were worth a hundred. Lugars or P38's used to be over a hundred and now they are down to 40 bucks. This last push we cleaned up on pistols and the price went down. The further back you go the more you can get. A few months ago an infantry man would give you a 10 spot for a Lugar. Field artillery would give you $25, Ordnance $60, and quartermaster $150. If you could get to the real 4F's in England you could get $300 for the same gun. I'll find a new racket if we stay here, as army pay isn't enough. You see some funny things here in the army. Guys make whiskey and sell it while it's still hot for $10 a quart. Others get $2 for pressing a pair of pants. That's where I spend my money. I get guys to wash my clothes and do my sewing. Before I go into battle I dress up like a general. It costs a lot of dough but I always said if they get me I'm going down looking like a soldier. Most of us tankers are the same way. I seen my asst driver shaving in the asst driver's seat while the shells were tearing the bed rolls off our tank. That's Fortney, you probably remember me mentioning him in my letters. He was a replacement at St. Jean June 15. He was 18 years old and green as they came. I picked him out of a bunch of 50 replacements. He couldn't drive, couldn't shoot, and didn't even know how to clean a mach gun. I liked him from the first day. He came to me to teach him all about the tanks and he learned fast. He got his basic training in the battle at St. Lo. I think Fortney kept me from breaking up in that battle when he started shining his shoes as we were leading the attack on hill 192. I had to laugh so much I forgot how to be scared. On the long spear heads across France I taught him all I knew about driving. I made him drive even during the rest periods. We went in the woods and practiced shooting pistols for hours at a time. He watched every move I made in the tank and copied it and became a darn good driver even if I do say so myself. Capt Bulvin wanted to make him a cpl driver in another tank but he refused to leave much to my liking. When we got here in Germany he had the same ideas I had. Make those rats pay. We burned the towns down. He would throw incendiary grenades in the houses as we rode by and by the time the infantry came along the Jerries were burned out and had to surrender or die. One day back in France we were dug in under a hedgerow. Just the two of us. Planes came over and dropped flares and lit up our area like day. We lay there covered in sweat. I said 'you scared?' 'Yeah', he says, and I said 'me too.' We pulled out the bible and read a few prayers that we already knew by heart and directly we dozed off to sleep while the anti personnel bombs came down like rain. Early the next morning as we climbed out of our hole, there not 10 feet away was a bomb crater. Neither of us heard it hit. Dave Stine a good friend of mine and Joe was in a five man hole a hundred feet away had the roof blown clean off his hole by a bomb but no one was hurt. Ray Pinlow ran through the field to his tank in the middle of the raid so he and his crew could pray together like they always do when the chips are down.

You probably are wondering why we are not the happiest bunch of guys in the world now that the Germans are wiped. Well we are thousands of miles from the front now but if you close your eyes and listen you can almost hear a group of G.I.'s in a foxhole saying the lord's prayer together as the bombs come raining down on a tiny island in the Pacific.

God bless you Mom and Dad

Your Loving Son

Bob

Germany

Sunday

Dear Mom, Dad,

Here are a few things that happened just after I mailed your letter yesterday that you may be interested in. At 10:30 yesterday morning the colonel sent for me to report to him at once. Well I thought I was really in trouble but I couldn't figure out what I had done that he knew about. For a minute I thought I was going to get a $65 fine but it turned out that all he wanted to do to me was pin the Purple Heart on me. When he gave me the medal I went in and took my Bronze Star out of cold storage so I can mail them both home together. When they get there please don't go showing them to everybody. It's nobody's business what I have or haven't got in this war.

Our company was just given another star for the battle of the Rhine and the Ruhr Valley. That along with the Purple Heart gives me 73 points. We also received the gold arrow head for being in the assault wave on Omaha Beach Normandy France on June 6. We get no points for it as that would leave the 4F boys out in the cold. We are also allowed to wear another arrow head for D Day H hour on the Rhine but you can only have 1 no matter how many invasions you make. That gives all our replacements that didn't land with us in France the arrow head anyway.

You wanted to know what I can wear now in the line of ribbons. Well here it is. Eto ribbon with 4 stars and 1 arrow head. Bronze Star ribbon, Purple Heart ribbon, Good Conduct ribbon. B.S. medal, P.H. medal (Expert, driver, mach gunner, sub mach gun, 75 and 37mm tank guns.) (Sharp shooter pistol, rifle, carbine) (Marksman, bazooka, anti tank rifle grenade). I can't see how you can be in doubt as to what I have now. But if there is just ask.

With those extra 10 pts I may be able to get home before going to the Pacific or may be able to stay here as Army of Occupation (I hope). Passes are starting for England, Paris, Brussels, and the French Riviera. I am going to take the first one that comes my way. All except the one for England. I never want to go there again. We were never allowed to tell it before but in England the people are rotten. They try to rob your money every chance they get. You have to pay enormous prices for hotel rooms while on pass. You pay twice as much for a meal as they charge to their own boys.

My last letter from Roy was 6 or 7 weeks old so I don't know whether or not he got away as lucky as I did in this war yet. I just would like to get a letter after VE day from him. Let me know as soon as you hear.

Well it's time I got to work so I'll sign off for today.

Your Loving Son

Bob

(over)

Monday

Well today I go to the hospital for a checkup and a few x-rays. I will be gone for a couple of days at least and if they find anything wrong I may stay for an operation. I am going to have my back and knees x-rayed to see if there is any bones out of place. Back in Julick I was climbing up on the tank and a shell landed near me and blew me off and I landed on my back. Ever since then it has bothered me but I didn't want to leave the boys till the war was over so I didn't turn in. Another time a sniper cut down on me and I had to dive into the turret head first and I caught my knees on the gun and since then they have been getting stiff when I have to drive very far.

As long as I am down there at the hosp I may as well have that piece of shrapnel taken out of my leg as it isn't doing any good where it is. It is just under the muscle and I can feel it rub. I'll let you know in a couple of days how everything is.

Jade Aldenberg is the name of the town we are in now. It is about 40 miles north of Bremen. You can see why we are having all the bad cold weather. The North See is just down the road a little ways, and the air coming in from it is damp and cold. The ground is soggy and wet all the time. It makes beautiful dairy country and they sure do make use of it. The fields are full of cows. Farming is poor as if you turn up a shovel full of dirt the hole fills with water instantly. We took over a town and moved most of the people out. We live in their houses. They aren't bad either. Huey and I have a nice upstairs room with two single beds and electric lights. There is a water driven washing machine downstairs and an electric pump on the well. The hospital I am going to is in Bremen so if they keep me you will know where I am. The town is pretty well flattened out but there are sections that aren't so bad. The heart of the city is just a pile of bricks and you have to go around it. It isn't half as bad as St. Lo or Vire or Julick though.

It is raining cats and dogs out now. There is a little thunder and lightening too.

Captain Bulvin is due back here tomorrow. The guys can't wait to see him either. He is a great guy. I know him better than any one else in this Btn as I drove his tank from the first day he came to this outfit until he left for home. He is noted all over the btns as being the bravest officer we have. He leads every tank spear head and usually gets us out alive. He received the Silver Star for our push we made together on Nov 18 to Nov 25. Remember when we went into Germany on Sept 11? He was chosen to take command of a combat patrol into Germany. We were told it would be a mission that we should not expect to come back from. Our tank was in need of repairs so he was given the Major's tank from HQ Company for the mission. I was tickled to death as I wasn't in any frame of mind to get killed that day as we figured the war was almost over. About an hour before they were to leave he was nervous as a cat and finally came over to my tank and said it would feel kind of funny going up there without us. Well I knew what he wanted then but I waited for him to ask us. Finally he asked me if I would drive for him. Well I didn't have the heart to say no, so I climbed aboard. When the rest of my crew seen me going they grabbed their stuff and jumped in too. Of course the Major's crew was tickled to death and so was Capt Bulvin. We left that nite for the front. Four o'clock the next morning our 5 tanks and two M10 tank destroyers, two jeeps and 50 foot soldiers started out. All by ourselves and twenty miles to go. The country was all hills and great planted pine forests. We hit strong opposition as soon as we left. The enemy couldn't see anything but the lead tank (mine) as the forest only had small dirt roads winding through it. They must have thought it was a strong armored spearhead as they ran. (Thank God).

Our scouts seen tank destroyers two more tanks about a mile and a half away down the valley. They got both of them with 12 shots. We then seen truck convoys loaded with Jerries going like mad up the St Vite highway towards the Siegfried line. We fired everything we had at them and smashed it. Eagle Eye Fortney spotted another tank about 4 miles away going up a dirt road. We could see it good with the glasses but they were out of range. A radio message brought a piper cub over in a short time and he directed long term fire on it and we seen the luckiest shots ever made. At eleven miles they hit it with the third shot.

Well we took a cigar box full of German soil and a couple of road signs which we hung on the outside of our tanks back to the General of the 28 inf div. He said he was proud of us and all that stuff and then back we went to the good old 29th which just got in from a rest.

I hope you don't mind me writing about this stuff once in a while, it sort of has to come out and I wouldn't tell it to anyone but you. You just can't stop fighting a war and just forget it. It will take years to change back to being like we were.

I just received your letter of May 18th. I'm glad you went to see Kitty. I guess she gets pretty lonely up there by herself.

You asked me if I remembered Grand Ma. How could anyone that knew her ever forget her? She was one grand person and I shall never forget her. Sometimes when I go to church and we sing the old hymns I can almost hear her singing in the Methodist church on Wood Ave.

Well you probably will have to read this letter in sections now so I had better close for now and get some sleep.

Your Loving Son
Bob

Germany
May 30
Dear Mother, Dad,

No more tanks was the verdict down at the hosp yesterday. It's about time too, don't you think? Two and a half years in one of those coffins is enough. They took X-rays of my back and found a few bones in the wrong place. They always were that way and always will be according to the doctors. He asked why I didn't turn in before this and get out of the fighting. Well I told him I wouldn't do it again for a million bucks and I wouldn't take a million for the experiences that I have had. They put me on light duty for the duration and by then everything should be back in shape. He said the muscles in my back and legs are all strained and what they need is rest. If the sun ever comes out again I'll take a sun bath once in a while, he said it would be good for me. I spent two days at the hospital and enjoyed it very much. I spent both nites walking around Bremen. It's quite a town too. You sure can get lost easy.

Down at the hosp, I met some of my pals that have been operated on. One guy 'Big Clark' an ex-marine just had a cyst removed from his spine. He was funny. They gave him pills to put him to sleep for the operation. The pills didn't even make him sleepy so they gave him a needle but he still kept talking so they ended up giving him gas. Well he was pretty shot when I first went in to see him but this morning just before I left he was having a fight with a red headed nurse. He wanted to get up and she wouldn't give him his pants. He is 6'3 and weighs about 240 and full of the devil. He came with us back on the Siegfried line as a replacement.

Capt Bulvin was back here when I came in today. He bought me a beer down the corner at our company bar. He looks good after 60 days at home. I told him I wasn't going to drive for him any more and he didn't seem to like the idea. By the time we get to the Pacific I will be able to drive but I'm not going to let them know it. That will give Fortney the job and he sure has earned it. Well you can take the star out of your window now as one of your sons is a 4F.

Your Loving Son

Bob

Germany

June 2

Dear Mom, Dad,

I haven't written to you in the past few days as we have just finished setting up another outpost. It's about 10 miles from the nearest village and the farm houses are a mile apart. We moved into half a farm house and let the family have the other half. We should kick them out altogether but they have some small kids and I can't hate kids even if they are German.

Last nite I woke up when something bit me on the leg. I got up and took a good look and found the bed was alive with fleas and little green bugs. I was so mad I woke up the woman and told her if that room wasn't clean and the beds and blankets washed by noon I was going to set fire to the house. Her and the old man started work on it 4 o'clock in the morning and by 9 o'clock they had everything out in the yard drying in the sun. That's the first time anything like that ever happened to me and it better be the last for their sake.

This part of the country is very low and the ground is always wet. Each house has a bridge going to it from the street as the gutters are about 10 feet wide and have about 3 to 6 feet of water in them. It is that way even in the towns. You can see what we have to put up with as far as mosquitoes are concerned. They grow as large as small birds and their stingers can go through the best armor plate. They hit you in formation sometimes 20 at a time and if you aren't careful they will pick you up and away you go.

There is no drinking water at all. The water from the well is the color of iodine and will color your clothing red if you use it for washing. We boiled eggs in it and they looked like Easter eggs when we were done. Even the small river down the street is red, I don't know if fish live in it or not but I doubt it. The people put out large wooden tubs to catch rain water for drinking. It doesn't seem to hurt the cows to drink the red water but the dogs and cats are given rain water.

This outpost is a joke. We are supposed to pick up German soldiers and check civilian passes but in two days all we have seen is 7 people and they were just out milking their cows. I'm not complaining though as we have no bars except me. Ain't that a joke. As far as I'm concerned the boys can do as they want. So far all they have done is eat and sleep. I send two of them out with the horse and buggy every morning after eggs and onions, potatoes. I am going to kill a young cow tomorrow as our meat supply is getting low. These guys and myself can polish off more meat in a day than a small town full of people back home. We ate a small pig (about 50 lbs) in two days. That is just the seven of us. I'll bet that cow won't last more than five days. Of course the patrols will stop in and have a bit twice a day. The kitchen sends our meals out to us but we always send most of it back all except the dessert.

Our patrol came in about an hour ago and brought us our mail. I got two letters from you dated May 22 and 25th. Your mail only takes about 5 or 6 days to come over. You had one enclosed too Dad. You said you haven't written for a couple of weeks Dad, well it was over a month. But anyway I was glad to hear from you. I'll bet you get tired of that nite shift pretty quick. I know the hours used to drag by for me during the nite. It isn't bad though, you ought to go on a nite patrol sometime. Cross country in mud and rain for five or six miles. Even that isn't so bad as just sitting in a fox hole for 6 or 7 days and nites in a row. The nite seems to last forever, but you are satisfied as you know as soon as it gets light you attack and one or two out of the gang aren't coming back. Most of the time you hope it's you that gets it as it will be all over.

I was going to answer Fritzie's letter tonite but according to tonite's mail they will be at our house before the letter could reach them. I'm glad they are coming to stay with you Mom. It will be some company and you and Fritzie can go out together and see all the shows in NY. I hope we get a furlough home before we leave for the Pacific so I can go along with you. I won't mind going so much if I can get to see you folks again first. Maybe Roy and I can get together down there in the Pacific and kill those rats together. I sure hope so. I got to admire those yellow rats though they don't give up like the Jerries. Why they give up in such large numbers we had to take them prisoner.

You asked about how I got all the junk I sent home, well there is no censor now so I can tell you. Three of the medals were off 4 German prisoners that I captured without a gun. I'll never live that experience down as long as I live. It was back in Schleiden across the Ruhr on Nov 22. We took the town (about 100 houses) after two days of heavy fighting. 7 of my pals were killed and eleven wounded in the town. We had the town and stopped to gas and reload our ammo. Fortney and I just finished handing in the last case of mach gun ammo when I seen a truck in the garage across the street. Well I walked over and took a look and there were Jerry field packs in the back of it so I got up and went looting through it. I found a swell shaving brush and razor and a couple pair of good wool socks. I then went in and pulled a drawer out of the desk and dumped the stuff on the floor and was kneeling down picking through it when I heard a noise in back of me. Well I looked around and there stood 4 German soldiers looking at me. Well I didn't know what to do so I just kept quiet until they said "Kamrad". It's a good thing they said it when they did as I was just going to say it myself. Well out I went, them following me. When I got outside an infantry boy took them back to the P.W. after I had taken their medals and a busted pen from them. Well I was pretty well shook up and it was quite some time before my knees stopped shaking. We went down the cellar of the house and found 1 bazooka, 2 machine guns, and a rifle. They could have hit our tank with the bazooka from the cellar window. Well after that none of us felt too good for a while.

The rest of the stuff I got in Munchen Gladbach. The silver iron cross medal in the little black case came from a SS officer that gave up to us after we killed his men in a two hour duel with a M VI. Grand Pa wants a medal so if you don't mind give him that one and tell him it came from a German soldier with plenty of guts. The SS knife came from a colonel who committed suicide. He led a counter attack against the 29th. The camera from a mansion in the outskirts of town where our bombers missed a few buildings. The other stuff I just picked up here and there.

I think you have a picture of Pop Hoffer that I took while we were on maneuvers. Well he was killed in that town while trying to shoot it out with an 88. Pop's shells were bouncing off the 88 and didn't even take the paint off it. He hit it 7 times before the German tank fired a shot. The 88 of course went in one side and out the other with the first shot. I sure would like to get some of those armchair generals who ship us our guns in a tank for a few maneuvers. It's heart breaking to see your tracer shells bounce off their tanks when you know theirs will go through yours at twice the range.

One pal of mine hit a M VI 22 times in a row at a mile and a half range and not one of them knocked it out. Then the German swung his 88 around and killed him with the first shot. Can you blame us for wanting to join the infantry? Well it's about three o'clock and time to change guards so I'll close for tonite and drop a few lines in a few days.

Your Loving Son,

Bob

June 6
Jadenburg
Dear Mom, Dad,

Well this is the first anniversary of D Day, the radio has been giving rebroadcasts of the news headlines of the landing. It's the first time I heard what they said about it on the air. It must have been quite a day for you people back there.

We are supposed to have a holiday today but I am still on outpost and haven't time to celebrate. There are only 6 of us left here that landed on D Day and only two of us that have been here all the time. The other four spent anywhere from 4 to 8 months in the hospital.

Last nite I only got one letter from the States. It was a vmail from Kitty. She was glad to see you when you were up to help her with her flowers.

I guess Fritzy and Bernie are up with you by now. How do they like living up among you Yankees? You asked who the girl was that I sent you the picture of. Well I don't know which one you mean but 9 out of 10 girls over here are named Hanna or Maria, so you can take your pick.

I can't wait to get out of here now. It's driving me nuts staying in one place so long. We have been here two weeks now.

There is no news on my pass yet, I guess they are waiting for me to come up and beg for it. Well they will have to wait a hell of a long time. They are after me pretty bad now. I turned down every job they want to give me. The other day they told me I would have to take over the 1st platoon and I told Capt Bulvin to mark me as AWOL as of now, as I was going over the hill so they would have to bust me. They backed down so it was OK, but they are still trying to find a way to make me take Staff Sgt. You see the job and rating I have now is the easiest in the army and that hurts them to see me having such a good time.

I haven't enough money to go on pass yet anyway and I don't want to borrow any. I have about $125 but that would only last half a day in Paris. I could borrow $500 in 5 minutes but it is too hard to pay back, as I only draw 18 bucks per mo. Maybe you are wondering why a guy needs so much money well here is the story. We get paid in Francs in France. Our gov values a franc at $.02 but the French value it at ¼ of a cent. That means dinner costs us about $12 or 24 bucks if you have a girl with you. A hotel room is around 25 bucks a nite. Maybe I will go to Paris for 1 day and then take off to Versailles and visit some friends. That way I could get away for about 200 bucks, or a pocket full of 'chaclada' chocolate to you. Chocolate is the magic word over here. One day as I was taking a walk down the main street in a town in Belgium there was a lot of noise in back of me. I looked around and there were dozens of kids and beautiful girls following me. I couldn't figure it out until a buddy of mine
June 8 I got called out on some trouble and didn't get to finish the other day so I'll continue now.

As I was saying a buddy of mine discovered I had two chocolate bars sticking out of my back pocket.

My pen disappeared, I guess someone borrowed it. It's the same pen you sent me in France. Whoever has it will give it back when he is done with it.

We had some trouble this morning with the people that live in the other half of our house. They came in our rooms while we were out playing ball and stole two bars of soap and a bar of chocolate. When you are in the army you can always tell when someone has been in your bags. It was Red's bag and he asked me if he could kill the guy. He has a bad temper so I took him with me to look around the house and see if we couldn't find the stuff. Well we found it in the people's bedroom. Red almost went mad. The people cried and begged us to forgive them. I gave them fifteen minutes to move out of the house and you ought to see them cry. We try to treat these people fair but sometimes you just can't. Well we have the whole house to ourselves now so there shouldn't be any more trouble.

Red came with us back in Schleiden Germany as a replacement. He was only 18 years old and full of fight. He has just seen enough action to make him cold blooded but not enough to tame him down. He is a swell kid though and will do anything in the world for me. He still doesn't know how to be scared. It's the same as we all used to be back in Normandy when we didn't know any better. Well that's the news from here.

Your loving son

Bob

Germany

June 10

Dear Mom, Dad,

It's past three o'clock in the afternoon and I'm not even wide awake yet. We had a party here last nite in our little home in the woods. We really had a good time too. We invited four or five of the boys from camp to the feast besides the 7 of us that are stationed out here. We had eggs, meat, chicken, coffee, and a few bottles of wine. Every one had a swell time. It broke up about four o'clock this morning. The first thing I heard this morning was the voice of Capt Bulvin as he pulled me out of bed. He was hollering for ten minutes before I could open my mouth. I had to bust out laughing at him as I never seen him mad before. I told him we had a party last nite when he finally quieted down. What the hell do you mean a party, he says? I said we were celebrating him coming to the outfit just a year ago. He knew that was a damn lie but he had to laugh. He then raised the roof because we did not invite him. Well everything was fine then until our maid came in and started to clean the house. He says 'Who the hell is that'? I said we have her come in every day at eleven o'clock to clean the house for us. He said some day I'm going to send you back to the States and break your heart. Then he left in disgust and I went back to sleep. When I got up a few minutes ago everything was in order, dishes washed and all. I went to the phone and called up Capt Bulvin and told him we were ready for inspection. He hung up in my face.

Well the sun is out at this minute but it will rain before another hour goes by. There is nothing else to write as I haven't received mail in a few days now. So I'll close now and fix up something to eat.
Your Loving Son,
Bob

June 10
Dear Mom, Dad,

The mail came in a little while ago and you letters of June 1-4 came in. The other letter I wrote today didn't have anything in it so I'll finish it now. You seemed to be worried about my back and knees. Well they are still a little stiff and sore but are getting along alright. What used to bother them most was when we couldn't get out of the tank for a week at a time. If you ever tried to sit in a steel chair with your knees up even with your chest 24 hours a day for a week or two you would find they would get pretty stiff. When you slept, your legs would go to sleep too and every half hour you have to wake up and rub them to get blood running again. In France one time my whole crew had to stay in the tank for 16 ½ days. When things got cool I tried to climb out but needed the help of 2 men to do it. Under those conditions you are bound to have trouble with your back and legs. The sun helps them when there is any sun.

You asked why I didn't go after the Purple Heart and clusters. Well I don't think you understand, but I will try to explain it. When you see your pals get their legs and arms blown off or get killed all they get is a Purple Heart. The way I look at it they should be the only ones to be able to wear it. Can you imagine how I would feel walking down the street in NY and seeing one of the boys with a leg off and me with the same medal on, that he got for a leg? What would Joe think if he seen me with clusters in my medal ribbon with nothing but a few hunks of shrapnel in my legs? I put off getting the medal until after I seen how many points I needed. It was the only way to boost my score over 70 so I took it, but I'm still half sorry I did. One reason I did it was because the only guys in my company with over 85 is the mess sgt, and the first cook. Each have 3 kids. It burns me up to see them go as they were always glad when we had to go to the front so they didn't have to cook for us. They never had to be shot at and never got close enough to the front so we could shoot them and get away with it.

Most of the boys won't go to the hospital when they get wounded as the hospital always sends home a telegram saying 'Your son is seriously wounded'. If the army would mind its own business we would be better off.

I just seen a good piece in the paper that sure builds up our morale. It's about the Russians. I'll send it to you. The lights are out now, I don't know what happened but we can't seem to get them back on. I am using the last candle so I had better finish this letter in the daylight tomorrow.
Hello again,

I just have enough paper here to wish you a very happy Birthday. There is no way in the world for me to give you a present this year but maybe I'll be able to make up for it next year.

Your Loving Son,

Bob

Germany

June 12

Dear Mother, Dad,

It's three o'clock in the morning and I realize it is one heck of a time to be writing a letter, but tonite I just feel like writing. Maybe it's because I'm afraid to go to sleep I don't know. It seems as though every nite about this time I have bad dreams and wake up in a sweat. Last nite I dreamt I got shot in the foot and in the hand. The funny part was I enjoyed that one as it would mean a trip to the States if it were true. One nite last week I dreamt I was driving down Gresser Ave in my tank and a big old tiger tank pulled out around Turners' old house and shot the gun off my tank. I backed up the street a ways and another tank started shooting at me from in front of Eldridges' house. That's all I remember of it but the next morning the guys told me I sure was giving somebody hell in my sleep. When I hear the boys talking in their sleep I listen to see if it sounds good or bad. If it's bad I wake them up. I wish they would do the same for me. Sometimes you can hear three of them talking in their sleep at the same time.

The old coo coo clock just struck 3:30 o'clock. That reminds me, I wanted to tell you about the coo coo clocks over here. There is one in every house, exactly like the one we used to have. During the day you can hear real coo coo birds all around in the woods. They sound exactly like the clock only very much louder. On a quiet day in the country you can hear one for half a mile or more. I don't know what they look like as they never coo when you are near them. The birds over here are all different from the ones you have at home. There are about seven different kinds of birds over here that I have seen. Some look the same as ours except for their different colors. Then there are some that are altogether different from anything we have. Down the street is a large tree with a nest as big as a bushel basket in it. It is full of baby cranes. The mother flies around our house all day getting food for them. It is the biggest bird I ever seen in Europe. The wing span is at least five feet from wing tip to wing tip.

The flowers are all in bloom now. The fields are covered with yellow flowers with millions of poppies and little blue flowers mixed with them. It's a very beautiful sight even in Germany.

I am laying on my stomach on the floor so if you can't read this you will know the reason why.

Well it's just a year ago today that I lost my first tank. Just about this time I was laying 20 feet from a Jerry machine gun nest without so much as a rock to defend myself. You will ever know how close you came to being 10,000 richer

271

that day. That day I seen four of my best pals get killed. Maybe you remember me speaking of them when I was home. They were Harry Clark, Joe Fimenala, Louie, Lt. Bailey. They all were killed as they climbed out of their tank when it was hit. The same machine gun that was next to me was the one that got them. After I seen that happen I had no more feelings for human life. (I'll finish tomorrow)

It's now three o'clock in the afternoon and I just crawled out of bed. I'd have been sleeping yet but the flies kept using my face for a landing field and it gets quite annoying after a while.

Your package with the shrimp, catsup, marshmallows and nuts came in today. When I woke up the boys were having a marshmallow roast over the kitchen stove. I'm going to open the shrimp for supper if I can hold off that long. I just took a poll of how many of the boys like shrimp and found that only three besides myself like them. That will give me an even break, as usually everybody around likes them.

The radio program for the rest of the day was just announced and I hear Bob Hope is on at 21 hours (that's 9 o'clock to you) or about two o'clock in the afternoon back in the States.

The latest news says that the 9th army is going to the Pacific and the 7th and 3rd stay here. I suppose we will be transferred to another army before long. Roy will no doubt be transferred also as he hasn't enough points to stay here in Europe. When those changes come the mail will be all mixed up and we will not hear from each other for a few weeks. When that time comes don't think because you are not receiving mail that I am coming home. There is only a very slim chance of me getting home before next year. I don't mind staying here though. The Germans do all our work and we live in houses. I don't even have anyone to give me orders any more and that's the best part. The only time I see an officer is when I go in to camp to turn in my report, or when Captain Bulvin comes out to see me. I handle all problems that arise around the civilians here. They all come to me with their problems just like I was Mr. Anthony. If something comes in that I can't handle we send them in to HQ. Something came up last nite that has me a little worried. Someone cut our telephone lines with the company. They cut the wire and then taped it up so we wouldn't notice it. I put on an extra guard just to play safe. It probably was only a kid trained by the army to disrupt our communications. They cause very little trouble but you have to be careful of them. We found piano wire stretched across the road at just the right height to cut a jeep driver's head off. That was one old trick the Jerries used down in Normandy. We learned about it the hard way but it wasn't long before all jeeps had steel poles welded on the front of the bumper to take the place of the driver's neck.

Well tomorrow is your birthday Mom. I wish I was home so I could take you to a show or something but that is out for this year. I hope you have a good time anyway.

Well it's time for supper so I'll close for now wishing you a very happy Birthday and God bless you.

Your Loving Son

Bob

Jadenburg

June 16, 1945

Dear Mother, Dad,

Just thought I'd drop you a few lines to let you know I'm still stationed in the same place. I am going nuts just sitting around doing nothing. All the books we were issued this month were either mysteries or just plain rotten so I read about three of the best and quit. The best one was "Wild is the River". It was about the army of occupation in New Orleans after and during the civil war. It was a good story besides being educational. There are USO shows in Breman but it is too much trouble to get there. The roads up here are very bad and traffic is about 20 miles per hour. The bridges are all blown out across the Wesser river and you either have to take a ferry boat or wait in line for a chance to go across a British built 'rumble bridge'. It's a sorry excuse for a bridge as it is one way at a time and not even safe at that.

We have been playing cards, pitching horse shoes, and reading. You get tired of that after a while though.

The weather is still the same. It's even worse than Normandy France. It rains at least four or five times a day and it hardly ever gets warm. I'll be glad when we go to southern Germany again where the weather is the best in Europe. I was out last nite until three o'clock and discovered the days are even longer than in France. It gets dark about 11:30 and gets light at 2:30 o'clock.

Thank God the war is over in Europe. I don't think we could last long fighting 23 hours a day. I know I couldn't.

There is no deer hunting around here like there is down south. It is just as well though as someone would surely get killed if we kept hunting like we were for a while. When a deer ran across an open field ten or fifteen guys would open up on it. It sounded like a full scale battle. The meat was delicious though, we had so much of it our kitchen was serving it for a while.

I hope you don't mind me writing you all the time about nothing. There is nothing to write but it helps to pass the time away.

I'm getting along pretty good learning German. I learn a few new words each day and they keep adding up. I can understand everything the people say if they speak slowly and I can answer them so they can understand. Of course it's not the best grammar but we get along. I can almost tell what a person wants before he opens his mouth. If they come up to with a basket of 'iss' (eggs) I know they want a pass. (It's all according to how many eggs they bring as to whether or not they get the pass.) Why they even have to come to me to get permission to milk their cows. I get a big kick out of Red, he checks passes to the letter. If they aren't exactly right he sends them in to me. I raise hell with them and holler at them in English. That gets them scared and you ought to see them follow the law to the letter. The tank corps is considered equal to the Germany SS troops. They are scared to death of us. Believe me we are doing our part to keep it that way. When someone gets out of line one of the boys pulls a gun on them and makes out like he is going to shoot them. The nearest guy to him always stops him and says give him or her another chance. One guy we caught out after curfew and pulled that gag on him. When I finally gave him permission to go he tripped over his own feet three times getting out the door. When Red walks down the street people jump through windows to get out of his way.

This is the first time since I have been in the army that I have given more orders than I receive. I never give an order to any of our boys, I just ask them to do it. They know better than to refuse.

I found out about the money I sent you. You can give away all the bills dated 1923 or under. 1924 to 1945 are good (some of them at least).

I believe either you or Fritzy said something about Bob Schneider going into the service. Well if I could lay my hands on him I would drag him to the Navy recruiting office the day he reaches 17. School or no school he is better off going without a year of school and living than finishing school and dieing. I don't know when he will be 17 but if the war is still on with Japan try to get him in the Navy before the Army can grab him. I spent five of the worst days the Navy ever had with them June 1st – 6th 1944. It is a joke comparing it with the army.

If he does get in the army he will be sure to get in the infantry just like Roy did. He may not be as lucky as Roy either. When Roy reached the front the infantry job was finished and the tanks did the work while Roy learned his job. If Roy had reached here a month earlier he would either have been killed or wounded long before now. His and most all our outfits were wiped out in the last months of the old year. A man with no experience like him couldn't have lived through it. He just seen enough action now to know how to take care of himself. Bob won't get that chance!

Here is another address I want you to keep along with the rest.

Louis C Ogden
RFD #1
Middletown New York
Phone 923065

Your Loving Son,
Bob

Germany
June 20 1945
Dear Mom, Dad,

This letter has been coming for a long time, that is I have been trying to write it for a long time. I started it yesterday and ended up by throwing it in the fire. Things just weren't going right. The weather was cold and rainy, people were complaining about the Russians looting their farms, others were after passes to Breman, (which is a pain in the neck) as I have to make a report on each one. The captain was down on me for letting a truck load of Russians (slave labor) get away with a truck load of loot. My telephone wires were cut and I couldn't get in touch with #1 outpost to stop them. Well anyway today was altogether different. The sun was out all day and it was warm enough for the boys to go swimming. There was no trouble of any sort. The best news I heard today was about the 87th division going to the states for furloughs. I hope Roy isn't gipped out of his.

You asked about why I only had three battle stars and Roy has two. Well the stars aren't really battle stars as even the WACs and nurses get them. You get them for being in a combat zone at a set date. The first one I got was for northern France. Everyone in France from D Day until the fighting stopped in France gets a star even if he was never within a hundred miles of the front. The same goes for the battle of the Rhine Valley, and eastern France, Luxembourg, Belgium, Holland inclusive. You get no more points for fighting than you do for pushing a pencil. In other words the combat man is a sucker. Well anyway I now have 4 stars and an arrowhead for the invasion. The arrowhead doesn't count a single point. That's why I'm not doing any more fighting. They just laugh at you and call you a sucker.

Roy was lucky he wasn't put in the 29th as I was just waiting for that. I was all set to go and visit him with my 45. A bullet in the leg would have sent him back to the states. I figured one Cadmus was enough in that outfit. The 29th is the outfit they use to get rid of all the extra manpower.

You asked if I had a fraulein to do my cooking. Well seeing as you put it that way, yes I have. I have been going with a girl from a nearby farm for the past three weeks. She bakes wonderful cakes with my flour and sugar. I am invited to her house tomorrow for a duck dinner. We have lots of fun together riding her father's horses and taking a buggy ride after super every nite. She is learning English fast (and how). All the slang I know and a little more. I am also getting a free lesson in German every time I take her out. She is also a great help in putting me wise to who's who in Jaderberg.

I suppose you are wondering what the latest rumor is as to what is to become of the dear old 747. Well here it is, we have been classed third rate. We have had so many men killed or wounded that all we have left is kids like Roy with 15 weeks training. Our drivers have no experience. (5 hours in a tank at Fort Knox). We have to make gunners out of guys that never fired the 75, Half of them can't even take the gun apart to clean it. Our officers were all killed in the last big battle (Julich to Munchen Gladback.) We now take orders from officers that were inducted in the army 6 months ago (I just love that).   They give us classes on tank tactics that they learned in school. I always wait until they get finished talking and then say in a deep voice 'It don't work that way' or 'where did you learn that, at Fort Knox?' Well as you can well imagine they hate my guts. I think that's why they put all us D Day men out here on outposts. We make fools out of them every time they open their mouths. Well anyway being a third rate outfit means we will be broken up and used as replacements in some armoured division. If true here is where I head for the infantry.

Well Dad they just announced over the radio that last Sunday was Fathers' Day. It's a heck of a time to tell us but still it's never too late to celebrate fathers' day. As far as I'm concerned every day is Mothers' and Fathers' day, as there is never a day goes by that I don't picture in my mind what you are doing and wish I were there doing it with you.

June 21

Mimi gave me some pictures of herself and her dog last nite. I'll send some of them to you. The dog's name is Ballow. He is even bigger than Wolf and knows more tricks than Wolf did. He is two years old and just full of the devil. He won't go out of his yard, or go into the kitchen or living room no matter how much you call him. Before he will eat anything Mimi must say it is all right. His mother had 5 more pups a few weeks ago and I am going to get one if we don't move out of here too soon. Mimi has to go get him in Brake, 21 kilometers from here. She makes the trip once a month and it will be two weeks before she goes again.

She gets mad at me because I pay more attention to the dog and her horse than I do to her. She wants me to marry her and live here on the farm,. She says her father will give me a good job in Ogdengberg, working in a factory for his brother. I tell her yes, sure we'll get married just as soon as I get out of the army. She says she will even go visit America with me in a few years. All the boys here on my outpost tell their girls the same thing. Some of them want to live in America and some want to stay here. It's going to be a sad day when we leave here. We all give them false names and addresses. I can just see their faces now when their letters are returned. One of my boys is engaged to three different girls. All of them live in this town too. God help him if they all get together. In this town there are only three German men that aren't married and one of them has a wooden leg and the other two are shell shocked. So you see we can pick out any girl we want and they are tickled to death to get one of us. They must figure it's their last and only chance to get married. I always pick out the girl who can cook the best. Some guys pick the girls with the best horses and others pick the best looking ones.

The company is swamped with letters from Belgium, Holland, France, girls all wanting to know when their boyfriends are coming back after them. The funny part is 90% of the guys are married already. I don't blame them a bit either. 75% of all the guys that are married in our outfit have received word from home that their wives are going out with 4F's back in the states. Seven guys in my company already have been divorced since coming to Germany. Some of them went crazy and took wild chances and got killed. The rest of them (guys that never looked at another girl) are going out with every girl that comes along. A few more are volunteering for the Pacific with the hope of getting killed. All I can say is I'm glad I never got married, and now I know better than to marry an American girl. Holland is the only country where the girls are true to their husbands.

Well the weather has finally changed and for the best. The sun is out all day every day. I don't know how long it will last but we are enjoying it now. I have a beautiful sunburn and it has helped my head a lot. I lay in the sun two hours every day. My knees don't bother me a bit now but I'll not tell that to the doctor.
Your Loving Son,
Bob

Germany
June 25
Dear Mom, Dad,
    Mail came in last nite for the first time in a week. I received your letters of June 12. I figured it was about time you were writing again Dad, thanks a lot. Mom you are acting just the way I thought you would when I told you about being wounded. In your letter you asked if the wounds still hurt and if I thought I would be sent home on account of them. I told you they were only small pieces of shrapnel and that it didn't bother me. I didn't even have them treated when I was hit. I took sulfur drug to keep it from getting infected and that's all. I have all the pieces out except for 1 piece on my lower ribs and it is only the size of a pill. I have no scars at all and no pain, and I am not coming home. So stop your worrying. What would you do if I were really wounded? If you act up when I get scratched what would you do if I got blown in half like most of the boys. One pal of mine has both legs and one arm blown off besides having the use of only one eye and he writes telling me how lucky he is not to have to fight any more. They are giving him wooden legs and arm and you won't be able to tell it when he gets out of the hospital. He has so much steel in him they call him 'Old Iron Sides' and he's having the time of his life. You told me to have all the fun I could over here Dad. Well you should know me by now. I have fun no matter where I am. If I have any more fun then I am having now I never would come home. As far as going out and having fun goes, I never had it as good in the states. Every day is filled from the time I get up til I fall asleep on my feet. I go fishing, horseback riding, ball playing, hunting and go to my girl's house for supper and then take her riding in a horse and buggy. Sometimes we go home early and play rummy at

her house. Some nites all the fellows bring their girl friends to one house and they play the piano and sing for us. Our favorite song is the famous German war song "Lili Marleen" which the Americans took over. All the girls over here have pretty voices and singing is their favorite pastime. We teach them the latest American songs. You ought to hear my girl sing "One Meat Ball". She doesn't know what the words mean but she loves the tune and sings it all day while she works. I had her listen to it over and over on the BBC and she can sing it better and lots funnier than the American girls on the radio. We have a recording of the Andrews Sisters singing "Don't Fence Me In", and the girls play it over and over and then copy it. Now they sing it the same style as on the record.

I had a funny thing happen to me the other nite that you will no doubt get a laugh out of. Every nite I leave Mimi's house about 1 o'clock and make that long lonely walk through the pasture and swamp to my outpost. It is dark as hell and a beautiful spot for an ambush so I always carry my pistol in my hand ready to shoot on the hike. Well for the past week I had the feeling I was being watched and once or twice I thought I saw a head duck in the weeds as I went by a particularly lonely spot. Well the nite before last I decided I'd carry my tommy gun just in case. Well sure enough just as I was coming by that same spot there was that head again. Well I let on like I didn't see it for a minute then I flopped on the ground and started to pump lead full automatic. When the gun was empty (30 rounds) I threw the gun and drew my pistol and ran and dove on the spot. Well I got up covered with blood and the damnedest feeling I ever had in my life. There on the ground was a billy goat cut almost in half. Well I didn't know what to do with the goat. If I left it there I would have to stop going to Mimi's house or else answer to her father for the goat. So I decided to take the goat home and bury it. I slung it over my shoulder and took off. I hadn't gone two hundred yards when here come my boys carrying the mail cross country. They heard the shooting and figured I was dead by now. Two of them fell in swamp mud up to their shoulders but got up and kept running. When I heard them coming I dropped the goat in the high grass and went to meet them. They were all excited and glad to see me alive but after seeing the blood all over me it was all I could do to keep them from killing every living soul within 5 miles. I told them to forget it and that I was alright. They kept after me but I wouldn't talk. We all went to bed and after I was sure they were all asleep I got up and headed for the swamp. Once again I started for home with the goat over my shoulder. It was just breaking day when Bob Cadmus could be seen pounding a stake in the ground with a sign on it 'Latrine Closed June 22, 1945'. When I woke up this morning I overheard one of the boys saying to the other, 'I wonder what he did with the body'. No I just couldn't stand the nickname 'Billy Goat Bob'.

Speaking of billy goats, Dad, your head must be as hard as a billy goat's. What are you going to tell the boss when that i-beam don't line up with the rest on account of the dent you put in it? Blame it on the steel mill no doubt.

Say Dad when you get time I wonder if you will let me know the number of bonds and their size that I have now. Also how much I have in the bank. What I want to do is get about $750 worth of bonds so I can lay my hands on $1000 ten years from now if I need. You can never tell when someone will need an operation or something and a thousand bucks would help out a hell of a lot. When I get that amount I am going to quit buying them and save the cash. What do you think of the idea?

Dad you asked me for about the hundredth time what I did to deserve the Bronze Star. Well I was already told about what I did to deserve it by one of your friends. It seems, sez she, some newspaper man must have seen me do some little thing and made a big story out of it so I was given a medal on the basis of his story. Well let's just let it go at that huh?

When I wrote and told you about the things I did and seen over here I didn't want you to get the idea I was a hero or anything like that. There isn't a thing over here that I seen or did that thousands of other boys didn't do and see the same and often more so than I did. I only write so you can get a true picture of how we live and die over here. I feel the same way as Ernie Pyle did. Maybe if the people know what war is really like they would try to prevent future wars. Even now with this war but half won the people are letting us down. From what I read in the papers the 'peacetime draft' has only half a chance of becoming a law. Even the VFW is fighting to make the law, if passed, so weak that it would be as good as none at all. What's the matter with the people in America? Don't they remember the death march on Rattan, or the Slaughter at Dunkirk? Each of which could have been prevented if we had troops to send in for support. I wish I could have been in some of those great battles just to see what it was like. I never fought in a battle with the knowledge that I was going to lose no matter how hard I fought. It must take a great man to fight under those circumstances. I wish I could say to myself I could do it. But there is only one way to find out for sure and that's the hard way.

Well the chow wagon just rolled up so I had better finish this letter up quick if I want to get anything to eat.

I hope you had a good time at the party's on Mothers Day. Write and let me know how it was.
Your Loving Son,
Bob

Germany
June 29
Dear Mother, Dad,

Roy's letter of June 19th just came in from Liege. He said he was about ready to leave the hospital in a day or so. If I only had known he was there I could have sent him the address of Clair Pierlot. He would have been able to live in class for a while, as Clair's father is the richest man in the city and one of the wealthiest men in all Europe. His brother was the Prime Minister of Belgium. He could have swam in her private swimming pool or played ping pong and done anything else he wanted. All he would have had to do is tell them he was my brother and he would have it made. I'm glad he found the ice cream store there. That was where I tasted ice cream for the first time in Europe. I couldn't pay for it either, Clair's father bought me all I could eat and then a pretty blond secretary from his factory bought me some more. When I broke down in front of their house I was a sorry looking sight. I hadn't shaved in over a month and my clothes were dirty and torn. They took me in and let me take a good hot bath in the first bathtub I ever seen in Europe. The maid washed and ironed my clothes and boy did I feel good being all cleaned up for the first time in months. They wanted me to quit the army and live with them. I was almost tempted to do it too. Boy wouldn't that be something. I would never have to work another day in my life.

Yes I'll always remember that visit to Liege as one of the highlights in my tour of Europe. There was one more thing about the family that I forgot to tell you. When Mr. Pierlot was taking me through one of his factories he took me down into an underground room containing hundreds of tons of tool steel all packed in grease which he had hidden from the Germans. It was the finest steel in Europe and vital to the German war industry. It all came from Luxembourg. Luxembourg is where Europe gets its finest steel.

If the Germans found out about him hiding the steel he would have been shot. You have to give a guy like that credit.

The weather has turned cold and windy again. It's the kind of cold that you feel no matter how much clothing you have on. Maybe after a good storm it will clear up again and get warm.

While I was over at Mimi's house last nite her father came in and said one of his bulls had fallen into one of the water filled ditches that surround every field over here. It's a mixture of water and mud and weeds. Well anyway we went out with a rope and pulled him out. All that was showing was his snout. When he got out he couldn't walk for a few minutes but finally managed to get up and shake the mud off himself. You should have seen him eat then. He was starved. Her father said it was probably in there over 24 hours. Mimi said they lose at least one or two cows a year that way. Her horse fell in about 6 months ago and all you could see was his nose sticking out. They managed to get him out with the help of a few neighbors. You ought to see our boys fall in those sink holes. Every day or so one of them come in covered with mud. The ground looks solid but when you step on it down you go. Most of the time they fall in when trying to jump the ditch. You pick out a spot on the other side that looks solid and get back and run as fast as you can and pray to God it's as solid as it looks. It doesn't take you long to find out after you land either. One of the boys has to cross 9 of those ditches to get to his girlfriend's house or else walk about 5 miles around to the bridges. So he got himself a long pole and pole vaults across. One nite while coming back in the dark he misjudged the jump and landed sideways right in the middle. He came home mad as hell and swore he never would go see his girl again. That nite he changed his mind and went anyway, and darned if he didn't fall in again.

Did my medals arrive yet? I hope they don't get lost in the mail as it takes months to get new ones. You said you were hoping Roy would miss the boat home, and maybe get to stay here as army of occupation. Well he hasn't a chance of staying here and what might happen is he will get attached to some other outfit that goes straight to the Pacific. I'm hoping he gets to his outfit before he sails. Besides he has a good job now and if he is put in another outfit he will no doubt be on the front lines again.

Well it's time for supper now so I'll close now and get this letter in tonite's mail.

Your Loving Son,

Bob

Dear Mother Dad,

I just wrote all the news to you this morning so I'll just say hello and good bye now. What I want to tell you is my address has changed. It is now APO 758 c/o P/M   NYC

I am now in the 7th seventh army. At present we are army of occupation. Maybe I will be lucky enough to stay in it.

God bless you both

Your Loving Son   Bob

Germany

June 30

Dear Mother, Dad,

Your letter of June 21 with the pictures just came in. Thanks a million Mom they turned out swell. You said you were sending one to Joe. Well if you haven't already sent it <u>don't do it</u>. I told you if he wanted one he would write and ask you for it. You see all but three of those guys in that picture are dead. One of them was Joe's driver and another one of his best friends. The rest were all guys that came in the army with us, including Harry Clark the tall skinny guy in the back row who was one of the best friends I ever had or ever will have. He saved my life on June 12 and got killed doing it. After his tank was knocked out he climbed up in plain view of the enemy to point out the gun to me. As he was pointing it out to me he was cut in half by machine gun fire from three different directions. Joe may not feel the same as I do about it. He may feel he was to blame for someone getting killed or it may bring back memories of the day he got hit. When a guy gets hit like he did his mind changes and they think different than you would expect. As for me, I'm proud of what my buddies have done and I want everyone to hear about what they have given in this war. I'll never forget what they have done for me and I don't want to forget it.

I just got a letter from Roy. He is in a redeployment center waiting to go back to his outfit. He met an old friend of mine back there. Ed Brady. Remember him? Ed is the guy I used to sleep with back in Camp Hood. He was with us until Thanksgiving when after seeing one of the worst sights in the world his nerves cracked. He was sent back to do a less hazardous job and ended up in a replacement Battalion as supply sgt. He issued Roy his clothing as he left the hospital. Roy says he is getting him out of all work while he is there. Ed would do anything for me. I'm glad Roy met him. Remember when I was home on furlough, it was his wife that called me up. I went to NY to see her. Yes Ed did a fine job over here, and he is one of the first guys I'm going to look up when I get back.

This living in a house isn't doing me any good Mom. I have a bad cold now for the first time since I came over seas. As long as I sleep outside in the mud and rain I'm ok, but as soon as we live like men instead of animals it's to bed we go, sick. I'll be alright in a day or two, I stay in the house all the time now to keep out of the damp windy weather we are having.

It's no use me writing Roy now until he gets back with some outfit as he will be moving so often the mail would never catch up with him. I'll write as soon as it is possible for him to receive the mail.

Pop Skelly wrote again (twice this week). He says Joe is getting some new kind of treatment for his eye. Let's wish him luck huh.
Your Loving Son,
Bob

Germany
July 2, 1945
Dear Mom, Dad,

There isn't much to write about, I'm just writing to pass the time away. It's raining like the dickens and the thunder and lightening make everything look like war. This will sure be a quiet 4th of July this year compared to last. At 12 noon last year every gun in France fired at once into the German lines. All our guns were fired into St. Lo.

Gosh I just got another letter from Roy, the third one this week. It was an old one, written when he first went to the hosp. He only writes about ten lines to a letter but I like to hear from him anyway. I had to write a letter to the M. Gen in Beale today. They wanted a full report on how the Russians were able to steal three cows, 2 pigs and a <u>Billy goat</u> without my patrols seeing them. I wrote and told them that the live stock must have been killed, butchered, and carried by hand cross country. I told them we have only enough men to patrol the roads and not the whole swamp and grazing land. Those darn Russians are such a lot of trouble to me, I tell them.

I don't suppose it is a secret any more about my trip from NY to Scotland. One of the sailors on my ship told me that our lead destroyer was named the Mahan. Does that name sound familiar to you Dad? That's the one that you took me to see when it was launched. You were on it when it slid down the weighs, or whatever you call them. The name of the ship that I was on was the Charles Carrol. Have you ever seen it? It was a Navy ship used for invasions. It carried LC1 landing craft on it. It was in on the invasions of Salerno.

Jack Benny is over here now and is on the radio at least twice a day. Not bad either. Charley McCarthy is on every nite too. The Andrew Sisters are on now. Phil Spitalny and his all girl orchestra just went off. Bob Hope is one, two or three nites a week. Amos and Andy are over here too but you have to be a magician to get to see any of them. I gave up all hopes of ever getting a pass so I think I'll send what money I have home. There is no sense in going to Paris anyway. It takes 6 months pay to spend a three day pass there. I think I'll just stay home here for the next couple of years and mark it down as lost time. If they ever do give me a pass I'll just go and look the town over and then take off for home.

July 4
Hello Again,

It's still raining and colder than ever. I went over to see Mimi last nite and met her three good looking cousins. Every time Mimi turned her back I would start fooling around with one of the cousins. During the nite I managed to date up two of them. One for Saturday the other for Sunday. Neither one of them knew about the other. It will be a good stunt if I don't get caught. They will come down and meet me at my house, as I can't get to their house without Mimi seeing me.

I was issued my new dress uniform yesterday. It consists of a Gen Ike jacket, a pair of pants to match, a tie and a cap. Boy it really looks good too. I haven't had time to have my stripes or Hershey bars sewn on yet and we can't get armored force patches. (Send me 5 or 6 if you can find any.) Well anyway I had on my purple heart ribbon, Bronze Star, Eto ribbon with 4 stars and arrow head and Honorable Service ribbon. The girls like that stuff. The people over here admire a soldier no matter what country he is from. They hate a loser, even their own sons and husbands. The prisoners that we have released can't even get food from their own mothers. The people hate them because we beat them. One guy just came home the other day after being a prisoner for three years. His wife refuses to live with him. She said he must have been yellow as he wouldn't have surrendered. Oh well, we should worry. That will teach them to start another war.

There isn't anything new so I'll close for now and finish tomorrow. Oh yes. I received your letter of June 25 yesterday.

July 5

Yesterday was the 4th of July but you would never know it, as there wasn't any noise of any kind. The boys back at the company area had a day off but we on the out posts resumed business as usual. Capt. Bulvin called me up on the telephone and asked me to dig up some food for the company as our rations have been cut

20%. There is practically no meat or potatoes coming in at all. We are getting rice instead. Of course that doesn't affect us out here as we have been finding food for ourselves anyway. I went out and bought 600 lbs of potatoes (30 marks) three bucks. I think that's a good price don't you? I have 1 hundred lbs of onions, and 1 hundred lbs of carrots coming tomorrow. $3 for both. The potatoes are small but it is rather early for new potatoes. When they are full grown they will cost $2 per hundred lbs. Tomorrow I'm going to buy a young cow for them if I can find a good one. It's funny how they always pick on me to find food when they go short. Every man in the company puts in a buck a month out of his pay for extra food, that's when I'll get the money I put out today. We also have a beer hall and they make a good profit on it. Beer is ½ a mark a glass, 5 cents. It costs them about 1 cent a glass from the Belgians. Wine is 10 cents a bottle, 1 qt. It costs the company nothing as it is captured stuff. So you see we have plenty of money in the company fund.

I don't think I ever told you about how the guys make money over here did I? Well anyway here's how it goes. The combat get nothing as we are too busy to loot most of the time. But it's the guys in back of us that make a fortune. Our gas truck driver for instance. We take a town and secure it, then he comes and gives us a load of gas. When his truck is empty he goes back to Holland for more gas. But before he leaves he loads his truck down with anything he can get. Yard goods were a big item in Munchen Gladback. He went into a clothing factory and took about a hundred rolls of cloth. Back in Holland he received $60 a roll from the shop keepers. One week he sent home $18,000 bucks. In Julich a guy got a truck load of leather from a shoe factory. He got $9000 bucks for it. Some take back clothing, dresses, suits (a hundred apiece). One guy goes into each house and removes the radio. Sometimes he takes back 20 radios at a time. He can get as high as $400 each. A guy got $1300 for an electric ice box. The only one I ever seen in Europe. I don't blame them a bit, I would do the same if I could. After all that's what the war was for, just to make money. Back in Holland money isn't worth anything. You can't buy anything at all with it. The people pay 6 and 8 bucks a pack for cigarettes so they can trade them off for meat or food of any kind. Cognac costs $40 a bottle if you slip him a cigarette with the money, but no cigarette no cognac for any amount. Well that's some nice news you don't read in the paper very often and that reminds me if I don't close this letter today this will look like a newspaper.

Give my regards to all the neighbors and tell Mrs. Dakter I was asking for her. I hope she gets well enough to enjoy herself after all the work she has done in the past 20 years.
Your Loving Son,
Bob

Germany
July 8
Dear Mom, Dad,

Your letter of June 26 just came after a week of no mail at all.

I sure hope you are right about Roy getting back to his outfit in time to catch the ship to the US. It would be swell if I could get home in time to see him before he leaves again, but that is impossible, so I'll just have to wait til he gets back from the Pacific or maybe meet him down there. I suppose I'll be heading for the 'big ditch' and the shortcut to hell before very many weeks. It's all for the best after all, I feel like a rat sitting here enjoying myself while those poor guys are still fighting down there. I know enough about that fighting to help those boys when they hit the beach for Tokyo. If we had some beachers with experience on Normandy we wouldn't have been stopped at St. Lo and there would have been less men killed on the beach itself. A new man can't realize that the faster he charges ahead the less danger there is. Once you stop you're done as you give the enemy time to organize and dig in. There is hardly a man alive today that landed on D Day and those that are can't fight any more. So you see the more guys like myself they have on the landing the better. You can't tell a guy what to do on an invasion you must show and lead him, and the only guys that can do that are the ones that done it before.

July 9/10

Well maybe I can finish this letter now without stopping if I'm lucky. The guys are all outside laying in the sun taking it easy.

I just finished taking a bath in a wash tub and it made me feel lots better as it is hot and sticky out today.

This afternoon I picked a gallon of red raspberries out in the yard. Boy they were swell. I know you would have liked them Dad. We had chicken for dinner and steak for supper, not bad chow for the army huh? We sent what was left of our cow into the company as we were afraid it would spoil with this warm weather. I am tired of steak anyway.

I received your letters of July 3 last nite. Thanks for writing Dad, I always like to hear from you. Don't worry about us not having fun Dad, except for a few bad days once in a while everything is swell. I go to Mimi's house almost every nite and we have lots of fun together. Her mother makes pudding or something every nite for us. Her Pop always opens a bottle of wine before I leave. It helps put me to sleep. I love the dog, he is almost the same as Wolf. He never gets tired of playing. I think I am going to get the pup sometime this week. Mimi's cousin is going to bring it to me from Beale the next time she goes in. I can't wait to see him, from what they say it ought to be a swell dog. I hear we are not allowed to take dogs home with us but we will see. If there is any kind of chance at all we'll both get home in a few years.

My points are still too low to do me any good Mom. 73 isn't very much. One darn kid would get me home for good. There are guys in my company with 3 kids and they still haven't enough. Most of the guys that came in with me have a kid and they are all set to leave as soon as their ship comes in. I sent you some flowers made of cloth that these Germans use to decorate their hats and dresses. I thought you might be able to use them so I sent them to you in an envelope. They usually put them in a bunch like a bouquet.

You said you were getting all set to give Roy a good time when he gets home. Well you are probably wasting your time as he will no doubt want to do things a little different than he used to. I know when I get home all I want to do is go to NY and see a good show without it being interrupted to change reels or because the generator broke down. Then I'm coming home and eat ice cream sodas til they come out of my ears. Most of all I want a roast beef dinner like you used to make every Sunday for dinner. The past few days I have had a longing for some of your potato salads, and boy what I wouldn't do for a doz ears of corn on the cob and a bowl of butter. It would help if Dad turned his back while I put the butter on. By the time I get home my plans will probably have changed again. So when I write and tell you I'm coming don't do anything til I get there. What the hell am I thinking of anyway, I won't be home for 2 years or more. So what's the use of thinking.

Well good nite and God bless you.
Your Loving Son,
Bob
P.S. send no packages until you get new address.

Germany
July12
Dear Mother Dad,
Yesterday was another one of those days, only a lot worse than ever. I received a phone call from Fortney saying the colonel was out making an inspection of all the outposts. Well I got the boys up and we cleaned the place up as best we could before he got here. He pulled up to my guard on the cross roads and asked him his orders and was well pleased. Then he came to the house. Well I seen him coming and ran out to meet him. I gave him a snappy salute and Sir'd him to death. He came in an looked around and was tickled to death with everything. He said (Cadmus! you have a fine outfit here.) He then turned in a report to Capt Belvin saying everything here was perfect. That only happens once in a sgt's army life if he is lucky. This all happened at 12:30 o'clock.

At 1 o'clock I was in the back yard picking berries when I heard a jeep pull up to the cross roads. I didn't pay any attention to it, but I still remember hearing it. Later when that guard came in he told me a captain from the 29th div was their and asked him his orders. Well I didn't think anything of it. At 3 o'clock a jeep pulled up with the Colonel, Capt Belvin. They both jumped out and came running in the house, and started jumping all over me. Who was on guard at 1 o'clock, says the colonel? I says, Corp Lang sir. He says get him out here. Well it was then that I found out that he had gone to sleep in the grass next to the road and the capt had to wake him up. Then Colonel Freeze started hollering at both of us. He said to me, what the hell kind of an outfit you running sergent!!!! Well anyway they first took Lang to the company guard house and decided to give me one more chance. He is getting a $2.50 fine and a month on the rock pile besides being busted from a cpl to pvt. Now their is an officer here three times a day to check the guards. I get everybody up at 8 o'clock in the morning to scrub the house till it shines. Here is what 's got me worried now. General Gerhart came back from the States last week and today he is going to inspect the good old 747. I would bet a thousand bucks my post will be his first stop. If he finds one thing wrong its the end of me. Well all I can do is hope. This is the part of the army that is really rotten. I get blamed for everything my men do. One guy gets in trouble and we all have to suffer for it. After going through the war with the stripes witch I didn't want it would be a shame to lose them now when the going is easy. That $33 bucks a month adds up after a while.

I received an air mail letter from Kitty yesterday (5 days) and she said you were up to see her and had my medals with you. Well I'm glad they got home alright but I don't like you showing them to everyone.

It is still nice and warm here, their is a cool breeze blowing in from the sea at nite and it makes sleeping good.

Well I think I'll take a nap until dinner time or until the General gets here.

Your Loving Son

Bob

July 13

Germany

Dear Mom Dad,

Their is still a few minutes yet before supper so I'll start another letter now and probably finish it tomorrow. Thanks for the info on my bank account Mom, I didn't think I had that much. $1623 altogether. Well its enough to buy a pretty good car anyway. Nelson Eddy is on the radio singing a crazy song called the Flea. He is on the radio every day over here. Bob Hope is on very often too. Bing Crosby is on from morning til nite. The best part about the radio over here is, their are no advertisements to listen to. Radio Luxemburg is contracted by U.S. but all the good programs come over the BBC. That is England's only big station and it is paid for from taxes and not by the soap companys. They have rotten programs of their own but they broadcast mostly all American programs. All they have of their own is 20 second news bulletins and opera and light classical. Grace Moare is on now singing the Blue Danube. You can hear that song at least 10 times a day over BBC.

I got to hand it to Tommy Albans, he is sure asking for trouble when he gets in the ground forces. Anybody can go to Paris and become an officer now but we have only had two guys in our company foolish enough to do it. They are begging for men to go to O.C.S now. All you have to do is say yes and they slap the bars on your shoulder. Their are very few soldiers who would lower themselves to the grade of an office after going through battle the hard way. So many officers are rotten bums and double crossers that it is really a disgrace to be an officer. After the war the guys aren't going to be to friendly with guys that were officers. Of course their are some good ones but they will have to suffer with the bad.

You asked about the Russians being in our area. Well it isn't the Russian soldiers that are around it is ex slave labor and prisoners of war. Most of them 2 or 3 million have been sent back to U.S.S.R. but their are thousands of them that are still running around. They disguise themselves as Germans and live off the land. They go around at nite and loot houses and steal what food they need. Others like it here with the German farmers, and refuse to leave. They live just like part of the family. Others from the cities, the ones used to work in factorys really hate the Germans and kill the ones they remember being bad to them during the war. Lots of them go way out in the country (mostly down south) kill two or three familys of Germans and then live in their houses and use the farm to raise food. When we first set the Russians free in the cities they went out and killed hundreds of towns people for revenge. We didn't try to stop them until we felt they had killed enough.

One Russian camp we had was really bad. The germans had worked them hard and then didn't feed them anything but potato soup. When we took that charge they had already killed everyone that ever looked crosseyed at them. When we took over the really bad Germans came back from hiding with the idea we would protect them. Well the Russians told us what the score was so we didn't guard the exits to good. Every morning you could see forty or fifty bodys laying around town. It was the funny'st thing you ever seen. The Russians at that camp all liked me and trusted me. They would tell me everything they did. Their one Russian that turned trator and was put in charge of all the Prisoners in the camp while the Germans were their. He use to beat them with a bull whip and send some to Nordhausen to be killed. Well one nite I was at one of their partys and I heard a lot of noise outside. I went out and their they were pounding the guy to death. There were to many people around so I stopped it. I sent the guy away, he lived with his wife in a beauty full house down the road. Then when it got dark I had the guard leave at the moors long enough for three or four of them to slip out. Well that's all we ever seen of the ex boss. That's the way we cleaned out a good part of Germany. We didn't trust the military gov and those kind of people had to be taken care of. The Russians are more like Americans than any other people in Europe (Even the English) they treat the Germans as good as we do (the good Germans) and respect the women as much as any other country. You people have been mislead as to the behavior of the Russians. They are just and honest, and independent. I never had a russian ask me for so much as a cigarette but when you offer it to them they go wild as they went 4 years without any. The French are the worst bums their are. They try to talk you out of everything you have. The English are the same way, but not as bad. In a french camp you cant pull out a pack of butts without 20 or 30 guys asking and begging for them. A Russian would die before asking for a favor. No I never have been in Berlin Mom. In fact I have never been east of the Elbe River. Nor do I desire to go. Well I hope Roy is home by the time this letter reaches you. When he gets their bust his leg for him if you can. All you got to do is hit it with a baseball bat while he is asleep. (But hit it hard) Take it easy in the bad weather Dad, you have already done more than your share in the war. Go out and enjoy your selves when you can.

Your Loving Son

Bob

Germany
July 16
Dear Mom Dad.
    Their hasn't been any mail for a couple of days but Im sure Ill get some tonite. I answered Kitty's letter yesterday, their wasn't anything to write so I just told her about the weather and things like that. Its hard to write to her as I don't do or see anything that she would be interested in. Summer is really here now! It's about 100 in the shade but their is a small breeze witch helps make it easy'er to stand. This is quite a change from the weather we were having up til last week.
    I had some more trouble with the guard last nite. About three oclock I was laying here in bed cussing the mosquitos and the heat. It was to much for me so I got up and made a cup of coffey and a few pancakes along with 6 or 8 eggs and a few slices of toast and butter. I figured the guard would like a cup of coffey so I carried out a cup to him and found him sound asleep in the grass next to the road. He had the alarm clock set to wake him when his turn was up. I was so mad I could have shot him in his sleep. I took his gun with out waking him up and came in and got another man up to go on guard. When I woke the guard up he didn't know what to say. If he wasn't so small I would have beat him to within an inch of his life. I brought him into my room and asked him if he wanted to go

into the company and be court marshalled or stay here and dig a hole 6x6x6 and stand the whole guard (12 hr) by him self tonite. He begged me to let him stay and dig. So today he is out in the back yard digging like mad. Tonite he goes on guard at 8 oclock and stays on til 8 in the morning. By then he should be pretty tired of standing. He is only 18 years old and never seen any combat. I told all of the boys that if any of them got caught sleeping I would be court marshalled as one guy was already caught last week. So I don't feel sorry for him at all. In fact I am giving him a break. If I turned him in he would get at least 6 months of hard labor. I believe after this he will be a good soldier, and if I sent him to the guard house he never would be any good as his records would always be against him.

Well the men fraternizing ban has been lifted. It only means we don't have to sneak around with the girls. Now we can go out in public with them.

Well Mimi will be here in a little wile so I had better close this letter and wash up a little. We are going riding along the coast and then go swimming at the pond in Ogdenburg. I will feel silly in her fathers bathing suit but its just the thing over here, so as long as my buddies don't see me in it I'm ok.
Well so long for today, I'll write soon.
Your Loving Son
Bob.

Germany
July 17
Dear Mom Dad,
Well the news that I have been waiting for for so long has finally come. Our outfit has been put back in Class A. We have fifty new replacements and are heading for some unknown training area. We are now the 747 AMPH Tank battalion. We are going to get new assault tanks made to go in water as well as land. They are going to be used to establish a beach head on (?) They have a 75 mm HOW and a 37 mm rifle. We will land a half hour before the inf to clear the beach so they can land. When the inf lands we will spearhead their attack. Our tanks will be launched from LCT's about 5 to 10 miles out at sea. I'm so excited I can hardly wait to get going. Just think I will have been in on two of the greatest attacks in the history of the world. Besides it will be my chance to kill some japs. I always wanted to kill a jap and now I got my chance to kill them by the hundreds like we did over here. You can tell Roy when he lands I'll be there to meet him.

We have a very small chance of getting to the States before we go. Now it looks like they are going to work hell out of us. The landing will probably come off in about 6 months. We are getting 15 weeks training. Maybe some of it will be in the States. We will know for sure in the coming week. I would like to see you before I leave but maybe it would be better not to get home first. It might be hard to leave home again. Mom please don't start worrying again now! A lot of things can happen in 6 months. Besides I really want to go now. I have had plenty of rest and this quiet life is driving me nuts. I would give a hundred bucks to hear a

1400 gun barrage again. The noise and excitement of war gets into you after so much of it. The sound of a thousand bombers going over is something to hear. And to see an invasion fleet of 4000 ships all open up with their ack ack guns at nite is worth a million bucks of anybody's money. Can you imagine what 25 thousand automatic anti aircraft guns all shooting tracer bullets would look like! I say 25000, there were probably a lot more. Even the smallest invasion boat had 4 mach guns and some of those battle ships must have had hundreds of them. Well its a great game this war, as much as I hate it, I can't help but want to see and hear some of those sights again. If I get the chance to come home, I'll sure be there so don't worry about that.

We are still an outpost doing army of occ work and I don't know when we will leave but I'll write you all the details so don't worry.

It is cool today and thundershowers are all around us. Well I'm going to wash and shave now as I have a date with Mimi tonite. Blacky and I have a buggy here with double seats so we are going out riding with our girls together.
God bless you both.
Your Loving Son
Bob

July 26, 1945
Gent, Belgium
Dear Mom Dad,
Well we got the bum's rush out of Germany the other day. We were loaded on trucks Monday morning and drove 300 miles to Gent by midnite. We came through Achimel and Antwerp and many other large cities in Germany, Holland and Belgium. It was a swell trip and the weather was fine. We expected to hit Antwerp and sail for the states to get our training. We drove right by the docks and seen all the boys loading up to sail for home. We sure felt good for a while. However the trucks never stopped and we ended up 50 miles away in this city. Our camp isn't ready for us yet so we are right here in the middle of the city. The city is as good as any city we have in America. Everything is modern. Neon signs, fluorescent street lights, doz's of movies all with American pictures. The stores all have plenty to sell and their doesn't seem to be a shortage of anything. Their are hundreds of cars, (all American) and they have gas for all. I can't understand it. The people all speak English and are not too hard to get along with. Yesterday I had ice cream for the first time since last year when I got it in Liege Belg. (about 10 months ago.) Their are ice cream stores on every block and I hit them all. They even have soda. The bars all have beer and plenty of whiskey. Shoe stores all have hundreds of pr of shoes on display in the windows. I have pictures of an old castle here that I'm going to send you. I was all through it and seen some strange sights. Their were torture chambers, dungeons with the bones of the prisoners still there. The castle was the strongest fort in Belgium in the 12th cen-

tury. The people came from miles around to be under its protections and thats why this is such a big city.

Well to get back to the point, we are going to a camp about 20 miles from here and train with the new AMPH tanks. Our training will end in Oct sometime then we will head for Marseilles France to get the ship for the SP. I hope by now Roy is home. He sure earned the break. Maybe I'll see him in Tokyo.

Well I'll close now as I have a date for three o'clock. We are going to see a movie then down to a swell joint for a chicken dinner. I'll write as soon as something else happens.

APO 562 (Third army)
Love
Bob

Holland
July 28, 1945
Dear Mom Dad,

We are now in our training area by the sea. It's just fifty feet to the canal (Gent) from my tent. One mile to the sea, and 40 miles to Antwerp, and 5 miles from the Belgium border. The canal is 100 feet wide and 173 feet deep. Large ocean liners go by my front door all day. Some are American and are on their way to home. We talk to the sailors as the ships go by. Our camp is nothing but tents that we put up in an open field and nothing else. It's enough to drive a guy crazy after living the way we did in Germany. We get paroles but no one has enough money to go on them. It costs a guy at least $100 a nite in town. I went broke in one nite after saving money since last November for a pass.

Our new Amph. tanks came in today and by tomorrow we will be training in them. They are going to take us ten or twenty miles out to sea in an LCT and let us drive back in at nite. That calls for a course in navigation which starts next week. That's how we are going to invade Japan. The first thing the japs will know about it is when they see our tanks drive up out of the water onto their beach. The inf. comes in an hour after we launch. The guys are not feeling too good about it now but after a while they will begin to forget the rotten deal we got and go to work with a smile. We figured we at least earned a trip home and were really counting on it. That's why we feel so bad about it. Then seeing all those Am. ships heading home every day doesn't make us feel any better either.

Well their isn't much to write about any more, so don't expect too many letters. I'll write once in a while but don't feel much like writing any more. A guy gets a little tired of being a sucker all the time. Don't get me wrong Mom, I want to go to the Pacific but I do feel we deserve a pass to the States first.
There has been no mail this week but some should come in soon now. Here is my new address.
APO 562
Your Loving Son   Bob

Holland
July 30
Dear Mom Dad,

Well everything is going full blast now. We have our new AM tanks and are training from dawn to dark. It won't be long before we are ready. Their has been a new change though. Their is now a 50/50 chance of coming home first. It might be just a lot of talk to boost our morale or it might be true I don't know. I quit smoking today, not because I wanted to either. It's just that I couldn't see smoking cigarettes when they are worth 18 cents each. A guy offered me 10 guilders (37 1/2 cents is a guilder) for a pack of cigarettes. Well I sold him my two weeks ration of 14 packs. That gave me 140 guilders or $53 for my two weeks smokes. I also sold my candy (6 bars) for $42 and my soap for $12 (3 bars of soap). The whole works cost me $1.15. Pretty good profit huh? Now I can go on pass for another couple of days. I'm going to have all the fun I can now that I know I'm in for another war. We get paid in a few days but I only draw $18 a month so it looks as if I will have to quit smoking for the duration.

We are all getting used to the idea of going to the Pacific now without a trip home so things are starting to look better now. We are wondering if we can finish off the japs before you people start another war with the Russians. All our officers have 85 points and are going home as they just made anybody that would take it an officer and away we go. Capt Bulvin has 87 pts because of his kid. It was a good thing he had that kid or he would be stuck too.

Fortney the guy that came with me on June 15 right after D day only has 53 pts so you can see how hard it is to get 85. A combat man just can't live long enough to get it unless he has the kids.

Their has been no mail so their is nothing for me to write. I hope you're having good time on your vacation this year. I'm glad Roy is staying home for a while. If I can find exactly where he is I may get to see him. He will have to tell me as I have no way of finding him any other way.

Well I'm going to dive out the front door into the canal for a swim before it gets too cold so good nite and God bless you.
Your Loving Son
Bob
P.S. We have a new chaplain now and I think he is from N.J. He is very good and everyone seems to like him.

Holland
August 02, 1945
Dear Mother and Dad,

The mail started to come in again. Last nite I got a letter from you and one from Kitty. Boy was I glad to hear about Roy. Good old Ed Brady, I'll never be able to thank him enough. It sure is a load off my mind to have him safe again for a wile. I was just assigned my new tank. It isn't the one I will use in the Pacific but it is one just exactly like it. their are only three of them in Europe and they just came over this week. It has no gun on it like the other tanks we just got. No gun except a couple of mach guns that is. In place of a gun it has the new rocket launcher on it. It has sixty barrels on it and can be fired one at a time or all sixty at once. Now my job will be to (drive or sail) my tank into the sea out of sight of land and sail up to with in 100 yds of the beach and let go all rockets at once then run like hell for the open sea before they shoot back. We then load up again and wait til inf and regular tanks in on the assault landing. When the beach is taken we will be finished until we are ready for another landing. It looks good to me so far so I'm not worrying so much. We were told to be ready to leave some time in (Sept) either for the Pacific direct or to the States and then the SP.

So you can expect to see me around the 1st of Oct or not at all. I sure hope I make it home first but if I don't, please don't let it worry you. I'll get home some day for sure.

If I knew exactly where Roy is I could go see him but up til now I have no idea how to find him.
Well that's it for today
Hope to see you soon
Your Loving Son
Bob

August 12
Holland
Dear Mom and Dad,

I am leaving for Brussels on a 15 hour pass tomorrow morning so I want to get rid of this money order before I go. The only reason I'm going is to see what the joint looks like. I'm only going to take $30. with me so that will be about all I will be able to do. Some of the guys went last Sunday and spent $200. I made up my mind that no amount of fun is worth that much.

There has been no change here as far as going home is concerned. The shipping orders are still for Sept 6 or 7, but if the war is really over the orders no doubt change. That doesn't bother me a bit. Now that things have changed I'll tell you what it means for me.

The new amph tank is a death trap and is certain death for any one who lands with one. As mines will blow them in half, a machine gun can cut them in half. Any kind of shell will sink them and we were told that and we have even seen it on the Rhine with the aligators. These are the same as the aligator except they have a gun on them and are not different. They are very good for landing as they do plenty of damage before they are discovered but once they discover us we would be wiped out to the last man. Now you can see why we didn't feel so good about it. We don't mind doing so much, its just the thought of not seeing home first after all we went through. When the war was on, we never did expect to live more than an hour or two and didn't care much. But when V E day comes and here I was still alive I first wanted to see home once more. We never even thought about being lucky enough to make it until V E day. Then the news about us going strait to the Pacific in a suicide out fit, well you can imagine how we felt. I did want to go but not until I seen you and Dad once more. I wanted to go with Roy in the inf. I felt I could save a lot of lives with my experience, maybe even Roys. Now with this new bomb, it will be safe to make the landing so I'm not worried even if it isn't over.

When we first got the news we were studying Jap tactics and things. Then we were issued the Momsen Lung for when our tank gets sunk. You see in these new tanks you are locked in and when she sinks you go down with it and it takes time to get your hatch open so they will give you these oxygen tank affairs to help you live long enough to escape. Well when we heard the news it was all we could do to hold back the tears. You can imagine how the other out fits next to us feel. They were given our shipping orders to go strait and we got theirs to go to N.S. first.

Well all our worrying are over for a while so we can sleep sound tonite.

Two of our boys got drunk and fell in the canal out side my tent and drowned. We haven't been able to find the bodies yet. We have been draging the canal for two days now with no luck. I'll let you know how we make out tomorrow,

Your Loving Son
Bob

August 13
Holland
Dear Mom and Dad,

I just received your letters July 31, and its sure swell to hear from you again once and a wile. Well the war is still on but there is no need to worry about it any more. As far as our new job is concerned anyway. With the new bomb we will be able to land any place we want along the jap beach, with no loss of life. We are continuing with our training first as if nothing had happened. It sure is a load off our minds to know we won't have to go through it all over again.

Yesterday was my pass day and I had a very nice time in Brussels, the capital of Belgium. We spent the best part of the day first sight seeing and eating. A few of the things we seen were, The Kings Palace, the tomb of the unknown soldier, Parliament, the Arch of Freedom, (the botanical gardens). The last was very beauty full and only went so I could tell you all about it when I get home. I'm sure you would have liked to seen it Every thing was beauty full as the weather was fine and all the flowers were in bloom. The whole city is covered with flowers and large beautiful trees. The buildings are all modern just as in the states. Their are (on the average) three ice cream stores to the block. They have every thing and any thing you want. All you need is enough money to pay for it. I'll tell you all about it in a few weeks when I get home. Every thing is still the same. We are supposed to sail early in Sept. Of course if the war should end orders are all going to be changed, but who cares.

I hope you two have a swell time on your vacation. It seems to be a funny way to spend a vacation just around home, but if that's what you like its the only thing to do.

You asked about the puppy. Well when I heard that we would take our training over here I decided not to take him as he would be too big to hide by the time we would sail. I wouldn't want to have to shoot him just before we leave as he is such a swell dog.

Its about time Mr Merrit died, I have been expecting that news for years and years.

Gee that picture sure looks good. That suit looks swell on you Dad. The sleeves look a little long but otherwise it's a fine looking job. You look as though you lost a little weight Dad. I put on about 40 lbs. since VE day. I'm now 242 but its starting to go down again now that I am sweating about coming home. Don't worry though, I'll be home before going to the Pacific. Even if I don't their is no longer any danger in any new jobs now that we have the new bomb.
The medals I sent you should have come by now. If they don't reach you by next week I'll send out a tracer.
God bless you both
Your Loving Son
Bob

August 16   **V-J DAY**
Holland
Dear Mom and Dad,
    Your mail along with the great news will make this a red letter day for me. We did no celebrating at all. It no doubt sounds funny to hear that from me, but news that it's over I sort of have a funny feeling in my stomach. It was all as useless, here we are in the same boat as before the war. Nothing gained and all those boys back there in a lonely grave for what! In a few months we will all be hunting for jobs again and the war will soon be forgotten. At least we did accomplish one thing. Now with the new bomb, it would be foolish to even think of another war. If we do have another war their will be no suffering, it won't last long for that.

    Dad I got your letter telling about you borrowing a few bucks from my account. Well I wish you would look at it as our account. I thought I made it clear before I left that when ever you needed any thing of mine you were just to take it and forget it. When I was down, you gave me all you had and never complained about it. Just forget about it and don't worry about paying it back. I don't need a dime of it. You mentioned that I would need it to get married with and all that bunk. Well I have no intentions of ever getting married as in all my life I have never met a girl that I would ever think of marrying and if I do find one she probably wouldn't have me so forget about it. If you ever need money again just take it and don't cash in any more of your bonds.

It looks like I'll just have to wait and see Roy when I get home as he is to far away for me to get to him with out getting my self in trouble. If the war didn't end when it did I was going to see him any way, but now it wouldn't pay. Boy you can't even imagine how much better I feel now that Roy is out of danger. I didn't mind the danger as much for my self, but when Roy came over it made things ten times as bad.

Last February when we crossed the Roer River at Julich, I figured my chances were about 10 to 1 against me making it. We knew the exact plans for the crossing three months in advance as the crossing was supposed to be made in the first week of Dec. Then came the big counter attack and the whole 9th army was transferred to the first army. All except the 29th div.

The Germans planned to cut north to Antwerp and trap us along with the British 2nd. Our tank btn. and the 29th were holding all the ground between Aachen and Julich. Well we were in a hell of a fix. We worked 14 hours a day in the rain snow and mud digging trenches, laying thousands of mines and stringing barbed wire across every inch of ground.

Well Christmas Eve, and Christmas day and the next day were the three days that saved us from being wiped out. Our planes had perfect weather those three days and knocked out most of the supply lines so the jerries couldn't make their final push to Antwerp. Well we were pretty safe then for about a week until they sent over every German plane that would fly. We got bombed day and nite. We couldn't sleep as paratroops were being dropped every nite and we had to guard against them.

New Years morning was the worst. Seven planes were shot down in our area and I seen all seven. It was some show. Then we started to get ready for the push across the river again. Every day we lost men on account of their nerves. The whole out fit was going mad. Then you wrote and told me Roy was over here. Well that was about all I could stand. I tried to find out where he was so I could shoot him in the leg but we pushed off before I found out. (Lucky for him now)

Once we took Julich and I heard the 3rd army tanks were on the roll I felt better. Once the tanks get going the inf. is safe. Then the news came of the 87 going to the Pacific. Roy wouldn't have had a chance. I put in a request to join the inf. in his out fit as I figured I could see to it that he wouldn't. I make any landing on the beach one way or another. Plans came the morning that we were frozen to this out fit and that we would also leave for the S.P. in these iron coffins. My nerves were really shot then. I got so bad for a while I thought I would have to go to a rest camp for a few months. Then you wrote and Ed Brady was taking care of Roy and my worries were over. I didn't mind going to the Pacific when I heard that, all I wanted was a furlough in the States before I left.

Then came news we would not get to the states. That hurt a lot so we all think we did at least deserve that much. Then they said we had a 50/50 chance of going home. Later came word we were going home.

Now this war is over and we probably won't come home for a few more months but I'm tickled to death anyway. Well I don't know what is the matter with me now but I am nervous as a cat. I stopped going to town as the ride almost drives me nuts. The drivers are always drunk and the road runs for 20 miles right along the edge of the Gent Canal and every time we make the trip we almost run in the water at least once. The water is 150 feet deep and we just had two guys drown in it just outside my tent. I'm even afraid to walk near the water in the day-time now.

If I have fetch out more dead men over here or see any more of the boys get killed I'll just have to quit and come home. The other day when the news first came that the war was over I quit getting up for revelry and I refused to go near those darn tanks. I gave orders if any one wakes me up before 9 in the morning I'll beat them to an inch of their life. So far no one came near my tent in the morning. Yesterday the first sgt. asked me to give a class on the new flame throw-er. I told him, - (well any way I don't think he will ask me again.)

There is nothing wrong with my eating though. I eat like a horse. I'll bet I put on at least 10 lbs. a week.

Well it's time I quit telling you my troubles and get some sleep so I'll finish in the morning.

August 19
Hello again,

I have been so busy the past few days I just couldn't get around to finishing this letter. I went and seen a couple of shows down in the little town down the road. Today I went to the dentist and had a wisdom tooth pulled and my jaw feels like it's broke. Maybe it would be a good thing if it was. I might lose a little weight.

I first got another of your letters from the lakes. It sure looked like a swell spot.

Gee I really feel lots better now that I got away from camp for a few days. When I get home I'm going fishing for about two weeks and I think I will be my self again. Fishing always did make me feel better, it sort of takes your mind off your trou-bles.

Well no matter what happens now, we should be home within a few months. I hope I get home by Christmas as I hate to be away at that time of the year. So far I have been lucky that way. Its only last Christmas that I missed. Lets hope we can all be together this next one.

The boys are coming in now and they are feeling a little high, so I had better go and put the worst ones to bed before they fall in the canal.

Guess what just happened today. I was finally offered a pass to Paris and I haven't got a dime so I had to turn it down. And I just sent you a money order for $50 too. I'll sell my pistol this week if I can't dig up some money some place. I hate to sell it as three men died for me first so I could have it. Poor boys? ha. ha. Did I ever tell you about my new one? Boy its a swell gun! It's a Belgium made gun with an American patent. It's all blue steel and shoots a 9mm bullet. It holds 15 shots. Maybe I'll keep it yet. Its the most accurate pistol I ever had.

Sunday

Well its about time I mailed this letter so I'll close now and mail it.

Your Loving Son

Bob

August 21

Terneuzen Holland

Dear Mom and Dad,

By now you are no doubt back from your vacation and all tired out. Well I have been getting enough rest for all of us anyway. We have to get up for revelry every morning at 6:30 but as yet I never have found enough ambition to get out of my sleeping bag before 9 o'clock. They did make a stink about it for a while but now they just got use to the idea.

Well the rainy season is here I guess, if it isn't the rainy season its a reasonable facsimile as it rains at least two thirds of every day. But don't get me wrong, I'm not kicking as when it rains we stay in bed all day.

There is still no news as to when we will move out of here, but we are hoping to come home very shortly. If we don't leave here soon then we would all like to go back to Germany for another vacation.

I got a letter from Kitty yesterday and answered it last nite. She says she hasn't had a letter from Roy in a long time. I explained to her that it is hard to write when you are running around like he is. I haven't even written to him in about three months. He knows every thing that I do about Europe so what use is their in writing.

Gee since I have been going out to the movies at nite I feel lots better. The shows are rotten and the sound is so poor you can't hear half the show but it is a change. Are all the pictures as bad as I think they are, or is it just me? I walk out on most of them. Well I think I will finish this letter tomorrow as their isn't anything else to write.

August 25

Hello Again,

Many days have gone by since I started this letter but aside from being busy, there hasn't been anything to write about. Our training has been doubled and they are more serious now then before the war ended. I'll explain why later.

We have a new company commander and he seems to be a swell guy. Captain Belvins seen him before he left and told him about me (I just found out). Well anyway I have been sleeping all morning and never going out in the tanks. A few days ago I was pulled out of bed and told the Captain wanted me. Well I thought the guy was a damned lire as the Captain never heard my name, or at least I didn't think he did, so I hit the guy with a 13EE and went back to sleep. Well about two minutes later up came the Captain and he told me I was his driver and to get ready to go to the motor pool. Well I didn't like losing my (rocket ship) but the capt has the best tank in the outfit so I didn't mind.

Well within the hour I was in my life preserver, had on my (breathing aperatus T-1) (something like Momsen lung) and on my way out to sea at the head of the fleet. It felt like old times leading the company again. We went out to sea in column formation and then swung into a V formation and then the inverted wedge. It looked fine. All formations are ordered over the radio in my tank and it is beauty full to watch all the tanks turn at once into a different formation. We went 14 miles out to sea <u>with</u> the <u>tide</u>. The wind was blowing with us and the sea was really rough but everything went fine until we turned around to come back. The waves came right over the tank and down the driver's hatch into my lap. It would almost wash me out of the seat every time they came over. My ear phones got wet and I couldn't hear a word from the turret so I had to drive opened up. Well the water hit me so fast I couldn't even breath much less see where I was going. In between waves I managed to keep on my course. Well the same thing was going on in all the other tanks to so you can picture in your mind what kind of formation we held. I finally pulled out the hand throdel and let it go its own way wile I took off my pants, shirt, and shoes. I then checked my Momsen lung and I made sure my life preserver was tied tight around my shoulders. There is nothing like being carefull as these tanks have a great habit of diving into and out of those big waves and keep right on going down. The corps XVI (that's 4 tank btns.) lost about 4 tanks a day that way. Some times the engine quits and when it quits the pumps stop, and when they stop it's time to start swimming. The pumps will pump out 5000 gall. per minute when they run but once they stop you got one hell of a time trying to splash the water out. Well after a two hour battle with the sea we made it back to land. We didn't lose a tank but we did almost lose a couple of them, a big English ship went right between two of them and they were only 75 yds apart. Well anyway we all were soaked and it was raining and cold (about 50 dg) so I decided to go in for a swim as the water is warm. I swam for about 2 hours and then put on my rain coat and we had classes for two hours. We were all sick by then but the Col said it was good for us and we would get used to it sooner or later any how.

We then had to practice diving with the (Lung). We dived down to a sunken tank, crawl in side of it and then come out and come to the top. We only go down 25 feet but you would be surprised at the pressure even at that depth. We have enough oxygen to last 6 minutes under water. Thats for when the tank sinks and you are traped inside. Their are two exits so with the extra oxygen tank you have plenty of time to get out.

Well we got back to our tents late that nite still wet and cold and sick. The doctor gave us the old stand by (codein and aspirin) and we were better before morning. That codein is great stuff.

Well that is what we are doing every day now. Monday we are to be put on review for all the big shots. We are to go out to sea in an English LCT and then get dumped off about 15 miles out. Then we will come in battle formation and attack Terneuzen. All during the week we will be inspected and next friday our training will be over. Then we are heading home early in Sept. Now here is the catch !!! I may or may <u>not</u> come with the out fit. They <u>may</u> take us high point men out of the out fit and use us for army of acc. They <u>may</u> take us to Caliphania and finish training their new men. The 747 <u>is</u> going to the Pacific and <u>I</u> may <u>have</u> to go with it, but I don't think I will. The out fit is going down their with the tanks and patroll the islands <u>and</u> their are <u>500</u> islands still held by the japs and only 1/2 are expected to surrender. (this is not public) (restricted)

So I will probably be home sometime in Sept or Oct. But their are a <u>1000</u> big IF's.

Good nite and God bless you

Your Loving Son

Bob

August 28, 1945

Brussels

Dear Mom and Dad,

I'm in Brussels on a 3 day pass again. So don't expect mail for a while. Our orders have been changed!! We won't be home in Sept. maybe Oct.

This red cross pen is rotten, so I had better sign off.

I am having a swell <u>time</u>.

Love

Bob

August 29

Holland

Dear Mother and Dad,

The big news started coming in the day before yesterday and been getting thicker and thicker with each passing hour. First the news account of the atom bomb. Then Russia, and now they say the Japs quit. The news came in this afternoon and I am still trying to keep myself from believing it until it is confirmed. If this new bomb is as good as they say, I hope those japs don't quit. If we wipe them out it will save a lot of trouble later.

Our orders up until tonite were to sail for NY on Sept 6th. But!! Now if the war is over all that is out. So I'll let you know everything as it happens.

I got a letter from you tonite for the first time in a week or two. It's finally starting to come in. I wrote you 3 long letters in the past week but things changed so fast that the letters were all wrong so I threw them in the fire before they got mailed!

I'll write soon as anything happens. Your Loving Son , Bob

August 29
Brussels
Dear Mom and Dad

(*smudged, unreadable*) my three day pass here in Brussels and having the time of my life. This is better town for a G.I. than either Paris or N.Y. Their are better nite clubs, more girls, better transportation and the best part is its all <u>free</u>. When you get a three day pass your taken care of by the army and Red Cross. The Hotel is free and every thing in it is for our convenience. We have nice beds with <u>sheets</u>, showers, dining room with swell chow, free beer and whiskey and Coca Cola for 5 cents a glass. Crullers for all hours of the day. You can sleep as long as you want, stay out all nite if you want and not an officer allowed in the joint. The army has a G.I. night club called (G.I. Joe) all you need is your 3 day pass for admission. You can take your girl friend in with you. They have a swell band and dance floor, Ice cream fountain, bar, and a hundred Belgian girls to keep the beer or Coca cola glasses full. Then down the street is the A.B.C. theater, run by the U.S. Army for all allied troops. You are also allowed to take a girl with you their. The show is all Belgium and it sure is good. Its a better stage show then you can see in Radio City.

Then their is civilian entertainment here is where you need <u>plenty</u> of (<u>gelt</u>) Every hundred feet is a nite club. Well you cant help but want to go in so you go in and take a seat and order a short beer so you can watch the floor show. Well its (<u>sounds</u>) cheap doesn't it? Well the beer costs 20 franks (43 cents) a glass plus 10% tip. Well thats a buck shot already and all you got is a seat and a beer for you and your girl. Well before your done you have three or four beers a piece and you find you have spent like seven or eight bucks and the nite is still <u>very</u> young. Next you go to the ice cream store and have a choc. sundae (200 franks) or $4.20) with a glass of water included. Next you hit a lunch wagon or Cafe where you will no doubt buy a stake or pork chop dinner. That sets you back 400 franks for you and the girl. Ah well thats 8 more bucks shot but you aren't hungry any more (Rice fills you up). So you take your girl home and make a date for the next nite. You now have a whole day to figure out how to dig up enough money for the next nite.

Well here is how I did it. I left camp with $18. bucks and 6 packs of butts. Now after spending 3 days and 2 nites here I still have 40 bucks. I sold the butts for $3.00 a pack. That gave me 36 dollars all to gether. I bought a pistle for 30 and sold it for 45. I sold my liquor ration ticket for 10 and bought 2 more for 5 each and in turn sold them for 10 each. Then I bought 2 cartons of cigaretts for 40 and sold them for 60. My rations came due yesterday so I got 7 more packs for

5 cents a pack and sold them for 3 dollars a pack. 1 plug of chewing tobbaco 5 cents and sold for 2 bucks. 6 packs of gum 50 cents a pack. I sold the sweatter you sent me when I was in Texas for 20 bucks. Well that and a few more items gave me a happy three day pass in the most modern city in Europe.

By the way order a pair of 13EE (Black) low-cut dress shoes from Chrisanti. Pay for them out of the $50 I just sent you. Four months have gone since VE day and that gives me 8 more points so now I have 81 The score is 80 so some day soon I should be strolling down Gresser Ave. Everything is a mess over here so don't expect me right away. We were supposed to sail on the 7th of Sept but now we will probably be held up for a while. I'll be going back to camp tomorrow nite and there better be some mail there for me.

Well I just have a half hour to meet Gara, so I had better sign off til I get back to camp. Gara Bushmen, thats the girl I am going with here.

God Bless you till we meet again

Your ever loving son

Bob

Sept 2, 1945

Holland

Dear Mom Dad,

Well I just returned from Brussels after an extended three day pass. I say extended as we did extend it to 5 days. We had a pretty good officer in charge and when we told him we didn't want to leave just yet, he said take another day. It happened again the next day and this afternoon he asked us if we wanted to stay until next Tuesday as we have Sunday and Monday off anyway. We were all broke so we decided to come back today and lay around until Tuesday.

I am going to ask for another pass Tuesday so I can go see some friends of mine in France. If I knew where Roy was I would go see him. He never wrote and told me how to get to him so I just won't go. I stand in pretty good with the Company now as they want me to drive the C.O. I can always get out of it by my orders from the hospital. They know that and are treating me royal so as to keep me driving. So I'm going to make the best of it while it lasts. I'm going to tell them some friend of mine is stationed in Mathieu France and is going to the S.P. and I want to see him before he leaves. You know who lives there don't you? Mme Jean La Hoste and Theresa the flying bomb. They have been writing to me and begging me to come pay them a visit.

If you remember, that was the town that I had to drive over the railroad trestle 200 feet above the Muse way. The jeries had tons of TNT all set to blow it up but Dr. La Hoste and his FF1 kept sniping the Germans off as they tried to light the fuse. And the place where the Germans had the 6 hostages locked in the church and we were preparing to shoot them when we arrived. Also the place where we rescued the 4 American priests who were hiding there for 7 months. Jean had seven copies of my picture made (you know the one I sent you) and gave them to the people that were locked in the church. They all asked Jean to write and ask me to come to their village for a visit. Well I have been thinking it over for a long time and have finally decided to <u>try</u> and go.

John Huey my buddy from Roselle went back to a little town that he was first to enter and the people made big banners and strung them across the street saying 'Liberator Returns!!' Then the whole town turned out and had a big chain dance and and later a wild party in his honor. Well he was embarrassed to death as those French people made such a big fuss for nothing it really scares you. So I'm not going to tell them I'm coming, if I can get away I'll go and if things look unsettled I'll hang around so as to be sure not to miss any ship heading my way.

Well this is a big day in Holland. It's the Queen's Birthday. So everybody is taking a three day vacation and doing things up in a big way. The town near here Terneuzen is decorated up beautiful. Millions of flowers decorate every phone pole the length of the town. Great orange paper lanterns are strung across the road every 25 feet or so. The front of each house is covered with flowers and the dogs are dressed up in red orange and blue paper. The kids are all dressed up in false faces, clown suits and big paper hats. All the hay wagons were decorated into floats, and the horses all have their shoes shined and have wreaths of flowers around their necks. The people are all singing and dancing in the streets. You can hear them here at camp four miles away. It's one of the greatest celebrations I ever seen. Sept 3rd the day after tomorrow is Liberation Day in Belgium. The 101st airborne div (The defenders of Bastogne) are putting on a big parade in Brussels and are getting a citation from the Belgium Gov. The 747 the (conquerers of Bastogne) get a day of rest, thanks to the Atom Bomb.

While I was away on pass, strange things were going on back here. Four men have gone crazy and the rest are nervous wrecks. It must be the war catching up with us. Remember a few weeks ago, I wrote you and said my nerves were going on me? Well I fought it and won. I thought it was only me and it really had me worried. I kept eating and tried to get lots of sleep and when I wasn't doing anything I would read all the funny books I could find. Well I'm back to normal now and fit as a fiddle. We made the trip in from Brussels in two hours (65 miles) and I didn't feel the least bit nervous. I wish I could do something for these boys, but I guess they will have to do like I did, fight it. It was the same thing in combat, when you felt yourself slipping you could let yourself go or you could fight it. Some did fight it but others felt sorry for themselves and ended up in a 4F outfit. Thats what kept me going, I could just picture myself with a white helmet and an MP arm band and it would make make me so mad I would feel better in no time. Some guys gave in and are back there now doing some women's job. Every one of them would give anything for a chance to get the 747 patch back on their shoulder.

I was wondering if the war really changed us guys much. Well I think I found out this week. Down at the Brussels leave center, we all lived together, combat men from the inf, paratroops, tanks, and recon. And service troops from artillery, quartermaster, engineers, air corp ground crews, and truck drivers. Well the combat men ate everything they served and enjoyed it. The service troops fussed around and complained about how it was cooked and served. The combat troops talked about the wonderful job Ike did running the war. The service troops complained they weren't going home fast enough. Up at the Red Cross club the combat troops said please pass the coffee and the others said Rotten coffee isn't it? So I guess there is a change in us but I don't think it is for the worse. All the combat men get together and are like one big happy family. The service troops don't even get along with one another. Wonder what's going to happen after we get home and the combat men are split up and there are 10 service men to each one of us. I know myself, for instance, if I hear some bird holler at a waiter because there is a fly in his soup I'll knock his darn head off.

We just got some replacements in from another outfit and you ought to hear them. I told two of them to grease the bogy roller on the tank. They said they just washed their hands and weren't going to get them dirty again. Did you ever hear of anything like that? Well it was all I could do to keep from beating them over the head with an axe or something. Yes there sure is a change because I remember when I was the same way.

Well I hope you enjoyed your trip to the mountains with Grand Ma and Pa. The first thing you know you will have another passenger in the back seat (namely me). The lights are about to go out so I'm going to close for tonite.
God bless you both
Your Loving Son
Bob

Sept 5th
Dear Mom, Dad,

It's a beauty full day in Holland! That's the biggest news I have, as there are only 10 days clear out of the year over here. Last nite I was put on Sgt of the Guard but much to my surprise, no one got into any trouble yet. The officer of the day and I checked the guard three times during the nite and for a change every one of them was on the ball. Its quite a job to check the guard now to as we have guards in ghent, Tarnazen, motor park and the btn area. I just about run the wheels off that jeep last nite. We have guards in Ghent to keep the boys out of trouble. Guards in Tarnazen to take care of the club. Their are at least ten fights a nite in Ghent. You see the town is full of English soldiers. Need I say more?

Well any way our boys and the Canadians get together and clean out the town every nite. The English are really sore about us stopping the (lend lease) just because the war is over. We laugh at them and they get mad because their familys will starve this winter with out our help. Of course their are two sides to the story. We stop feeding them and at the same time Ike says we will import food from the States to feed the Germans. But here is our side of it. President Truman says until England lifts trade restrictions between India, Australia and the rest of her colonys we will cut them short of all aide. As soon as England lifts the restrictions we will lend England (I should say give) 10,000,000,000 dollars to restore her purchasing power, witch in turn will set our world trade in tip top shape. Any way I get a kick out of it, just seeing England squirm for a wile under U.S. pressure. We are all tickled to death with Truman so far. He sure is a wizard at international politics. He even has (Uncle Joe) on his guard, and that's a hard thing to do, as Joe isn't any body's fool.

The part about feeding the Germans is hard to get through your head also. You see Every thing the Germans produce is going into the hands of the Allies. They can't produce unless they are healthy and any way a boat load of wheat is cheaper then a boat load of medicine.

I just finished reading three books. (Anna and the King of Siam) was the first and dirtyest, but very educational. (Whistle Stop) was best, and (Gentle Annie) next best. I feel lots better when I am reading or doing something rather than just sitting around.

I just cleaned my pen, it sure needed it. It has been dropped in the sand a doz times since I cleaned it last.

Well my points finally went over the mark. The score is now 80 and I have 81 I didn't make it by much but it is just enough to get me out of the army by Christmas. It may take Roy a little longer but he will be home soon too. Maybe even before me.

Im suppose to go diving tomorrow, down to the bottom of the bay. We are practicing getting dead men out of sunken tanks. It sort of gives you a funny feeling, as it would have been me they were practicing for if it weren't for the Atom Bomb. Yes Sir, it sure feels good to know that no Jap or German is going to put a slug in your head. The only bad part is I never even got to kill a Jap. Its just as well though, as one of them first just might have got me before I got any of them and that really would have broken my heart.

Boy I sure had a bad dream last nite. I dreamt their were two plains dropping Atom bombs as big as pills all over Linden and I was running like mad to get away from them. My ears were bursting from the concussion and it was so real, when I woke up I thought I was deaf. I had to laugh after it was over as those Atom Bombs as big as pills were inventions of my imagination. I was thinking of what would happen if a B29 started dropping millions of them on Japan and then darned if I didn't dream of it the other way around.

I have a picture of one of our nice Amph Tanks here that I am going to send you.
Lots of fun on your time off and God bless you both.
Your Loving Son
Bob

Holland
Sept 7
Dear Mom Dad,

Well you can see by the letter that plans were changed about our outfit going home. All training stopped and we are unattached from XVI corps as of 10th of Sept. We are going to be a service outfit but I don't know where yet. I am not worrying about it anyway as I have enough pts to come home even if the outfit stays here a year.

If I were you I would stop writing regular mail about the middle of Oct and just send a vmail once a week in case something should happen to keep me here longer than I expect. I have been getting a big kick out of your letters telling me what you are going to feed me when I get home. Well it doesn't make any difference what you give me as I love everything you cook. But here are a few things you better not forget. Clam Chowder and plenty of it. My tongue is hanging out for it. Also potato salad is something I haven't had since you gave it to me last. For breakfast I want eggs, sausage, hard rolls, sugar buns, and two quarts of milk. Of course we will make a trip to Elizabeth and have some Texas weenies, and over to NY to Kellys Clam Bar for shrimp. I also want plenty of chicken chow mien while I'm in NY. That big ice cream soda you told me you were going to make sounds like a good deal too. Don't forget it.

I got a letter from Pop Skelly today and he said Joe was going to get his discharge soon. The doctor said he wasn't quite ready. He still hasn't the use of one eye.

It's cold and windy here now and it still rains at least half of each day. I sure hope I can get out of Europe next month for sure. This weather makes you feel rotten all the time.

You asked how we spent VJ day. Well I'll send you a cartoon that will explain it very clearly.

I can't think of another thing to write and before I started writing tonite I could think of a million things to write about. Well I'll close now and if I think of anything I'll add to this in the morning.

Sunday

Well the guys forgot to wake me up for church this morning so I slept until dinner time. We had spaghetti and meatballs for dinner. Boy I'm sure putting on all the weight I lost back in France during the war. All we do is eat day and nite. By the way can you get oysters in the winter time? I just have to have some fried oysters the very day I come home. I can't sleep nites just thinking of them. I dream about oysters in every shape or form, and if it isn't oysters it's shrimp with good sauce. Oh well it won't be long now. I guess I can wait a few more months.

Sept 17

I forgot to mail this letter last week when I wrote it and it just turned up when I was cleaning my duffel bag of all extra junk. And you can imagine what I had in it. Everything from a beer mug to 8 pair of dirty socks. Well in the past few days things have changed again. We are no longer going to La Havre. Our outfit is staying here for the time being and us high pt men will be shipped out any day now either to Antwerp or La Havre to catch a ship. Don't be surprised to see me home any time now. It will come quick when it comes.

It stopped raining the past few days and today it got so hot you couldn't breath. Tonite it will be cold enough to freeze you to death.

I haven't had any mail from you in almost two weeks. I guess you stopped writing when you heard I was supposed to come home soon.

Well I haven't any more news so I'll close for now.

Hoping to see you soon
Your Loving Son
Bob

Sept 12
Dear Mom and Dad,

Monday we are leaving for La Havre France. The outfit is going to do MP duty and the high pt men will go home from there as their numbers come up. So you can expect me any time now. It may be the end of Sept or early in Oct. Then it may not be until November. Anyway it looks good to me as La Havre is the biggest port here for debar-cation. I am writing a regular letter and will give you all the dope.
Your Loving Son
Bob

Sept 20 1945
Dear <u>Mother</u>

I am scheduled to return to the United States sometime before the end of December so please hold any Christmas parcels you have for me.

Until I advise you otherwise, continue to send my letters but <u>DO NOT SEND ANY MORE PACKAGES.</u>
Bob

Sept 24
Terneuzen Holland
Dear Mother and Dad,

Gee I'm sorry about not writing to you for the past week or so but we have been so disgusted that it would only have been a miserable letter if I had written. We were told we were to leave last Monday and then it was changed to Wednes-

day and when Wednesday came along it was cancelled altogether. Now we are supposed to join some anti aircraft outfit in Brussels and go home with them. It sure hurts to be in an orphan btn, in combat or out. We will be lucky to be on or way home by Christmas. It looks like my 88 pts are as good as none at all. Do you think it would be wise for me to join up for 3 more years and stay here or come home to no job and starve? Up until a month ago I had two wonderful jobs to come back to, but first Pat got killed and then Carl drowned so that lets me out of those two jobs. I sure hate to think of working my head off in Mather Springs for the rest of my life. Maybe if I stay here for three more years I can save enough money to buy a job on the police force or something.

The mail is something else to drive you nuts. I've sweated out every mail call for three weeks and received exactly three letters. One from you, one from Kitty, and one from Helen. It isn't all your fault as no one seems to get mail any more. It has us in so bad a mood that they are afraid to ask us to do anything any more. I haven't stood reveille in two weeks and I haven't any intentions of doing so from here on either. sleep until noon and then eat and go back to bed until about two.. Then wash and shave and play cards until two in the morning.

I never go to town as the guys all get drunk and at least one truck is smashed a nite with an average of two killed per smashup. Last nite a truck went into the canal and 4 men and the truck have been pulled out so far. There are so many men AWOL that they don't know how many more are at the bottom. Well we will know in another three days when they rise to the surface. Then next in the line of danger are the fights in town between the English and us. Every morning there are at least 4 men beat up so badly they have to go to the hospital. So you can plainly see why I stay in camp, it's too late now to get my head split open. And I always have been afraid of that canal. The road twists and turns along it for 20 miles and its too deep for fooling around.

The weather is another bad thing to contend with. It rains now on the average of 20 hours a day, enough alone to get you disgusted. Boy would I love to be back in Germany where the country (central) is beautiful and the weather the best in Europe. My pen is almost out of ink so don't be surprised if I stop writing in a very abrupt manner.
The boys taught me to play pinochle about three days ago and I have been playing with great success almost ever since. Last nite I lost 17 games in a row, which made me very unhappy and almost disgusted with the game in general. The first nite was the best though, even if I did get my partner a little cut up at times. (New pen) How was I supposed to know that jack of something queen of another double was good. And one time I bid 20 and lost with a double ace double 10 strait of hearts. Oh well I'm learning fast now so look out when I get home.

You seemed worried in your last letter about me diving to the bottom of the bay out here with the Momsen Lung! Well the first time I went down I was a little worried myself but Columbus took a chance and I couldn't afford to miss out on that trip to the Pacific. I never would have slept another wink if Roy and my buddies here had to go and I was left out. It just isn't in me as much as I hate war to stay behind while my pals are doing their best. Its hard when you see the dead laying along the road if you can't say to yourself 'well I did my best'. It's also swell not to have to bend your head when you see a guy that had to do your job for you. There is not a man in the btn that can name a 747 battle that I wasn't in. That is the finest feeling there is when it comes time to think of your dead buddies. Well anyway the training is finally over and it didn't hurt my ear a bit.

I guess Roy is going to be over here even longer than me if possible. There is something else I have learned over here in the past few months. That is to roll my own cigarettes. Maybe its because $40 a carton is too much money to give up a week for butts. All that has stopped now though. Holland money is no longer worth anything. Last week it was down from .37 a guilder to .03 a guilder. I think it has all been recalled now. I just got rid of the last I had at the old rate the day it went down. Boy I was sweating for a while too. I would have lost my shirt in another day. That is the second time I was saved by the bell. The last time was when I sold a 45 pistol for $100 one day and the next day an army order came down saying you were not allowed to carry one unless your job called for one. That day 45's were sold for as little as 5 bucks each. You see you always have to carry a gun and a sub machine gun is too heavy to carry around in the rear area so everybody wants a pistol. I never could see where the extra weight was worth a hundred bucks to get rid of. So I always sold my pistol and bore the weight and extra protection of the good old M3 Sub.

Well I've sure filled in a lot of paper so far but never did say anything so I think its about time I cut the chatter and climb into my M1 sleeping bag between three M2 blankets and the M4 cat and G.I. wish the hell I was home.
Your Loving and very forgetful Son
Bob.

Happy birthday to the best Dad a guy ever had.

Sept 25
Moving out for PoE in morning. Wait for <u>new</u> address.
Bob

1945

Dear MomDad,

   We are at camp Wright Tie near Brussels. The outfit is alerted to go home on the 20th of Oct. We have it fine here except for the rain. It rains all the time. It has not stopped once in the 4 days we have been here. We don't have to do a thing as we have three German prisoners to each tent to do all our work for us. They make our beds, shine our shoes and wash our clothes and shave and cut our hair.

We can even have our meals brought to us in bed. I'll see you around Oct 30 or the 1st of Nov. Of course it could be postponed again but I don't think so.

Stop writing to me now
Your Loving Son
Bob

P.S.   I just got my honored service medal yesterday. I will send it as soon you let me know weather or not my other two medal's arrived. It looks like this.

October 11, 1945
Brussels

Bob and Roy Cadmus 1945, Brussels

Dear Mom and Dad,

I know you will be surprised to hear who is with me in Brussels. Yesterday I brought Roy back here from Campiegne (Camp Icon) France. I went down and got him in a jeep the day before. He sure looks good and has he changed. I hardly knew him by his voice and actions. He has learned to hurry up a little, althoughhe still has plenty of his old actions about him.

We got him a three day pass besides the day he took off when I was down at his <u>home</u>. He slept with me last nite at Camp Wright Tie to and met all the boys from my out fit. He will have plenty of time as his pass is good until tomorrow afternoon. I'll tell you about every thing when I get home so until then so long and God bless you
Your Loving Son   Bob

Oct. 13 1945
Brussels

We spent the nite in our hotel here in town so we had an early start this <u>afternoon</u>. We got up about eleven and went and bought a steak dinner. We got these pictures taken yesterday and boy do they show up that 40lbs I gained.

Roy is going to start back as soon as I finish this letter. I'm going to try and find a truck going back to Paris. I would take him back my self but I'm afraid I may miss the boat. He will have plenty of time as his pass is good until tomorrow afternoon.

I'll tell you about everything when I get home so until then so long and God bless you
Your Loving Son, Bob

Oct 13, 1945 Brussels, Belgium

Dear Mom & Dad,

I have a lot of things to tell you but as you already know Bob & I met at last. He just walked in on me with no warning. the first thing I did was to take him and his two buddies to see Ed Brady. We talked and for once wasn't just telling stories. We knew the others weren't phonies, but real veterans. Bob only had a 24 hour pass so we had to come back here the next day. I went in and got a 3 day pass in about 5 minutes. So I came up here to see him. I met some of his buddies, I think they were a little disappointed. Bob told them I was twice the size of him and when they found out he is twice the size of me, well you can see.

I've got to go now but first Nelson didn't go home. Let me have his address <u>tonite</u>. Tell you all about it later.

as ever,

Roy

Nov 2 1945

Paris

Dear Mom Dad,

Well at long last I made my way to Paris. You are probably wondering why I am in Paris instead of on a ship heading for the U.S.A. Well its a long sad story. We were to board ship Nov 1st and then at the last minute as usual it was canceled for at least 30 days. Now we no longer have any priority's as the 70 pt men have the right of way in now. Well it made me pretty mad the other day when they told us, so a friend of mine came along with me to Paris with a pocket full of blank passes. Well you know me, when I get back to camp I'll be there. It probably will be within a week or two as money goes fast in (Gay Parie)

I started out with $18. and three cartons of cigaretts and a complete uniform. I sold the cigarettes for $16 a carton and then the sun came out so I sold my rain coat for $30. Now its raining again so I am here in my (Hotel) room keeping dry.

The first thing I seen as I entered Paris was the Arch of Tryump, under witch was a brass band playing (Oh Susanna) I guess it was for some General or something, I didn't stop to investigate. Any way from there I went down to the Red Cross and picked up an American WAC (homley as hell) but so am I so what the dif? Any way I figured she would know all of the cheap places to eat and she did. (that is cheap for Paris) We are going sight seeing tomorrow at one oclock (cheap way to spend the day)(60 francs). The day after tomorrow I think I will go to Versailles about 10 miles from here, to see a family I met when we we fought there last August, (a year ago) I'll see how the food holds out and stay accordingly. I may go up and see Roy again some day if he is still there and then hop a plain to Le Harve an see if their is any more orders to move out. If not, I will take off to Isigny and visit the graves of our boys that died on the beach. Harry Clark's wife wrote and asked me to do it if I could. She is anxious to know if the grave is in good order. I can also see Sid Creig's grave wile I am there beside the guys in my company. Than if we don't move in time to get home for Christmas I will reinlist for 6 months and go back to Germany. From there I can visit Austria, Switzerland, Russia, and maby China.

If I reinlist I'll take a tech sgt job and make $135. a month. Now that I am in France I make $110. per mo but if I go to Germany it goes to $93. With $135 a mo I can save and even $100 a month and it shouldn't be to long before I get a new car at that rate. Of course it is a hard way to make money but its honest. Well any way their is still a chance to make for home for Christmas so I'll wait and see what happens. I will never get mail from you over here again so its no use of you writing. I'll try to get to England in a couple of weeks and I can call you up from their, but I'll try to think of something to say if I do as it will be costing me $4. per minute. Its a good buy though, 6 minutes for $24. I would do it any day, (given half a chance) I know it sure sounded good to here Roy's voice over the phone even if I didn't recognize it. Boy has his voice changed. He is a real man now. He is still a wise guy but not half as bad as he was.

Well so long and God Bless you both
Your Loving Son
Bob

Dear Mother,
    I am scheduled to return to the United States sometime before the end of December so please hold any Christmas parcels you have for me.
    Until I advise you otherwise, continue to send my letters, but <u>DO NOT SEND ANY MORE PACKAGES</u>.

                    Bob

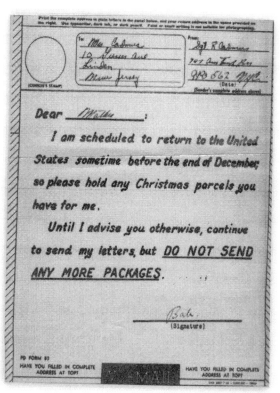

V mail letter

ENLISTED RECORD AND REPORT OF SEPARATION

HONORABLE DISCHARGE

55

1. LAST NAME - FIRST NAME - MIDDLE INITIAL		2. ARMY SERIAL NO.	3. GRADE	4. ARM OR SERVICE	5. COMPONENT
Cadmus Rynier R		32 603 063	Tec 4	ARMD	AUS
6. ORGANIZATION		7. DATE OF SEPARATION	8. PLACE OF SEPARATION		
Co A 747th Tk Bn		24 Dec 45	SEP CTR FT DIX NJ		
9. PERMANENT ADDRESS FOR MAILING PURPOSES		10. DATE OF BIRTH	11. PLACE OF BIRTH		
10 Gresser Ave Linden NJ		27 Mar 23	Bayonne NJ		
12. ADDRESS FROM WHICH EMPLOYMENT WILL BE SOUGHT		13. COLOR EYES	14. COLOR HAIR	15. HEIGHT	16. WEIGHT	17. NO. DEPEND.
See 9		green	brown	6	3	250	2

18. RACE W 19. MARITAL STATUS S 20. U.S. CITIZEN YES X 21. CIVILIAN OCCUPATION AND NO. Machine Parts Inspector 4-94.343

MILITARY HISTORY

22. DATE OF INDUCTION	23. DATE OF ENLISTMENT	24. DATE OF ENTRY INTO ACTIVE SERVICE	25. PLACE OF ENTRY INTO SERVICE
28Dec42		4 Jan43	Newark NJ

26. SELECTIVE SERVICE DATA ► | 27. LOCAL S.S. BOARD NO. 12 | 28. COUNTY AND STATE Union NJ | 29. HOME ADDRESS AT TIME OF ENTRY INTO SERVICE See 9

30. MILITARY OCCUPATIONAL SPECIALTY AND NO.	31. MILITARY QUALIFICATIONS AND DATE (i.e., Infantry, aviation and marksmanship badges, etc.)
Medium Tank Crewman 2736	Carbine M1 marksman 157 10Dec43

32. BATTLES AND CAMPAIGNS Central Europe   Rhineland GO 33 WD 45 as amended

33. DECORATIONS AND CITATIONS Bronze Star Medal GO 68 Hq 29th Inf Div 23 Jul 44 American Service Medal European-African-Middle Eastern Service Medal Good Conduct Medal Purple Heart Sec II GO 172 Hq 29th Inf Div 9May45 World War II Victory Medal

34. WOUNDS RECEIVED IN ACTION E T O   22 Nov 44

35. LATEST IMMUNIZATION DATES				36.		37. SERVICE OUTSIDE CONTINENTAL U.S. AND RETURN		
SMALLPOX	TYPHOID	TETANUS	OTHER (specify)		DATE OF DEPARTURE	DESTINATION	DATE OF ARRIVAL
7Jan44	10Dec44	1Nov44	None		11Feb44	E T O	23Feb44

38. TOTAL LENGTH OF SERVICE						39. HIGHEST GRADE HELD			
CONTINENTAL SERVICE			FOREIGN SERVICE						
YEARS	MONTHS	DAYS	YEARS	MONTHS	DAYS				
1	2	19	1	9	3	Tec 4	6Nov45	U S A	13Nov45

40. PRIOR SERVICE None

41. REASON AND AUTHORITY FOR SEPARATION Convenience of the Govt AR-615-365 15Dec44 and RR 1-1 Demobilization

42. SERVICE SCHOOLS ATTENDED None | 43. EDUCATION (Years) 8 0 0

PAY DATA

44. LONGEVITY FOR PAY PURPOSES			45. MUSTERING OUT PAY		46. SOLDIER DEPOSIT	47. TRAVEL PAY	48. TOTAL AMOUNT, NAME OF DISBURSING OFFICER
YEARS 2	MONTHS 11	DAYS 27	TOTAL 300	THIS PAY't 100	None	3.00	$220.46 J HARRIS COL FD

INSURANCE NOTICE

IMPORTANT If premium is not paid when due or within thirty-one days thereafter, insurance will lapse. Make checks or money orders payable to the Treasurer of the U.S. and forward to Collector of Internal Revenue, Washington 25, D.C.

49. KIND OF INSURANCE		50. HOW PAID		51. Effective date of Allotment Discontinuance	52. Date of Next Premium Due	53. PREMIUM DUE	54. INTENTION OF VETERAN TO
Nat. Serv.	U.S. Govt.	None	Allotment	Direct to V.A.	31dec45	31Jan45	6.50	Continue X

55. | 56. REMARKS (This space for completion of above items or entry of other items specified in W. D. Directives)

Lapel button issued

Inactive ERC from 28Dec42 to 3 Jan 43

ASR Score 2Sep45   81

56. SIGNATURE OF PERSON BEING SEPARATED *Rynier R Cadmus*

57. PERSONNEL OFFICER (Type name, grade and organization - signature) J E WHITE JR CAPT   AC   *J. E. White*

This form supersedes all previous editions of WD AGO Forms 53 and 55 for enlisted persons entitled to an Honorable Discharge, which will not be used after receipt of this revision.

Army of the United States

Honorable Discharge

This is to certify that

RYNIER R CADMUS 32 603 063 TECHNICIAN FOURTH GRADE

COMPANY A 747TH TANK BATTALION

Army of the United States

is hereby Honorably Discharged from the military service of the United States of America.

This certificate is awarded as a testimonial of Honest and Faithful Service to this country.

Given at SEPARATION CENTER
FORT DIX NEW JERSEY

Date 24 DECEMBER 1945

L R WALKER
LT COL. AC

RÉPUBLIQUE FRANÇAISE

Guerre 1939-1945

CITATION

EXTRAIT DE LA DECISION Nº 268

LE PRESIDENT DU GOUVERNEMENT PROVISOIRE DE LA REPUBLIQUE

CITE A L'ORDRE DE L'ARMEE

29th Infantry Division

747th Tank Battalion

"Splendide Unité animée des plus hautes vertus militaires, a, au cours des Opérations de Débarquement du 6 juin 1944 fait montre d'un héroïsme extraordinaire.

Ayant reçu pour mission de s'emparer de positions fortement tenues par un ennemi décidé à se défendre à tout prix, a débarqué sur une plage abondamment minée et soumise à de violents feux d'armes de tous calibres.

Après s'être emparé des falaises d'une importance vitale, a continué ses attaques en direction de St-LAURENT-S-MER.

Malgré de fortes pertes en personnel et matériel, s'est accroché au terrain occupé couvrant ainsi l'avance sur ISIGNY.

En s'emparant des objectifs qui lui avaient été assignés, a contribué pour une large part à la défaite de l'ennemi et à la Libération de la FRANCE.

CETTE CITATION COMPORTE L'ATTRIBUTION DE LA CROIX DE GUERRE AVEC PALME.

Paris, le 22 juillet 1946
Signé: BIDAULT.

COPIE CERTIFIEE CONFORME
Washington, le 2 juin 1992
L'Attaché de Défense Adjoint
près l'Ambassade de France aux Etats-Unis

TRANSLATION

THE REPUBLIC OF FRANCE

1939-1945 WORLD WAR

CITATION

ORDER N° 268

THE PRESIDENT OF THE PROVISIONAL GOVERNMENT OF THE FRENCH REPUBLIC

CITES TO THE ORDER OF THE ARMY

the 29th Infantry Division

A splendid unit animated by the highest military virtues. During the landing operations of 6 June 1944, it displayed extraordinary heroism. Its mission was to seize positions strongly held by an enemy determined to defend itself at any cost. This unit landed on a heavily mined beach and was subjected to violent fire from weapons of every caliber. After having seized cliffs of vital importance, it attacked and seized St. Laurent-S-Mer. In spite of heavy losses in personnel and matériel, it defended the occupied ground, which covered the advance on Isigny. By seizing its assigned objectives, it contributed in a great measure to the defeat of the enemy and the liberation of France.

THESE CITATIONS INCLUDE THE AWARD OF THE CROIX DE GUERRE WITH PALM.

Paris, July 22, 1946
Signed: BIDAULT

318

Photo by Nancy Cadmus Franklin of Dad standing in front of a tank similar to his. We think the tank is or was on exhibit at a VFW in Foley, Alabama

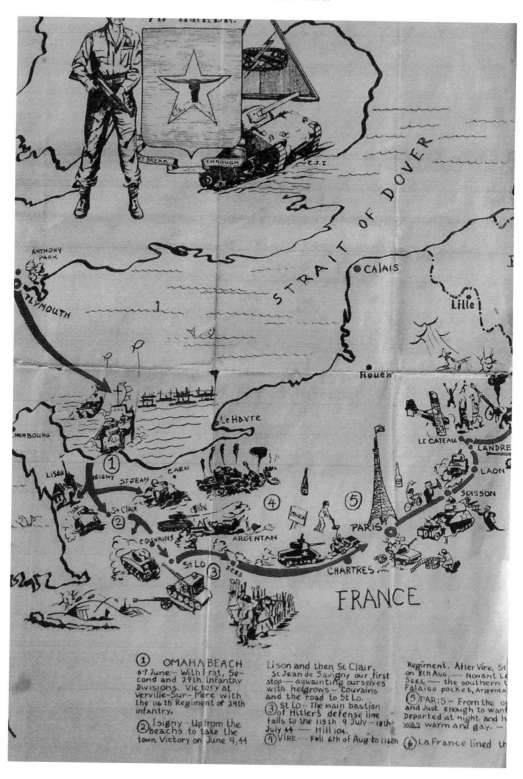

① OMAHA BEACH
6-7 June — With first, Second and 29th Infantry
Divisions. Victory at
Verville-Sur-Mere with
the 116th Regiment of 29th
infantry.

② Isigny — Up from the
beachs to take the
town. Victory on June 9,44

Lison and then St Clair.
St Jean de Savigny our first
stop — aquainting ourselves
with hedgrows — Couvains
and the road to St Lo.

③ St Lo — The main bastion
of Hitler's defense line
falls to the 115th 9 July — 18th
July 44 — Hill 104.

④ VIRE — Fell 6th of Aug to 116th

Regiment. After Vire, St
on 8th Aug. — Nonant L
Sees, — the southern t
Falaise pocket, Argenta

⑤ PARIS — From the o
and Just enough to want
Departed at night and h
was warm and gay. —

⑥ La France lined th

747ᵗʰ TANK BATTALION

FROM "D" DAY TO VICTORY

Long ride ended with collection of eggs, wine and even chickens from a grateful people.

7 Point of Spearhead virtually ran into tail of German retreat. Victory after five hour skirmish. March continued.

8 The Siegfried Line on 11th of September 44. Pill boxes, and heavy artillery fire came down like rain drops. 21 pillboxes were taken on the first day —— bucked the line for two weeks —— next Amburge, Alsdorf, —— The push to the Roer River —— Schleiden our first permanent home —holding the line at the Roer— Christmas and New Years "digging in" during the "Bulge"– 21st November – 18th February – Fanatic resistance crushed at Sports Platz marked end of fighting west of the Roer River.

9 Roer crossed – Victory at Julich Setterrich, Mersch, Pattern, Titz, and Munchen Gladbach Rheydt. Drinks furnished by the Late Dr. Goebbels at Schloss Rheydt, his home town.

10 Crossing the 30th Inf. Div. over the Rhine River March 23-24 "Driving Alligators in the assault wave.

11 Rear Security with 29th for 9th Army. D.P. Camps.

12 Nordhausen – underground factory for V bombs- the horrors of a German Concentration Camp— a

Hanover and back to Munster while we were at Munster 13 VICTORY was proclaimed. 7 May 1945.

SIGNATURES ON THE BACK OF THE 747 BATTALION CO. A
CAMPAIGN MAP

Stanley A Basik
Cleveland, Ohio

Joe Sullivan
Rt. 2 Box 125-B
Bakersfield,
California

Wayne H. Barrow
Kahoka, Mo.

L. Ferguson
Bklyn, N.Y.

Henry M Padgett
30 Smith St.
Sanders?? C.

Jamie E Bailet
Aurora,
Missouri

Wm. G. Moore (F.C.M)
Starkville, Miss.

Vernon Black
Route 5
Dahlonega, Ga.

Joe Roth
1111 W. Columbia Ave
Philadelphia, Pa

Luke Cutrera
Patterson, La.

John McConnally
Waldenburg
N.C.

"Slats" C.J. Hoverlaus

James J. Mielle
949 Genesee St.
Waukesha, Wisc.

Onald C. "Jr." Kavanagh
259 Farrington St.
St. Paul, Minnesota

Fred Rages
Huntington, L.I.
New York

Carl L. Lange Jr.
4842 Hutchinson
Chicago 41, Ill.

Morris T. Davis
Springfield, Mo.

Joe Skelly
2781 Y. Concourse
NY 58 N.Y.

Mein
Lehm
OLDE

Richard M. Williamson
508 - forbien St. apt. 301
San Francisco
California

Ray Bailey
Meadowbrook
West Va

Glen E. Bowling
Box 591
Borger, Texas
(The Texas Kid)

Richard C. Miller
Box 26 R.D. #1
Harmony Pa.

James J. Soderberg
1453 Redondo Ave.
Salt Lake City 5, Utah

Thad Weghenmeyer
mountaintop
R.D. #1   Pa.

Raymond Pingloca
200 Grant Ave
Grantwood N.J.

Buddy Gregson
c/o 118 Butler Ave.

Carl Schwartz
Solen North
Dakota R.R.1.
Louis C Crippen
343 2o Detroit ave
Toledo, Ohio (8)

S. Thomas Amato
Washington Hts N.J.

Seymour Teichter
1019 Walcher
Norfolk, Va.

Homer M. Clark
26 lines St.
Worcester 2, Mass.

Mr. De Santi
1640 Clark St
San Leandro
cal.

Buster Ackerman
Menton N.J.
122 High St.

John Catly
Salem J. N.Y. L.I.

Walter Bacroyer
Salisbury N.Y.

Louis Di Paul
R.R.#
Middletown

SAMPLE LETTERS

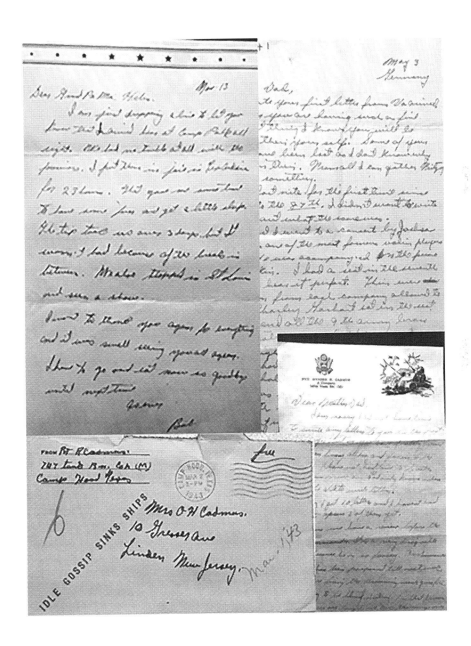

A letter from Joe Skelly written in November of 1999 to Mom when he sent the citation and medal of the Croix de Guerre. (since Dad had passed on, Joe received Dad's along with his at a special ceremony)

Dear Natalie,

Enclosed is the most sought after Croix de Guerre (cross of war) awarded by the government of France to certain units for exceptional heroism on Omaha Beach and Normandy. I am very proud and I know Bob would also. After all he and I practically won the war single handed.

Have a good Thankgiving ....
Joe

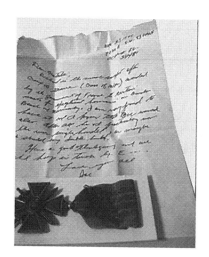

BRONZE STAR

GOOD CONDUCT MEDAL

CROIX DE GUERRE
with Palm

MARKSMANSHIP 1,2,3

PURPLE HEART   **TANK MEDAL**

DAD'S MEDALS (We photographed all
we had, but after reading the letters it seems
there were more)

An article and letter from one of his assistant drivers in 1998 shortly after Dad suffered a major heart attack ·Letter written by Ken Fortney

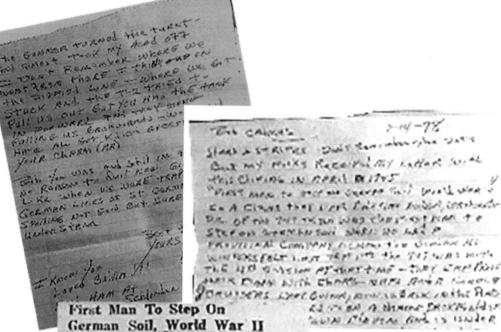

First Man To Step On German Soil, World War II

Co. A claims that Capt. Boleslau Bulvin, Washington, D. C., f the 747th Tank Battalion, was 1e first man to step on German soil when he led a provisional ·ompany across. the border at Winterspelt last Sept. 11th. The 747th was with the 4th Division at the time.

They can prove their claim with charts, maps and a couple of six-foot bruisers!

Capt. Bulvin, now back in the States on rotation, used to be a champ buckfielder on the Georgetown eleven, and is under post-war contract to the Cleveland Rams. Bucking the line is an old story to the Captain who, inci-

TRANSCRIPTION OF THE LETTER FROM KEN FORTNEY

Bob Cadmus   *1-14-98*

Stars & Stripes - Don't remember the date but my folks received my letter with this clipping in April 1945

"First man to step on German soil. World War II"
Co A claims that Capt. Boleslau Bulvin, Washington D.C. of the 747 TK BN was the first man to step on German soil when he led a provisional company across the border at Wintersfelt last Sept 11th the 747 was with the 4th Division at that time - they can prove their claim with charts-maps and a couple of 6 foot bruisers. Capt. Bulvin, is now back in the States on rotation, used to be a champ backfielder on the Georgetown Eleven and is under post-war contract to the Clevland Rams. Bucking the line is an old story to the Captain who, incidentally brought back a match box full of German soil to Co Headquarters.

I trust you remember this day - we went thru St. Vite & Bastone the day before. Also this was when I had that machine gun going every way possible I burned out the barrel - it got so hot. Remember we sat in that little river at the bottom of the hill and the Germans lobed in smoke shell on us the gunner turned the turret and almost took my head off. I don't remember where we went from there. I think up on the Sigfied line - where we got stuck and theT-2 tried to pull us out but you had the tank in forward and they were pulling us backwards - we could have all got killed except for your charm (HA)

Bob you was and still am a fighter. No reason to quit now. Give hell like when we were traped behine German lines at St. Germain. Spelling not good but suryou understand.

Best to you and yours

Ken

I know you loved Bulvin!!!
and ham at Schlindar

MEMORIES OF RICHARD (DICK) CAMPLONE

From: **A tape of memories recorded by Richard Camplone, 747 Tank Battalion Company A**

The following first hand account was found on a cassette tape sent to Bob Cadmus from Richard Camplone around 1997. Mr Camplone had decided to write a book about his life and memories of service during WWII. He drove a T2 tank. Richard and Bob served in the same tank battalion and remained friends the rest of their lives. I have not found any evidence of said book, so we decided to incorporate some of his memories from the tapes.

'We went for 3 days without any sleep or food. It seemed like an eternity. Company C was sent ahead of us. When they turned the curve, the Royal Air Force fighters attacked them with bombs and rockets. Lots of guys got killed trying to put out identification planks. Now to A Company. We went on down the road past the burning tanks with blood in our eyes. We were mad as hell. We drove two abreast firing at anything that moved on both sides of the road, including houses, barns, even bathhouses.

The lead tanks were very fast, trying to catch up to the company commander tank, which was a mistake, as it was at the back of the battalion. There was a lieutenant in the turret of a tank on my right who had just come along for the ride. He never stopped shooting all the way. I don't know who he was and never saw him again. We were moving too fast for the infantry to keep up.

We got into the town at 1AM probably much before we were supposed to get there. While we were in town the Navy started sending in 16" shells with the battle wing still in the harbor. Five story apartment houses were coming down with one shot. Each time the shells went off, the tanks would jump two feet off the ground. By days end the whole town was burning.

My company commander bawled me out for being too close to the town. You see, when we lose a T2, we lose the crew and that is a very important part of the company. It keeps our artillery guns, radio, tanks in repair. We did all the mine sweeping work and demolition work too.

You used to lie down to smoke and wipe butts with shells.

They were pulling us back because our front and side flanks were not covered. The tanks made a sharp turn in, in the rear of a church yard. By the time the T2 got there there were already large ferrels in the turns, made by the heavy tanks. We got stuck in the ferrels and could not move. I sent one guy after the tanks on foot to get help. I sent two guys up a building behind where we were stuck to set up a machine gun nest.

I started walking around and found a cafe. I kicked in the door. A woman and four kids were inside. They were shell shocked. I assured them that everything was ok.

I went on to meet two nuns by the church. They were very upset by the town being destroyed. 'Why did we do such a thing?' One of the nuns spit in my face. I could understand their anger, but they were lucky they were nuns. There was a staircase on my left as I entered the back of the church. Behind the staircase was a German officer trying to get his pistol out. My machine gun started going off into the ground in front of me, then shot up the steps and into the officer still trying to get his pistol out. First time I killed someone at close range.

The Germans were pouring troops into the town via bridges over the canals. A tank was coming to save us. His camouflage net in the rear was on fire. he got out to put the fire out and was wounded. One of many times he was wounded.

Now the battle for St. Lo. A Company lost more tanks and men than you could believe. We went out every day for about four weeks. We lost approximately 10% of our men and tanks every day. I don't know where they got the tanks and supplies, but every night when we got back to our company there were tanks ready and replacements for the men who were killed or wounded. Replacements must have come from Fort Knox training. Most had only been in the army five or six months. They were poorly trained. They had never even seen an M4 Sherman tank before. Sometimes we never got a chance to get acquainted or learn their names before they were killed or wounded.

We started fighting in hedgerow country. It's almost the equivalent to jungle fighting. On the morning of July 14, my T2 gets a call that Lieutenant Wilkes' tank broke down on a road close by us. Donald B. was dri-

ving across an open field. There was a large explosion about 6 feet in front of us. Donald goes nuts and starts acting like a wild man. They're dropping shells all around us. I went down to the turret and shut down the engines. Then I calmed Donald down and told him how to get to the disabled tank.

When we got to the cross roads we blew up two anti tank mines. It was a very large explosion. All the guys got out except me. I was numb, with no feelings. I could not feel my legs. —- came back for me and helped me out of the tank. I lay flat along the road for about three hours. The feeling in my legs returned. Now I go back to the T2 and clear the cross road of about 10 antitank mines. I knew exactly how to handle them.

The next day Ray—— comes walking down the road. There were at least ten dead soldiers no one had bothered to move.

To my right there was a tank that had burned the day before. I went there to see if I could salvage a turn buckle for the disabled tank. Crawling through those Hedgerows was very dangerous. Everyone was firing at me, even our own G.I.s Crawling out of the hedgerow I felt something soft. I picked it up. It was a hand with half an arm attached. I still dream of that arm. The tank was completely gutted, nothing salvageable inside. Later I find out there was still a man in the tank. He was cremated.

I managed to back the disabled tank out. The infantry major made me stay there with the tank.

The worst fighting I ever saw took place the next two days. There were dead and wounded soldiers everywhere. The Germans send word to call a truce for a few hours to remove the dead and wounded from the hedgerows. The commander of the 29th Division, General Gerhardt said no way. Maybe the bastards are getting tired and they should surrender instead.

I watched for two days. Bombers came over to bomb a corridor in St. Lo. 2,400 bombers a day, sometimes they made three trips in a day over the corridor. They tried to open up St. Lo so that General Patton and his 3rd Army could break through to Southern France. About a week later St. Lo was taken at a very high price in lives and support material. Records show the cost of taking Normandy was 37,000 lives of American soldiers. What a price to pay for democracy.

Now we got 2 days to rest. A chance to wash and clean, get new clothes, food and sleep. and mail. Rumors were flying around. The one I like best is that the Normandy was sunk in NY Harbor, raised at Pier 57 in NY and refitted for a troop carrier that was going to pick us up and carry us back to the USA.

After two days rest they sent us to St. Germaine. We got there at dusk to get ready to attack in the morning. Went down a long hill about a half mile long zig zagging the whole way into a valley. Half the tanks on one side and half on mine. We picked up about twenty prisoners. All night long artillery was used against us. Joe Skelly and I figured they must have sent us to the wrong place as we were far into enemy lines. We were surrounded by German tanks, paratroopers, SS troops. Two tanks on the other side of the road were already burned. The assault gun was right behind us. Several lost legs and were killed. Joe Skelly lay wounded and helpless in front of the T2. While my men tried to get Skelly back in the tank—— was calling for help from his tank. I went out after him but a machine gun opened up a can of C Rations behind me. I ducked back in. After Skelly got back in the T2 I looked out again. There were two German soldiers about ten feet from the tank with bazookas getting ready to fire into the side. The fastest gun I carry is a luger I carry on the shoulder. I shot one soldier right in the eye. The second dropped his bazooka and ran. I shot him in the head. He went down. His helmet came off. He started running again. I emptied my luger on him and then threw it to the bottom of the tank. We took off up the hill. I was throwing smoke grenades out the turret. To this day I don't know how they missed us. We could hear the shells whizzing by.

We got back to a medic half track. Skelly looked like a piece of chopped meat. The medics didn't even want to waste plasma on him. (I went to his wedding after the war)
We lost 12 tanks that morning and plenty of men.

We were involved in the ____ of the _____Gap where we had a whole German army in a trap and took many prisoners. German planes kept bombing us 2-3 days in a row. They kept dropping personal bombs. I think they were trying to break down our morale with bombs called 'screaming meemies'.

The 747 was only a battalion. The Germans must have thought we were a large corps of tanks because we were always used and in the thick of things.

We started to fight to get to Paris. Our objective was to bypass the Paris suburbs and keep going east. We started in pitch black of night. The only thing you could follow was the exhaust from the tank in front of you. At that time we had a new driver. We went over a cliff and rolled over three and a half times. Thank God it didn't roll another half. I was suspended in mid air hanging out the turret. I couldn't believe I was not hurt. We spent the next few days patching each other up. No one knew where we were. We got the T2 back on its tracks. Cleaned and repaired it and tried to catch up with our company about 3 days ahead of us.

This was one of the best times we ever had. We would ride into a French town, and they would put out American flags. We were the first Americans they saw. We stopped to pick up the goodies they offered us: champagne, bread, eggs, cheese-We would stop and hug and kiss all the girls, especially the pretty ones. They looked behind us for the rest of the tanks. I assured them they would be here shortly. We got gas from houses and put it in our diesel engines. Paris was finally taken after our outfit went through it.

We took enough ground around Paris so that when General DeGaulle took his victory parade there would be no chance he would get shot. After 14 days we caught up with our outfit. The commander could not believe we were able to find them.

We were the first troops to enter Germany. We hit the Sigfield Line. The first day we captured 20 pillboxes, bucked the Siegfried Line the next two weeks. We were sent north to the 9th infantry and our old friends the 29th. At that time we were under the English General Montgomery. The English always used a lot of artillery. One night it looked like the sun was coming up in the west. The traffic of outgoing shells was unbelievable. When we got to the German army they seemed unaffected by the artillery. We were no match for the German tanks on open ground. We were designed to support the infantry. Our main artillery was the 75 mm guns which bounced off their tanks. The Germans called our tanks 'American matchboxes'. Any hit would set them on fire. When the ammunition exploded you were cremated in your tank. We lost most of our company in a couple of days. The brass wanted all burned tanks out of sight to save the morale of the troops.

We went hungry many days. Bob Cadmus broke into the kitchen area one night and stole a ham, some loaves of bread and a gallon of marmalade jam. They only had two hams for the whole company of 125 men. Bob and myself ate the whole ham. We were caught the next day and supposedly punished.

Now we cross the Rhine River. Pretty tough going. The terrain was very muddy. We worked hard pulling tanks out of mud and got caught in a barrage. I drove into a bomb crater which had about 3 inches of ice in it. I almost drowned. We went on to capture a large town named munchen____. There we found Goebbel's private wine cellar and boy did we get sloshed. We supported the infantry divisions crossing the Rhine. By now I was wondering if there was anyone besides us that was in the army.

We captured one of their concentration camps called Nordhausen. The smell was so bad I did not want to go into the camp. Dave S. forced me to go through the camp. The sights were unbelievable. Most of the men in this command displayed extraordinary heroism and we never got the the credit we deserved. A separate tank battalion, we had no big brass in command. Anytime anyone needed someone to go first we were sent. We were moved so fast helping other divisions the mail had a hard time catching up to us.

The war ended when we were in Munster.

Everyone was looking forward to going home. They sent us to a town named Bumenhausen to see what they were going to do with us. We were declared as essential. You wouldn't believe how bad the morale was. We were exhausted and really down in the dumps. They put us in an amphibious army corps. We started training on the North Sea for the invasion of Japan. It was hard to believe what they were doing to us. Our Colonel kept telling us how lucky we was to make the assault on Tokyo Bay.

Thank God for the atom bomb and to President Truman for using it. Without the atom bomb I don't think any of us would have made it home.

July 4: Commendation
Formal Commanding Officer, 747 Tank Battalion :

Sir, through you and to you veterans of the 747 Separate Tank Battalion are hereby commended for the following feats of arms and administration while supporting the 1st, 2nd, 4th, 28th, 29th, 79th, and 90th infantry divisions plus two Ranger Battalions, one Belgium Brigade from June 6, 1944 to May 9 1945. In addition you served the military Government of several areas. Omaha Beach, simultaneously supporting 3 infantry divisions and one ranger battalion while also providing the 5th Corps 2 reserve; Holland: supported 1st Brigade taking direct fire; Battle of the Bulge; taking indirect fire as a division on the 9th army front; Rhine River Crossing: transporting and helping infantry divisions across the river; Military Government: served as such in numerous areas after the Rhine River Crossing when military government teams were not available. Your deeds in the interest of great principles of the American Constitution were so extraordinary as to sometimes border on fantasia. For your companions who fell in action.
Homer D. Wilkes

Bob Cadmus was one of the best tank drivers. He once lay in a grave with a bunch of cadavers playing dead til he could get out and get back to the company.

Everything written here is the whole truth, the best that I can remember it."

Richard Camplone

Marion man remembers D-Day invasion

BY FRANCES DEVORE
STAFF WRITER

When Joseph Skelly wakes tomorrow, it will be to one more beautiful, peaceful day at On Top of The World, but it's certain his thoughts will be centered on another June 6 — 52 years ago — when he was part of an incredible Allied invasion force that made its move to take Europe back from the German war machine.

"The long wait was finally over," he says, thinking back to his tank company hitting Omaha Beach on the Normandy coast and rolling straight into hell.

"In the first light of morning we saw that we were surrounded by thousands of ships and landing craft, many flying barrage balloons to thwart air attack. Flotilla commanders shouted back and forth, using megaphones to keep some semblance of order in our attack pattern. Destroyers were seen running up and down the beach front rapidly firing their five-inch guns. They looked so close to the beach you would think that they were on wheels. We made our first pass, only to be ordered off because the gallant infantrymen of the 29th Division

Joseph Skelly was part of a D-Day invasion force in World War II.

KYLE DANACEAU/STAR-BANNER

were pinned down suffering tremendous casualties. Later as the attack became tenable our LCTs began the assault.

"The carnage on the beach and adjacent waters was totally devastating. Tangled barbed wire and all kinds of concrete and steel obstacles had been planted to stop our advance. The most horrendous sight of all was the great number of dead infantrymen, floating face down, so closely packed you could walk ashore on their backs without getting your feet wet. Our LCT commander made a pass at the beach and lowered the ramp, but we were too far out. He gave the signal to go. If we had complied, we would have sunk in water that was too deep and probably most of our crews would have drowned.

"Our platoon commander jumped onto the bridge to persuade the captain to get closer. He was yelling "I don't want to lose my ship," and our lieutenant was poking him in the side with a 45 automatic. We were offloaded near the shore but at a precarious angle. Our tracks finally gripped the bottom and we moved forward with the hulk of the tank completely submerged.

"We now focused our attention on the beach. The sight was more devastating than seeing the floating bodies. I stuck my head out of the hatch to size up the situation and was hit in the face with a bloody mangled arm not attached

to a body. The tank on my left was trying to climb a steep incline and dragging and chewing up a body in its tracks. Meanwhile enemy fire was pounding our position. My best buddy, a driver, became physically ill because he couldn't avoid driving over the dead without mangling them even more. Our only hope was to get off the beach and up the steep cliff. The devastation on the beach is a very painful and vivid recollection which will remain etched in my mind forever.

Once on the top of the cliff, the company regrouped, right in front of the deepest crater Skelly had ever seen, probably caused by offshore shelling. Sledgehammers had to be used to dislodge the tank's breathing stacks for 360-degree firing. Meanwhile, the men were standing on the deck exposed to all kinds of fire, friendly and unfriendly. Then the tank moved on down to a small village called Colville sur Mer and went on the defensive with a French cheering section.

"Snipers were popping away at our infantry from all sides and in back of us, but the 75 mm gun

PLEASE SEE SKELLY ON 2D

Skelly remembers Allied invasion

CONTINUED FROM 1D

could not be fired for fear of killing or wounding our own men. I succeeded in dislodging the enemy from the upper windows with my 50 caliber and coaxial 30 caliber machine guns. Almost immediately we began taking fire from our left, from a small stone building. Since we could not stop to aim, I fired on the run, luckily hitting the door dead center. This destroyed the building, and its German occupants." Skelly feared their cohorts would somehow recognize his tank, Abie's Irish Rose, and make it a special target.

He said the next few days were about the same — "you shoot me and I shoot you," with enemy booby traps, mined roads and very accurate artillery fire. The Germans had previously marked their coordinates on specific targets such as main roads and intersections, he explained.

"Fields and roads were dotted with the bloated and sinking carcasses of farm animals and the bodies of enemy soldiers with their skins turning blue and the unforgettable odor of death," he said.

Skelly was wounded and permanently put out of action two months later in St. Germain. The enemy attacked early in the morning and since the tank company lacked infantry and artillery support, it was practically destroyed. Two of his crew died and the remaining three were wounded and burned. He was returned to the United States on a hospital ship called Saint Olaf and spent about 18 months in different hospitals. The 747th Tank Battalion fought to the end of the war, however, and immediately went into training with Amphibious Tanks to prepare for the assault on the Japanese mainland. Skelly said he thanks

God that they never had to go.

Out of 600 combatants, 271 were killed in France, he says. "Quick figuring brings you very close to 50 percent killed in action. We were suitably bemedaled with a preponderance of Purple Hearts. The President of France awarded our unit with the Croix de Guerre with Palm," (its highest award) for our contribution on D-Day and the liberation of France.

"Those of us still living have had yearly reunions for most of the past 52 years. We know the meaning of real comradeship. Most of us suffer from some form of post war syndrome. I am severely handicapped as a result of this conflict and am living out my life here, with my wife, Claire." The couple married in 1948 and have two children. Skelly retired from Brooks Brothers and moved to Ocala from Vero Beach three years ago.

The 747th Tank Battalion was activated in Bowie, Texas, Jan. 3, 1943, a separate unit made up of approximately 600 men, 60 tanks and a variety of half tracks, jeeps and trucks, according to Skelly.

"The men were Irish, Italians and Jews from Brooklyn, the Bronx, and a number of Polish and German men from New Jersey and Pennsylvania. Others were a few foreign-born from Greece, Czechoslovakia, Pakistan and China. Hard-nosed basic training and maneuvers ended with transportation aboard the U.S. Navy Attack Transport Charles Carroll, with seasickness the order of the day in the miserable February crossing. Further training followed in Scotland and England and the rest is history.

Marion Man Remembers D-Day Invasion

1996 Newspaper interview with Joe Skelly: a first person account of the D-Day invasion

Marion Man Remembers D-Day Invasion
by Frances Devore, Staff Writer

When Joseph Skelly wakes tomorrow, it will be to one more beautiful, peaceful day at On Top of The World, but it's certain his thoughts will be centered on another June 6 - 52 years ago - when he was part of an incredible Allied invasion force that made its move to take back Europe from the German war machine.

"The long wait was finally over," he says, thinking back to his tank company hitting Omaha Beach on the Normandy coast and rolling straight into hell.

"In the first light of morning we saw that we were surrounded by thousands of ships and landing craft, many flying barrage balloons to thwart air attack. Flotilla commanders shouted back and forth, using megaphones to keep some semblance of order in our attack pattern. Destroyers were seen running up and down the beach front rapidly firing their five - inch guns. They looked so close to the beach you would think they were on wheels. We made our first pass, only to be ordered off because the gallant infantrymen of the 29th division were pinned down suffering tremendous casualties. Later, as the attack became tenable our LCTs began the assault.

"The carnage on the beach and adjacent waters was totally devastating. Tangled barbed wire and all kinds of concrete and steel obstacles had been planted to stop our advance. The most horrendous sight of all was the great number of dead infantrymen floating face down, so close you could walk ashore on their backs without getting your feet wet. Our LCT commander made a pass at the beach and lowered the ramp, but we were too far out. He gave the signal to go. If we had complied, we would have sunk in water that was too deep and probably most of our crews would have drowned."

"Our platoon commander jumped onto the bridge to persuade the captain to get closer. He was yelling "I don't want to lose my ship." and our lieutenant was poking him in the side with 45 automatic. We were offloaded near the shore but at a precarious angle. Our tracks finally gripped the bottom and we moved forward with the hulk of the tank completely submerged."

"We now focused our attention on the beach. The sight was more devastating than seeing the floating bodies. I stuck my head out of the hatch to size up the situation and was hit in the face with bloody mangled arm not attached to a body. The tank on my left was trying to climb a steep incline and dragging and chewing up a body in its tracks. Meanwhile enemy fire was pounding our position. My best buddy, a driver, became physically ill because he couldn't avoid driving over the dead without mangling them up even more. Our only hope was to get off the beach and up the steep cliff. The devastation on the beach is a very painful and vivid recollection which will remain etched in my mind forever."

Once on top of the cliff, the company regrouped, right in front of the deepest crater Skelly had ever seen, probably caused by offshore shelling. Sledgehammers had to be used to dislodge the tank's breathing stacks for 360-degree firing. Meanwhile, the men were standing exposed to al kinds of fire, friendly and unfriendly. Then the tank moved on down to a small village called Coalville sur Mer and went on the defensive with a French cheering section.

"Snipers were popping away at our infantry from all sides and in back of us, but the 75 mm gun could not be fired for fear of killing our own men. I successfully dislodged the enemy from the upper windows with my 50 caliber and my coaxial 30 caliber machine guns. Almost immediately we started taking fire from our left, from a small stone building. Since we could not stop to aim, I fired on the run, luckily hitting the door dead center. This destroyed the building and its German occupants." Skelly feared their cohorts would somehow recognize his tank, Abie's Irish Rose, and make it a special target.

He said the next few days were about the same - "you shoot me and I shoot you," with enemy booby traps, mined roads, and very accurate artillery fire. The Germans had previously marked their coordinates on specific targets such as main roads and intersections, he said.

"Fields and roads were dotted with the bloated and, stinking carcasses of farm animals and the bodies of enemy soldiers with their skins turning blue and the unforgettable odor of death," he said.

Skelly was wounded and permanently put out of action two months later in St. Germain. The enemy attacked early in the morning and since the tank company lacked infantry and artillery support, it was practically destroyed. Two of his crew died and the remaining three were wounded and burned. He was returned to the United States on a hospital ship called Saint Olaf and spent about 18 months in different hospitals. The

747th Tank Battalion fought to the end of the war, however, and immediately went into training with Amphibious Tanks to prepare for the assault on the Japanese mainland. Skelly said he thanks God that they never had to go.

"Those of us still living have had yearly reunions for most of the past 52 years. We know the meaning of real comradeship. Most of us suffer from some form of post war syndrome. I am severely handicapped as a result of this conflict and am living out my life here, with my wife Clare." The couple married in 1948 and have two children. Skelly retired from Brooks Brothers and moved to Ocala from Vero Beach three years ago. The 747th Tank Battalion was activated in Bowie, Texas, Jan 3, 1943, a separate unit made up of approximately 600 men, 60 tanks and a variety of half tracks, jeeps, and trucks, according to Skelly. "The men were Irish, Italians, and Jews from Brooklyn, the Bronx and a number of Polish and German men from New Jersey and Pennsylvania. Others were a few foreign born from Greece, Czechoslovakia, Pakistan and China. Hard-nosed basic training and maneuvers ended with transportation aboard the U.S. Navy Attack Transport Charles Carroll, with seasickness the order of the day in the miserable February crossing. Further training followed in Scotland and England and the rest is history.

Epilogue

Bob Cadmus was back home in New Jersey by Christmas, 1945. He returned to work at Mather Springs, in Linden, as a machinist. After a few months, he decided to take a vacation and drive to Georgia to see an Army buddy. Well, he never made it to Georgia. While passing through the Shenandoah Valley in Virginia, he happened to spend the night at The Quiet Retreat, a bed & breakfast in New Market, VA. During his sta, he saw a picture of a young lady on the mantel and inquired who she was. It turned out Natalie was the niece of the two spinster aunts who ran The Qui
et Retreat. Bob decided he just had to meet her. As luck would have it, she was staying with her mother and sister on the farm where she grew up which was just down the lane. One thing led to another and they were married in February 1947 and settled down to start a family in Roselle, NJ.

Bob worked hard to provide for his family and soon an opportunity came along that he couldn't refuse. He went in with his father and bought a rowboat rental business on Barnegat Bay in Bayville, NJ.and moved his family down to the shore. Ten rowboats, a bait stand, a small storefront that sold fishing supplies, snacks and breakfast to the fishermen. The small house across the street was where his parents stayed. They grew the business over the years to 100 boats and 50 motors. He bought out his father's share and went on to improve the property by building a larger bait stand, a motor shed, large restroom area and relocated the take out stand. All of us kids had jobs to do and we worked 7 days a week all summer. Betty cut and sold bait; Shirley got the boats ready for the customers ; and I worked in the stand selling coffee, refreshments, and fishing and crabbing supplies. Dad rented out the boats and managed the staff, while Mom took care of the traffic and parking. When we opened up at 5AM, there would be a line of cars waiting so she would make sure they parked just right so that all the customers had a place to park. It could get pretty crazy out there because most weekends when the crabs were running, we were out of boats by 6AM. Mom also kept the books and took care of payroll.

In the early days, during the winter, Dad found a job building boats. Mom worked as a secretary to the Board of Education at the high school we attended. This helped get us through until the boat works (Dick's Landing) opened up again in the Spring. After a time, Dad built his own shop and started building cedar picnic tables and cedar sheds during the winter months. We had enough land up on the highway where the shop and house was, that we were able to sell them to the passers by. No internet at that time. Mostly by word of mouth, the customers would find their way down Route 9.

Dad was so successful in his businesses that they were able to help the three of us go to college and retired at age 50. Mom and Dad went on a lot of adventures after they retired. They bought an RV and drove to Alaska and eventually visited 49 states plus Canada, making all kinds of friends along the way. They designed and had a 34 ft.Garvey built and took it up the Hudson River and St. Lawrence Seaway twice. The second time, they went all the way to the Mississippi and came down it to Mobile to get to their place in Bon Secour, AL. He then had the boat retrofitted with a net and went shrimping. Many hours were spent fishing in the gulf and the inland waterways.

The experiences Dad had in the war were certainly horrific at times, however, the man that emerged after the war knew the value of hard work and study. He appreciated all that America had to offer and if you went after it, you could achieve your dreams. He did not take anything for granted and didn't care for those who did.

Nancy Cadmus Franklin

ABOUT THE AUTHOR

Shirley Cadmus earned a BA and MA from Madison College, Harrisonburg, Va. She taught art at George Washington High School, Averett University and Danville Community College, all located in Danville, Virginia. After 40 years of teaching, she now devotes her time to pottery, painting and photography, while operating her art gallery in Milton, North Carolina. This is her first published book.

SHIRLEY CADMUS

I hesitate to call myself the author. My father, unknowingly, wrote this book while he lived its pages. If he'd had his way, this book wouldn't exist. When my sisters and I started reading the letters about ten years after his death, we were stunned. Dad wrote letters? A whole box of letters? We couldn't dig through them fast enough. Since Betty was in possession of the letters and the three of us live a distance from one another, we had to rely on her to sort through, type, and put them in order. Quite a task! We anxiously awaited her emails containing attachments of letters. The three of us got together and put each page and envelope in plastic sleeves and arranged them by date into albums. Having met at our mom's/Betty's home in Pennsylvania we sat around the dining room table, each with matching computers and piles of letters spread out among us. We would read aloud interesting or funny portions to each other. The work was tedious, but I don't remember ever having so much fun working with my sisters toward a common goal.

The more I read, the more the letters impressed me. They read like a novel. We were determined to get everything in order so we could read our dad's work as a whole, and to preserve the originals. We finally got to know and sympathize with our father. We had never understood why, on the major holidays, as well as random days he would retreat to his room and not speak to us. In addition, we laughed at some of the habits and quirks he exhibited in his letters that continued in our lives. We photographed all the medals we had in our possession, tho there may have been more.

We sure would love to have seen all the photographs Dad mentioned in his letters!!

We lost Dad in 1998, and Mom in 2016. Betty is living in Pennsylvania; Nancy, her son, Robert Clausius, and her husband, Chuck, are living in Houston, Texas. Shirley lives in Caswell County, North Carolina.

This book reads like a first person account of Robert Cadmus' service in the US Army from Boot Camp through Japan's surrender. Reading this collection of letters and interviews will surely take the reader on their own journey through WWII.

Shirley Cadmus
rakupotter@me.com

Made in the USA
San Bernardino, CA
16 August 2017